"A man does not make a nation, but a nation at its birth may find its vibrant and triumphant voice in a man."
—**José Martí**

"Fidel has his own special way of fusing himself with the people, [which] can be appreciated only by seeing him in action. At the great public mass meetings one can observe something like the dialogue of two tuning forks whose vibrations interact, producing new sounds. Fidel and the mass begin to vibrate together in a dialogue of growing intensity until they reach a climax in an abrupt conclusion crowned by our cry of struggle and victory."
—**Che Guevara**

FIDEL CASTRO READER

FIDEL CASTRO READER

EDITED BY
DAVID DEUTSCHMANN
AND DEBORAH SHNOOKAL

Ocean Press
Melbourne ▪ New York ▪ London
www.oceanbooks.com.au

ISBN 978-1-925317-99-2 paper

Library of Congress Catalog Card Number
    First edition 2007
    Second edition 2017

PUBLISHED BY OCEAN PRESS
Australia: PO Box 1015, North Melbourne, Victoria 3051, Australia
                E-mail: info@oceanbooks.com.au

OCEAN PRESS TRADE DISTRIBUTORS
United States: **Consortium Book Sales and Distribution**
                Tel: 1-800-283-3572   www.cbsd.com
Canada: Publishers Group Canada
                Tel: 1-800-663-5714   E-mail: customerservice@raincoast.com
Australia and New Zealand: **Ocean Press**
                E-mail: orders@oceanbooks.com.au
UK and Europe: **Turnaround Publisher Services**
                E-mail: orders@turnaround-uk.com
Cuba and Latin America: **Ocean Sur**
                E-mail: info@oceansur.com

www.oceanbooks.com.au
info@oceanbooks.com.au

CONTENTS

Fidel Castro Biographical Note   ix

Editors' Preface to the Second Edition   xi

Editors' Preface to the First Edition   xiii

Chronology   1

Foreword: Tributes to Fidel by President Raúl Castro   31

1. History Will Absolve Me
   Santiago de Cuba, October 16, 1953   41

2. On the Triumph of the Revolution
   Céspedes Park, Santiago de Cuba, January 2, 1959   103
   Camp Columbia, Havana, January 8, 1959   129

3. At the United Nations General Assembly
   New York, September 26, 1960   133

4. The Bay of Pigs Invasion and the Proclamation of the
   Socialist Character of the Revolution
   Colón Cemetery, Havana, April 16, 1961   185
   May Day, Havana, May 1, 1961   190

5. Words to Intellectuals
   Havana, June 30, 1961   209

6. Manifesto for the Liberation of the Americas:
   "The Second Declaration of Havana"
   Havana, February 4, 1962   237

7. The October Missile Crisis
   The Five Points of Dignity, October 28, 1962   265
   On the Missile Crisis, November 1, 1962   266

8. Formation of the Cuban Communist Party and Che's Farewell Letter
    Chaplin Theater, Havana, October 3, 1965   271

9. On the Latin American Revolution
    Havana, August 10, 1967   289

10. The Death of Che Guevara
    Revolution Plaza, Havana, October 18, 1967   311

11. One Hundred Years of Struggle for Cuban Independence
    La Demajagua Monument, Manzanillo, October 10, 1968   323

12. Revolution and Counterrevolution in Allende's Chile
    National Stadium, Santiago de Chile, December 2, 1971   355

13. On behalf of the Movement of Nonaligned Countries
    UN General Assembly, New York, October 12, 1979   383

14. Rectifying the Errors of the Cuban Revolution
    Karl Marx Theater, Havana, April 19, 1986   413

15. Cuban Internationalism and the Collapse of the Socialist Bloc
    Havana, December 7, 1989   427

16. Return of Che Guevara's Remains to Cuba
    Santa Clara, Cuba, October 17, 1997   439

17. Inauguration of President Chávez in Venezuela: "The Battle of Ideas"
    University of Venezuela, Caracas, February 3, 1999   443

18. Response to the US Declaration of the "War Against Terrorism"
    Havana, September 22, 2001   473

19. Assessing Half a Century of the Cuban Revolution
    Revolution Plaza, Havana, May 1, 2003   479

20. In Answer to the Empire: Letters to President George W. Bush
    Proclamation by an Adversary of the US Government, May 14, 2004   495
    Second Epistle, June 21, 2004   500

Epilogue: Fidel Castro on the Cuban Revolution After Fidel   507

Index   517

Further reading

FIDEL CASTRO

Fidel Castro Ruz was born in Birán, in the former province of Oriente, on August 13, 1926. Born into a well-off landowning family, he received his primary education in a rural school, later attended private Jesuit schools in Santiago de Cuba and Havana, and graduated from law school at the University of Havana.

While at university, he joined a student group against political corruption. He was a member of the Cuban People's Party (also known as the Orthodox Party) in 1947 and became a leader of its left wing. That same year, he volunteered for an armed expedition against the Trujillo dictatorship in the Dominican Republic (the expeditionaries were unable to leave Cuba to carry out their plans). As a student leader, Fidel Castro was in Colombia to help organize a Latin American anti-imperialist student congress and participated in the April 1948 popular uprising in Bogotá.

After Fulgencio Batista's coup d'état of March 10, 1952, Fidel Castro began to organize a revolutionary organization to initiate armed insurrection against the US-backed Batista dictatorship. He organized and led an unsuccessful attack on the Moncada army garrison in Santiago de Cuba on July 26, 1953, for which he and over two dozen others were captured, tried, found guilty, and imprisoned; more than 60 revolutionaries were murdered by Batista's army during and immediately after the Moncada attack. While in prison, Fidel Castro edited his defense speech from the trial into the pamphlet *History Will Absolve Me*, which was distributed in tens of thousands of copies and became the program of what was to become the July 26 Movement. Originally sentenced to 15 years, he and his comrades were released from prison 22 months later, in May 1955, as a result of a growing public campaign.

On July 7, 1955, Fidel Castro left for Mexico, where he began to organize a guerrilla expedition to Cuba to launch the armed insurrection. On December 2, 1956, along with 81 other fighters, including his brother Raúl, Che Guevara, Camilo Cienfuegos, Juan Almeida and Jesús Montané, Fidel reached the Cuban coast aboard the cabin cruiser *Granma*. For the next two years, Fidel Castro directed the operations of the Rebel Army, in addition to continuing as central leader of the July 26 Movement. After an initial setback, the guerrillas were able to reorganize their forces and by late 1958 had successfully extended the struggle from the Sierra Maestra mountains to the heart of the island.

On January 1, 1959, Batista fled Cuba. In response to a call by Fidel, hundreds of thousands of Cubans launched an insurrectionary general strike that ensured the victory of the revolution. Fidel Castro arrived triumphantly in Havana on January 8 as commander-in-chief of Cuba's victorious Rebel Army. On February 13, 1959, he was named prime minister, a position he held until December 1976, when he became president of the Council of State and the Council of Ministers.

He has been first secretary of the Central Committee of the Cuban Communist Party since its founding in 1965.

On July 31, 2006, shortly before his 80th birthday, Fidel Castro handed over all his positions in the Cuban government and Communist Party to his brother Raúl, minister of defense and first vice-president of the Council of State.

PREFACE TO THE SECOND EDITION

Fidel Castro died on November 25, 2016, at the age of 90. He was buried in Santiago de Cuba on December 4, 2016, after leaving instructions that no monuments, busts or statues of him should be erected and no public buildings, parks, plazas, institutions, streets or avenues should bear his name.

His death sparked an unprecedented wave of both emotion and political reaffirmation among the Cuban people. A visit to Cuba by the editors of this anthology happened to coincide with the death of Fidel Castro, one of the political giants in the 20th century. There we witnessed a gathering of a million people in Havana's Revolution Plaza and the millions more who celebrated the life of Fidel Castro as the caravan with his ashes traveled across the island in a reverse journey to the one Fidel took in January 1959 at the head of the youthful, unshaven rebel army that had defeated the U.S.-backed dictatorship. It was striking to see how, within days, the slogan *Yo soy Fidel* [I am Fidel] first raised by students at the University of Havana, became the cry of literally millions and millions of Cubans as they reaffirmed their commitment to their revolution.

We have included in this new, updated edition the tributes to Fidel by President Raúl Castro at both the gigantic rally in Havana and the 500,000-strong gathering in Santiago de Cuba, the final destination of the caravan. We would like to remind readers of Fidel's words in January 1959 when he addressed a great mass of jubilant fellow citizens explaining that this time it would be a "real" revolution. He promised that Cuba's dignity and sovereignty, which had long been abused and trampled, first by its Spanish colonial rulers and then by its powerful northern neighbor, would now be redeemed. He committed himself to defending the right to dignity, not just for the Cuban people but for all humanity.

Fidel urged Cubans to have confidence that the new government would fulfill its obligations to the people, even though, he explained, there may be many obstacles. No one could have foreseen the obstacles the bold Cuban revolutionary project on a tiny island so close to the imperial power of the United States would face—and survive: invasion, blockade, near nuclear annihilation, regular natural disasters, multiple assassination attempts, and almost total economic ruin after the collapse of the socialist bloc. Fidel concluded that historic speech at Camp Columbia on January 8, 1959, by commenting: "I know that there will never be such a crowd again, except on one occasion—the day I'm buried. I'm sure that there will be a large crowd then, too, to take me to my grave, because I will never defraud the people."

We dedicate this updated edition of the *Fidel Castro Reader* to both Fidel Castro and to the heroic Cuban people as they approach the 60th anniversary of their revolution.

Fidel Castro profoundly shaped the lives of the editors of this anthology and we are forever in his debt.

The editors
December 2016

PREFACE TO THE FIRST EDITION

Addressing the Millennium Summit at the United Nations in September 2000, Fidel Castro playfully put a handkerchief over the little warning light that was illuminated to advise the speaker when their five minutes were up.

This incident highlights the dilemma faced by the editors of this book: How can a selection be made of the words of one of history's greatest orators, encompassing over five decades of speeches? Many of Fidel Castro's single speeches alone would fill an entire book. And how can a selection be made to truly represent all the ideas and issues he has articulated during half a century on the world political stage?

Fidel Castro gave more than 5,000 speeches over a 48-year period, in addition to countless interviews and political statements of one sort or another. The selection published here is quite different from the initial selection made when this editorial project was first conceived. Undoubtedly, the contents of this volume would have been quite different if selected five years before or five years hence, as it would inevitably be shaped by the circumstances of the moment, as this selection is. The editors of this volume acknowledge that the present selection is partly framed by two considerations: firstly, the dramatic changes in the political landscape in Latin America in the first decade of the 21st century, and secondly, the ongoing consequences of the "crisis of socialism" and the debate over the future of the socialist project.

These events over the last decade especially, and Fidel's decision to temporarily hand over power to his brother Raúl in July 2006, have influenced our choice of speeches. Nevertheless, we are confident it is both representative of Fidel's political thinking and reflective of the process of the Cuban revolution itself.

There are 20 chapters and an epilogue in this volume, encompassing some 28 separate speeches and interventions. Some of these are printed in full, others are excerpted. For this volume, we have included several speeches addressed to audiences outside Cuba. A comprehensive chronology will also guide readers through the history of the period reflected in this anthology.

A selection such as this must inevitably exclude some if not many of Fidel's classic speeches made at key moments of the revolution. It also neglects in part a number of important themes he has returned to over the years, such as Cuba's involvement in Africa, the Third World debt crisis and the environmental disaster threatening humanity.

Special mention needs to be made of a parallel publishing project to this anthology. Ocean Press's sister publisher, Ocean Sur — a new Latin American book publisher with several offices in the continent — has embarked on an ambitious project to publish a series of thematic selections of Fidel Castro's speeches, interviews and writings in order to make these works available in Spanish to readers in Latin America and elsewhere. This will include multi-volume anthologies of Fidel Castro on culture and education, Latin America, Chile during the Allende era, Venezuela and Chávez, political portraits of world and historical figures, socialism, political economy, Africa and solidarity.

* * *

As a witness to the spectacle of Fidel Castro's mass oratory, his close collaborator Che Guevara observed that Fidel "has his own special way of fusing himself with the people [which] can be appreciated only by seeing him in action. At the great public mass meetings one can observe something like the dialogue of two tuning forks whose vibrations interact, producing new sounds. Fidel and the mass begin to vibrate together in a dialogue of growing intensity until they reach a climax in an abrupt conclusion crowned by our cry of struggle and victory."

Hopefully, the printed pages of this book convey to the reader some sense of this dynamic relationship between Fidel Castro and the Cuban revolution.

His old friend, Gabriel García Márquez, described Fidel as "a man of austere ways and insatiable illusions, with an old-fashioned formal education, of cautious words and simple manners, and incapable of conceiving any idea which is not out of the ordinary."

Fidel has never ceased to engage in what he has called "the battle of ideas," arguing:

> I believe there is something more powerful than weapons: ideas, reason and the morality of a cause... What can bring about the downfall of a military power with hundreds of bases all over the world? Ideas that are just, at the right moment, and in the appropriate historical circumstances.

Since his withdrawal from daily responsibilities in the Cuban government, Fidel has echoed this earlier statement by expressing his total confidence that his ideas would outlive him. Writing to the Union of Young Communists (UJC) in June 2007, he said:

> Are ideas born of human beings? Do they perish with an individual? Ideas have come into being throughout the history of the human species. They will exist as long as our species does.

We leave the reader to witness throughout this volume the extraordinary voice of one of the major political figures of the 20th century, who speaks not only for Latin America and the Third World, but also for a humanity clamoring for an alternative.

The editors
August 2007

CHRONOLOGY

1926

August 13 Fidel Castro Ruz is born on the Manacas farm, in Birán, Mayarí, Oriente province.

1933

August 12 The dictatorship of Gerardo Machado is overthrown by a general strike and a provisional government assumes power.

September 4 Fulgencio Batista leads the "Sergeants Revolt" and the provisional government is replaced by a government of President Ramón Grau San Martín.

1934

January 15 Batista overthrows President Grau.

1945

June Fidel graduates from Belén College, Havana. His final school report notes: "Fidel has what it takes and will make something of himself."

1947

July-September Fidel trains for an expedition to the Dominican Republic to fight against the dictator Rafael Leonidas Trujillo. The plan is intercepted and aborted.

1948

March 31 On an organizing tour of Latin America to prepare for a student solidarity conference, Fidel arrives in Bogotá, Colombia.

April 9 While Fidel is in Colombia, he participates in a popular uprising known as the "Bogotazo" that occurs in response to the assassination of political leader Eliécer Gaitán.

1950

June Fidel completes his studies at the University of Havana and graduates with a doctorate in law.

1951

August 16 Eduardo Chibás, founder of the Orthodox Party and campaigner against government corruption, commits suicide at the end of his regular radio broadcast.

1952

March 10 General Fulgencio Batista takes power in a military coup.

1953

July 26 Fidel Castro leads the attack by 165 young militants on the Moncada barracks in Santiago de Cuba, in the hope of sparking an uprising against the Batista dictatorship. The attack fails, many are killed, and Fidel narrowly escapes capture.

August 1 Fidel is surprised and captured by an army patrol.

October 16 At his trial for the Moncada attack, Fidel outlines the revolutionary political program that is later published and widely distributed as *History Will Absolve Me*. He is condemned to 15 years' imprisonment.

1955

May 15 Fidel and his compañeros involved in the Moncada attack are released from prison after a widespread amnesty campaign. (The two women political prisoners, Haydée Santamaría and Melba Hernández, had been released the previous year on February 20.)

June 12 The July 26 Movement is formally established as an underground organization, headed by Fidel Castro.

July 7 With legal avenues closed in the fight against Batista, and threats against his life, Fidel leaves Cuba for exile in Mexico.

July In Mexico, Fidel meets Ernesto Che Guevara, who had been befriended by some Cubans in Guatemala before the overthrow of President Árbenz in a Central Intelligence Agency (CIA)-sponsored coup the previous year.

1956

November 25 Fidel, Che Guevara and 80 Cubans leave the Mexican port of Tuxpan aboard the cabin cruiser *Granma*, with the intention of launching an armed struggle against Batista in the Sierra Maestra mountain range in eastern Cuba.

November 30 The urban wing of the July 26 Movement, led by Frank País, initiates an uprising against Batista in Santiago de Cuba.

December 2 The *Granma* expeditionaries land at Las Coloradas beach and the revolutionary war begins.

December 5 The guerrillas are dispersed after being surprised by Batista's troops at Alegría de Pío. Of the *Granma* expeditionaries, only a handful survive.

December 18 Fidel, Raúl Castro and six others reunite at Cinco Palmas. A few days later, they are joined by Juan Almeida, Che Guevara, Ramiro Valdés and four others from the *Granma*.

1957

January 17 The guerrillas and some new peasant recruits capture the army base at La Plata.

January 22 A significant victory over Batista's forces under the command of Lt. Angel Sánchez Mosquera is scored at Arroyo del Infierno.

February 17 *New York Times* journalist Herbert Matthews interviews Fidel in the Sierra Maestra. The same day, the first meeting of the July 26 Movement since the start of the revolutionary war is held.

March 13 A group of students attack the Presidential Palace and seize a major Havana radio station. José Antonio Echeverría, Federation of

University Students (FEU) president and leader of the Revolutionary Student Directorate (DRE), is shot and killed in the attack.

May 28 The battle of El Uvero takes place in which Che Guevara stands out among the combatants. A few weeks later, he is the first to be named "commander" by Fidel to lead his own guerrilla column.

July 30 Frank País, the young leader of the urban underground in Santiago de Cuba, is killed.

August 20 Fidel leads Column One (José Martí) in the battle of Palma Mocha.

September 17 The first battle of Pino del Agua takes place.

November–December The Rebel Army conducts the "winter offensive" against Batista's forces in the Sierra Maestra.

1958

February 16–17 A significant victory is won by the rebels at the second battle of Pino del Agua.

March 1 Raúl Castro and Juan Almeida lead columns that open up second and third fronts in Oriente province.

April 9 The national general strike called by the July 26 Movement is defeated.

May 25 Batista's army launches a military offensive against the Rebel Army, but it fails after two-and-a-half months of intensive fighting.

July 11–21 At the battle of El Jigüe, Fidel personally leads the rebel forces in inflicting a decisive defeat on Batista's army, which is expelled from the Sierra Maestra. This allows the Rebel Army to significantly expand its operational zone.

August 31 Commanders Che Guevara and Camilo Cienfuegos lead columns west toward the center of the island of Cuba, opening new battle fronts in Las Villas province.

November 15 Fidel leaves the Sierra Maestra to direct the Rebel Army's final offensive in Santiago de Cuba. By the end of the month, Batista's elite troops are defeated at the battle of Guisa.

December 28 Che Guevara's guerrilla column initiates the battle of Santa Clara, successfully taking control of the city within a few days.

1959

January 1 Fidel reaches Santiago de Cuba as the military regime collapses. He calls for a general strike for January 2. Batista and several cronies flee to Santo Domingo, leaving General Cantillo in charge.

January 2 In the early hours, Fidel addresses the people of Santiago de Cuba in Céspedes Park. Che Guevara and Camilo Cienfuegos reach Havana.

January 8 Fidel arrives in Havana after a triumphant march across the island. A revolutionary government is installed headed by judge Manuel Urrutia as president and José Miró Cardona as prime minister. Fidel assumes the post of commander-in-chief of the Revolutionary Armed Forces.

January 23–27 Fidel visits Venezuela and addresses 300,000 people in the Plaza del Silencio in Caracas.

February 7 The 1940 constitution is reinstated.

February 9 Argentine-born Che Guevara is declared a Cuban citizen.

February 16 Fidel replaces Miró Cardona as prime minister in the revolutionary government.

March 22 At a mass rally in Havana, Fidel explains that the revolutionary government will be outlawing racial discrimination and adopting measures to protect workers in the lowest paid jobs.

April Gambling casinos are closed and Mafia boss Santos Trafficante, Jr., is arrested.

April 21 All private beaches are opened to the public.

April 15–27 At the invitation of the Association of Newspaper Editors, Fidel visits the United States, where he has a three-hour meeting with Vice-President Richard Nixon. Nixon later concludes that Fidel is "either incredibly naive about communism or under communist discipline."

May 8 In a televised speech, Fidel summarizes his perspective, saying "This revolution is neither capitalist nor communist!... We want to liberate humanity from dogmas, and free the economy and society, without terrorizing or binding anyone."

May 17 The Agrarian Reform Law is proclaimed, placing a limit on the maximum land holding allowed.

June 26 Cuba breaks diplomatic relations with the Dominican Republic, but dictator Rafael Trujillo continues to back plots against the Cuban revolutionary government.

July 16 After a confrontation with Prime Minister Fidel Castro, President Urrutia resigns. Osvaldo Dorticós is appointed president.

July 26 To celebrate the anniversary of the 1953 attack on the Moncada barracks, the people of Havana open their homes to welcome thousands of peasant families in an effort to breach the country-city divide.

October 7 Che Guevara is designated head of the Department of Industry of the National Institute of Agrarian Reform (INRA).

October 21 Two planes flying from the United States strafe Havana, cause two deaths and wound dozens. Former Cuban air force chief Pedro Luis Díaz Lanz later admits involvement.

October 26 Announcing the formation of the National Revolutionary Militias to incorporate workers and peasants into the defense of the revolution, Fidel says "the revolution is here to stay."

October 28 After successfully negotiating an end to a counterrevolutionary plot led by Huber Matos, Camilo Cienfuegos is killed in a plane accident flying from Camagüey to Havana.

October At the end of this month, President Eisenhower approves a CIA covert action program against Cuba.

November 25 Che Guevara is appointed director of the National Bank of Cuba.

December 11 Col. J.C. King, head of the CIA's Western Hemisphere division, sends a memo to CIA chief Allen Dulles about the possibilities for eliminating Fidel Castro.

December The CIA proposes to recruit Cuban exiles and train them for paramilitary attacks against Cuba.

1960

February Soviet Vice-Premier Anastas Mikoyan visits Cuba and the first major trade agreements are signed.

March 4 An explosion on board *La Coubre*, a French vessel bringing Belgian arms to Cuba, results in 101 deaths and more than 200 wounded.

March 5 At the funeral for the victims of the previous day's terrorist attack, Fidel first uses the slogan, *"Patria o muerte"* [Homeland or death]. Alberto Korda snaps a photograph of Che Guevara on the platform that becomes the iconic image of the revolutionary guerrilla.

March 17 President Eisenhower approves the CIA's plans for a "Program of Covert Action Against Castro" — a comprehensive plan of military action and propaganda to overthrow the Cuban revolutionary government.

May 8 Diplomatic relations between Cuba and the Soviet Union are restored, having been broken previously by Batista.

May 17 First broadcasts by the CIA-run radio station on the Swan Islands, off the coast of Honduras.

June 28-July 1 The revolutionary government nationalizes foreign oil companies that refuse to refine Soviet oil, including Shell, Texaco and Esso.

July 6 Cuba's US sugar quota is suspended. The Soviet Union agrees to buy Cuban sugar.

July 23 Cuba's first commercial treaty with China is signed.

August 6 Cuba nationalizes other US businesses, including oil refineries, sugar mills and US electricity and telephone companies.

August 7 The Cuban Catholic bishops issue a pastoral letter warning about "communism," marking a serious rift between the church and the revolutionary government.

August 28 The United States imposes an embargo on trade with Cuba.

September 2 In response to the hostile "Declaration of San José" issued by the Organization of American States (OAS), a "National General Assembly of the People of Cuba" in Revolution Plaza, a gigantic mass rally, adopts the "Declaration of Havana," calling for the end of exploitation of human beings and the exploitation of the underdeveloped world by imperialist finance capital.

September 17 Cuba nationalizes all US banks.

September 26 Fidel Castro addresses the United Nations General Assembly in New York for four-and-a-half hours. At his hotel in Harlem, Fidel meets with Egyptian President Nasser, Indian Prime Minister Nehru, Soviet Prime Minister Khrushchev and African American leader Malcolm X.

September 28 Establishment of the Committees for the Defense of the Revolution (CDRs).

October 13 Large commercial and industrial enterprises in Cuba are nationalized. The Urban Reform Law is proclaimed, ending commercial real estate.

October 19 President Eisenhower prohibits all US exports to Cuba except food and medicines.

October 21 Che Guevara leaves on an extended visit to the Soviet Union, the German Democratic Republic, Czechoslovakia, China and North Korea.

November CIA broadcasts from the Swan Islands off Honduras warn Cubans of an imminent plan by the revolutionary government to remove parents' rights over their children.

November 9 John F. Kennedy defeats Richard Nixon in the US presidential election.

December 2 Cuba establishes diplomatic relations with the Democratic Republic of Vietnam (Hanoi).

December 16 President Eisenhower reduces Cuba's sugar quota for 1961 to zero.

1961

January 1 Cuba's national literacy campaign begins. Over 100,000 high school students are mobilized for the task in the Conrado Benítez Brigades.

January 3 Washington breaks diplomatic relations with Havana.

February 23   The revolutionary government establishes the Ministry of Industry headed by Che Guevara.

March 12   As part of a terrorist bombing campaign, an oil refinery in Santiago de Cuba is attacked.

March 13   President Kennedy proposes the "Alliance for Progress" to counter the influence of the Cuban revolution in Latin America.

April 15   Bombing raids are simultaneously launched on three Cuban air fields by planes with fake Cuban insignia.

April 16   At the ceremony to bury the victims of the previous day's terrorist attack, Fidel proclaims the socialist character of the revolution. This same day the first literacy *brigadistas* arrive at the Varadero training camp.

April 17   The invasion of 1,500 mercenaries (Brigade 2506), trained and armed by the CIA, begins at the Bay of Pigs on the southern coast of Cuba.

April 19   With more than 1,200 mercenaries captured, the Bay of Pigs invasion is defeated.

May 1   At an enormous May Day rally in Havana, Fidel sums up the lessons of the Bay of Pigs invasion and assesses the stage reached in the unfolding revolutionary process.

June 30   Fidel addresses the final session of a three-day meeting of Cuban writers and artists, explaining, "Within the revolution, everything; against the revolution, nothing."

July   Formation of the Integrated Revolutionary Organizations (ORI) as a fusion of the July 26 Movement, the Revolutionary Directorate (DR) and the Popular Socialist Party (PSP).

August 8   Che Guevara denounces President Kennedy's "Alliance for Progress" at the OAS meeting in Punta del Este, Uruguay.

September 2   Cuba is the only Latin American country to participate in the founding meeting of the Movement of Nonaligned Countries in Bandung, Indonesia.

November 30   A new CIA covert action program against Cuba dubbed "Operation Mongoose" is approved by President Kennedy.

December 2 In a television broadcast, Fidel says he has "always been and will always remain a Marxist-Leninist."

December 22 A huge celebration is held in Revolution Plaza to mark the completion of the national literacy campaign, and Cuba is declared a "territory free of illiteracy."

1962

January 22-31 The OAS meeting in Punta del Este, Uruguay, decides to expel Cuba from the organization.

February 3 President Kennedy announces the total blockade of Cuba to take effect on February 7.

February 4 The "Second Declaration of Havana," a manifesto for the liberation of the Americas, is proclaimed by more than one million Cubans, stating, "The duty of a revolutionary is to make the revolution."

March 12 The ration book system is established in Cuba.

March 26 Fidel Castro denounces sectarianism within the ORI, and a new party, the United Party of the Socialist Revolution (PURS), is established.

August 27–September 7 Che Guevara makes his second visit to the Soviet Union.

October 22 After US spy planes discover Soviet missile installations in Cuba, the international crisis unfolds that brings the world to the brink of nuclear war.

November 2 President Kennedy announces that the Soviet missiles in Cuba are being dismantled.

December 24 The mercenaries captured during the Bay of Pigs invasion are sent back to the United States in exchange for medicines and baby food worth $54 million.

1963

April 27 Fidel Castro arrives in Moscow on his first state visit to the Soviet Union.

October 4 Hurricane Flora devastates Cuba, especially the eastern provinces.

November 22 President Kennedy is assassinated in Dallas, Texas. Almost immediately, a media campaign attempts to link the assassin, Lee Harvey Oswald, to Cuba.

December 20 Cuba initiates a campaign in solidarity with Vietnam.

1964

January A conflict between Washington and London arises over a British company's plan to sell 450 buses to Cuba.

March 25 Che Guevara speaks at the UN Conference on Trade and Development (UNCTAD) conference in Geneva, at which the Group of 77 (a caucus of Third World countries) is born.

December 11 Che Guevara addresses the UN General Assembly in New York, condemning the US war in Vietnam and supporting the independence movements from Puerto Rico to the Congo.

December 17 Che Guevara embarks on an extended trip to Egypt and several other African countries.

1965

February 22–27 Che Guevara makes a controversial speech at the Afro-Asian conference in Algeria, urging the socialist countries to do more to support Third World struggles for independence.

March 13 Discussing the Sino-Soviet split at a meeting at the University of Havana, Fidel says, "Division in the face of the enemy was never a revolutionary or intelligent strategy."

March 25 Che Guevara returns to Cuba and shortly afterwards drops from public view.

April Che Guevara leaves Cuba, along with a brigade of almost 100 Cubans, on a mission to support the liberation movements in Africa.

October 3 The newly formed Cuban Communist Party holds its first Central Committee meeting, where Fidel reads Che's farewell letter.

October 10 Because of the US suspension of flights from Cuba, the port of Camarioca is opened for boats coming from the United States to take Cubans wishing to emigrate.

November 21 Che Guevara leaves the Congo and writes up his account of the mission, which he describes as a "failure."

1966

January First Tricontinental Conference of Solidarity with the Peoples of Africa, Asia and Latin America (OSPAAAL) is held in Havana.

September 28 At a ceremony on the sixth anniversary of the establishment of the CDRs, Fidel says "We will never build a communist consciousness with a dollar sign in the hearts and minds of men."

November 2 US Congress adopts the Cuban Adjustment Act that encourages illegal departures from Cuba.

November 4 Che Guevara arrives in Bolivia to begin the revolutionary struggle it is hoped will spread throughout the continent of Latin America.

December 31 Che Guevara meets with Mario Monje, the Bolivian Communist Party leader. There is a serious disagreement about perspectives for the guerrilla movement.

1967

March 13 Speaking at the University of Havana, Fidel criticizes several Latin American communist parties, saying, "Those who are not revolutionary fighters cannot be called communists."

April 16 Che Guevara's "Message to the Tricontinental" is published in Cuba, calling for the creation of "two, three, many Vietnams."

April 19 On the sixth anniversary of the Bay of Pigs invasion, in the year designated the "Year of Heroic Vietnam," Fidel argues, "Our people have no other path to liberation than that of armed struggle."

August 10 Fidel addresses the Latin American Solidarity Organizations (OLAS) conference reaffirming armed struggle as the "fundamental road" for Latin American revolutionaries. Che Guevara is elected honorary chair of the organization.

October 8   Che Guevara is wounded in combat and captured. This date becomes known in Cuba as the "Day of the Heroic Guerrilla."

October 9   Che Guevara is assassinated in cold blood by Bolivian Army Rangers under instructions from Washington.

October 15   In a television appearance, Fidel confirms news of Che Guevara's death in Bolivia.

October 18   Fidel delivers a memorial speech for Che Guevara to almost one million people gathered in Havana's Revolution Plaza.

1968

January   The trial of 35 members of the "pro-Soviet micro-faction" led by Aníbal Escalante takes place.

March 13   The revolutionary government confiscates virtually all private businesses, except small family farms. At the University of Havana, Fidel explains, "We did not make a revolution to establish the right to trade."

July   Che Guevara's *Bolivian Diary* is published and distributed free to the Cuban people. It is simultaneously published around the world.

August 21   The Soviet Union invades Czechoslovakia. Fidel responds with cautious approval.

October 10   Cuba commemorates the 100th anniversary of the struggle for independence at the Demajagua monument, Manzanillo, Oriente province.

1969

July 26   Fidel Castro announces the campaign for a 10-million-ton sugar harvest.

1970

May 20   The failure of the campaign to achieve a 10-million-ton sugar harvest is acknowledged.

1971

November 10–December 4 Fidel visits Chile and tours the country extensively at the time of the Popular Unity government, led by Salvador Allende.

December 2 Fidel gives a farewell speech to a huge crowd in the National Stadium in Santiago de Chile.

1972

July 11 Cuba joins the socialist trading bloc, the Council of Mutual Economic Assistance (CMEA).

1973

September 9 The Cuban exile terrorist group Omega-7 claims responsibility for bombing Cuba's UN Mission in New York, and further bomb attacks in October and November.

September 11 President Allende of Chile is overthrown in a coup led by General Augusto Pinochet, openly backed by the CIA and US Secretary of State Henry Kissinger.

1974

January Soviet Premier Leonid Brezhnev visits Cuba.

March 26 Vietnamese Prime Minister Pham Van Dong visits Cuba and Fidel gives a speech emphasizing the importance of international solidarity.

November Cuban and US officials begin talks seeking a solution to the migration problem.

1975

January 27 A US Senate Commission headed by Senator Frank Church is established to investigate the activities of US intelligence agencies against foreign governments and political leaders, including Fidel Castro.

February 14 Introduction of the Cuban Family Code, affirming women's rights in the workplace and in the home.

November 5 As part of "Operation Carlota" Cuba sends troops to support Angola's independence against a South African invasion.

December 17-22 The first congress of the Cuban Communist Party is held. Fidel addresses the closing ceremony, saying, "We are the privileged heirs to what others have done."

1976

February 24 Cuba adopts a new socialist constitution after it has been put to a referendum in which 98 percent of voters participated.

October 6 A Cubana airlines plane explodes in mid-air off the coast of Barbados, killing all 73 passengers, including Cuba's national fencing team. Cuban exiles Orlando Bosch and Luis Posada Carriles, known agents of the CIA, are arrested in Venezuela and charged with the crime. Cuba cancels the skyjacking agreement signed with the United States in 1973.

December 2 The first National Assembly of People's Power is held and elects Fidel Castro as president of the Council of State.

1977

September 1 Under the presidency of Jimmy Carter, Cuba and the United States agree to open diplomatic offices ("interests sections") in their respective countries.

October The African National Congress (ANC) leader in exile Oliver Tambo and Mozambican President Samora Machel visit Cuba this month. Fidel is welcomed in Jamaica by Prime Minister Michael Manley.

1978

February 9 The US Senate Select Committee on Intelligence proposes legislation to prohibit political assassinations by US agents.

August 1 Five Cuban exiles are indicted for assassinating Chilean diplomat Orlando Letelier and his driver Ronnie Moffitt in Washington on September 21, 1976.

December 23 The first contingent of the Antonio Maceo brigade (a group of young Cuban Americans) arrives in Havana for a three-week visit.

1979

January 1 As a result of a new dialogue on migration issues between Washington and Havana, Cuban Americans are permitted to visit Cuba. More than 100,000 visit Cuba during this year.

March 13 A revolution occurs in the Caribbean island of Grenada led by Maurice Bishop and the New Jewel Movement.

July 19 The Sandinistas overthrow the Somoza dictatorship in Nicaragua. At the July 26 celebrations, Fidel says, "No two revolutions are the same."

September 3–9 Fidel Castro is elected chair of the Movement of Nonaligned Countries at its sixth summit in Havana.

October 12 Fidel Castro addresses the UN General Assembly in New York on behalf of the Movement of Nonaligned Countries, which he explains represents "the great majority of humanity."

1980

April A new migration crisis unfolds as a group of would-be émigrés crash a bus through the gates of the Peruvian embassy in Havana. Cuba responds by opening the port of Mariel for boats to come and take people to the United States. At a gigantic rally, called the "March of the Fighting People," Fidel states that the revolution and the construction of socialism must be the task of "free men and women."

May 1 Sandinista leader Daniel Ortega and Grenadian Prime Minister Maurice Bishop attend the May Day celebrations in Havana. Fidel describes Cuba, Nicaragua and Grenada as "three giants rising up."

July 19 Fidel attends the first anniversary celebrations of the Nicaraguan revolution and promises Cuba's support for the Sandinista government against Washington's "dirty war."

September 11 Cuban diplomat Félix García is assassinated in New York by the terrorist organization Omega-7.

1981

January 20 Formation of the Territorial Troop Militia.

October 22 The North-South Summit in Cancun, Mexico, is pressured to exclude Fidel Castro, even though he heads the Group of 77 developing nations.

1982

April 2–June 13 War between Britain and Argentina over the Malvinas (Falkland) Islands.

October 18 French President Mitterrand intervenes to secure the release of Armando Valladares from a Cuban prison after serving 22 years for acts of terrorism.

1983

October 25 The United States invades Grenada after the assassination of Prime Minister Maurice Bishop. Some 600 Cubans working on the island are arrested and sent back to Cuba, while others die fighting.

1984

December Cuba and the United States reach agreement on migration issues.

1985

March 15 Mikhail Gorbachev becomes prime minister in the Soviet Union and announces a policy of *glasnost* (transparency) and *perestroika* (restructuring) of Soviet political and economic life.

May 19 US-sponsored "Radio Martí" begins hostile broadcasts from Florida to Cuba.

July 18 In a dialogue with delegates to a Latin American trade union conference on the debt crisis, Fidel says the choice is either "to pay tribute to the empire or to pay tribute to your homeland."

August 3–7 Fidel Castro addresses a conference in Havana on the debt crisis in Latin America, the debt now spiralling to $360 billion.

1986

February 4-7 At the closing ceremony of the third congress of the Cuban Communist Party, Fidel says, "Our homeland is stronger, our economy more solid, our experience richer."

February 26 Fidel goes to Moscow to meet Prime Minister Gorbachev.

April 19 On the 25th anniversary of the Bay of Pigs, Fidel Castro announces a campaign to wipe out corruption, economism, individualism and bureaucratism in the Cuban Communist Party, a campaign that becomes known as the "rectification" campaign.

December 20 Cuba releases counterrevolutionary leader Eloy Menoyo Gutiérrez from prison.

1987

October 8 On the 20th anniversary of Che Guevara's death in Bolivia, Fidel urges a return to study Che's writings on political economy and the transition to socialism.

1988

March 23 Cuban troops play a major role in the victory against the South African army at Cuito Cuanavale, Angola, paving the way for the independence of Namibia and the downfall of the apartheid regime in Pretoria.

July 26 Fidel rejects *perestroika* as anathema to the principles of socialism, saying "Capitalist methods will never build socialism."

1989

April 2-5 Prime Minister Gorbachev visits Cuba. This is the first state visit by a Soviet leader since Brezhnev in 1974.

June 14 General Arnaldo Ochoa and other key officials in Cuban state security are put on trial for drug trafficking.

July 26 Fidel warns of the possible collapse of the Soviet Union but declares that even if the Soviet Union disappears, the Cuban revolution will continue to advance.

October 18 Cuba is elected for a two-year term as a non-permanent member of the UN Security Council.

November 9 The collapse of the Berlin Wall marks the beginning of the downfall of the European socialist bloc.

December 7 Cuba honors the heroes of its internationalist missions at a ceremony for the Cubans who died fighting in southern Africa. Facing the imminent collapse of the European socialist bloc, Fidel says the choice for Cuba is "Socialism or death!"

December 20 US military intervention in Panama captures and imprisons President Manuel Noriega. Thousands of people are killed. More than one million Cubans protest at the US interests section in Havana.

1990

February Florida's governor, Republican Bob Martínez, appoints a "Free Cuba Commission" headed by Cuban American National Foundation (CANF) chairman Jorge Mas Canosa.

March The first group of child victims from the 1986 Chernobyl nuclear plant disaster arrive in Cuba for treatment.

April The Sandinista government is defeated in elections in Nicaragua.

August The Cuban government adopts drastic measures in the face of the looming economic crisis referred to as the "Special Period in time of peace."

1991

February The CMEA, which had accounted for 85-88 percent of Cuba's foreign trade, formally disbands.

July 18 The first Ibero-American summit is held in Mexico City.

July 26 ANC leader Nelson Mandela attends the Moncada anniversary celebrations and thanks Cuba for its support in the struggle against apartheid.

September 11 Prime Minister Gorbachev announces the withdrawal of Soviet military advisors from Cuba.

October 10 Fidel addresses the opening session of the fourth congress of the Cuban Communist Party, saying "The only situation in which we would have no future would be if we lost our homeland, the revolution and socialism."

October 14 The Cuban Communist Party congress ends, marking a significant shift toward developing a new, younger party leadership, and making a change in the party rules to accept as members those practicing their religious beliefs.

November 25 Following the military coup against President Aristide in Haiti, the United States announces that the Guantánamo naval base will be used to accommodate thousands of Haitian refugees.

December The Soviet government collapses.

1992

January 1 First year of the "Special Period" is declared and many predictions are made about the imminent collapse of the Cuban revolution.

April 1 "TV Martí" broadcasts from Florida to Cuba, escalating the battle of the airwaves.

June 11 Fidel participates in the Earth Summit in Rio de Janeiro, Brazil, arguing "tomorrow is too late" to address the environmental crisis. "Let hunger, not humanity, disappear from the face of the earth," Fidel states.

July Somewhat prematurely, US commentators publish various books and articles predicting the "final hour" of Fidel Castro and the Cuban revolution.

July 24 At the second Ibero-American summit in Madrid on the 500th anniversary of the colonization of the Americas, Fidel stresses the need for solidarity among the peoples of the continent.

September 3 In a speech in Cienfuegos, Fidel acknowledges Cuba is facing a severe economic crisis, having lost 70 percent of its purchasing power.

September 7 The 10th summit of the Movement of Nonaligned Countries demands an end to the US blockade of Cuba and US withdrawal from the Guantánamo naval base.

October 3 US Congress approves the "Cuban Democracy Act" (proposed by Democrat Robert Torricelli), extending the US economic blockade against Cuba to third countries.

November 24 The UN General Assembly approves for the first time a Cuban resolution opposing the US economic blockade with a vote of 59 to 3, with 71 abstentions and 42 absentees. Cuba estimates that the blockade has cost it $30 billion over three decades.

1993

February 24 The first direct elections are held to Cuba's National Assembly, with 99.62 percent of eligible voters participating.

July 26 Fidel announces the legalization of the US dollar and other major economic changes, including the approval of free farmers' markets. "Cuba will neither sell out nor surrender," Fidel states.

1994

May 10 Fidel attends the inauguration of Nelson Mandela as president of the new democratic South Africa.

August 11 A new crisis of Cubans seeking to cross the Florida Straits on rafts leads to a new migration agreement between the United States and Cuba.

1995

October 22 In a speech at the United Nations, Fidel condemns the fact that 20 million people die each year of curable diseases and that the arms race continues although the Cold War is over.

1996

February 24 Two planes flown by counterrevolutionary "Brothers to the Rescue" pilots flying from the United States are shot down over Cuban territorial waters.

March 5 US Congress passes the "Libertad" (Helms-Burton) Act, which is signed into law by President Bill Clinton on March 12.

1997

April–September A series of bombs explode at hotels in Havana and Varadero, with one fatality: an Italian tourist.

September 10 Salvadoran citizen Raúl Cruz León is arrested for these bombings and admits links to the Miami Cuban exile terrorists, including Luis Posada Carriles.

October 10 The fifth congress of the Cuban Communist Party concludes with the slogan, "Save our homeland, the revolution and socialism."

October 17 The remains of Che Guevara and other combatants killed in Bolivia 30 years earlier are returned to Cuba and placed in a mausoleum in Santa Clara.

December 13 The National Assembly of People's Power votes to make some significant changes to the Cuban constitution.

1998

January 21–25 Pope John Paul II visits Cuba and urges that "Cuba should open itself up to the world and the world should open up to Cuba."

May 6 Nobel prize-winning author Gabriel García Márquez takes a message from Fidel Castro to President Clinton providing information about the activities of counterrevolutionary terrorist groups based in the United States.

July 12 In an article in the *New York Times*, Luis Posada Carriles admits involvement in the terrorist bombings of Cuban hotels in 1997, saying they were financed by the Cuban American National Foundation (CANF).

September 2 Speaking at the summit of the Movement of Nonaligned Countries in South Africa, Fidel says, "There is no end of history."

September 4 Fidel addresses the South African parliament and receives an enthusiastic welcome in Soweto the following day.

September 12 Five Cubans are arrested in Miami on espionage charges, having infiltrated exile organizations in order to avert terrorist attacks against Cuba.

December 6 In Venezuela, Hugo Chávez is elected president with a clear majority vote. Chávez makes his first state visit to Cuba the following month.

1999

February Fidel attends the inauguration of President Chávez in Venezuela and speaks about the "battle of ideas" at a meeting at the university.

May 31 Cuba issues a lawsuit against the US government claiming $181.1 billion in damages for aggression and terrorist acts over 40 years.

September 19 Fidel sends a message to the Group of 77 saying globalization is "an irreversible reality."

November 25 Five-year-old Elián González is rescued off the coast of Florida after his mother and several other Cubans drowned in their attempt to reach the United States. The boy is immediately taken hostage by his Miami relatives and every attempt by his father and the Cuban government to effect his return to Cuba is blocked.

November 30–December 3 The World Trade Organization (WTO) summit in Seattle becomes the scene of mass protests against neoliberal globalization.

2000

April 14 At the closing ceremony of the South Summit in Havana, Fidel calls for the abolition of the International Monetary Fund (IMF).

June 28 Elián González is finally returned to his father and family in Cuba.

September 6 Fidel participates in the Millennium Summit at the United Nations in New York, stating, "Chaos rules in our world... and blind laws are offered up as divine norms that will bring the peace, order, well-being and security our planet needs so badly."

September 8 Fidel speaks to an overflowing crowd at the Riverside Church in Harlem, New York.

October 28-30 During a state visit to Caracas, President Castro addresses the Venezuelan National Assembly and signs important accords for economic cooperation between Cuba and Venezuela.

November Cuban intelligence discovers a plot to assassinate Fidel at the 10th Ibero-American Summit in Panama. Luis Posada Carriles and three others are arrested by Panamanian authorities.

2001

January 25–30 The first World Social Forum is held in Porto Alegre, Brazil, raising the slogan "Another world is possible."

April 17 Fidel sends a message of support to protests in Quebec against the Free Trade Area of the Americas (FTAA).

June 8 The five Cubans arrested for espionage in 1998 are sentenced in the US federal court in Miami to four life sentences and 75 years collectively.

June 23 During a three-hour speech, Fidel suffers a fall, giving rise to widespread speculation about his health.

September 1 Fidel addresses the World Conference against Racism, Racial Discrimination, Xenophobia and Intolerance in Durban, South Africa, arguing that racism is "not a natural, instinctive human reaction but a social, cultural and political phenomenon."

September 11 Terrorists use hijacked aircraft to attack the Pentagon in Washington and the World Trade Center in New York. On behalf of the Cuban government, Fidel offers his sympathy and assistance to US authorities.

2002

January 7 Cuba is informed that the Guantánamo naval base will be used to hold "enemy combatants" captured in the "war on terror" in Afghanistan.

April 11 President Hugo Chávez is the victim of an attempted coup in Venezuela.

May 6 President George W. Bush makes unfounded accusations that Cuba is developing biological weapons.

May 12–17 Former US President Jimmy Carter visits Cuba and addresses a large audience at the University of Havana.

May 21 Cuba is included in President Bush's list of countries "supporting terrorism."

2003

May 13 Washington expels 14 Cuban diplomats.

May 26 Fidel attends the inauguration ceremony of President Néstor Kirchner in Argentina and addresses a large, enthusiastic meeting at a university.

June 26 After more than eight million Cubans sign a petition, the National Assembly votes to amend the constitution to make socialism "irrevocable."

October 10 President Bush announces a Commission for Assistance to a Free Cuba (CAFC) to prepare for a "transition to democracy" at the same time as tightening restrictions on US travel to the island.

October In response to severe hurricane damage, the US sale of food and agricultural products to Cuba is authorized.

2004

January 1 Cuba celebrates the 45th anniversary of the revolution.

January 29 Fidel Castro accuses President Bush of plotting his assassination.

April 29 A US State Department report accuses Cuba of maintaining links with "international terrorism."

May 8 The Bush administration plan to "accelerate the transition to democracy in Cuba" is released to the public. Fidel responds on May 14 with his letter titled, "Proclamation by an adversary of the US government."

May 18 A meeting with moderate exile leaders is held in Havana.

June 10 Five opposition leaders are released from prison in Cuba, followed by the release of others.

June 21 Addressing over one million Cubans in front of the US interests section in Havana, Fidel reads his "Second Epistle" to President Bush.

July The US administration further tightens travel restrictions to Cuba.

August 26 Cuba breaks diplomatic ties with Panama after the outgoing President Mireya Moscoso grants an amnesty to Luis Posada Carriles and his three accomplices in the plot to kill Fidel Castro.

October 20 Fidel breaks his arm and fractures his knee in a fall.

November 8 The circulation in Cuba of the US dollar is suspended and replaced with a special currency for use in the tourist market.

November 23 Chinese premier Hu Jintao visits Cuba and signs several significant trade agreements.

December 14 In the spirit of ALBA (the Bolivarian Alternative for the Americas) — a counterproposal to Washington's FTAA (Free Trade Area of the Americas) — presidents Castro and Chávez agree to close economic cooperation.

2005

March 17 The Cuban peso is revalued against the US dollar as a result of the excellent performance of the Cuban economy.

May 17 More than one million Cubans accuse the United States of harboring Luis Posada Carriles, who was convicted for the terrorist bombing of the Cubana airplane in 1976.

July 28 US Secretary of State Condoleezza Rice names Caleb McCarry as the coordinator of the "transition" in Cuba.

August 9 An Atlanta court orders a new trial for the five Cubans convicted of espionage in 1998, declaring the original trial in Miami invalid.

October 14–15 The Ibero-American Summit in Salamanca, Spain, condemns the blockade against Cuba and demands that US authorities facilitate the trial of Luis Posada Carriles.

October 15 A brigade of young social workers are put in charge of gas stations in Havana in an anti-corruption campaign.

November 8 The UN General Assembly condemns the US blockade against Cuba for the 14th time.

November 17 In a speech at the University of Havana, Fidel says that the revolution can only be destroyed from within, after he had criticized the "nouveau riche" for corruption and illegal trading in a speech a few weeks earlier.

November 23 Cuba reaches the goal of 2 million tourists for 2005.

December 18 Evo Morales, leader of the Movement toward Socialism (MAS), is elected president in Bolivia. Evo Morales comes to Havana on December 30 to sign cooperation accords.

December 31 The year ends with an announcement that Cuba has achieved economic growth of 11.8 percent.

2006

July 31 Prior to major intestinal surgery, Fidel temporarily hands over his government and party responsibilities to Raúl Castro, minister for defense and first vice-president of the Council of State.

August 1 Fidel's message to the Cuban people from hospital is published.

November 5 Sandinista leader Daniel Ortega wins the presidential election in Nicaragua.

2007

March 28 Fidel writes his first column for *Granma* since his illness, "Reflections of the Commandante."

July 31 Fidel sends his message "The Eternal Flame."

2008

February 18 Fidel announces he will not seek reelection as president of the Council of State. Consequently, Raúl Castro is elected president by Cuba's National Assembly on February 24.

2013

March 5 Venezuelan President Hugo Chávez dies at the age of 58 and is replaced by Vice-President Nicolás Maduro.

2014

December 14 President Obama and President Raúl Castro announce the restoration of diplomatic relations between Cuba and the United States and an agreement to release the five Cuban political prisoners held in the United States since 1998. Most of the harsh conditions of the US blockade against Cuba remain in force and the United States continues to illegally occupy Cuban territory at Guantánamo in eastern Cuba.

2016

March 21 President Obama visits Cuba with his family.

April 19 Fidel addresses the 7th congress of the Cuban Communist Party, suggesting this will probably be his last public speech.

August 13 Fidel attends a special event in Havana's Karl Marx Theater to commemorate his 90th birthday.

November 25 Fidel Castro dies and is cremated the next day.

November 28 Nearly one million Cubans participate in a mass rally in Havana's Revolution Plaza, addressed by many world leaders who traveled to Cuba to pay their respects.

November 29 A caravan with Fidel Castro's ashes sets out from Havana to travel across the island to Santiago de Cuba in the east, and hundreds of thousands of Cubans line the route.

December 3 A mass gathering of 500,000 people is held in Santiago to honor the passing of the leader of the Cuban revolution.

December 4 Fidel's ashes are buried in Santiago de Cuba, next to the remains of José Martí.

TRIBUTES TO FIDEL

RAUL CASTRO

The following are remarks made by President Raúl Castro in Havana's Revolution Plaza on Tuesday, November 29, 2016, after the death of Fidel a few days earlier.

Dear people of Cuba:

Although it will be my responsibility to present the final speech in a few days' time, when we gather in Antonio Maceo Plaza of the Revolution in Santiago de Cuba, I wish to express, at this time, in the name of our people, party, and government, as well as the family, our sincere gratitude for your presence here at this event, for the moving words you have expressed, and also for the extraordinary, innumerable demonstrations of solidarity, affection, and respect received from the entire planet, in this hour of pain and commitment.

Fidel dedicated his entire life to solidarity, and led a socialist revolution "of the humble, by the humble, for the humble" that became a symbol of the anti-colonial, anti-apartheid, anti-imperialist struggle, for the emancipation and dignity of peoples.

His vibrant words resound in this plaza today, as they did in the gathering of *campesinos* on July 26, 1959, in support of the agrarian reform, which [for Washington] meant we crossed the Rubicon and a death sentence for the revolution was therefore proclaimed. Here, Fidel reaffirmed the agrarian reform would proceed. And we did it. Today, 57 years later, we are honoring the person who conceived it and led it.

In this plaza, we voted to approve, together with Fidel, the First and Second Declarations of Havana, in 1960 and 1962, respectively. Faced with aggression from the Organization of American States (OAS), Fidel proclaimed that "standing behind the homeland, behind the free flag, behind the redeeming revolution… there is an honorable people, ready to defend its independence and the common destiny of a liberated Latin America."

I was with Fidel in the building now occupied by the Ministry of the Revolutionary Armed Forces [on one side of the plaza], when we heard the explosion of the French ship *La Coubre*, which had brought the first and only weapons we had been able to purchase in Europe. We left for the docks immediately in order to aid the victims, because we knew that the explosion must have come from the ship that was unloading those weapons. Only a few minutes after our arrival, a second explosion occurred as a lethal trap for the rescuers, the two explosions causing 101 deaths and numerous injuries.

Here, with Fidel, in December 1961, Cuba was declared a Territory Free of Illiteracy at the conclusion of the literacy campaign that was carried out by more than 250,000 teachers and students, while that same year, veterans of the Rebel Army and the newly formed National Revolutionary Militias battled the mercenaries at the Bay of Pigs and armed bands infiltrated from abroad into the mountainous regions, where, among many other vile acts, they murdered 10 young literacy teachers. A victory was won at the Bay of Pigs, while at the same time, the entire country learned to read and write, in order to ensure, as Fidel said, "The young would hold the future in their hands."

With great emotion, it was here, too, we heard the *comandante en jefe*, during the solemn wake of October 1967 pay tribute to the unforgettable *Comandante* Che Guevara, and we returned here again, 30 years later, during the most difficult stage of the Special Period, to commit ourselves, before Che's remains, to follow his immortal example.

Shaken and indignant, we attended the painful farewell to the 73 persons murdered by state terrorism in the bombing of the Cubana Airlines plane over Barbados, among them the young gold medalists in the 4th Central American and Caribbean Fencing Championships. On that occasion, we repeated with Fidel, "When an energetic and virile people weeps…" [The crowd shouts, "Injustice trembles!"] Exactly, "Injustice trembles!"

This is the plaza of important May Day marches: in 1996, against the Helms-Burton Act, which is still in effect; the enormous march of 1999, and the open tribunal of youth, students, and workers of 2000, when Fidel explained his conception of revolution, which millions of Cubans have made their own with their signature over the last few days in a sacred act of commitment.

This is also the place where we have come to support the agreements reached at our congresses of the Communist Party of Cuba.

In this same spirit, the people have come over these last few days, including many of our youth, to render heartfelt tribute and swear loyalty to the ideas and work of the *comandante en jefe* of the Cuban revolution.

Dear Fidel:

Alongside the monument to José Martí, national hero and intellectual author of the [July 26, 1953] assault on the Moncada Garrison, where we have gathered for over half a century in moments of extraordinary pain— and to honor our martyrs, proclaim our ideals, revere our symbols, and consult the people regarding important decisions—in this plaza, where we commemorate our victories, we say to you, together with our self-sacrificing, combative, heroic people: *Hasta la victoria siempre!* [Onward to victory, always!]

The following is the speech given by President Raúl Castro in Santiago de Cuba's Antonio Maceo Plaza on Saturday, December 3, 2016. The next day Fidel's ashes were buried near the monument to José Martí in the Santa Ifigenia cemetery in Santiago..

Dear people of Cuba:

This afternoon, on reaching this heroic city, the funeral procession transporting Fidel's ashes that retraced in reverse the route of the Caravan of Liberty of [January] 1959, and visited iconic sites in Santiago de Cuba, birthplace of the revolution, was met with demonstrations of love by the Cuban people, just as it was throughout the rest of the country.

Tomorrow, his ashes will be laid to rest in a simple ceremony in the Santa Ifigenia Cemetery, located very close to the mausoleum of National Hero José Martí; his *compañeros* in the struggle at Moncada, from the *Granma* and Rebel Army, from the clandestine campaign and internationalist missions. The tombs of Carlos Manuel de Céspedes, father of the homeland, and the legendary Mariana Grajales, mother of the Maceo brothers and, I might suggest, who was also the mother of all Cuban men and women, are located just a few meters away. Also close by is the pantheon where the remains lie of the unforgettable Frank País García, a young man from Santiago, who was murdered by Batista's henchmen at only 22 years of age, one month after his younger brother Josué, who had died fighting in an operation in this city. Frank's young age did not prevent him from displaying exemplary resistance to the dictatorship; he stood out as the leader of the armed uprising in Santiago de Cuba on November 30, 1956, in support of the landing of the *Granma* expedition, and he played a decisive role in organizing the sending of weapons and combatants to the nascent Rebel Army in the Sierra Maestra.

Ever since the news of the passing of the historic leader of the Cuban revolution, late on the evening of November 25, pain and sadness have overwhelmed the Cuban people who, deeply moved by his decease, have shown integrity, patriotic conviction, discipline, and maturity by attending, en masse, the tribute activities organized, and by swearing to uphold the oath of loyalty to the conception of revolution articulated by Fidel on May 1, 2000.

On November 28 and 29, millions of compatriots signed their names in support of the revolution. Amidst the pain of these days we have once again felt pride and comfort in the outstanding reactions of children and young Cubans, who reaffirmed their willingness to be loyal continuators of the ideals of the leader of the revolution.

On behalf of our people, the party, state, government, and family members, I reiterate our most heartfelt thanks for the countless displays of respect and affection toward Fidel, his ideas and his work, which continue to arrive from all corners of the globe.

Ever faithful to Martí's philosophy that "all the glory of the world fits into a kernel of corn," the leader of the revolution rejected any manifestation of a cult of personality, and remained true to this position until the last hours of his life, insisting that, after his death, his name and likeness never be used to designate institutions, plazas, parks, avenues, streets, or other public spaces, insisting also that no monuments, busts, statues, and other such tributes to him be erected.

In accordance with *compañero* Fidel's decision, during the next session of the National Assembly of People's Power, we will present the necessary legislative proposals to ensure his will is upheld.

Our dear friend Bouteflika, president of Algeria, rightly said that Fidel possessed the extraordinary ability to travel into the future, return, and explain it. On July 26, 1989, in the city of Camagüey, the *comandante en jefe* predicted, two-and-a-half years in advance, the disappearance of the Soviet Union and socialist camp, and proclaimed to the world that, if this were the case, Cuba would continue to defend the banner of socialism.

Fidel's authority and his close relationship with the people were key to the country's heroic resistance during the dramatic years of the Special Period, when the nation's Gross Domestic Product fell 34.8 percent and the Cuban people's food situation deteriorated significantly, when we suffered blackouts lasting 16 to 20 hours a day, and a good part of our industry and public transport was paralyzed. Despite this, however, we were able to safeguard public health and education for the entire nation.

I recall the party meetings in the different regions—east, in the city of

Holguín; central, in the city of Santa Clara; and west in the capital of the republic, Havana — held in July 1994 to analyze how to tackle, with greater efficiency and cohesion, the challenges of the Special Period, the growing imperialist blockade and media campaigns geared toward sowing despair among our citizens. We all left these meetings convinced that with the combined strength and intelligence of the masses under the leadership of the party, it would be, and was, possible to transform the Special Period into a new victorious battle in the country's history.

At that time, few people in the world would have wagered on our ability to resist and overcome in the face of such adversity and the intensification of the enemy blockade. Our people, however, under Fidel's leadership, provided an unforgettable lesson in resolve and loyalty to the principles of the revolution. Recalling those difficult moments, I think it right and fitting to return to what I said about Fidel on the Isle of Youth on July 26, 1994, one of the most difficult years over 22 years ago. Speaking of Fidel, I said: "The most illustrious son of Cuba this century showed us that the attempt to capture the Moncada Garrison was possible; that we were able to turn that setback into a victory," which, I might add, we achieved five years, five months and five days later, on that glorious January 1 of 1959.

He showed us, "Yes, it was possible to reach the coast of Cuba in the *Granma* yacht; that yes, it was possible to resist the enemy, hunger, rain and cold, and organize a revolutionary army in the Sierra Maestra following the Alegría de Pío debacle; that yes, it was possible to open new guerrilla fronts in the province of Oriente, with ours and Almeida's columns; that yes, it was possible to defeat [Batista's] great offensive of over 10,000 soldiers with only 300 rifles..." after which Che wrote in his campaign diary that the backbone of the army of the tyranny had been broken.

Fidel showed us "that yes, it was possible to repeat the feats of Maceo and Gómez, extending with Che and Camilo's columns the struggle from the east to the west of the island; that yes, it was possible to defeat, with the support of the entire people, the tyranny of Batista, backed by US imperialism.

"He was the man who showed us that yes, it was possible to defeat in 72 hours," or even less, "the mercenary invasion at the Bay of Pigs and, at the same time, continue the campaign to eradicate illiteracy in one year," as happened in 1961. "That yes, it was possible to proclaim the socialist character of the revolution some 90 miles from the empire, and when its warships advanced toward Cuba, following the brigade of mercenary troops; that yes, it was possible to resolutely uphold the inalienable principles of our sovereignty, fearlessly confronting the threat of nuclear aggression by the United States during those days of the October 1962 missile crisis.

"He also showed us that yes, it was possible to offer solidarity assistance to other sister peoples struggling against colonial oppression, external aggression and racism. That yes, it was possible to defeat the racist South Africans, saving Angola's territorial integrity, forcing Namibia's independence and delivering a harsh blow to the apartheid regime. That yes, it was possible to turn Cuba into a medical power, reduce infant mortality first, to the lowest rate in the Third World, and then to a level comparable to that of rich countries; now, at least on this continent, our rate of infant mortality of children under one year of age is lower than Canada's and the United States; and at the same time, we were able to significantly increase the life expectancy of our population.

"Fidel showed us that yes, it was possible to transform Cuba into a great scientific center, to advance in the modern and decisive fields of genetic engineering and biotechnology; to insert ourselves within the powerhouse of international pharmaceuticals; to develop tourism, despite the US blockade; to build causeways in the sea to make Cuba increasingly more attractive, obtaining greater monetary benefit from our natural beauty.

"Above all, he showed us that yes, it is possible to resist, survive, and develop without renouncing our principles or the achievements of socialism in the unipolar world that emerged after the fall of the socialist camp in Europe and the disintegration of the Soviet Union.

"Fidel's enduring lesson is that yes, it is possible, that humans are able to overcome the harshest conditions as long as their willingness to triumph does not falter, they accurately assess every situation, and do not renounce their just and noble principles."

Those are the words I spoke more than two decades ago about a man, who, following the first disastrous battle at Alegría de Pío—which, the day after tomorrow, will celebrate its 60th anniversary--never lost faith in victory, so that 13 days later, by December 18, already in the mountains of the Sierra Maestra, with seven rifles and a handful of combatants, pronounced: "Now we have won the war!"

This is the undefeated Fidel who brings us together and who, through his example, showed us, yes, it was possible, yes, it is possible, and yes, it will be possible! [The crowd applauds and shouts, "Yes, we can!"]. So, I repeat, he showed us, yes, it was possible, yes, it is possible, and yes, it will be possible to overcome any obstacle, threat or disruption in our resolute effort to build socialism in Cuba, that is to say, to guarantee the independence and sovereignty of the homeland!

Here, with Fidel's remains, in the Antonio Maceo Plaza of the Revolution, in this heroic city of Santiago de Cuba, we swear to defend the homeland and socialism! And together we all reaffirm what the Bronze Titan [Antonio Maceo] said: "Whoever attempts to conquer Cuba, will gather the dust of her blood-soaked soil, if he does not perish in fight!" [The crowd recites Maceo's words along with Raúl.]

Fidel, Fidel! *Hasta la victoria!* [The crowd responds, *Siempre!*]

1. HISTORY WILL ABSOLVE ME

SANTIAGO DE CUBA, OCTOBER 16, 1953

On July 26, 1953, Fidel Castro led a group of young rebels (including two women) to attack the Moncada military garrison in Santiago de Cuba, in the eastern province of Oriente, in the hope of sparking a popular uprising against General Batista who had seized power in a coup on March 10, 1952. The attack failed and 70 of the young rebels were brutally tortured or murdered in cold blood. Fidel Castro and 28 others were captured, tried and convicted. The following is a reconstruction of Fidel's courtroom defense speech that was smuggled out of prison and published as the political platform of the Cuban revolutionary movement with the title "History will absolve me." Fidel was sentenced to 15 years' imprisonment but freed in 1955 after a broad amnesty campaign.

Honorable Judges:

Never has a lawyer had to practice his profession under such difficult conditions; never have so many overwhelming irregularities been committed against an accused man. In this case, counsel and defendant are one and the same. As attorney, he has not even been able to take a look at the indictment. As accused, for the past 76 days he has been locked away in solitary confinement, held totally and absolutely incommunicado, in violation of every human and legal right.

He who speaks to you hates vanity with all his being, and his temperament and frame of mind are not inclined toward courtroom posturing or sensationalism of any kind. If I have had to assume my own defense before this court it is for two reasons. First, because I have been denied legal aid almost entirely, and second, only one who has been so deeply wounded, who has seen his country so forsaken and justice so vilified, can speak at a moment like this with words that spring from the blood of his heart and the essence of truth.

There was no lack of generous compañeros who wished to defend me, and the Havana Bar Association appointed a courageous and competent jurist, Dr. Jorge Pagliery, dean of the bar in this city, to represent me in this case. However, he was not permitted to carry out his task. As often as he tried to see me, the prison gates were closed on him. Only after a month and a half, and through the intervention of the court, was he finally granted a 10-minute interview with me in the presence of a sergeant from the Military Intelligence Service (SIM). One supposes that a lawyer has a right to speak with his defendant in private, and this right is respected throughout the world, except in the case of a Cuban prisoner of war in the hands of an implacable dictatorship that abides by no code of law, be it legal or humane. Neither Dr. Pagliery nor I were willing to tolerate such dirty spying on our means of defense for the oral trial. Perhaps they wanted to know beforehand the methods we would use in order to reduce to dust the incredible fabric of lies they had woven around the events at the Moncada barracks? How were we going to expose the terrible truth they would go to such great lengths to conceal? It was then that we decided to take advantage of my profession as a lawyer and that I would assume my own defense.

This decision, overheard by the sergeant and reported by him to his superior, provoked a real panic. It looked like some mocking little imp was telling them that I was going to ruin all their plans. You know very well, Honorable Judges, how much pressure has been brought to bear on me in order to strip me also of this right that is ratified by long Cuban tradition. The court could not give in to such machinations, for that would have left the accused unable to defend himself. The accused, who is now exercising this right to plead his own case, will under no circumstances refrain from saying what he must say. I consider it essential that I explain, in the beginning, the reason for the terrible isolation in which I have been kept; the purpose of keeping me silent; what was behind the plots to kill me, plots with which the court is familiar; what grave events are being hidden from the people; and the truth behind all the strange things which have taken place during this trial. I propose to do all this with the utmost clarity.

You have publicly called this case the most significant in the history of the republic. If you sincerely believed this, you should not have allowed your authority to be stained and degraded. The first court session was September 21. Among 100 machine guns and bayonets, scandalously invading the hall of justice, more than 100 people were seated in the prisoner's dock. The great majority had nothing to do with what had happened. They had been under preventive detention for many days, suffering all kinds of insults and abuses in the chambers of the repressive units. But the rest of the accused, the minority, were brave and determined, ready to proudly confirm their part in the battle for freedom, ready to offer an example of unprecedented self-sacrifice and to wrench from the jail's claws those who in deliberate bad faith had been included in the trial. Those who had met in combat confronted one another again. Once again, with the cause of justice on our side, we would wage the terrible battle of truth against infamy! Surely the regime was not prepared for the moral catastrophe that awaited it!

How to maintain all its false accusations? How to keep secret what had really happened, when so many young people were willing to risk everything—prison, torture and death, if necessary—in order that the truth be told before this court?

I was called as a witness at that first session. For two hours I was questioned by the prosecutor as well as by 20 defense attorneys. I was able to prove with exact facts and figures the sums of money that had been spent, the way this money was collected and the arms we had been able to round up. I had nothing to hide, for the truth was that all this was accomplished through sacrifices without precedent in the history of our republic. I spoke of the goals that inspired us in our struggle and of the humane and generous treatment that we had at all times accorded our adversaries. If I accomplished my purpose of demonstrating that those who were falsely implicated in this trial were neither directly nor indirectly involved, I owe it to the complete support of my heroic compañeros. For, as I said, the consequences they might be forced to suffer at no time caused them to repent as revolutionaries and patriots. I was never once allowed to speak with these compañeros of mine during the time we were in prison, and yet we planned to act in the same way. The fact is, when people carry the same ideals in their hearts, nothing can isolate them—neither prison walls nor the sod of cemeteries, for a single memory, a single spirit, a single idea, a single conscience, a single dignity will sustain them all.

From that very moment, the structure of lies the regime had erected about the events at the Moncada barracks began to collapse like a house of cards. As a result, the prosecutor realized that keeping in prison all those persons named as instigators was completely absurd, and he requested their provisional release.

At the close of my testimony in that first session, I asked the court to allow me to leave the dock and sit among the counsel for the defense. This permission was granted. At that point, what I consider my most important mission in this trial began: to totally discredit the cowardly, malicious and treacherous lies that the regime had hurled against our fighters; to reveal with irrefutable evidence the horrible, repugnant crimes they had committed against the prisoners; and to show the nation and the world the infinite misfortune of the Cuban people who are suffering the cruelest, the most inhuman oppression in all their history.

The second session was convened on Tuesday, September 22. By that time only 10 witnesses had testified, and they had already clarified the murders in the Manzanillo area, specifically establishing and placing on record the direct responsibility of the captain commanding that post. There were 300 more witnesses to testify. What would happen if, with an overwhelming mass of facts and evidence, I should proceed to cross-examine the very military men who were directly responsible for those crimes? Could the regime permit me to go ahead before the large audience attending the trial? In front of journalists and lawyers from all over the island? And in front of the party leaders of the opposition, who they had stupidly seated right in the prisoner's dock where they could hear so clearly everything that might be exposed here? They would rather have blown up the court house, with all the judges, than allow that!

And so they devised a plan by which they could eliminate me from the trial and they proceeded to do just that, *manu militari* [by force of arms]. On Friday night, September 25, the eve of the third session of the trial, two prison doctors visited me in my cell. They were visibly embarrassed. "We have come to examine you," they said. I asked them, "Who is so worried about my health?" Actually, from the moment I saw them I realized what they had come for. They could not have treated me with greater respect, and they explained their predicament to me. That afternoon Colonel Chaviano had appeared at the prison and told them I was "doing the government terrible damage with this trial." He had told them they must sign a certificate declaring that I was ill and was, therefore, unable to appear in court. The doctors told me that for their part they were prepared to resign from their posts and risk persecution. They put the matter in my hands, for me to decide. I found it hard to ask those people to sacrifice themselves. But neither could I, under any circumstances, consent to be part of that plan. Leaving the matter to their own consciences, I told them only: "You know your duty; I certainly know mine."

After leaving the cell they signed the certificate. I know they did so believing in good faith that this was the only way they could save my life, which they considered to be in grave danger. I was not obliged to keep our conversation secret, for I am bound only by the truth. Telling the truth in this instance may jeopardize the material interests of those good doctors, but I am removing all doubt about their honor, which is worth much more. That same night, I wrote the court a letter denouncing the plot; requesting that two court physicians be sent to certify my excellent state of health, and to inform you that if to save my life I must take part in such deception, I would a thousand times prefer to lose it. To show my determination to fight alone against this whole degenerate frame-up, I added to my own words one of the Master [José Martí]'s lines: "A just cause even from the depths of a cave is stronger than an army." As the court knows, this was the letter Dr. Melba Hernández submitted at the third session of the trial on September 26. I managed to get it to her in spite of the heavy guard I was under. That letter, of course, provoked immediate reprisals. Dr. Hernández was subjected to solitary confinement, and since I was already incommunicado I was sent to the most inaccessible corner of the prison. From that moment on, all the accused were thoroughly searched from head to foot before they were brought into the courtroom.

Two court physicians certified on September 27 that I was, in fact, in perfect health. Yet, in spite of the repeated orders from the court, I was never again brought to the hearings. Furthermore, anonymous persons daily circulated hundreds of apocryphal pamphlets which announced my rescue from jail. This stupid alibi was invented so they could physically eliminate me and pretend I had tried to escape. Since the scheme failed as a result of timely exposure by vigilant friends, and after the first affidavit was shown to be false, the regime could only keep me away from the trial by open and flagrant contempt of court.

This was an incredible situation, Honorable Judges. Here was a regime literally afraid to bring an accused man to court; a regime of bloodshed and terror that shrank in fear of the moral conviction of a defenseless man — unarmed, slandered and isolated. And so, after depriving me of everything else, they finally deprived me even of the trial in which I was the main defendant. Remember that this was during a period in which individual rights were suspended and the Public Order Act as well as censorship of radio and press were in full force. What unbelievable crimes this regime must have committed to so fear the voice of one accused man!

I must dwell on the insolence and disrespect the army leaders have at all times shown toward you. As often as this court has ordered an end to the inhuman isolation in which I was held; as often as it has ordered my most elementary rights to be respected; as often as it has demanded that I be brought before it, this court has never been obeyed! Worse yet, in the very presence of the court, during the first and second hearings, a praetorian guard was stationed beside me to prevent me from speaking to anyone, even during the brief recesses. In other words, not only in prison, but also in the courtroom and in your presence, they ignored your decrees. I had intended to mention this matter in the following session, as a question of elementary respect for the court, but I was never brought back. And if, in exchange for so much disrespect, they bring us before you to be imprisoned in the name of a legality that they and they alone have been violating since March 10, sad indeed is the role they would force on you. The Latin maxim "*Cedant arma togae*" [Let arms yield to the toga] has certainly not been observed on a single occasion during this trial. I beg you to keep that situation well in mind.

Moreover, these tricks were in any case quite useless; my brave compañeros, with unprecedented patriotism, did their duty to the utmost.

"Yes, we set out to fight for Cuba's freedom and we are not ashamed of having done so," they declared, one by one, on the witness stand. Then, addressing the court with impressive courage, they denounced the hideous crimes committed upon the bodies of our brothers. Although absent from court, I was able, in my prison cell, to follow the trial in every detail, thanks to the inmates at Boniato Prison. In spite of all threats, these men found ingenious methods of getting me newspaper clippings and all kinds of information. In this way they avenged the abuses and immoralities perpetrated against them both by Taboada, the warden, and the supervisor, Lieutenant Rosabal, who drove them from sun up to sun down building private mansions and starved them by embezzling the prison food budget.

As the trial went on, roles were reversed. Those who came to accuse found themselves accused, and the accused became the accusers! It was not the revolutionaries who were judged there; judged once and forever was a man named Batista—*monstruum horrendum!* [horrible monster]—and it matters little that these valiant and worthy young people have been condemned, if tomorrow the people condemn the dictator and his henchmen! Our people were consigned to the Isle of Pines Prison, in whose circular galleries Castells's ghost still lingers and where the cries of countless victims still echo; there our young men have been sent to expiate their love of liberty, in bitter confinement, banished from society, torn from their homes and exiled from their country. Is it not clear to you, as I have said before, that in such circumstances it is difficult and disagreeable for this lawyer to fulfill his duty?

As a result of so many turbid and illegal machinations, due to the will of those who govern and the weakness of those who judge, I find myself here in this little room at the Civilian Hospital, where I have been brought to be tried in secret, so that I may not be heard and my voice may be stifled, so that no one may hear what I am going to say. Why, then, do we need that imposing Palace of Justice which the Honorable Judges would without doubt find much more comfortable? I must warn you: It is unwise to administer justice from a hospital room, surrounded by sentinels with fixed bayonets; the citizens might suppose that our justice is sick, and that it is captive.

Let me remind you, your laws of procedure provide that trials will be "public hearings"; however, the people have been barred altogether from this session of court. The only civilians admitted here have been two attorneys and six reporters from newspapers where the censorship of the press will prevent printing a word I say. I see, as my sole audience in this chamber and in the corridors, nearly 100 soldiers and officers. I am grateful for the polite and serious attention they give me. I only wish I could have the whole army before me! I know, one day, this army will seethe with rage to wash away the terrible, shameful bloodstains splattered across the military uniform by the present ruthless clique in its lust for power. On that day, what a fall awaits those mounted so arrogantly on their noble steeds! That is, if the people have not dislodged them long before that!

Finally, I would like to add that I was allowed no treatise on penal law in my cell. I have at my disposal only this tiny code of law lent to me by my learned counsel, Dr. Baudillo Castellanos, the courageous defender of my compañeros. In the same way they prevented me from receiving the books by Martí; it seems the prison censorship considered them too subversive. Or is it because I said Martí was the inspiration for July 26? Reference books on any other subject were also denied me during this trial. But it makes no difference! I carry the teachings of the Master in my heart, and in my mind the noble ideas of all those who have defended the people's freedom everywhere!

I am going to make only one request of this court; I trust it will be granted as a compensation for the many abuses and outrages the accused has had to tolerate without protection of the law. I ask that my right to express myself be respected without restraint. Otherwise, even the merest semblance of justice cannot be maintained, and the final episode of this trial would be, more than all the others, one of ignominy and cowardice.

I must admit that I am somewhat disappointed. I had expected that the Honorable Prosecutor would come forward with a grave accusation. I thought he would be ready to justify to the limit his contention, and his reasons why I should be condemned in the name of law and justice — what law and what justice? — to 26 years in prison. But no. He has limited himself to reading Article 148 of the Social Defense Code. On the basis of this, plus aggravating circumstances, he requests that I be imprisoned for the lengthy term of 26 years! Two minutes seems a very short time in which to demand and justify that a person be put behind bars for more than a quarter of a century. Can it be that the Honorable Prosecutor is, perhaps, annoyed with the court? Because as I see it, his laconic attitude in this case clashes with the solemnity with which the Honorable Judges declared, rather proudly, that this was a trial of the greatest importance! I have heard prosecutors speak 10 times longer in a simple narcotics case asking for a sentence of just six months. The Honorable Prosecutor has supplied not a word in support of his petition. I am a just man. I realize that for a prosecuting attorney under oath of loyalty to the constitution of the republic, it is difficult to come here in the name of an unconstitutional, statutory, de facto government, lacking any legal much less moral basis, to ask that a young Cuban, a lawyer like himself and perhaps as honorable as he, be sent to jail for 26 years. But the Honorable Prosecutor is a gifted man and I have seen much less talented persons write lengthy diatribes in defense of this regime. How then can I suppose that he lacks the reason with which to defend it, at least for 15 minutes, however contemptible that might be to any decent person? It is clear that there is a great conspiracy behind all this.

Honorable Judges: Why such interest in silencing me? Why is every type of argument foregone in order to avoid presenting any target whatsoever against which I might direct my own brief? Is it that they lack any legal, moral or political basis on which to put forth a serious formulation of the question? Are they so afraid of the truth? Do they hope that I, too, will speak for only two minutes and that I will not touch on the points which have caused certain people sleepless nights since July 26? Since the prosecutor's petition was restricted to the mere reading of five lines of an article of the Social Defense Code, might they suppose that I, too, would limit myself to those same lines and circle round them like some slave turning a millstone? I will by no means accept such a gag, for in this trial there is much more than the freedom of a single individual at stake. Fundamental matters of principle are being debated here: The right of people to be free is on trial, the very foundations of our existence as a civilized and democratic nation are in the balance. When this trial is over, I do not want to have to reproach myself for any principle left undefended, for any truth left unsaid, for any crime not denounced.

The Honorable Prosecutor's famous little article hardly deserves a minute of my time. I will limit myself for the moment to a brief legal debate against it, because I want to clear the field for an assault against all the endless lies and deceits, the hypocrisy, banalities and moral cowardice that have set the stage for the crude comedy which since March 10—and even before then—has been called justice in Cuba.

It is a fundamental principle of criminal law that an imputed offense must correspond exactly to the type of crime described by law. If no law applies exactly to the point in question, then there is no offense.

The article in question reads:

> A penalty of imprisonment of three to 10 years will be imposed on the perpetrator of any act aimed at bringing about an armed uprising against the constitutional powers of the state. The penalty will be imprisonment from five to 20 years, in the event that insurrection actually be carried out.

In what country is the Honorable Prosecutor living? Who has told him that we have sought to bring about an uprising against the constitutional powers of the state? Two things are self-evident: First of all, the dictatorship that oppresses the nation is not a constitutional power, but an unconstitutional one; it was established against the constitution, over the constitution, violating the legitimate constitution of the republic. The legitimate constitution is that which emanates directly from a sovereign people. I will demonstrate this point fully later on, notwithstanding all the subterfuges contrived by cowards and traitors to justify the unjustifiable. Secondly, the article refers to powers, in the plural, as in the case of a republic governed by a legislative power, an executive power, and a judicial power which balance and counterbalance one another. We have fomented a rebellion against one single power, an illegal one, which has usurped and combined both the legislative and executive powers of the nation, and so has destroyed the entire system that was specifically safeguarded by the code now under analysis. As to the independence of the judiciary after March 10, I will not allude to that for I am in no mood for joking... No matter how Article 148 may be stretched, shrunk or amended, not a single comma applies to the events of July 26. Let us leave this statute alone and await the opportunity to apply it to those who really did foment an uprising against the constitutional powers of the state. Later I will come back to the code to refresh the Honorable Prosecutor's memory about certain circumstances he has unfortunately overlooked.

I warn you, I am just beginning! If there is in your hearts a vestige of love for your country, love for humanity, love for justice, listen carefully. I know that I will be silenced for many years; I know that the regime will try to suppress the truth by all possible means; I know that there will be a conspiracy to bury me in oblivion. But my voice will not be stifled — it will rise from my breast even when I feel most alone, and my heart will give it all the fire that callous cowards deny it.

From a shack in the mountains on Monday, July 27, I listened to the dictator's voice on the airwaves while there were still 18 of our people in arms against the government. Those who have never experienced such moments will never know that kind of bitterness and indignation. While the long-cherished hopes of freeing our people lay in ruins about us we heard those crushed hopes gloated over by a tyrant more vicious, more arrogant than ever. The endless stream of lies and slanders, poured forth in his crude, odious, repulsive language, may only be compared to the endless stream of pure, young blood that had flowed since the previous night — with his knowledge, consent, complicity and approval — being spilled by the most inhuman gang of assassins it is possible to imagine. To have believed him for a single moment would have sufficed to fill a person of conscience with remorse and shame for the rest of their life. At that time I could not even hope to brand his miserable forehead with the mark of truth to condemn him for the rest of his days and for all time to come. Already a circle of more than 1,000 men, armed with weapons more powerful than ours and with peremptory orders to bring in our corpses, was closing in around us. Now that the truth is coming out, now that speaking before you I am carrying out the mission I set for myself, I may die peacefully and content. So I will not mince my words about those savage murderers.

I must pause to consider the facts for a moment. The government itself said the attack showed such precision and perfection that it must have been planned by military strategists. Nothing could have been further from the truth! The plan was drawn up by a group of young people, none of whom had any military experience at all. I will reveal their names, omitting two who are neither dead nor in prison: Abel Santamaría, José Luis Tasende, Renato Guitart Rosell, Pedro Miret, Jesús Montané and myself. Half of them are dead, and in tribute to their memory I can say that although they were not military experts they had enough patriotism to have given — had we not been at such a great disadvantage — a good beating to that entire bunch of generals, those generals of March 10 who are neither soldiers nor patriots. Much more difficult than the planning of the attack was our organizing, training, mobilizing and arming people under this repressive regime with its millions of dollars spent on espionage, bribery and disinformation services. Nevertheless, all this was carried out by those people and many others like them with incredible commitment, discretion and discipline. Still more praiseworthy is the fact that they gave this task everything they had, and ultimately, their very lives.

The final mobilization of our people who came to this province from the most remote towns of the entire island was accomplished with admirable precision and in absolute secrecy. It is equally true that the attack was carried out with magnificent coordination. It began simultaneously at 5:15 a.m. in both Bayamo and Santiago de Cuba; and one by one, with exact timing, the buildings surrounding the barracks fell to our forces. Nevertheless, in the interests of truth—even though it may detract from our accomplishment—I am also going to reveal for the first time a fatal fact: Due to a most unfortunate error, half of our forces, and the better armed half at that, got lost on entering the city and were not there to help us at the decisive moment. Abel Santamaría, with 21 people, had occupied the Civilian Hospital; with him went a doctor and two of our women compañeras to attend to the wounded. Raúl Castro, with 10 combatants, occupied the Palace of Justice, and it was my responsibility to attack the barracks with the rest, 95 men. Preceded by an advance group of eight who had forced gate three, I arrived with the first group of 45 men. It was precisely here that the battle began, when my car ran into an outside patrol armed with machine guns. The reserve group, which had almost all the heavy weapons (the light arms were with the advance group), turned down the wrong street and lost its way in an unfamiliar city. I must clarify the fact that I do not doubt for a moment the courage of those people; they experienced great anguish and desperation when they realized they were lost. Because of the type of action it was and because the contending forces were wearing identically colored uniforms, it was not easy for these people to reestablish contact with us. Many of them, captured later on, met death with true heroism.

Everyone had instructions, first of all, to be humane in the struggle. Never was a group of armed people more generous to the adversary. From the beginning we took numerous prisoners—nearly 20—and there was one moment when three of our people—Ramiro Valdés, José Suárez and Jesús Montané—managed to enter a barracks and hold nearly 50 soldiers prisoner for a short time. Those soldiers testified before the court, and without exception they all acknowledged that we treated them with absolute respect, that we didn't even subject them to one insulting remark. In line with this,

I want to give my heartfelt thanks to the prosecutor for one thing in the trial of my compañeros: When he made his report he was fair enough to acknowledge as an incontestable fact that we maintained a high spirit of chivalry throughout the struggle.

Discipline among the soldiers was very poor. They finally defeated us because of their superior numbers — 15 to one — and because of the protection afforded them by the defenses of the fortress. Our combatants were much better marksmen, as our enemies themselves conceded. There was a high degree of courage on both sides.

In analyzing the reasons for our tactical failure, apart from the regrettable error already mentioned, I believe we made a mistake by dividing the commando unit we had so carefully trained. Of our best-trained combatants and boldest leaders, there were 27 in Bayamo, 21 at the Civilian Hospital and 10 at the Palace of Justice. If our forces had been distributed differently the outcome of the battle might have been different. The clash with the patrol (purely accidental, since the unit might have been at that point 20 seconds earlier or 20 seconds later) alerted the camp, and gave it time to mobilize. Otherwise it would have fallen into our hands without a shot fired, since we already controlled the guard post. On the other hand, except for the .22-caliber rifles, for which there were plenty of bullets, our side was very short of ammunition. Had we had hand grenades, the army would not have been able to resist us for 15 minutes.

When I became convinced that all efforts to take the barracks were now useless, I began to withdraw our people in groups of eight and 10. Our retreat was covered by six expert marksmen under the command of Pedro Miret and Fidel Labrador; heroically they held off the army's advance. Our losses in the battle had been insignificant; 95 percent of our casualties came from the army's brutality after the struggle. The group at the Civilian Hospital only had one casualty; the rest of that group was trapped when the troops blocked the only exit; but our young combatants did not lay down their arms until their very last bullet was gone. Among them was Abel Santamaría, the most generous, beloved and intrepid of our young combatants, whose glorious resistance immortalizes him in Cuban history. We will soon see the fate they met and how Batista sought to punish the heroism of our youth.

We planned to continue the struggle in the mountains in case the attack on the regiment failed. In Siboney, I was able to gather a third of our forces; but many of these people were now discouraged. About 20 of them decided to surrender; later we will see what became of them. The rest, 18 men, with what arms and ammunition were left, followed me into the mountains. The terrain was completely unknown to us. For a week we held the heights of the Gran Piedra range and the army occupied the foothills. We could not come down; they didn't risk coming up. It was not force of arms, but hunger and thirst that ultimately overcame our resistance. I had to divide the combatants into smaller groups. Some of them managed to slip through the army lines; others were surrendered by Monsignor Pérez Serantes. Finally only two compañeros remained with me—José Suárez and Oscar Alcalde. While the three of us were totally exhausted, a force led by Lieutenant Sarría surprised us in our sleep at dawn. This was Saturday, August 1. By that time the slaughter of prisoners had ceased as a result of the people's protest. This officer, a man of honor, saved us from being murdered on the spot with our hands tied behind us.

I need not deny here the stupid statements by Ugalde Carrillo and company, who tried to besmirch my name in an effort to mask their own cowardice, incompetence and criminality. The facts are clear enough.

My purpose is not to bore the court with epic narratives. All that I have said is essential for a more precise understanding of what is yet to come.

Let me mention two important facts that facilitate an objective judgment of our attitude. First, we could have taken over the regiment simply by seizing all the high-ranking officers in their homes. This possibility was rejected for the very humane reason that we wished to avoid scenes of tragedy and struggle in the presence of their families. Second, we decided not to take over any radio station until the army camp was under our control. This attitude, unusually magnanimous and considerate, spared the citizens a great deal of bloodshed. With only 10 combatants I could have seized a radio station and called the people to revolt. There is no question about the people's willingness to fight. I had a recording of Eduardo Chibás's last message over the CMQ radio network, and patriotic poems and battle hymns capable of moving even the least sensitive, especially with the sounds of live battle in their ears. But I did not want to use them although our situation was desperate.

The regime has insisted that our movement did not have popular support. I have never heard an assertion so naive, and at the same time so full of bad faith. The regime seeks to show submission and cowardice on the part of the people. They all but claim that the people support the dictatorship; they do not know how offensive this is to the brave people of Oriente. Santiago thought our attack was only a local disturbance between two factions of soldiers; not until many hours later did they realize what had really happened. Who can doubt the valor, civic pride and limitless courage of the rebellious and patriotic people of Santiago de Cuba? If Moncada had fallen into our hands, even the women of Santiago de Cuba would have risen in arms. Many rifles were loaded for our fighters by the nurses at the Civilian Hospital. They fought alongside us. That is something we will never forget.

It was never our intention to engage the soldiers of the regiment in combat. We wanted to seize control of them and their weapons in a surprise attack, arouse the people and call on the soldiers to abandon the odious flag of the dictatorship and to embrace the banner of freedom; to defend the supreme interests of the nation and not the petty interests of a small clique; to turn their guns and fire on the people's enemies and not on the people, among whom are their own sons and fathers; to unite with the people as brothers instead of opposing the people as the enemies the government tries to make of them; to march behind the only beautiful ideal worthy of sacrificing one's life—the greatness and happiness of one's country. To those who doubt that many soldiers would have followed us, I ask: What Cuban does not cherish glory? What heart is not set aflame by the promise of freedom?

The navy did not fight against us, and it would undoubtedly have come over to our side later on. It is well known that this branch of the armed forces is the least dominated by the dictatorship and that there is a very intense civic conscience among its members. But, as to the rest of the nation's armed forces, would they have fought against a people in revolt? I declare that they would not! A soldier is made of flesh and blood; he thinks, observes, feels. He is susceptible to the opinions, beliefs, sympathies and antipathies of the people. If you ask his opinion, he may tell you he cannot express it; but that does not mean he has no opinion. He is affected by exactly the same problems that affect other citizens—subsistence, rent, the education of his children, their future, etc. Everything of this kind is an inevitable point of contact between him and the people and everything of this kind links him to the present and future of the society in which he lives. It is foolish to imagine that the salary a soldier receives from the state—a modest enough salary at that—should resolve the vital problems imposed on him by his needs, duties and feelings as a member of his community.

This brief explanation has been necessary because it is basic to a consideration to which few people, until now, have paid any attention: soldiers have a deep respect for the feelings of the majority of the people! During the Machado regime, in the same proportion as popular antipathy increased, the loyalty of the army visibly decreased. This was so true that a group of women almost succeeded in subverting Camp Columbia. But this is proven even more clearly by a recent development. While [Ramón] Grau San Martín's regime was able to preserve great popularity among the people, unscrupulous ex-officers and power-hungry civilians attempted innumerable conspiracies in the army, and none of them found a following in the rank and file.

The March 10 coup took place at the moment when the civil government's prestige had dwindled to its lowest ebb, a circumstance of which Batista and his clique took advantage. Why did they not strike their blow after June 1? Simply because, had they waited for the majority of the nation to express its will at the polls, the troops would not have responded to the conspiracy!

Consequently, a second assertion can be made: The army has never revolted against a regime with a popular majority behind it. These are historical truths, and if Batista insists on remaining in power at all costs against the will of the majority of Cubans, his end will be more tragic than that of Gerardo Machado.

I have a right to express an opinion about the armed forces because I defended them when everyone else was silent. And I did this neither as a conspirator nor from any kind of personal interest—for we then enjoyed full constitutional prerogatives. I was prompted only by humane instincts and civic duty. In those days, the newspaper *Alerta* was one of the most widely read because of its position on national political matters. In its pages I campaigned against the forced labor to which the soldiers were subjected on the private estates of high civil personages and military officers. On March 3, 1952, I supplied the courts with data, photographs, films and other proof denouncing this state of affairs. I also pointed out in those articles that it was elementary decency to increase army salaries. I would like to know who else raised their voice on that occasion to protest against all this injustice done to the soldiers. Certainly not Batista and company, living well protected on their luxurious estates, surrounded by all kinds of security measures, while I ran a thousand risks with neither bodyguards nor arms.

Just as I defended the soldiers then, now — when all others are once more silent — I tell them that they allowed themselves to be miserably deceived; and to the deception and shame of March 10 they have added the disgrace, the thousand times greater disgrace, of the dreadful and unjustifiable crimes of Santiago de Cuba. From that time the uniform of the army has been splattered with blood. As last year I told the people and denounced before the courts that soldiers were working as slaves on private estates, today I make the bitter charge that there are soldiers stained from head to toe with the blood of the young Cubans they have tortured and slain. And I say also that if the army serves the republic, defends the nation, respects the people and protects the citizenry then it is only fair that the soldier should earn at least 100 pesos a month. But if the soldiers slay and oppress the people, betray the nation and defend only the interests of one small group, then the army deserves not a cent of the republic's money and Camp Columbia should be converted into a school with 10,000 orphans living there instead of soldiers.

I want to be fair above all else, so I can't blame all the soldiers for the shameful crimes that stain a few evil and treacherous military men. But every honorable and upright soldier who loves his career and his uniform is duty bound to demand and to fight for the cleansing of this guilt, to avenge this betrayal and to see the guilty punished. Otherwise the soldier's uniform will forever be a mark of infamy instead of a source of pride.

Of course, the March 10 regime had no choice but to remove the soldiers from the private estates. But it did so only to put them to work as doormen, chauffeurs, servants and bodyguards for the whole rabble of petty politicians who make up the party of the dictatorship. Every fourth- or fifth-rank official considers himself entitled to the services of a soldier to drive his car and to watch over him as if he were constantly afraid of receiving the kick in the pants he so justly deserves.

If they had been at all interested in promoting real reforms, why did the regime not confiscate the estates and the fortunes of men like Genovevo

Pérez Dámera, who acquired their riches by exploiting soldiers, driving them like slaves and misappropriating the funds of the armed forces? But no—Genovevo Pérez and others like him no doubt still have soldiers protecting them on their estates because the March 10 generals, deep in their hearts, aspire to the same future and can't allow that kind of precedent to be set.

March 10 was a miserable deception, yes... After Batista and his band of corrupt and disreputable politicians had failed in their electoral plan, they took advantage of the army's discontent and used it to climb to power on the backs of the soldiers. And I know there are many military men who are disgruntled because they have been disappointed. At first their pay was raised, but later, through deductions and cuts of every kind, it was lowered again. Many of the old elements, who had drifted away from the armed forces, returned to the ranks and blocked the way of young, capable and valuable people who might otherwise have advanced. Good soldiers have been neglected while the most scandalous nepotism prevails. Many decent military men are now asking themselves why the armed forces had to assume the tremendous historic responsibility of destroying our constitution merely to put a group of immoral men in power, men of bad reputation, corrupt, politically degenerate beyond redemption, who could never again have occupied a political post had it not been at the point of a bayonet; and they weren't even the ones with the bayonets in their hands...

On the other hand, soldiers endure a worse tyranny than civilians. They are under constant surveillance and not one of them enjoys the slightest security in his job. Any unjustified suspicion, any gossip, any intrigue or denunciation is sufficient to bring transfer, dishonorable discharge or imprisonment. Did not [General] Tabernilla, in a memorandum, forbid them to talk with anyone opposed to the government, that is to say, with 99 percent of the people? What a lack of confidence! Not even the vestal virgins of Rome had to abide by such a rule! As for the much publicized little homes for enlisted men, there aren't 300 on the whole island; yet with what has been spent on tanks, guns and other weaponry every soldier might have a place to live. Batista isn't concerned with taking care of the army, but that the army takes care of him! He increases the army's power of oppression and killing but does not improve living conditions for the soldiers. Triple guard duty, constant confinement to barracks, continuous anxiety, the enmity of the people, uncertainty about the future—this is what has been given to the soldier. In other words: "Die for the regime, soldier, give it your sweat and blood. We will dedicate a speech to you and award you a posthumous promotion (when it no longer matters) and afterwards... we will go on living in luxury, making ourselves rich. Kill, abuse, oppress the people. When the people get tired and all this comes to an end, you can pay for our crimes while we go abroad and live like kings. And if one day we return, don't you or your children knock on the doors of our mansions, for we will be millionaires and millionaires do not mingle with the poor. Kill, soldier, oppress the people, die for the regime, give your sweat and blood..."

But if blind to this sad truth, a minority of soldiers had decided to fight the people, the people who were going to liberate them from tyranny, victory still would have gone to the people. The Honorable Prosecutor was very interested in knowing our chances for success. These chances were based on considerations of a technical, military and social nature. They have tried to establish the myth that modern arms render the people helpless in overthrowing tyrants. Military parades and the pompous display of war machines are used to perpetuate this myth and to create a complex of absolute impotence in the people. But no weaponry, no violence, can vanquish the people once they are determined to win back their rights. Both past and present are full of examples. The most recent is the revolt in Bolivia, where miners with dynamite sticks smashed and defeated regular army regiments.

Fortunately, we Cubans need not look for examples abroad. No example is as inspiring as that of our own land. During the war of 1895 there were nearly half a million armed Spanish soldiers in Cuba, many more than the dictator counts on today to hold back a population five times greater. The arms of the Spaniards were, incomparably, both more modern and more powerful than those of our *mambises* [independence fighters]. Often the Spaniards were equipped with field artillery and the infantry used breech-loaders similar to those still in use by the infantry of today. The Cubans were usually armed with no more than their machetes, for their cartridge belts were almost always empty. There is an unforgettable passage in the history of our War of Independence, narrated by General Miró Argenter, chief of Antonio Maceo's general staff. I managed to bring it copied on this scrap of paper so I wouldn't have to depend on my memory:

> Untrained men under the command of Pedro Delgado, most of them
> equipped only with machetes, were virtually annihilated as they threw
> themselves against the solid rank of Spaniards. It is not an exaggeration
> to assert that of every 50 men, 25 were killed. Some even attacked the
> Spaniards with their bare fists, without machetes, without even knives.
> Searching through the reeds by the Hondo River, we found 15 more dead
> from the Cuban party, and it was not immediately clear what group
> they belonged to. They did not appear to have shouldered arms, their
> clothes were intact and only tin drinking cups hung from their waists;
> a few steps further on lay a dead horse, all its equipment in order. We
> reconstructed the climax of the tragedy. These men, following their
> daring chief, Lieutenant Colonel Pedro Delgado, had earned heroes'
> laurels. They had thrown themselves against bayonets with bare hands,
> the clash of metal which was heard around them was the sound of their
> drinking cups banging against the saddlehorn. Maceo was deeply moved.
> This man so used to seeing death in all its forms murmured this praise: "I
> had never seen anything like this, untrained and unarmed men attacking
> the Spaniards with only drinking cups for weapons. And I called it
> *impedimenta!*"

This is how people fight when they want to win their freedom; they throw
stones at airplanes and overturn tanks!

As soon as Santiago de Cuba was in our hands we would have immediately prepared the people of Oriente for war. Bayamo was attacked precisely to place our advance forces along the Cauto River. Never forget that this province, which has a million and a half inhabitants today, is the most rebellious and patriotic in Cuba. It was this province that sparked the 30-year fight for independence and paid the highest price in blood, sacrifice and heroism. In Oriente you can still breathe the air of that glorious epic. At dawn, when the cocks crow like bugles calling soldiers to reveille, and when the sun rises radiant over the rugged mountains, it seems that once again we will live the days of Yara or Baire!

I stated that the second consideration on which we based our chances for success was of a social nature. Why were we sure of the people's support? When we speak of the people we are not talking about those who live in comfort, the conservative elements of the nation, who welcome any repressive regime, any dictatorship, any despotism, prostrating themselves before the masters of the moment until they grind their foreheads into the ground. When we speak of struggle and we mention the people we mean the vast unredeemed masses, those to whom everyone makes promises and who are deceived by all; we mean the people who yearn for a better, more dignified and more just nation; who are moved by ancestral aspirations to justice, for they have suffered injustice and mockery generation after generation; those who long for great and wise transformations in all aspects of their life; people who, to attain those changes, are ready to give even the very last breath they have when they believe in something or in someone, especially when they believe in themselves. The first condition of sincerity and good faith in any endeavor is to do precisely what no one else ever does, that is, to speak with absolute clarity, without fear. The demagogues and professional politicians who manage to perform the miracle of being right about everything and of pleasing everyone are, necessarily, deceiving everyone about everything. Revolutionaries must proclaim their ideas courageously, define their principles and express their intentions so that no one is deceived, neither friend nor foe.

In terms of struggle, when we talk about the people we're talking about the 600,000 Cubans without work, who want to earn their daily bread honestly without having to emigrate from their homeland in search of a livelihood; the 500,000 farm laborers who live in miserable shacks, who work four months of the year and starve the rest, sharing their misery with their children, who don't have an inch of land to till and whose existence would move any heart not made of stone; the 400,000 industrial workers and laborers whose retirement funds have been embezzled, whose benefits are being taken away, whose homes are wretched hovels, whose salaries pass from the hands of the boss to those of the moneylender, whose future is a pay reduction and dismissal, whose lives are endless labor and whose only rest is the tomb; the 100,000 small farmers who live and die working land that is not theirs, looking at it with the sadness of Moses gazing at the promised land, who die without ever owning it, who like feudal serfs have to pay for the use of their parcel of land by giving up a portion of its produce, who cannot love it, improve it, beautify it nor plant a cedar or an orange tree on it because they never know when a sheriff will come with the rural guard to evict them; the 30,000 teachers and professors who are so devoted, dedicated and so necessary to improve the destiny of future generations and who are so badly treated and paid; the 20,000 small business people weighed down by debts, ruined by the crisis and harangued by a plague of grafting and venal officials; the 10,000 young professionals: doctors, engineers, lawyers, veterinarians, school teachers, dentists, pharmacists, journalists, painters, sculptors, etc., who finish school with their degrees anxious to work and full of hope, only to find themselves at a dead end, all doors closed to them, where no ears hear their clamor or supplication. These are the people, the ones who know misfortune and, therefore, are capable of fighting with limitless courage! To these people whose desperate roads through life have been paved with the bricks of betrayal and false promises, we were not going to say: "We will give you…" but rather: "Here it is, now fight for it with everything you have, so that liberty and happiness may be yours!"

The five revolutionary laws that would have been proclaimed immediately after the capture of the Moncada barracks and would have been broadcast to the nation by radio must be included in the indictment. It is possible that Colonel Chaviano may deliberately have destroyed these documents, but even if he has, I remember them.

The first revolutionary law would have returned power to the people and proclaimed the 1940 constitution as the supreme law of the state until such time as the people should decide to modify or change it. And in order to effect its implementation and punish those who violated it—there being no electoral organization to carry this out—the revolutionary movement, as the circumstantial incarnation of this sovereignty, the only source of legitimate power, would have assumed all the faculties inherent therein, except that of modifying the constitution itself. In other words, it would have assumed the legislative, executive and judicial powers.

This attitude could not be clearer or more free of vacillation and sterile charlatanry. A government acclaimed by the mass of rebel people would be vested with all powers, everything necessary in order to proceed with the effective implementation of popular will and real justice. From that moment, the judicial power—which since March 10 had placed itself in contradiction to and outside the constitution—would cease to exist and we would proceed to its immediate and total reform before it would once again assume the power granted it by the supreme law of the republic. Without these previous measures, a return to legality by putting its custody back into the hands that have crippled the system so dishonorably would constitute a fraud, a deceit, one more betrayal.

The second revolutionary law would give non-mortgageable and non-transferable ownership of the land to all tenant and subtenant farmers, lessees, share croppers and squatters who hold parcels of five *caballerías* [approximately 165 acres] of land or less, and the state would indemnify the former owners on the basis of the rental which they would have received for these parcels over a period of 10 years.

The third revolutionary law would have granted workers and employees the right to share 30 percent of the profits of all the large industrial, mercantile and mining enterprises, including the sugar mills. The strictly agricultural enterprises would be exempt in consideration of other agrarian laws which would be put into effect.

The fourth revolutionary law would have granted all sugar planters the right to share 55 percent of sugar production and a minimum quota of 40,000 *arrobas* for all small tenant farmers who have been established for three years or more.

The fifth revolutionary law would have ordered the confiscation of all holdings and ill-gotten gains of those who had committed fraud during previous regimes, as well as the holdings and ill-gotten gains of all their legatees and heirs. To implement this, special courts with full powers would gain access to all records of all corporations registered or operating in this country, in order to investigate concealed funds of illegal origin, and to request that foreign governments extradite persons and attach holdings rightfully belonging to the Cuban people. Half of the property recovered would be used to subsidize retirement funds for workers and the other half would be used for hospitals, asylums and charitable organizations.

Furthermore, it was declared that the Cuban foreign policy in the Americas would be one of close solidarity with the democratic peoples of this continent, and that all those politically persecuted by bloody tyrannies oppressing our sister nations would find generous asylum, fraternity and bread in the land of Martí, not the persecution, hunger and treason they find today. Cuba should be the bulwark of liberty and not a shameful link in the chain of despotism.

These laws would have been proclaimed immediately. As soon as the upheaval ended and prior to a detailed and far-reaching study, they would have been followed by another series of laws and fundamental measures, such as agrarian reform, educational reform, nationalization of the electricity trust and the telephone company, the refund to the people of the illegal and repressive rates these companies have charged, and payment to the treasury of all taxes brazenly evaded in the past.

All these laws and others would be based on exact compliance with two essential articles of our constitution: one of them outlawing large estates, indicating the maximum area of land any one person or entity may own for each type of agricultural enterprise, adopting measures which would tend to revert the land to Cuban ownership. The other categorically demands that the state use all means at its disposal to provide jobs and ensure a decent livelihood to each manual or intellectual laborer. None of these laws can be called unconstitutional. The first popularly elected government would have to respect them, not only because of a moral obligation to the nation, but because when people achieve something they have yearned for throughout generations, no force in the world is capable of taking it away again.

The problem of the land, the problem of industrialization, the problem of housing, the problem of unemployment, the problem of education and the problem of the people's health.These are the six problems we would take immediate steps to solve, along with the restoration of civil liberties and political democracy.

This exposition may seem cold and theoretical if one does not know the shocking and tragic conditions of the nation with regard to these six problems, along with the most humiliating political oppression.

Eighty-five percent of the small farmers in Cuba pay rent and live under constant threat of being evicted from the land they till. More than half of our most productive land is in the hands of foreigners. In Oriente, the largest province, the lands of the United Fruit Company and the West Indian Company link the northern and southern coasts. There are 200,000 peasant families who do not have a single acre of land to till to provide food for their starving children. On the other hand, nearly 300,000 *caballerías* of cultivable land owned by powerful interests remain uncultivated. If Cuba is above all an agricultural state, if its population is largely rural, if the city depends on these rural areas, if the people from our countryside won our War of

Independence, if our nation's greatness and prosperity depend on a healthy and vigorous rural population that loves the land and knows how to work it, if this population depends on a state that protects and guides it, then how can the present state of affairs be allowed to continue?

Except for a few food, lumber and textile industries, Cuba continues to be primarily a producer of raw materials. We export sugar to import candy, we export hides to import shoes, we export iron to import plows... Everyone agrees with the urgent need to industrialize the nation, that we need steel industries, paper and chemical industries, that we must improve our cattle and grain production, and the technology and processing in our food industry in order to defend ourselves against the ruinous competition from Europe in cheese products, condensed milk, liquors and edible oils, and from the United States in canned goods; that we need cargo ships; that tourism should be an enormous source of revenue. But the capitalists insist that the workers remain under the yoke. The state sits back with its arms crossed and industrialization can wait forever.

Just as serious or even worse is the housing problem. There are 200,000 huts and hovels in Cuba; 400,000 families in the countryside and in the cities live cramped in huts and tenements without even the minimum sanitary requirements; 2.2 million urban dwellers pay rents which absorb between one-fifth and one-third of their incomes; and 2.8 million rural and urban residents lack electricity. We have the same situation here: If the state proposes the lowering of rents, landlords threaten to freeze all construction; if the state does not interfere, construction goes on so long as landlords get high rents; otherwise they would not lay a single brick even though the rest of the population would have to live totally exposed to the elements. The utilities monopoly is no better; they extend lines as far as it is profitable and beyond that point they don't care if people have to live in darkness for the rest of their lives. The state sits back with its arms crossed and the people have neither homes nor electricity.

Our education system perfectly matches everything I've just mentioned. Where the peasant doesn't own the land, what need is there for agricultural schools? Where there is no industry, what need is there for technical or vocational schools? Everything follows the same absurd logic; if we don't have one thing we can't have the other. In any small European country there are more than 200 technical and vocational schools; in Cuba only six such schools exist, and their graduates have no jobs for their skills. The little rural schoolhouses are attended by a mere half of the school-age children — bare-footed, half-naked and undernourished — and frequently the teacher must buy necessary school materials from his or her own salary. Is this the way to make a nation great?

Only death can liberate one from so much misery. In this respect, however, the state is most helpful — in providing early death for the people. Ninety percent of the children in the countryside are affected by parasites which filter through their bare feet from the ground they walk on. Society is moved to compassion when it hears of the kidnapping or murder of one child, but it is indifferent to the mass murder of so many thousands of children who die every year from lack of services, in agonizing pain. Their innocent eyes, death already shining in them, seem to look into some vague infinity as if entreating forgiveness for human selfishness, as if asking God to stay his wrath. And when the head of a family works only four months a year, with what can he purchase clothing and medicine for his children? They will grow up with rickets, with not a single good tooth in their mouths by the time they reach 30; they will have heard 10 million speeches and will finally die of misery and deception. Public hospitals, which are always full, accept only patients recommended by some powerful politician who, in return, demands the votes of the unfortunate one and his family so that Cuba may continue forever in the same or worse condition.

With this background, is it not understandable that from May to December over a million persons are jobless and that Cuba, with a population of 5.5 million, has a greater number of unemployed than France or Italy with a population of 40 million each?

When you try a defendant for robbery, Honorable Judges, do you ask him how long he has been unemployed? Do you ask him how many children he has, which days of the week he ate and which he didn't, do you investigate his social context at all? You just send him to jail without further thought. But those who burn warehouses and stores to collect insurance do not go to jail, even though a few human beings may have gone up in flames. The insured have money to hire lawyers and bribe judges. You imprison the poor wretch who steals because he is hungry; but none of the hundreds who steal millions from the government has ever spent a night in jail. You dine with them at the end of the year in some elegant club and they enjoy your respect. In Cuba, when a government official becomes a millionaire overnight and enters the fraternity of the rich, he could very well be greeted with the words of that opulent character out of Balzac — Taillefer — who in his toast to the young heir to an enormous fortune, said:

> Gentlemen, let us drink to the power of gold! Mr. Valentine, a millionaire six times over, has just ascended the throne. He is king, can do everything, is above everyone, as all the rich are. Henceforth, equality before the law, established by the constitution, will be a myth for him; for he will not be subject to laws, the laws will be subject to him. There are no courts nor are there sentences for millionaires.

The nation's future, the solutions to its problems, cannot continue to depend on the selfish interests of a dozen big businessmen or on the cold calculations of profits that 10 or 12 magnates draw up in their air-conditioned offices. The country cannot continue begging on its knees for miracles from a few golden calves, like the biblical one destroyed by the prophet's fury. Golden calves cannot perform miracles of any kind. The problems of the republic can be solved only if we dedicate ourselves to fight for it with the same energy, honesty and patriotism our liberators had when they founded it. Statesmen like Carlos Saladrigas, whose statesmanship consists of preserving the status quo and mouthing phrases like "absolute freedom of enterprise," "guarantees to investment capital" and "law of supply and demand," will not solve these problems. Those ministers can chat away in a Fifth Avenue mansion until not even the dust of the bones of those whose problems require immediate solution remains. In this present-day world, social problems are not solved by spontaneous generation.

A revolutionary government backed by the people and with the respect of the nation, after cleansing the different institutions of all venal and corrupt officials, would proceed immediately to the country's industrialization, mobilizing all idle capital, currently estimated at about 1.5 billion pesos, through the National Bank and the Agricultural and Industrial Development Bank, and submitting this mammoth task to experts and people of absolute competence, totally removed from all political machines, for study, direction, planning and realization.

After settling the 100,000 small farmers as owners on the land that they previously rented, a revolutionary government would immediately proceed to resolve the land problem. First, as set forth in the constitution, it would establish the maximum amount of land to be held by each type of agricultural enterprise and would acquire the excess acreage by expropriation, recovery of swampland, planting of large nurseries, and reserving of zones for reforestation. Secondly, it would distribute the remaining land among peasant families with priority given to the larger ones, and would promote agricultural cooperatives for communal use of expensive equipment, freezing plants and unified professional technical management of farming and cattle raising. Finally, it would provide resources, equipment, protection and useful guidance to the peasants.

A revolutionary government would solve the housing problem by cutting all rents in half, by providing tax exemptions on homes occupied by the owners; by tripling taxes on rented homes; by tearing down hovels and replacing them with modern apartment buildings; and by financing housing all over the island on a scale previously unheard of, with the criterion, just as each rural family should possess its own tract of land, that each city family should own its own house or apartment. There is plenty of building material and more than enough labor power to make a decent home for every Cuban. But if we continue to wait for the golden calf, a thousand years will have gone by and the problem will remain the same. On the other hand, today possibilities of taking electricity to the most isolated areas on the island are greater than ever. The use of nuclear energy in this field is now a reality and will greatly reduce the cost of producing electricity.

With these three projects and reforms, the problem of unemployment would automatically disappear and the task of improving public health and fighting against disease would become much less difficult.

Finally, a revolutionary government would undertake a thorough reform of the education system, bringing it into line with the projects just mentioned with the idea of educating those generations that will have the privilege of living in a happier land. Never forget the words of the Apostle [José Martí]: "A grave mistake is being made in Latin America: In countries that live almost completely from the produce of the land, people are being educated exclusively for urban life and are not prepared for rural life."

"The happiest country is the one that has educated its children best, both in how to think for themselves and how to develop their sensibilities." "An educated country will always be strong and free."

The soul of education, however, is the teacher, and in Cuba the teaching profession is miserably underpaid. Despite this, no one is more dedicated than the Cuban teacher. Who among us has not learned their ABCs in the little public schoolhouse? It is time we stopped paying pittances to these young men and women who are entrusted with the sacred task of teaching our youth. No teacher should earn less than 200 pesos, no secondary teacher should make less than 350 pesos, if they are to devote themselves exclusively to their noble calling without suffering want. Moreover, all rural teachers should have free use of the various systems of transportation; and, at least once every five years, all teachers should enjoy a sabbatical leave of six months with pay so they may attend special refresher courses at home or abroad to keep abreast of the latest developments in their field. In this way, the curriculum and the teaching system can be easily improved. Where will the money be found for all this? When there is an end to the embezzlement of government funds, when public officials stop taking graft from the large companies that owe taxes to the state, when the enormous resources of the country are brought into full use, when we no longer buy tanks, bombers and guns for this country (which has no borders to defend and where these instruments of war, now being purchased, are used against the people), when there is more interest in educating the people than in killing them there will be more than enough money.

Cuba could easily provide for a population three times as great as it has now, so there is no excuse for the abject poverty of a single one of its present inhabitants. The markets should be overflowing with produce, pantries should be full, all hands should be working. This is not inconceivable. What is inconceivable is that anyone should go to bed hungry while there is a single inch of unproductive land; that children should die for lack of medical attention; what is inconceivable is that 30 percent of our campesinos cannot write their names, and that 99 percent of them know nothing about Cuban history. What is inconceivable is that the majority of our rural people are now living in worse circumstances than the Indians Columbus discovered in the fairest land human eyes had ever seen.

To those who would call me a dreamer, I quote the words of Martí:

A real man does not seek the path where advantage lies, but rather the path of duty, and this is the only way to be a practical person, whose dream of today will be the law of tomorrow; because looking back on the essential course of history and seeing the inflamed and bleeding peoples seethe in the cauldron of the ages one knows, without exception, that the future lies on the side of duty.

Only when we understand that such a noble ideal inspired them can we conceive of the heroism of the young people who fell in Santiago. The meager material means at our disposal were all that prevented success. When the soldiers were told that Prío had given us a million pesos, this was just the regime's attempt to distort the most important fact: Our movement had no link with past politicians; that this movement is a new Cuban generation with its own ideas, rising up against tyranny; that this movement is made up of young people who were barely seven years old when Batista perpetrated his first crimes in 1934. The lie about the million pesos could not have been more absurd. If, with less than 20,000 pesos, we armed 165 people and attacked a regiment and a squadron, then with a million pesos we could have armed 8,000 people to attack 50 regiments and 50 squadrons—and Ugalde Carrillo still would not have known anything until Sunday, July 26, at 5:15 a.m. I assure you that for every combatant who fought, 20 well-trained others were unable to fight for lack of weapons. When these young people marched along the streets of Havana in the student demonstration of the Martí centennial, they solidly packed six blocks. If even 200 more people had been able to fight, or we had possessed 20 more hand grenades, perhaps this honorable court would have been spared all this inconvenience.

The politicians spend millions buying consciences, whereas a handful of Cubans who wanted to save their country's honor had to face death bare-handed for lack of funds. This shows how the country, to this very day, has been governed not by generous and dedicated people, but by political racketeers, the scum of public life.

With the greatest pride I tell you that in accordance with our principles we have never asked a politician, past or present, for a penny. Our means were assembled with incomparable sacrifice. For example, Elpidio Sosa, who sold his job and came to me one day with 300 pesos "for the cause";

Fernando Chenard, who sold the photographic equipment with which he earned his living; Pedro Marrero, who contributed several months' salary and who had to be stopped from actually selling the very furniture in his house; Oscar Alcalde, who sold his pharmaceutical laboratory; Jesús Montané, who gave his five years' savings, and so on with many others, each giving the little they had.

One must have great faith in one's country to act in such a way. The memory of these acts of idealism brings me straight to the most bitter chapter of this defense: the price the tyranny made them pay for wanting to free Cuba from oppression and injustice.

> *Beloved corpses, you that once*
> *Were the hope of my Homeland,*
> *Cast upon my forehead*
> *The dust of your decaying bones!*
> *Touch my heart with your cold hands!*
> *Groan at my ears!*
> *Each of my moans will*
> *Turn into the tears of one more tyrant!*
> *Gather around me! Roam about,*
> *That my soul may receive your spirits*
> *And give me the horror of the tombs,*
> *For tears are not enough*
> *When one lives in infamous bondage!*

Multiply the crimes of November 27, 1871,* by 10 and you will have the monstrous and repulsive crimes of July 26, 27, 28 and 29, 1953, in the province of Oriente. These are still fresh in our memory, but some day when years have passed, when the skies of the nation have cleared once more, when tempers have calmed and fear no longer torments our spirits, then we will begin to see the magnitude of this massacre in its shocking dimension, and future generations will be struck with horror when they look back on these acts of barbarity, unprecedented in our history. But I do not want to let anger blind me. I need a clear mind and serenity in my heavy heart in order to relate the facts as simply as possible, in no sense overdramatizing them, but just as they took place. As a Cuban I am ashamed that heartless men should have perpetrated such unthinkable crimes, dishonoring our nation before the rest of the world.

The tyrant Batista was never a man of scruples. He has never hesitated to tell his people the most outrageous lies. To justify his treacherous coup of March 10, he concocted stories about a fictitious uprising in the army, supposedly scheduled to take place in April, and which he "wanted to avert so that the republic might not be drenched in blood." A ridiculous little story no one ever believed! And when he himself wanted to drench the republic in blood, when he wanted to smother in terror and torture the just rebellion of Cuban youth, who were not willing to be his slaves, then he contrived even more fantastic lies. How little respect one must have for a people when one tries to deceive them so miserably! On the very day of my arrest I publicly assumed the responsibility for our armed movement of July 26. If there had been one iota of truth in even one of the many statements the dictator made against our combatants in his speech of July 27, it would have been enough to undermine the moral impact of my case. Why, then, was I not brought to trial? Why were medical certificates forged? Why did they violate all procedural laws and ignore so scandalously the rulings of the court? Why were so many things done, things never before seen in a court of law, in order to prevent my appearance at all costs? In contrast, I cannot begin to tell you everything I went through in order to appear. I asked the court to bring me to trial in accordance with all established principles, and I denounced the underhanded schemes that were used to prevent it. I wanted to argue with them in person. But they did not wish to face me. Who was afraid of the truth, and who was not?

The statements made by the dictator at Camp Columbia might be considered amusing if they were not so drenched in blood. He claimed we were a group of hirelings and that there were many foreigners among us. He said that the central part of our plan was an attempt to kill him — him, always him. As if those who attacked the Moncada barracks could not have killed him and 20 like him if they had approved of such methods. He stated that our attack had been planned by ex-president Prío, and that it had been financed with Prío's money. It has been irrefutably proven that no link whatsoever existed between our movement and the former regime. He claimed that we had machine guns and hand grenades. Yet the military technicians have stated right here in this court that we only had one machine gun and not a single hand grenade. He said that we had beheaded the sentries. Yet death certificates and medical reports of all the army's casualties show not one death caused by the blade. But above all and most important, he said that we stabbed patients at the Military Hospital. Yet the doctors from that hospital — army doctors — have testified that we never even occupied the building, that no patient was either wounded or killed by us, and that the hospital lost only one employee, a janitor, who imprudently stuck his head out of an open window.

Whenever a head of state, or anyone pretending to be one, makes declarations to the nation, he speaks not just to hear the sound of his own voice. He always has some specific purpose and expects some specific reaction, or has a given intention. Since our military defeat had already taken place, insofar as we no longer represented any actual threat to the dictatorship, why did they slander us like that? If it is still not clear that this was a blood-drenched speech, that it was simply an attempt to justify the crimes that they had been perpetrating since the night before and that they were going to continue to perpetrate, then, let figures speak for me: On July 27, in his speech from the military headquarters, Batista said that the assailants suffered 32 dead. By the end of the week the number of dead had risen to more than 80 people. In what battles, where, in what clashes, did these young people die? Before Batista spoke, more than 25 prisoners had been murdered. After Batista spoke, 50 more were massacred.

What a great sense of honor those modest army technicians and professionals had, who did not distort the facts before the court, but gave their reports adhering to the strictest truth! Surely these are soldiers who honor their uniform; surely these are men! Neither a real soldier nor a real man degrades his code of honor with lies and crime. I know that many of the soldiers are indignant at the barbaric assassinations perpetrated. I know that they feel repugnance and shame at the stench of homicidal blood that permeates every stone of the Moncada barracks.

Now that he has been contradicted by men of honor within his own army, I defy the dictator to repeat his vile slander against us. I defy him to try to justify before the Cuban people his July 27 speech. Let him not remain silent. Let him speak. Let him say who are the assassins, who are the ruthless, the inhumane. Let him tell us if the medals of honor, which he went to pin on the breasts of his heroes of that massacre, were rewards for the hideous crimes they had committed. Let him, from this very moment, assume his responsibility before history. Let him not pretend, at a later date, that the soldiers were acting without direct orders from him! Let him offer the nation an explanation for those 70 murders. The bloodshed was so great. The nation needs an explanation. The nation seeks it. The nation demands it.

It is common knowledge that in 1933, at the end of the battle at the National Hotel, some officers were murdered after they surrendered. *Bohemia* magazine protested energetically. It is also known that after the surrender of Fort Atarés, the besiegers' machine guns cut down a row of prisoners, and that one soldier, after asking who Blas Hernández was, blasted him with a bullet directly in the face, for which cowardly act he was promoted to the rank of officer. It is well known in Cuban history that the assassination of prisoners was fatally linked to Batista's name. How naive we were not to foresee this! However unjustifiable as those killings of 1933 were, they took place in a matter of minutes, in no more time than it took for a round of machine gun fire. Moreover, they took place while nerves were still on edge.

This was not the case in Santiago de Cuba. Here all types of vicious outrages and cruelty were deliberately excessive. Our people were killed not in the course of a minute, an hour or a day. Throughout an entire week the bashings and torture continued, people were thrown from rooftops and shot. All methods of extermination were ceaselessly perpetrated by well-skilled artisans of crime. The Moncada barracks were turned into a workshop of torture and death. Some shameless individuals turned their uniforms into butcher's aprons. The walls were splattered with blood. Bullets imbedded in the walls were encrusted with singed bits of skin, brains and human hair, the grisly reminders of rifles shot at point-blank range. The grass around the barracks was dark and sticky with human blood. The criminal hands that are guiding the destiny of Cuba had written for the prisoners at the entrance to that den of death the very inscription of hell: "Abandon here all hope."

They never even attempted a cover-up. They did not bother in the least to conceal what they were doing. They thought they had deceived the people with their lies and they ended up deceiving themselves. They felt themselves lords and masters of the universe, with power over life and death. So the fear they had experienced on our attack at daybreak was dissipated in a festival of corpses, in a drunken orgy of blood.

Chronicles of our history, down through four and a half centuries, tell us of many acts of cruelty: the slaughter of defenseless Indians by the Spaniards; the plundering and atrocities of pirates along the coast; the barbarities of the Spanish soldiers during our War of Independence; the shooting of prisoners of the Cuban army by Weyler's forces; the horrors of the Machado regime, and so on up to the bloody crimes of March 1935. But never has such a sad and bloody page been written in numbers of victims and in the viciousness of the victimizers as in Santiago de Cuba. Only one person in all these centuries has spilled so much blood in two separate periods of our history and has dug his claws into the flesh of two generations of Cubans. To release this river of blood, he waited for the centennial of the Apostle, just after the 50th anniversary of the republic, whose people fought for freedom, human rights and happiness at the cost of so many lives. Even greater is his crime and even more deplorable because the man who perpetrated it had already, for 11 long years, lorded over his people—a people who, through such deep-rooted sentiment and tradition, loves freedom and repudiates evil. Moreover, this man has never been sincere, loyal, honest or chivalrous for a minute in his entire public life.

He was not content with the treachery of January 1934, the crimes of March 1935 and the $40 million fortune that crowned his first regime. He had to add the treason of March 1952, the crimes of July 1953 and the millions of other crimes that only time will reveal. Dante divided his inferno into nine circles. He put criminals in the seventh, thieves in the eighth and traitors in the ninth. What a difficult dilemma the devils will be faced with when they try to find an appropriate place for this man's soul—if this man has a soul. The man who instigated the atrocities in Santiago de Cuba cannot even have a heart.

I know many details of the way in which these crimes were carried out, from the lips of some of the soldiers who, filled with shame, told me about the scenes they had witnessed.

When the fighting was over, the soldiers descended like savage beasts on Santiago de Cuba and they took the first fury of their frustrations out against the defenseless population. In the middle of a street, and away from the scene of the fighting, they shot through the chest an innocent child who was playing beside his doorstep. When the father approached to pick him up, they shot him through the head. Without a word they shot the Cala child, who was on his way home with a loaf of bread in his hands. It would be a never-ending task to relate all the crimes and outrages perpetrated against the civilian population. And if the army dealt thus with those who had taken no part at all in the action, you can imagine the terrible fate of the prisoners who had participated or who were believed to have participated. Just as, in this trial, they accused many people in no way involved in our attack, they also killed many prisoners who had no involvement whatsoever. The latter are not included in the statistics of victims released by the regime; those statistics refer exclusively to our combatants. Some day the total number of victims will be known.

The first prisoner killed was our doctor, Mario Muñoz, who bore no arms, wore no uniform, and was dressed in the white smock of a physician. He was a generous and competent person who would have given the same devoted care to a wounded adversary as to a friend. On the road from the Civilian Hospital to the barracks they shot him in the back and left him lying there, face down in a pool of blood. But the mass murder of prisoners did not begin until after 3:00 in the afternoon. Until this hour they awaited orders. Then General Martín Díaz Tamayo arrived from Havana and brought specific instructions from a meeting he had attended with Batista, along with the head of the army, the head of military intelligence and others. He said: "It is humiliating and dishonorable for the army to have lost three times as many people in combat as the insurgents did. Ten prisoners must be killed for each dead soldier." This was the order!

In every society there are those with base instincts. The sadists, brutes, conveyors of all the ancestral atavisms go about in the guise of human beings, but they are monsters, only more or less restrained by discipline and social customs. If they are offered a drink from a river of blood, they will not be satisfied until they drink the river dry. All these men needed was the order. At their hands the best and noblest Cubans perished: the most valiant, the most honest, the most idealistic. The tyrant called them mercenaries. There they were dying as heroes at the hands of those who collect a salary from the republic and who, with the arms the republic gave them to defend her, serve the interests of a clique and murder her best citizens.

Throughout their torturing of our compañeros, the army offered them the chance to save their lives by betraying their ideology and falsely declaring that Prío had given them money. When they indignantly rejected that proposition, the army continued with its horrible tortures. They crushed their testicles and they tore out their eyes. But no one yielded. No complaint was heard and no favor asked. Even when they had been deprived of their virile organs, our people were still a thousand times more men than all their tormentors put together. Photographs, which do not lie, show the bodies torn to pieces. Other methods were used. Frustrated by the valor of the men, they tried to break the spirit of our women. With a bleeding eye in their hands, a sergeant and several other men went to the cell where our compañeras Melba Hernández and Haydée Santamaría were held. Addressing the latter, and showing her the eye, they said: "This eye belonged to your brother. If you will not tell us what he refused to say, we will tear out the other." Haydée, who loved her valiant brother above all else, replied full of dignity: "If you tore out an eye and he did not speak, much less will I." Later they came back and burned the women prisoners' arms with cigarettes until at last, full of malice, they told the young Haydée Santamaría: "You no longer have a fiancé because we've killed him too." But still imperturbable, she answered: "He is not dead, because to die for one's country is to live forever." Never had the heroism and the dignity of Cuban womanhood reached such heights.

There wasn't even respect for those wounded in combat in the various city hospitals. There they were hunted down like prey pursued by vultures. In the Centro Gallego Hospital they broke into the operating room at the very moment when two of our critically wounded were receiving blood transfusions. They pulled them off the tables and, as the wounded could no longer stand, they were dragged down to the first floor where they arrived as corpses.

They could not do the same in the Colonia Española Hospital, where Gustavo Arcos and José Ponce were patients, because Dr. Posada bravely told them they could enter only over his dead body.

Air and camphor were injected into the veins of Pedro Miret, Abelardo Crespo and Fidel Labrador in an attempt to kill them at the Military Hospital. They owe their lives to Captain Tamayo, an army doctor and true soldier of honor who, pistol in hand, wrenched them from the hands of their merciless captors and transferred them to the Civilian Hospital. These five young men were the only ones of our wounded who survived.

In the early morning hours, groups of our combatants were removed from the barracks and driven to Siboney, La Maya, Songo and elsewhere. Then they were taken out — tied, gagged, already disfigured by the torture — and murdered in isolated spots. They are recorded as having died in combat against the army. This went on for several days, and few of the captured prisoners survived. Many were compelled to dig their own graves. One of our men, while he was digging, wheeled around and slashed the face of one of his assassins with his pick. Others were even buried alive, their hands tied behind their backs. Many solitary spots became the graveyards of the brave. On the army target range alone, five of our combatants lie buried. Some day these men will be disinterred, so they can be carried on the shoulders of the people to a place beside the tomb of Martí; their liberated land will surely want to erect a monument to honor the memory of the martyrs of the centennial.

The last youth they murdered near Santiago de Cuba was Marcos Martí. He was captured with our compañero Ciro Redondo in a cave at Siboney on the morning of Thursday, July 30. These two men were led down the road, with their arms raised, and the soldiers shot Marcos Martí in the back. After he had fallen to the ground, they riddled his body with bullets. Redondo was taken to the camp. When Major Pérez Chaumont saw him he exclaimed: "And this one? Why have you brought him to me?" The court learned of this incident from Redondo himself, the young man who survived thanks to what Pérez Chaumont called "the soldiers' stupidity."

It was the same throughout the province. Ten days after July 26, a newspaper in this city printed the news that two young men had been found hanged on the road from Manzanillo to Bayamo. Later the bodies were identified as Hugo Camejo and Pedro Vélez. Another extraordinary incident took place there. There were three victims — they had been dragged from Manzanillo barracks at 2:00 that morning. At a certain spot on the highway they were taken out, beaten unconscious and strangled with a rope. But after they had been left for dead, one of them, Andrés García, regained consciousness and hid in a farmer's house. Thanks to this, the court learned the details of this crime, too. Of all our combatants taken prisoner in the Bayamo area, he is the only survivor.

Near the Cauto River, in a spot known as Barrancas, at the bottom of a pit, lie the bodies of Raúl de Aguiar, Armando del Valle and Andrés

Valdés. They were murdered at midnight on the road between Alto Cedro and Palma Soriano by Sergeant Montes de Oca—in charge of the military post at Miranda barracks—Corporal Maceo, and the lieutenant in charge of Alto Cedro where the murdered combatants were captured. In the annals of crime, Sergeant Eulalio Gonzáles—better known as the "Tiger" of the Moncada barracks—deserves a special place. Later, this man didn't have the slightest qualms in bragging about his unspeakable deeds. It was he who, with his own hands, murdered our compañero Abel Santamaría. But that didn't satisfy him. One day as he was returning from the Puerto Boniato Prison, where he raises pedigree fighting cocks in the rear courtyard, he got on a bus on which Abel's mother was also traveling. When this monster realized who she was, he began to brag about his grisly deeds, and—in a loud voice so that the woman dressed in mourning could hear him—he said: "Yes, I have gouged out many eyes and I expect to continue gouging eyes out." The unprecedented moral degradation to which our nation has sunk is beyond the power of words, and expressed in that mother's sobs of grief before the cowardly insolence of the very man who had murdered her son. When mothers went to the Moncada barracks to ask about their sons, they were told with incredible cynicism and sadism: "Of course madam, you may see him at the Santa Ifigenia Hotel where we have put him up." Either Cuba is not Cuba, or those responsible for these deeds will have to face their reckoning one day. Heartless men, they crudely insulted the people who bared their heads in reverence as the corpses of the revolutionaries were carried by.

There were so many victims that the government still has not dared make public the complete list. They know their figures are false. They have all the victims' names, because prior to every murder they recorded all the vital statistics. The whole long process of identification through the National Identification Bureau was a huge farce, and there are families still waiting for word of their sons' fate. Why has this not been cleared up, after three months?

I wish to state for the record here that all the victims' pockets were picked to the very last penny and that all their personal effects, rings and watches,

*   In 1871 eight medical students were accused of desecrating the tombstone of Spanish newspaperman Gonzalo Castañón. They were executed on November 27, despite public outrage.

were stripped from their bodies and are brazenly being worn today by their assassins.

Honorable Judges, a great deal of what I have just related, you already know from the testimony of many of my compañeros. But please note that many key witnesses have been barred from this trial, although they were permitted to attend the sessions of the previous trial. For example, I want to point out that the nurses from the Civilian Hospital are absent, even though they work in the same place where this hearing is being held. They were kept away from this court so that under my questioning, they would not be able to testify that—besides Dr. Mario Muñoz—20 more of our combatants were captured alive. The regime fears that from the questioning of these witnesses some extremely dangerous testimony could find its way into the official transcript.

But Major Pérez Chaumont did appear here and he could not elude my questioning. What we learned from this man, a "hero" who fought only against unarmed and handcuffed men, gives us an idea of what might have been learned at the courthouse if I had not been kept out of the proceedings. I asked him how many of our combatants had died in his celebrated skirmishes at Siboney. He hesitated. I insisted and he finally said 21. Since I knew such skirmishes had never taken place, I asked him how many of our combatants had been wounded. He answered: "None. All of them were killed." It was then that I asked him, in astonishment, if the soldiers were using nuclear weapons. Of course, where people are shot point blank, there are no wounded. Then I asked him how many casualties the army had sustained. He replied that two of his men had been wounded. Finally I asked him if either of these men had died, and he said no. I waited. Later, all of the wounded army soldiers filed by and it was discovered that none of them had been wounded at Siboney. This same Major Pérez Chaumont, who hardly flinched at having assassinated 21 defenseless young people, has built a palatial home in Ciudamar Beach. It's worth more than 100,000 pesos—his savings after only a few months under Batista's new rule. And if this is the savings of a major, imagine how much generals have saved!

Honorable Judges: Where are our combatants who were captured on July 26, 27, 28 and 29? It is known that more than 60 combatants were captured in the area of Santiago de Cuba. Only three of them and the two women have been brought before the court. The rest of the accused were seized later. Where are our wounded? Only five of them are alive; the rest were murdered. These figures are irrefutable. On the other hand, 20 of the soldiers whom we held prisoner have been presented here and they themselves have declared that they received not even one offensive word from us. Thirty soldiers who were wounded, many in the street fighting, also appeared before you. Not one was killed by us. If the army suffered losses of 19 dead and 30 wounded, how is it possible that we should have had 80 dead and only five wounded? Who ever witnessed a battle with 21 dead and no wounded, like these famous battles described by Pérez Chaumont?

We have here the casualty lists from the bitter fighting sustained by the invasion troops in the war of 1895, both in battles where the Cuban army was defeated and where it was victorious. The battle of Los Indios in Las Villas: 12 wounded, none dead. The battle of Mal Tiempo: four dead, 23 wounded. Calimete: 16 dead, 64 wounded. La Palma: 39 dead, 88 wounded. Cacarajícara: five dead, 13 wounded. Descanso: four dead, 45 wounded. San Gabriel de Lombillo: two dead, 18 wounded... In all these battles the number of wounded is twice, three times and up to 10 times the number of dead, although in those days there were no modern medical techniques by which the percentage of deaths could be reduced. How then, now, can we explain the enormous proportion of 16 deaths per wounded man, if not by the government's slaughter of the wounded in the hospitals, and by the assassination of the other helpless prisoners they had taken? The figures are irrefutable.

"It is shameful and dishonorable for the army to have lost three times as many men in combat as those lost by the insurgents; we must kill 10 prisoners for each dead soldier." This is the concept of honor held by the petty corporals who became generals on March 10. This is the code of honor they wish to impose on the national army. A false honor, a feigned honor, an apparent honor based on lies, hypocrisy and crime; a mask of honor molded by those assassins with blood. Who told them that to die fighting is dishonorable? Who told them the honor of an army consists of murdering the wounded and prisoners of war?

In war, armies that murder prisoners have always earned the contempt and abomination of the entire world. Such cowardice has no justification, even in a case where national territory is invaded by foreign troops. In the words of a South American liberator: "Not even the strictest military obedience may turn a soldier's sword into that of an executioner." The honorable soldier does not kill the helpless prisoner after the fight, but rather, respects him. He does not finish off a wounded man, but rather, helps him. He stands in the way of crime and if he cannot prevent it, he acts as did that Spanish captain who, on hearing the shots of the firing squad that murdered Cuban students, indignantly broke his sword in two and refused to continue serving in that army.

The soldiers who murdered their prisoners were not worthy of the soldiers who died. I saw many soldiers fight with courage — for example, those in the patrols that fired their machine guns against us in almost hand-to-hand combat, or that sergeant who, defying death, rang the alarm to mobilize the barracks. Some are alive. I am glad. Others are dead. They believed they were doing their duty and in my eyes this makes them worthy of admiration and respect. I deplore only the fact that the valiant should fall for an evil cause. When Cuba is freed, we should respect, shelter and aid the wives and children of those courageous soldiers who perished fighting against us. They are not to blame for Cuba's miseries. They, too, are victims of this nefarious situation.

But what honor was earned by the soldiers who died in battle was lost by the generals who ordered prisoners to be killed after they surrendered. Men who became generals overnight, without ever having fired a shot; men who bought their stars with high treason against their country; men who ordered the execution of prisoners taken in battles in which they didn't even participate. These are the generals of March 10 — generals who would not even have been fit to drive the mules that carried the equipment in Antonio Maceo's army.

The army suffered three times as many casualties as we did because our men were expertly trained, as the military men themselves have admitted; and also because we had prepared adequate tactical measures, another fact recognized by the army. The army did not perform brilliantly; despite the millions spent on espionage by the SIM, they were totally taken by surprise, and their hand grenades failed to explode because they were obsolete. And this is all due to generals like Martín Díaz Tamayo and colonels like Ugalde Carrillo and Albert del Río Chaviano. We were not 17 traitors infiltrated into the ranks of the army, as was the case on March 10. Instead, we were 165 people who had traveled the length and breadth of Cuba to look death boldly in the face. If the army leaders had a notion of real military honor they would have resigned their commands rather than trying to wash away their shame and incompetence in the blood of their prisoners.

To kill helpless prisoners and then declare that they died in battle—that is the military capacity of the generals of March 10. That was the way the worst butchers of Valeriano Weyler behaved in the cruelest years of our War of Independence. The *Chronicles of War* include the following story:

> On February 23, officer Baldomero Acosta entered Punta Brava with some cavalry when, from the opposite road, a squad of the Pizarro regiment approached, led by a sergeant known in those parts as "Barriguilla" (Pot Belly). The insurgents exchanged a few shots with Pizarro's men, then withdrew by the trail that leads from Punta Brava to the village of Guatao. Followed by another battalion of volunteers from Marianao, and a company of troops from the Public Order Corps, who were led by Captain Calvo, Pizarro's squad of 50 men marched on Guatao... As soon as their first forces entered the village they commenced their massacre— killing 12 of the peaceful inhabitants... The troops led by Captain Calvo speedily rounded up all the civilians that were running about the village, tied them up and took them as prisoners of war to Havana... Not yet satisfied with their outrages, on the outskirts of Guatao they carried out another barbaric act, killing one of the prisoners and horribly wounding the rest. The Marquis of Cervera, a cowardly and palatine soldier, informed Weyler of the pyrrhic victory of the Spanish soldiers; but Major Zugasti, a man of principle, denounced the incident to the government and officially called the murders perpetrated by the criminal Captain Calvo and Sergeant Barriguilla an assassination of peaceful citizens.

Weyler's intervention in this horrible incident and his delight on learning the details of the massacre may be palpably deduced from the official dispatch that he sent to the Ministry of War concerning these cruelties: "Small column organized by commander Marianao with forces from garrison, volunteers and firemen led by Captain Calvo, fought and destroyed bands of Villanueva and Baldomero Acosta near Punta Brava, killing 20 of theirs, who were handed over to Mayor of Guatao for burial, and taking 15 prisoners, one of them wounded, we assume there are many wounded among them. One of ours suffered critical wounds, some suffered light bruises and wounds. Weyler."

What is the difference between Weyler's dispatch and that of Colonel Chaviano detailing the victories of Major Pérez Chaumont? Only that Weyler mentions one wounded soldier in his ranks. Chaviano mentions two. Weyler speaks of one wounded person and 15 prisoners in the enemy's ranks. Chaviano records neither wounded nor prisoners.

Just as I admire the courage of the soldiers who died bravely, I also admire the officers who bore themselves with dignity and did not drench their hands in this blood. Many of the survivors owe their lives to the commendable conduct of officers like Lieutenant Sarría, Lieutenant Campa, Captain Tamayo and others, who were real gentlemen in their treatment of the prisoners. If men like these had not partially saved the name of the armed forces, it would be more honorable today to wear a dishrag than to wear an army uniform.

For my dead compañeros, I claim no vengeance. Since their lives were priceless, the murderers could not pay for them even with their own lives. It is not by blood that we may redeem the lives of those who died for their country. The happiness of their people is the only tribute worthy of them.

Moreover, my compañeros are neither dead nor forgotten; they live today, more than ever, and their murderers will watch with dismay the victorious spirit of their ideas rise from their corpses. Let the Apostle speak for me: "There is a limit to the tears we can shed at the graveside of the dead, which is the infinite love for the homeland and its glory, a love that never falters, loses hope or grows dim. For the graves of the martyrs are the highest altars of our reverence."

> ...When one dies
> In the arms of a grateful homeland
> Agony ends, prison chains break — and
> At last, with death, life begins!

Up to this point I have confined myself almost exclusively to relating events. Since I am well aware that I am before a court convened to judge me, I will now demonstrate that all legal right was on our side alone, and that the verdict imposed on my compañeros — the verdict now being sought against me — has no justification in reason, in social morality or in terms of true justice.

I wish to be duly respectful to the Honorable Judges, and I am grateful that you find in the frankness of my plea no animosity toward you. My argument is meant simply to demonstrate what a false and erroneous position the judicial power has adopted in the present situation. To a certain extent, each court is nothing more than a cog in the wheel of the system, and therefore must move along the course determined by the vehicle, although this by no means justifies any individual acting against his principles. I know very well that the oligarchy bears most of the blame. The oligarchy, without dignified protest, abjectly yielded to the dictates of the usurper and betrayed their country by renouncing the autonomy of the judicial power. Individuals who constitute noble exceptions have attempted to mend the system's mangled honor with their individual decisions. But the gestures of this minority have been of little consequence, drowned as they were by the obsequious and fawning majority. This fatalism, however, will not stop me from speaking the truth that supports my cause. My appearance before this court may be a pure farce in order to give a semblance of legality to arbitrary decisions, but I am determined to rip away with a firm hand the infamous veil that hides so much shamelessness. It is curious: The very men who have brought me here to be judged and condemned have never heeded a single decision of this court.

Since this trial may be, as you said, the most important trial since we achieved our national sovereignty, what I say here will perhaps be lost in the silence that the dictatorship has tried to impose on me, but posterity will often look again at what you do here. Remember that today you are judging an accused man, but that you yourselves will be judged not once, but many times, as often as these days are submitted to scrutiny in the future. What I say here will then be repeated many times, not because it comes from my lips, but because the problem of justice is eternal and the people have a deep sense of justice above and beyond the hairsplitting of jurisprudence. The people wield simple but implacable logic, against everything that is absurd and contradictory. Furthermore, if there is in this world a people that utterly abhors favoritism and inequality, it is the Cuban people. To them, justice is symbolized by a maiden with a scale and a sword in her hands. Should she cower before one group and furiously brandish that sword against another group, then to the people of Cuba the maiden of justice will seem nothing more than a prostitute wielding a dagger. My logic is the simple logic of the people.

Let me tell you a story: Once upon a time there was a republic. It had its constitution, its laws, its freedoms, a president, a congress and courts of law. Everyone could assemble, associate, speak and write with complete freedom. The people were not satisfied with the government officials at that time, but they had the power to elect new officials and only a few days remained before they would do so. Public opinion was respected and heeded and all problems of common interest were freely discussed. There were political parties, radio and television debates and forums and public meetings. The whole nation pulsated with enthusiasm. The people had suffered greatly and although they were unhappy, they longed to be happy and had a right to be happy. They had been deceived many times and looked on the past with real horror. This country innocently believed that such a past could not return; the people were proud of their love of freedom and they carried their heads high in the conviction that liberty would be respected as a sacred right. They felt confident that no one would dare commit the crime of violating their democratic institutions. They wanted a change for the better, aspired to progress, and they saw all this at hand. All their hope lay in the future.

Poor country! One morning the citizens woke up dismayed; under the cover of darkness, while the people slept, the ghosts of the past had conspired and had seized the citizenry by its hands, its feet, and its neck. That grip, those claws were familiar: those jaws, those death-dealing scythes, those boots. No, it was no nightmare; it was a sad and terrible reality: A man named Fulgencio Batista had just perpetrated the appalling crime that no one had expected.

Then a humble citizen of that people, a citizen who wished to believe in the laws of the republic, in the integrity of its judges, whom he had seen vent their fury against the underprivileged, searched through a Social Defense Code to see what punishment society prescribed for the author of such a coup, and he discovered the following:

> Whosoever shall perpetrate any deed destined through violent means directly to change in whole or in part the constitution of the state or the form of the established government will incur a sentence of six to 10 years' imprisonment.
>
> A sentence of three to 10 years' imprisonment will be imposed on

the author of an act directed to promote an armed uprising against the constitutional powers of the state. The sentence increases to between five and 20 years if the insurrection is carried out.

Whosoever shall perpetrate an act with the specific purpose of preventing, in whole or in part, even temporarily, the Senate, the House of Representatives, the president, or the Supreme Court from exercising their constitutional functions will incur a sentence of six to 10 years' imprisonment.

Whosoever shall attempt to impede or tamper with the normal course of general elections, will incur a sentence of four to eight years' imprisonment.

Whosoever shall introduce, publish, propagate or try to enforce in Cuba instructions, orders or decrees that tend… to promote the nonobservance of laws in force, will incur a sentence of two to six years' imprisonment.

Whosoever shall assume command of troops, posts, fortresses, military camps, towns, warships, or military aircraft, without the authority to do so, or without express government orders, will incur a sentence of from five to 10 years' imprisonment.

A similar sentence will be passed on anyone who usurps the exercise of a function held by the constitution as properly belonging to the powers of state.

Without telling anyone, code in one hand and a deposition in the other, that citizen went to the old city building, that old building which housed the court, competent and under obligation to bring cause against and punish those responsible for this deed. He presented a writ denouncing the crimes and asking that Fulgencio Batista and his 17 accomplices be sentenced to 108 years in prison as decreed by the Social Defense Code; considering also the aggravating circumstances of repeated offense, malice and stealth.

Days and months passed. What a disappointment! The accused remained unchallenged; he strode up and down the country like a great lord and was called "Honorable Sir" and "General"; he dismissed and appointed judges at will. The very day the courts opened, the criminal occupied the seat of honor in the midst of our august and venerable patriarchs of justice.

More days and months rolled by, the people wearied of the mockery and abuses. There is a limit to tolerance! A struggle began against this man who was disregarding the law, who had usurped power by the use of violence against the will of the people, who was guilty of aggression against the established order, who had tortured, murdered, imprisoned and prosecuted those who had taken up the struggle to defend the law and to restore freedom to the people.

Honorable Judges: I am that humble citizen who one day demanded in vain that the courts punish the power-hungry men who had violated the law and torn our institutions to shreds. Now it is I who am accused for attempting to overthrow this illegal regime and to restore the legitimate constitution of the republic. I am held incommunicado for 76 days and denied the right to speak to anyone, even to my son. I am led through the city between two heavy machine guns. I am transferred to this hospital to be tried secretly with the greatest severity, and the prosecutor with the code in his hand solemnly demands that I be sentenced to 26 years in prison.

You will answer that on the former occasion the courts failed to act because force prevented them from doing so. Well then, confess, this time force will compel you to condemn me. The first time you were unable to punish the guilty; now you will be compelled to punish the innocent — the maiden of justice twice raped.

So much charlatanry to justify the unjustifiable, to explain the inexplicable and to reconcile the irreconcilable! The regime has reached the point of asserting that "Might is right" is the supreme law of the land. In other words, that using tanks and soldiers to take over the presidential palace, the national treasury and the other government offices, and aiming guns at the heart of the people, entitles them to govern the people! The same argument the Nazis used when they occupied the countries of Europe and installed puppet governments.

I sincerely believe revolution to be the source of legal right; but the nocturnal armed assault of March 10 could never be considered a revolution. In everyday language, as José Ingenieros said, it is common to call "revolutions" those small disorders promoted by a group of dissatisfied persons in order to grab from those in power both political sinecures and economic advantage. The usual result is no more than a change of hands, the dividing up of jobs and benefits. This is not the criterion of a philosopher, and cannot be that of a cultured person.

Leaving aside the problem of fundamental changes in the social system, not even on the surface of the public quagmire were we able to discern the slightest motion that could lessen the rampant putrefaction. The previous regime was guilty of petty politics, theft, pillage and disrespect for human life; but the present regime has increased political skullduggery five-fold, pillage ten-fold and a hundred-fold the lack of respect for human life.

It was known that Barriguilla had plundered and murdered, that he was a millionaire, that in Havana he owned a good number of apartments, countless stocks in foreign companies, fabulous accounts in US banks, that he agreed to divorce settlements to the tune of 18 million pesos, that he was a frequent guest in the most lavishly expensive hotels for Yankee tycoons. But no one would ever think of Barriguilla as a revolutionary. Barriguilla is that sergeant of Weyler's who assassinated 12 Cubans in Guatao. Batista's men murdered 70 in Santiago de Cuba. *De te fabula narratur* [History will be written about this].

Four political parties governed the country before March 10: the Autén-tico, Liberal, Democratic and Republican parties. Two days after the coup, the Republican Party gave its support to the new rulers. A year had not yet passed before the Liberal and Democratic parties were again in power. Batista did not restore the constitution, did not restore civil liberties, did not restore Congress, did not restore universal suffrage, did not restore in the last analysis any of the uprooted democratic institutions. But he did re-store Verdeja, Guas Inclán, Salvito García Ramos, Anaya Murillo and the top hierarchy of the traditional government parties, the most corrupt, ra-pacious, reactionary and antediluvian elements in Cuban politics. So went Barriguilla's "revolution"!

Lacking even the most elementary revolutionary content, Batista's regime represents in every respect a 20-year regression for Cuba. Batista's regime has exacted a high price from all of us, but primarily from the humble classes which are suffering hunger and misery. Meanwhile the dictatorship has laid waste the nation with chaos, ineptitude and anguish, and now engages in the most loathsome forms of ruthless politics, concocting scheme after scheme to perpetuate itself in power, even if this is over a pile of corpses and a sea of blood.

Batista's regime has not instigated a single nationwide program for the people's benefit. Batista delivered himself into the hands of the great financial interests. Little else could be expected from a person of his mentality, utterly devoid as he is of ideals and principles, and utterly lacking the faith, confidence and support of the masses. His regime merely brought with it a change of hands and a redistribution of the loot among a new group of friends, relatives, accomplices and parasitic hangers-on that constitute the political retinue of the dictator. What great opprobrium the people have been forced to endure so that a small group of egoists, altogether indifferent to the needs of their homeland, may find in public life an easy and comfortable modus vivendi.

How right Eduardo Chibás was in his last radio speech, when he said that Batista was encouraging the return of the colonels, castor oil and the law of the fugitive! Immediately after March 10, Cubans again began to witness acts of veritable vandalism which they had thought banished forever from their nation. There was an unprecedented attack on a cultural institution: A radio station was stormed by the thugs of the SIM, together with the young hoodlums of [Batista's] Unitary Action Party (PAU), while broadcasting the "University of the Air" program. And there was the case of the journalist, Mario Kuchilán, dragged from his home in the middle of the night and brutally tortured until he was nearly unconscious. There was the murder of the student Rubén Batista and the criminal volleys fired at a peaceful student demonstration next to the wall where Spanish volunteers shot the medical students in 1871. And many cases, such as that of Dr. García Bárcena, where right in the courtrooms people have coughed up blood because of the barbaric tortures inflicted upon them by the repressive security forces. I will not enumerate the hundreds of cases where groups of citizens have been brutally clubbed—men, women, children and the elderly. All of this was occurring even before July 26. Since then, as everyone knows, even Cardinal Arteaga himself was not spared such treatment. Everyone knows he was a victim of repressive agents. According to the official story, he fell prey to a "band of thieves." For once the regime told the truth, because what else is this regime?

People have just contemplated with horror the case of the journalist who was kidnapped and subjected to torture by fire for 20 days. Each new case brings forth evidence of unheard-of effrontery, of immense hypocrisy: the cowardice of those who shirk responsibility and invariably blame the enemies of the regime. Such governmental tactics are to be envied only by the worst gangster mobs. Even the Nazi criminals were never so cowardly.

Hitler assumed responsibility for the massacres of June 30, 1934, stating that for 24 hours he himself had been the German Supreme Court; the henchmen of this dictatorship—which defies all comparison because of its baseness, maliciousness and cowardice—kidnap, torture, murder and then outrageously put the blame on the adversaries of the regime. Typical tactics of Sergeant Barriguilla!

Not once in all the cases I have mentioned, Honorable Judges, have the agents responsible for these crimes been brought to court to be tried for them. How is this? Was this not to be the regime of public order, peace and respect for human life?

I have related all this in order to ask you now: Can this state of affairs be called a "revolution," capable of formulating law and establishing rights? Is it or is it not legitimate to struggle against this regime? And must there not be a high degree of corruption in the courts of law when these courts imprison citizens who try to rid the country of so much infamy?

Cuba is suffering from a cruel and base despotism. You are well aware that resistance to despots is legitimate. This is a universally recognized principle and our 1940 constitution expressly makes it a sacred right, in the second paragraph of Article 40: "It is legitimate to use adequate resistance to protect previously granted individual rights." And even if this prerogative had not been provided by the supreme law of the land, it is a consideration without which one cannot conceive of the existence of a democratic collectivity. Professor Infiesta, in his book on constitutional law, differentiates between the political and legal constitutions, and states: "Sometimes the legal constitution includes constitutional principles which, even without being so classified, would be equally binding solely on the basis of the people's consent, for example, the principle of majority rule or representation in our democracies." The right of insurrection in the face of tyranny is one such principle, and whether or not it is included in the legal constitution, it is always binding within a democratic society. The presentation of such a case to a high court is one of the most interesting problems of general law. Duguit has said in his *Treatise on Constitutional Law*: "If an insurrection fails, no court will dare to rule that this unsuccessful insurrection was technically not a conspiracy, not a transgression against the security of the state, inasmuch as, the government being tyrannical, the intention to overthrow it was legitimate." But please take note: Duguit does not state, "the court ought not to rule." He says, "no court will dare to rule." More explicitly, he means that no court will dare, that no court will have enough courage to do so, under a tyranny. If the court is courageous and does its duty, then yes, it will dare.

Recently there has been a violent controversy concerning the 1940 constitution. The Court of Social and Constitutional Rights ruled against it in favor of the so-called statutes. Nevertheless, Honorable Judges, I maintain that the 1940 constitution is still in force. My statement may seem absurd and extemporaneous to you. But do not be surprised. It is I who am astonished that a court of law should have attempted to deal a death blow to the legitimate constitution of the republic. Adhering strictly to facts, truth and reason—as I have done all along—I will prove what I have just stated. The Court of Social and Constitutional Rights was instituted according to Article 172 of the 1940 constitution, and the supplementary act of May 31, 1949. These laws, by virtue of which the court was created, granted it, insofar as problems of unconstitutionality are concerned, a specific and clearly defined area of legal competence: to rule in all matters of appeals claiming the unconstitutionality of laws, legal decrees, resolutions, or acts that deny, diminish, restrain or adulterate the constitutional rights and privileges or that jeopardize the operations of state agencies. Article 194 established very clearly the following: "All judges and courts are under the obligation to find solutions to conflicts between the constitution and the existing laws in accordance with the principle that the former will always prevail over the latter." Therefore, according to the laws that created it, the Court of Social and Constitutional Rights should always rule in favor of the constitution. When this court caused the statutes to prevail above the constitution of the republic, it completely overstepped its boundaries and its established field of competence, thereby giving a decision which is legally null and void. Furthermore, the decision itself is absurd, and absurdities have no validity in law nor in fact, not even from a metaphysical point of view. No matter how venerable a court may be, it cannot assert that circles are square or, what amounts to the same thing, that the grotesque offspring of the April 4 statutes should be considered the official constitution of a state.

The constitution is understood to be the basic and supreme law of the nation, defining the country's political structure, regulating the functioning of its government agencies, and determining the limits of their activities. It must be stable, enduring and, to a certain extent, inflexible. The statutes fulfill none of these qualifications. To begin with, they harbor a monstrous, shameless and brazen contradiction in regard to the most vital aspect of all: the integration of the republican structure and the principle of national sovereignty. Article 1 reads: "Cuba is a sovereign and independent state constituted as a democratic republic." Article 2 reads: "Sovereignty resides in the will of the people, and all powers derive from this source." But then comes Article 118, which reads: "The president will be nominated by the cabinet." So it is not the people who choose the president, but rather the cabinet. And who chooses the cabinet? Article 120, Section 13: "The president will be authorized to nominate and reappoint the members of the cabinet and to replace them when occasion arises." So, after all, who nominates whom? Is this not the classic old problem of the chicken and the egg that no one has ever been able to solve?

One day, 18 hoodlums got together. Their plan was to assault the republic and loot its 350 million peso annual budget. Behind peoples' backs and with great treachery, they succeeded. "Now what do we do next?" they wondered. One of them said to the rest: "You name me prime minister, and I'll make you generals." When this was done, he rounded up a group of 20 men and told them: "I will make you my cabinet if you make me president." In this way they named each other generals, ministers and president, and then took over the treasury and the republic.

Moreover, it was not simply a matter of usurping sovereignty at a given moment in order to name a cabinet, generals and a president. This man ascribed to himself, through these statutes, not only absolute control of the nation, but also the power of life and death over every citizen—control, in fact, over the very existence of the nation. Because of this, I maintain that the position of the Court of Social and Constitutional Rights is not only treacherous, vile, cowardly and repugnant, but also absurd.

The statutes contain an article which has not received much attention, but which gives us the key to this situation and is the one from which we will derive decisive conclusions. I refer specifically to the modifying clause included in Article 257, which reads: "This constitutional law is open to reform by the cabinet with a two-thirds quorum vote." This is where the farce reaches its climax. Not only did they exercise sovereignty in order to impose a constitution upon a people without that people's consent, and to install a regime which concentrates all power in their own hands, but also, through Article 257, they assume the most essential attribute of sovereignty: the power to change the basic and supreme law of the land. And they have already changed it several times since March 10. Yet, with the greatest gall, they assert in Article 2 that sovereignty resides in the will of the people and that the people are the source of all power. Since these changes may be brought about by a vote of two-thirds of the cabinet and the cabinet is named by the president, then the right to make and break Cuba is in the hands of one man, a man who is, furthermore, the most unworthy of all the creatures ever to be born in this land. Was this then accepted by the Court of Social and Constitutional Rights? And is all that derives from it valid and legal? Very well, you will see what was accepted: "This constitutional law is open to reform by the cabinet with a two-thirds quorum vote." Such a power recognizes no limits. Under its aegis, any article, any chapter, any section, even the whole law may be modified. For example, Article 1, which I have just mentioned, says that "Cuba is a sovereign and independent state constituted as a democratic republic," although today it is in fact a bloody dictatorship. Article 3 reads: "The national boundaries include the island of Cuba, the Isle of Pines, and the surrounding keys..." and so on. Batista and his cabinet under the provisions of Article 257 can modify all these other articles. They can say that Cuba is no longer a republic but a hereditary monarchy and he, Batista, can anoint himself king. He can dismember the national territory and sell a province to a foreign country, as Napoleon did with Louisiana. He may suspend the right to life itself, and like Herod, order the decapitation of newborn children. All these measures would be legal and you would have to incarcerate all those who opposed them, just as you now intend to do with me. I have put forth extreme examples to show how sad and humiliating our present situation is. To think that all these absolute powers are in the hands of those truly capable of selling our country along with all its citizens!

As the Court of Social and Constitutional Rights has accepted this state of affairs, what more are they waiting for? They may as well hang up their judicial robes. It is a fundamental principle of general law that there can be no constitutional status where the constitutional and legislative powers reside in the same body. When the cabinet makes the laws, the decrees and the rules—and at the same time has the power to change the constitution at any time—then I ask you: Why do we need a Court of Social and Constitutional Rights? The ruling in favor of this statute is irrational, inconceivable, illogical and totally contrary to the republican laws that you, Honorable Judges, swore to uphold. When the Court of Social and Constitutional Rights supported Batista's statutes over the constitution, the supreme law of the land was not abolished but rather the Court of Social and Constitutional Rights placed itself outside the constitution, renounced its autonomy and committed legal suicide. May it rest in peace!

The right to rebel, established in Article 40 of the constitution, is still valid. Was it established to function while the republic was enjoying normal conditions? No. This provision is to the constitution what a lifeboat is to a ship at sea. The lifeboat is only launched when the ship has been torpedoed by enemies laying wait along its course. With our constitution betrayed and the people deprived of all their prerogatives, there was only one way open, one right which no power may abolish. The right to resist oppression and injustice. If any doubt remains, there is an article of the Social Defense Code which the Honorable Prosecutor would have done well not to forget. It reads, and I quote: "The appointed or elected government authorities that fail to resist sedition with all available means will be liable to a sentence of interdiction of six to eight years." The judges of our nation were under the obligation to resist Batista's treacherous military coup of March 10. It is understandable that when no one has observed the law and when no one else has done their duty, those who have observed the law and have done their duty should be sent to prison.

You will not be able to deny that the regime forced upon the nation is unworthy of Cuba's history. In his book, *The Spirit of the Law*, which is the foundation of the modern separation of governmental power, Montesquieu makes a distinction between three types of government according to their basic nature: "The republican form wherein the whole people or a portion thereof has sovereign power; the monarchical form where only one person governs, but in accordance with fixed and well-defined laws; and the despotic form where one person without regard for laws or rules acts as they please, regarding only their own will or whim." And then he adds: "People whose five senses constantly tell them that they are everything and that the rest of humanity is nothing are bound to be lazy, ignorant and licentious... As virtue is necessary to democracy, and honor to a monarchy, fear is of the essence to a despotic regime, where virtue is not needed and honor would be dangerous."

The right of rebellion against tyranny, Honorable Judges, has been recognized from the most ancient times to the present day by all creeds, ideas and doctrines.

It was so in the theocratic monarchies of remote antiquity. In China it was almost a constitutional principle that when an emperor governed badly and despotically he should be deposed and replaced by a virtuous prince.

The philosophers of ancient India upheld the principle of active resistance to arbitrary authority. They justified revolution and very often put their theories into practice. One of their spiritual leaders used to say that "an opinion held by the majority is stronger than the king himself. A rope woven of many strands is strong enough to hold a lion."

The city states of Greece and republican Rome not only admitted but defended the meting-out of violent death to tyrants.

In the Middle Ages, John of Salisbury says in his *Book of the Statesman* that when a prince does not govern according to law and degenerates into a tyrant, violent overthrow is legitimate and justifiable. For tyrants, he recommends the dagger rather than poison.

St. Thomas Aquinas, in the *Summa Theologica*, rejects the doctrine of tyrannicide, and yet upholds the thesis that tyrants should be overthrown by the people.

Martin Luther proclaimed that when a government degenerates into a tyranny that violates the law, its subjects are released from their obligations to obey. His disciple, Philippe Melanchthon, upholds the right of resistance when governments become despotic. Calvin, the outstanding thinker of the Reformation with regard to political ideas, postulates that people are entitled to take up arms to oppose any usurpation.

No less a person that Juan Mariana, a Spanish Jesuit during the reign of Philip II, asserts in his book, *De Rege et Regis Institutione*, that when a governor usurps power, or even if he were elected, when he governs in a tyrannical manner, it is licit for a private citizen to exercise tyrannicide, either directly or through subterfuge with the least possible disturbance.

The French writer, François Hotman, maintained that between the government and its subjects there is a bond or contract, and that the people may rise in rebellion against the tyranny of government when the latter violates that pact.

About the same time, a booklet that came to be widely read appeared under the title *Vindiciae Contra Tyrannos*, and it was signed with the pseudonym Stephanus Junius Brutus. It openly declared that resistance to governments is legitimate when rulers oppress the people and that it is the duty of honorable judges to lead the struggle.

The Scottish reformers John Knox and John Poynet upheld the same point of view. And, in the most important book of that movement, George Buchanan stated that if a government achieves power without taking into account the consent of the people, or if a government rules their destiny in an unjust or arbitrary fashion, then that government becomes a tyranny and can be divested of power or, in a final recourse, its leaders can be put to death.

Johannes Althusius, a German jurist of the early 17th century, stated in his treatise on politics that sovereignty as the supreme authority of the state is born from the voluntary concourse of all its members; that governmental authority stems from the people and that its unjust, illegal or tyrannical exercise exempts them from the duty of obedience and justifies resistance or rebellion.

Thus far, Honorable Judges, I have mentioned examples from antiquity, from the Middle Ages, and from the beginnings of our times. I selected these examples from writers of all creeds. Moreover, you can see that the right to rebellion is at the very root of Cuba's existence as a nation. By virtue of it you are today able to appear in the robes of Cuban judges. Would it be that those garments really served the cause of justice!

It is well known that in England during the 17th century two kings, Charles I and James II, were dethroned for despotism. These actions coincided with the birth of liberal political philosophy and provided the ideological base for a new social class, which was then struggling to break the bonds of feudalism. Against divine right autocracies, this new philosophy upheld the principle of the social contract and of the consent of the governed, and constituted the foundation of the English revolution of 1688, the American revolution of 1775 and the French revolution of 1789. These great revolutionary events ushered in the liberation of the Spanish colonies in the New World — the final link in that chain being broken by Cuba. The new philosophy nurtured our own political ideas and helped us to develop our constitutions, from the constitution of Guáimaro up to the constitution of 1940. The latter was influenced by the socialist currents of our time; the principle of the social function of property and of a person's inalienable right to a decent living were built into it, although large vested interests have prevented fully enforcing those rights.

The right of insurrection against tyranny then underwent its final consecration and became a fundamental tenet of political liberty.

As far back as 1649, John Milton wrote that political power lies with the people, who can enthrone and dethrone kings and who have the duty to overthrow tyrants.

John Locke, in his essay on government, maintained that when the natural rights of man are violated, the people have the right and the duty to alter or abolish the government: "The only remedy against unauthorized force is to oppose it by force."

Jean-Jacques Rousseau said with great eloquence in his *Social Contract*:

> While a people sees itself forced to obey and obeys, it does well; but as soon as it can shake off the yoke and shakes it off, it does better, recovering its liberty through the use of the very right that has been taken away from it...
>
> The strongest person is never strong enough to be master forever, unless he converts force into right and obedience into duty. Force is a physical power; I do not see what morality one may derive from its use. To yield to force is an act of necessity, not of will; at the very least, it is an act of prudence. In what sense should this be called a duty?...
>
> To renounce freedom is to renounce one's status as a man, to renounce one's human rights, including one's duties. There is no possible compensation for renouncing everything. Total renunciation is incompatible with human nature and to take away all free will is to take away all morality of conduct. In short, it is vain and contradictory to stipulate on the one hand an absolute authority and on the other an unlimited obedience...

Thomas Paine said that "one just person deserves more respect than a rogue with a crown."

The people's right to rebel has been opposed only by reactionaries like that clergyman of Virginia, Jonathan Boucher, who said: "The right to rebel is a censurable doctrine derived from Lucifer, the father of rebellions."

The Declaration of Independence of the Congress of Philadelphia, on July 4, 1776, consecrated this right in a beautiful paragraph which reads:

> We hold these truths to be self-evident: that all men are created equal, that they are endowed by their Creator with certain inalienable rights, that among these are life, liberty and the pursuit of happiness; that to secure these rights, governments are instituted among men, deriving their just powers from the consent of the governed; that whenever any form of government becomes destructive of these ends, it is the right of the people to alter or abolish it and to institute a new government, laying its foundation on such principles and organizing its powers in such form as to them will seem most likely to effect their safety and happiness.

The famous French Declaration of the Rights of Man bequeathed this principle to the coming generations: "When the government violates the rights of the people, insurrection is for them the most sacred of rights and the most imperative of duties." "When a person seizes sovereignty, he should be condemned to death by free men."

I believe I have sufficiently presented my argument. I have called forth more reasons than the Honorable Prosecutor raised in demanding that I be condemned to 26 years in prison. All these arguments favor those who struggle for the freedom and happiness of the people. None support those who oppress the people, revile them and rob them blind. Therefore, I have been able to expound many reasons and he could not adduce even one. How can Batista's power be justified when he gained it against the will of the people and by violating the laws of the republic through the use of treachery and force? How could anyone consider legitimate a regime of blood, oppression and ignominy? How could anyone describe as revolutionary a regime that has gathered the most reactionary men, methods and ideas of public life around it? How can anyone consider legally valid the high treason of a court whose duty was to defend the constitution? With what right do the courts send to prison citizens who have tried to redeem their country by giving their own blood, their own lives? All this is monstrous in the eyes of the nation and in the face of the principles of true justice!

Still, there is one argument more powerful than all the others. We are Cubans and to be Cuban implies a duty; not to fulfill that duty is a crime, it is treason. We are proud of the history of our country; we learned it in school and have grown up hearing of freedom, justice and human rights. We were taught to venerate the glorious example of our heroes and martyrs. Céspedes, Agramonte, Maceo, Gómez and Martí were the first names engraved in our minds. We were taught that the Titan [Antonio Maceo] once said liberty is not begged for but won with the blade of a machete. We were taught that for the guidance of Cuba's free citizens, the Apostle [Martí] wrote in his book *The Golden Age*:

> The person who abides by unjust laws and permits anyone to trample and mistreat the country in which he or she was born is not an honorable person... In the world there must be a certain degree of honor just as there must be a certain amount of light. When there are many without honor, there are always others who bear in themselves the honor of many. These are those who rebel with great force against those who steal the people's freedom, that is to say, against those who steal honor itself. In those individuals, thousands more are contained, an entire people is contained, human dignity itself is contained...

We were taught that October 10 and February 24 are glorious anniversaries of national rejoicing because they mark days on which Cubans rebelled against the yoke of infamous tyranny. We were taught to cherish and defend the beloved flag of the lone star, and to sing every afternoon the verses of our national anthem: "To live in chains is to live in disgrace and in opprobrium," and "To die for one's homeland is to live forever!" All this we learned and will never forget, even though today in our land there is murder and prison for those who practice the ideas taught to them from the cradle. We were born in a free country that our parents bequeathed to us, and the island will first sink into the sea before we consent to be the slaves of anyone.

It seemed that the Apostle would die during his centennial. It seemed that his memory would be extinguished forever. So great was the affront! But he is alive; he has not died. His people are rebellious. His people are worthy. His people are faithful to his memory. There are Cubans who have fallen defending his doctrines. There are young combatants who in magnificent selflessness came to die beside his tomb, giving their blood and their lives so that he could keep on living in the heart of his nation. Cuba, what would have become of you had you let your Apostle die?

I now come to the close of my defense, but I will not end it as lawyers usually do, asking that the accused be freed. I cannot ask for freedom for myself while my compañeros are already suffering in the ignominious prison of the Isle of Pines. Send me there to join them and to share their fate. It is understandable that honest people should be dead or in prison in a republic where the president is a criminal and a thief.

To you, Honorable Judges, my sincere gratitude for having allowed me to express myself free from contemptible restrictions. I hold no bitterness toward you, I recognize that in certain aspects you have been humane, and I know that the chief justice of this court, a man of impeccable character, cannot disguise his repugnance at the current state of affairs that compels him to dictate an unjust verdict. Nevertheless, a more serious problem remains for the Court of Appeals: the indictments arising from the murders of 70 combatants, that is to say, the greatest massacre we have ever known. The guilty remain at liberty and with weapons in their hands, weapons that continue to threaten the lives of all citizens. If all the weight of the law does not fall upon the guilty because of cowardice or because of domination of the courts, and if then all the judges do not resign, I pity Your Honor. And I regret the unprecedented shame that will besmirch judicial power.

I know that imprisonment will be harder for me than it has ever been for anyone, filled with cowardly threats and hideous cruelty. But I do not fear prison, as I do not fear the fury of the miserable tyrant who took the lives of 70 of my compañeros. Condemn me. It does not matter. History will absolve me.

2. ON THE TRIUMPH OF THE REVOLUTION

As the rebel forces swept across Cuba in late 1958, General Batista and General Cantillo conspired to establish a military junta in a last-ditched effort to thwart the revolution. Meanwhile, Fidel Castro won the cooperation of Santiago de Cuba's military chief, Colonel Rego Rubido. In the early hours of January 1, 1959, Batista and some of his henchmen fled the country, leaving General Cantillo in charge. He immediately appointed elderly Supreme Court magistrate Dr. Carlos Piedra as head of a civilian-military junta. But on the same day, Fidel Castro called a general strike for the following day (January 2), saying: "This time nothing and no one can impede the triumph of the revolution."

CÉSPEDES PARK, SANTIAGO DE CUBA
JANUARY 2, 1959

In the early hours of January 2, Fidel Castro addressed the people of Santiago de Cuba in Céspedes Park, outlining the events that led up to the victory of the revolutionary forces.

People of Santiago, compatriots of all Cuba:

We have finally reached Santiago de Cuba. The road was long and difficult, but we finally made it. It was rumored that they expected us in the capital of the republic [Havana] at 2 p.m. today. No one was more amazed than I was at this treacherous blow, which would place me in the capital of the republic this morning. Besides, I had intended to be in the capital of the republic, that is, in the new capital of the republic, because Santiago de Cuba, in accordance with the wishes of the provisional president, in accordance with the wishes of the Rebel Army, and in accordance with the wishes of the worthy people of Santiago de Cuba, Santiago will be the new provisional capital of Cuba.

This measure may surprise some people. Admittedly, it is a change, but the revolution is characterized precisely by its newness, by the fact that it will do things that have never been done before.

In making Santiago de Cuba the provisional capital of the republic, we are fully aware of our reasons for doing so. This is no attempt to cajole a specific area by demagogy. It is simply that Santiago de Cuba has been the strongest bulwark of the revolution.

The revolution begins now. It will not be an easy task, but a difficult and dangerous undertaking, particularly in the initial phases. And in what better place could we establish the government of the republic than in this fortress of the revolution?

So that you may understand that this will be a government solidly supported by the people of this heroic city, located in the foothills of the Sierra Maestra—because Santiago de Cuba is a part of the Sierra Maestra— Santiago de Cuba and the Sierra Maestra will be the two strongest fortresses for the revolution. But there are other reasons that motivate us, and one is the military revolutionary movement, the true military revolutionary movement that did not take place in Camp Columbia [in Havana].

In Camp Columbia they prepared a puny little uprising against the revolution, principally with Batista's assistance. Since it is necessary to tell the truth and since we came here with a view to orienting the people, I can assure you that the military uprising in Camp Columbia was an attempt to deprive the people of power, to rob the revolution of its triumph and to allow Batista to escape, to allow General Tabernilla to escape, to allow the Tabernilla family to escape together with the Pilar Garcías, to allow the Salas Cañizares and the Venturas to escape. The uprising was an ambitious and treacherous blow that deserves the lowest epithets.

We must call a spade a spade and put the blame where it belongs. I am not going to be diplomatic. I will say outright that General Cantillo betrayed us, and I am not only going to say it, but I am going to prove it to you.

We always said that there would be no point in resolving this matter at the last moment with a puny little military uprising, because even if there was a military uprising, behind the people's backs, our revolution will go forward and this time cannot be crushed. It will not be like 1895 when the North Americans came and took over, intervening at the last moment, and afterwards did not even allow Calixto García to assume the leadership, although he had fought in Santiago de Cuba for 30 years.

It will not be like 1933, when the people began to believe that the revolution was going to triumph, but then along came Mr. Batista to betray the revolution, seize power and establish an 11-year dictatorship.

Nor will it be like 1944, when the people took courage, believing that they had finally reached a position where they could take power, while those who assumed power proved to be thieves. We will have no thievery, no treason, no intervention. This time it is a true revolution, even though some might not desire it. At the very moment the dictatorship fell, as a consequence of our military victories, when they could not hold out even for another 15 days, Mr. Cantillo appears on the scene as a paladin of freedom. Naturally, we have never refused any offer of collaboration that might prevent bloodshed, providing the aims of our revolution were not imperiled by it. Naturally, we have always appealed to the military in our search for peace, but it must be peace with freedom and peace with the triumph of our revolution. This is the only way to obtain peace.

Thus, on December 24, when we were told of General Cantillo's desire to meet us, we agreed to the interview. And I must confess, given the course of events, the extraordinary development of our military operations, that I had very little interest in speaking with the military. Nevertheless, I felt that it was the duty of those of us with responsibility not to allow ourselves to be carried away by our feelings. I also thought that if triumph could be achieved with minimum bloodshed, it was my duty to listen to the proposals made by the military.

I went to meet Mr. Cantillo, who spoke on behalf of the army. We met on [December] 28 at the Oriente mill, where he arrived in a helicopter at 8 p.m. We talked for four hours and I will not invent any stories about what took place, since there were several exceptional witnesses to the meeting. There was Dr. Raúl Chibas, there was a Catholic priest, and there were several military men, whose evidence cannot be questioned on any grounds whatsoever. After reviewing all of Cuba's problems, and considering every detail, General Cantillo agreed to create a military revolutionary movement with us.

The first thing I said to him was this: After carefully studying the situation, the situation of the army, the situation in which it had been placed by the dictatorship, after explaining to him that he did not have to concern himself with Batista, or with the Tabernillas, or with the rest of those people because none of them had shown any concern for the Cuban military forces, we argued that the military had been led into a campaign against the masses, a campaign that would never be victorious because no one can win a war against the mass of the population.

After telling him that the military forces were the victims of the regime's immorality, that the budgetary allocations for the purchase of arms had been embezzled, that the soldiers were being constantly defrauded, that those people did not deserve the consideration of honorable military men, that the army had no reason to bear the blame for crimes committed by Batista's gang of villains, I told him quite clearly that I did not authorize anything that would enable Batista to escape. I warned him that if Batista got away with the Tabernillas and the rest of them it would be because we had been unable to prevent it. We had to prevent Batista's flight.

Everyone knows that our first requirement in the event of an uprising by the military — that is, a military uprising coordinated with our movement — was the surrender of the war criminals. This is an essential condition. We could have captured Batista and all his accomplices; and I said loudly and clearly that I would not accept Batista's escape. I explained to him quite clearly what course of action would have to be taken and that I did not give any support [to Batista's escape], and neither would the July 26 Movement, nor would the people support a coup d'état [on such terms]. The fact is that the people won their own freedom by conquest; the people did it themselves.

Our freedom was taken from us by a coup d'état; but in order to finish once and for all with coups, it was necessary to achieve freedom through the people's sacrifice. We could achieve nothing by an uprising today and another tomorrow and another in two years and another three years later, because here in Cuba it is the people, and the people alone, who must decide who is to govern them.

The military forces must unconditionally obey the people's orders and be subject to the people, the constitution and the laws of the republic. If there is a bad government that embezzles and does the wrong thing, the only thing to do is to wait for the next election when that bad government can be turned out of office. That is why in democratic, constitutional regimes, governments have a fixed mandate. If they are bad, they can be ousted by the people, who can vote for a better government. The function of the military is not to elect governments, but to defend the law and to guarantee the rights of citizens. That is why I warned him that a coup d'état was out of the question, but that a military revolutionary movement was acceptable and that it should take place in Santiago de Cuba and not in Camp Columbia.

I told him quite clearly that the only way of forming a link with the people and joining them, of uniting the military and the revolutionaries, was not a coup d'état in the early hours of the dawn in Camp Columbia—at 2 or 3 a.m.—about which no one would know anything, as is the usual practice of these gentlemen. I told him it would be necessary to arouse the garrison at Santiago de Cuba, which was quite strong and adequately armed, in order to start the military movement, which would then be joined by the people and the revolutionaries. Given the situation in which the dictatorship found itself, such a movement would prove irresistible because all the other garrisons in the country would certainly join it immediately.

That was what was agreed to and not only was it what was agreed to, but I made him swear on it. He had planned to go to Havana the next day and we did not agree with this. I told him, "It is risky for you to go to Havana." And he replied, "No, no there's no risk." I insisted, "You are running a great risk of arrest because if there is a conspiracy, everyone knows about it here."

"No, I am sure they will not arrest me," he replied. And, of course, why would they arrest him if this was a Batista coup d'état?

My thoughts were: "Well, all this seems so easy that it cannot be right," so I said to him, "Will you promise me that in Havana you will not be persuaded by those supporting you to carry out a coup d'état in the capital? Will you promise me that you won't do it?" He said, "I promise I won't." I insisted, "Will you swear to me that you won't?" He replied again, "I swear I won't!"

I believe that the primary requisite for a military man is honor, that the primary requisite for a military man is his word. This gentleman not only proved that he is dishonorable and that his word is worth nothing, but also that he lacks intelligence. I say this because a movement that could have been organized from the start with the support of the whole population, with its victory assured from the outset, did nothing more than dive into space. He believed that it would be only too easy to fool the people and to mislead the revolution.

He understood a couple of things. He understood, for instance, that when we told the people that Batista had left in a plane the people would flock into the streets, wild with happiness. He assumed that the people were not sufficiently mature to distinguish between Batista's flight and the revolution. Because if Batista left and Cantillo's friends assumed control, it was quite likely that Dr. Urrutia would also have to go within three months. Just as they were betraying us now, so they would betray us later on. The truth of the matter is that Mr. Cantillo already betrayed us before the revolution. He had already given signs of this, and I can prove it.

We agreed with General Cantillo that the uprising would take place on December 31 at 3 p.m., and it was agreed that the armed forces would give unconditional support to the revolutionary movement. The president was to appoint the revolutionary leaders and establish the positions to which the revolutionary leaders would assign the military. They were offering unconditional support and every detail of the plan was agreed to. At 3 p.m. on December 31 the garrison at Santiago de Cuba was to rise in revolt. Immediately after this, several rebel columns would enter the city and the people would fraternize with the military and the rebels, immediately issuing a revolutionary proclamation to the country as a whole and calling on all honorable military men to join the movement.

It was agreed that the tanks in the city would be placed at our disposal and I personally offered to advance toward the capital with an armed column preceded by the tanks. The tanks were to be handed over to me at 3 p.m., not because it was considered that any fighting would be necessary but to guard against the possibility that in Havana the movement might fail, which made it necessary to place our vanguard as close as possible to the capital.

It was evident that with the hatred for the repressive forces created by the horrendous crimes committed by Ventura and Pilar García, Batista's overthrow would create considerable upheaval among the people. Moreover, the police force would inevitably feel that it lacked the moral strength to restrain the populace, as in fact happened. A series of excesses occurred in the capital. There was looting, shooting and fires, the responsibility for which falls on the shoulders of General Cantillo, who betrayed his word of honor and failed to carry out the plan which had been agreed to. He believed that appointing police captains and commanders, many of whom had already deserted when they were appointed — proof that they had guilty consciences — would be enough to solve the problem.

How different things were in Santiago de Cuba! How orderly and civic-minded! How disciplined the behavior of the masses! There was not a single attempt at looting, not a single example of personal vengeance, not a single person dragged through the streets, not a single fire! The behavior of the population of Santiago de Cuba was admirable and exemplary, despite the fact that Santiago de Cuba was the city that had suffered the most, where there had been the greatest terror and where, consequently, one would expect the people to be most outraged. Despite our statements of this morning that we did not agree with the coup d'état, the population in Santiago de Cuba behaved in an exemplary fashion and this is a matter of pride for the people, the revolutionaries and the military.

One can no longer say that revolution means anarchy and disorder; this happened in Havana because of treason, but that was not the case in Santiago de Cuba, which we can hold up as a model every time the revolution is accused of anarchy and disorganization.

The people should know about the negotiations between General Cantillo and me. After the agreements were made, when we had already suspended operations in Santiago de Cuba — because by December 28 our troops were quite close to the city and were ready for the assault — we were obliged to make a series of changes, abandoning the Santiago operation. Instead, we were to direct our troops elsewhere, in fact, to a place where it was believed that the movement might not be victorious immediately.

When we had completed all our maneuvers, the column which was to march on the capital received the following note from General Cantillo, just a few hours before it was due to leave. The text of the note read as follows: "Circumstances have changed considerably and now are favorable to a national solution."

This was strange, because the major factors already could not have been more favorable and everything pointed to victory. It was therefore strange that he should come and say that circumstances had changed greatly and favorably. The circumstances were that Batista and Tabernilla had come to an agreement, assuring the success of the coup.

Cantillo recommended, "nothing be done at the moment and that we should await the course of events over the next weeks, up to [January] 6." Obviously, given the indefinite truce, they would take care of everything in Havana.

I responded immediately: "The tenor of the note entirely contradicts our agreement. Moreover, it is ambiguous and incomprehensible and has made me lose confidence in the seriousness of the agreements. Hostilities will commence tomorrow at 3 p.m., the date and time agreed to for the launching of the movement."

Something very curious happened immediately afterwards. On receiving the very short note, I advised the commanding officer in Santiago de Cuba, through a messenger, that if hostilities were to break out because the agreements were not complied with and we had to attack Santiago de Cuba, they would have no option but to surrender.

But the messenger did not convey my message correctly. He told Colonel Rego Rubido that I demanded the surrender of the town as a precondition to any agreement. He did not explain that I had said, "in the event of our launching an attack." I had not said that I demanded the surrender of the town as a condition from General Cantillo. As a result of this message, the commanding officer at Santiago de Cuba [Colonel Rubido] sent me a very enigmatic and punctilious reply that I will read to you, indicating, naturally, that he felt very offended with what had been mistakenly conveyed to him:

> The solution is neither a coup d'état nor a military revolt. Nevertheless, we believe that it is the most advisable solution for Dr. Fidel Castro, in accordance with his ideas, and one which would place the destiny of the country in his hands within 48 hours. It is not a local but a national solution and any indiscretion might compromise or destroy this and lead to chaos. Therefore, we hope that you will have confidence in our decision and that there will be a solution before January 6.
>
> As for Santiago, because of the note and the messenger's report, it

will be necessary to change the plan and not enter the city. This caused a certain amount of ill-feeling among the key personnel, who would never surrender their arms without a fight. Arms are not surrendered to an ally and they are not surrendered without honor.

A beautiful phrase spoken by the commander of the garrison of Santiago de Cuba.

> If there is no confidence in us, or if Santiago de Cuba is attacked, this will be regarded as equivalent to breaking the agreements, which will disrupt the negotiations, and thereby formally absolve us from any commitments. It is our hope, given the time required to act in one way or another, that the reply arrives in time to be sent to Havana with the Viscount leaving this afternoon.

I responded to Colonel José Rego Rubido's note as follows:

Free Territory of Cuba, December 31, 1958

Colonel Sir:

A regrettable error has occurred in the transmission of my message to you, due perhaps to the haste with which I replied to your note. This is what I surmise from the conversation I have since held with its bearer. I did not tell him that the conditions of our agreement required the surrender of the garrison of Santiago de Cuba to our forces. This would have been a discourtesy and an unworthy and offensive proposal to the military forces who approached us so cordially.

The question is something entirely different. An agreement was reached between the leader of the military and ourselves which was to go into effect from 3 p.m. on December 31. The plan included details established after careful analysis of the problems, and was to begin with the revolt of the Santiago garrison. I persuaded General Cantillo of the advantages to be derived from beginning in Oriente [province] rather than in Camp Columbia, because the mass of the people greatly feared any coup starting in the barracks in Havana, stressing how difficult it would be, in that case, to ensure that the people joined that movement. He expressed his full agreement with my point of view and said he was only concerned about maintaining order in the capital; so we jointly agreed on measures necessary to keep order. Specifically, this involved the advance of our column toward Santiago de Cuba. It was to be a combined effort of the military, the people and ourselves, a sort of revolutionary movement which, from the outset, would have the support of the entire nation.

In accordance with this agreement, we suspended the operations that were underway and deployed our forces in other directions—such as Holguín, where the presence of some [of Batista's] well-known henchmen virtually ensured resistance to the revolutionary military movement.

When all our preparations were completed, I received yesterday's message [from Cantillo], indicating that the plan of action agreed to was not to be carried out.

Apparently there were other plans of which I was not informed because, in fact, the matter was no longer in our hands. Therefore, all we could do was wait. Everything was changed unilaterally, putting our own forces at risk, although according to our understanding and what was being said, they were being sent off on difficult operations...

We remained dependent on General Cantillo, who took many risks on his frequent trips to Havana. Militarily, these trips might well prove to be a disaster for us. You must realize that everything is very confused at this moment, and Batista is an artful, crafty individual who knows how to maneuver.

How can we be asked to renounce all the advantage we have gained during the past few weeks, and stand by, waiting patiently, for events to unfold?

I made it quite clear that it could not be a unilateral military operation. We did not experience the horror of two years of war just to stand by with our arms crossed, doing nothing, at the most critical moment. They cannot expect this of combatants who have known no rest in seven years of struggle against oppression.

This cannot happen, even though it is your intention to hand over power to the revolutionaries. It is not power that is important to us, but the accomplishment of the revolution. I am also concerned that the military, through an unjustifiable excess of scruples, might facilitate the flight of the principal criminals, letting them escape abroad with their vast fortunes, to then, from some foreign country, do further harm to our country.

I should add, that personally, I am not interested in power and do not envisage taking any post. All that I plan to do is ensure that the sacrifices of so many compatriots are not in vain, whatever the future may hold in store for me. I hope you will understand that I have every respect for the dignity of the military. Rest assured, this is not a matter of ambition or insolence.

I have always acted with loyalty and frankness. What has been gained underhandedly or with duplicity cannot be called a victory; the language of honor you have heard from my lips is the only language I know. Never in the course of the meetings with General Cantillo did we refer to the word "surrender."...

All I meant [in my letter] was that once the blood of our forces had been shed in the attempt to conquer a given objective, no other solution would be acceptable. Even though the cost might be extremely heavy, in view of the present conditions of the forces defending the regime, since these forces cannot support Santiago de Cuba, the latter must inevitably fall into our hands.

This was the basic objective of our whole campaign over the past two months and such a plan cannot be suspended for a week without grave consequences, should the military movement fail. Moreover, it would mean losing the most opportune time—which is the present—when the dictatorship is suffering severe losses in the provinces of Oriente and Las Villas.

We are faced with the dilemma of either renouncing these advantages or exchanging an assured victory for a doubtful one. Do you believe that in the face of yesterday's ambiguous and laconic note [from Cantillo], presenting a unilateral decision, I could hold myself responsible for delaying the plans?

As a military man, you must admit that is too much to ask of us. You have not stopped digging trenches for a single moment and those trenches could be used against us by a Pedraza, or Pilar García or Cañizares… If General Cantillo is relieved of his command, along with his trusted lieutenants, you cannot expect us to remain idle. We have no alternative but to attack because we, too, have sacred obligations.

We hope that these honorable military men will be much more than mere allies. We want them to be our compañeros in a single cause, the cause of Cuba. Above all, I hope that you and your compañeros do not misunderstand me. With respect to the tactical ceasefire in Santiago, to leave no possible room for doubt, I confirm that although at any time before the fighting begins we can renew our negotiations, as of today it must be made clear that operations can begin at any time and that nothing will convince us to alter our plans again.

Colonel Rego sent a punctilious, dignified reply as follows:

Sir,

I beg to acknowledge receipt of your letter of today's date, and believe me, I wish to thank you most sincerely for the explanation regarding the previous message. I must confess that I had felt some error of interpretation must have been involved since I have observed your line of conduct for some time and know that you are a person of principle.

I ignored the details of the original plan because I was only informed of the first part of it. I might add that I am also not aware of some of the details of the present plan. I believe you are partly right in your analysis of the first part of the original plan.

But I believe that a few more days might be necessary before it could be consummated and we would never be able to prevent some of the major, middle-level and minor guilty parties from escaping. I am among those who believe it is absolutely essential that Cuba provides an example to all those who abuse the positions of power they occupy to commit every possible type of offense. Unfortunately, history is plagued with similar cases and rarely are the criminals brought to account because rarely do revolutions do what they have to do.

I am fully aware of your concern for those who bear little responsibility for the course of historical events...

I have no reason whatsoever to believe that any person is attempting to facilitate the escape of the guilty, and, personally, I might add that I am opposed to their flight. Should that happen, the historic responsibility will fall on the shoulders of those who facilitated the escape, and no one else.

I believe that everything will take place in accordance with your ideas, and that it will be for the good of Cuba and for the revolution which you have initiated.

I heard of a young student who had been murdered and whose body was found in the cemetery. Today, I took it upon myself to ensure that a thorough investigation was made to identify the perpetrator and what the circumstances of his death were, and how it took place, just as I had done a few days ago, not sparing any effort until I can put those guilty of such crimes at the disposal of the appropriate authorities.

Lastly, I should advise you that I sent a message to the general, letting him know that I had obtained a plane to carry your note to him. Do not be impatient for I feel sure that you will be in Havana even before the date mentioned. When the general left here, I asked him to let me have the helicopter and a pilot, just in case you might like to fly over Santiago de Cuba on Sunday afternoon.

With sincerest greetings and my warmest wishes for a happy new year,

[Signed] Colonel Rego Rubido

This was the state of our negotiations when Colonel Rego, the commander of Santiago de Cuba, and I were equally surprised by the coup d'état in Camp Columbia, which completely contradicted everything that had been agreed to. The first and most criminal aspect of all was that Batista was allowed to escape, and with him Tabernilla, and the other major criminals. They were allowed to escape with their millions of pesos; yes, they were allowed to flee with the 300 or 400 million pesos they had stolen. This will prove very costly for us because now, from Santo Domingo and from other countries, they will be directing propaganda against the revolution, plotting all the damage they can inflict against our cause. For a good many years we will have them over there, threatening our people, and forcing the people to remain in a constant state of alert because they will be conspiring against us and paying others to do the same.

What did we do as soon as we learned of the blow when we heard about this on Radio Progreso? At that time I was making a statement when I was told that Batista had left for Santo Domingo. Could it be just a rumor? A mistake? I wondered. Could it be a trick? I sent someone out to confirm the story and was informed that Batista and his entourage had indeed left for Santo Domingo. The most astonishing thing of all was that General Cantillo declared that this had taken place thanks to the patriotism of General Batista, who had resigned in order to avoid bloodshed. What do you think about that?

There is something else I have to tell you in order to demonstrate what kind of a coup had been planned. Pedraza had been appointed a member of the junta and then he left. I hardly need to say anything else about the nature of those responsible for carrying out the coup. They did not appoint Urrutia to the presidency, that is, the man supported by the movement and by all the revolutionary organizations. The person they chose was none other than the oldest member of the Supreme Court bench [Piedra], and all his colleagues are quite old themselves. And besides, he has already been a president: a president of the Supreme Court of Justice, which has never dispensed any justice, which never dispensed any kind of justice.

What would the result of all this be? Only half a revolution. A compromise, a caricature of a revolution. This nobody — or whatever you want to call this Mr. Piedra — if he has not resigned by now he should be preparing to do so, because we are going to make him resign in Havana. I don't believe he will last 24 hours in office. It will break all records. They appoint this gentleman, and isn't it marvelous: Cantillo becomes a national hero, the defender of Cuba's freedom, the lord and master of Cuba, and there is Mr. Piedra… It would simply mean replacing one dictator with another.

Every point contained in the documents from Camp Columbia indicated that it was to be a counterrevolutionary uprising. In every point, the general trend was away from the aims of the people, and in every point there was something suspect. Mr. Piedra immediately made an appeal, or stated that he was going to make an appeal, to the rebels and to a peace commission. Meanwhile, we were supposed to be so calm and trusting; we were to lay down our guns and abandon everything and go and pay homage to Mr. Piedra and Mr. Cantillo.

It is obvious that both Cantillo and Piedra were out of touch with reality. I believe that the Cuban people have learned a great deal and we rebels have also learned something.

That was the situation this morning, but it is not the situation this evening, because many things have changed. Given these events, given this betrayal, I ordered all the rebel commanders to continue marching toward their targets, and consequently, I also immediately ordered all the columns assigned to Santiago de Cuba to advance on that city.

I want you to know that we were determined to take Santiago de Cuba by force. This would have been regrettable because it would have led to considerable bloodshed, and then tonight would not have been a night of celebration and joy, as it is; it would not have been a night of peace and fraternization, as it is. I must acknowledge that if a bloody battle did not take place here in Santiago de Cuba, it is due largely to the patriotism of army Colonel José Rego Rubido, to the commanders of the frigates *Máximo Gómez* and *Maceo* and to the chief of the Santiago de Cuba naval district, as well as to the officer who was acting as chief of police.

Citizens, it is only just that we should recognize these facts here and now and be thankful to those responsible for them. They contributed to averting a bloody battle and to converting this morning's counterrevolution into the revolutionary movement of this afternoon.

We had no alternative but to attack because we could not allow the Camp Columbia coup to be consolidated. Moreover, we had to attack without delay. When the troops were already marching toward their objectives, Colonel Rego used a helicopter to try to locate me. The navy commanders contacted us and placed themselves unconditionally at the service of the revolution.

With the support of their two vessels, equipped with heavy weaponry, and of the naval district and the police, I called a meeting of all the army officers stationed in Santiago de Cuba—and there are over 100 of these officers. I explained that I was not the least worried by the thought of addressing them because I knew I was right, and I knew they would understand my arguments and that we would reach an agreement in the course of the meeting. Indeed, in the early evening, just at nightfall, I went to the meeting at the Escandel which was attended by nearly all the army officers in Santiago de Cuba. Many of them were young men who were clearly anxious to fight for the good of their country.

I met with these military men and explained our aims for our country, what we wanted for the country, the manner in which we had always dealt with the military, and all the harm done to the army by the tyrants. I said I did not think it fair that all military men be regarded equally, that the criminals were only a small minority, that there were many honorable men in the army who I knew abhorred the crimes, the abuses and the injustice...

It was clear that when the top ranks of the army were filled by Tabernilla, Pilar García and the like, relatives and blind followers of Batista, there was a generalized sense of fear in the army. One could not ask an individual officer to accept any responsibility. We are familiar with two types of military men: There are military men like Sosa Blanco, Cañizares, Sánchez Mosquera and Chaviano, known for their crimes and the cowardly murder of unfortunate peasants; and then there are military men who conducted honorable campaigns, who never murdered anyone or burned down houses, men such as Commander Quevedo, who was our prisoner after his heroic resistance at the battle of El Jigüe and who is still an army officer. Men like Commander Sierra and many other officers who never in their lives burned down a single house. However, this type of officer got no promotion. Those who were promoted were the criminals because Batista always made a point of rewarding crime.

For example, we have the case of Colonel Rego Rubido who does not owe his position to the dictatorship since he was already a colonel when the March 10 coup took place. The fact is that I asked the army officers in Santiago de Cuba for support and they gave their unconditional backing to the Cuban revolution. When the navy, army and police officers met together, they agreed to condemn the Camp Columbia uprising and to support the legitimate government of the republic because it has the support of the majority of the population, and is represented by Dr. Manuel Urrutia Lleó. Thanks to their attitude, we were able to prevent a lot of bloodshed; thanks to their attitude, this afternoon we saw the birth of a truly revolutionary movement.

I fully understand that among the people there may be many justifiably passionate feelings. I appreciate the concern for justice evinced by our people. And we will have justice. But I want to ask that our people here, above all else, remain calm. Right now, we must consolidate power, before we do anything else. First and foremost, power must be consolidated. After that, we will appoint a commission, made up of reputable military men and officers of the Rebel Army, to take the necessary measures. These will include identifying those culpable. No one will oppose such measures because it is precisely the army and the armed forces who most want to ensure that the guilt of a few should not be borne by the whole corps. They are the ones most interested in ensuring that to wear a uniform is not shameful, and that the guilty are punished so that the innocent do not bear the dishonor of others.

Have confidence in us! This is what we ask of the people because we know how to fulfill our obligations.

Those were the circumstances surrounding the meeting held this afternoon—a meeting that proved to be a truly revolutionary movement in which the people, the military and the rebels participated.

The enthusiasm of the military in Santiago de Cuba was indescribable. As proof of their trust, I asked the military to join me in entering Santiago de Cuba, and so here I am with all the army officers. And here are the tanks that now are at the service of the revolution. Here is the artillery at the service of the revolution. And there are the frigates, now at the service of the revolution.

I do not need to say that the revolution can depend on the people because everyone knows this. I should say, however, that the people, who in the beginning had only shotguns, now have artillery, tanks and frigates, and many trained army technicians to help us handle them. Now the people are properly armed. And let me assure you that if, when we were only 12 people, we never lost faith, now that we have 12 tanks, how could we possibly lose faith?

Let me say that today, tonight, as of this dawn—because it is almost daybreak—the eminent magistrate Dr. Manuel Urrutia Lleó will take over the presidency of the republic. Does Dr. Urrutia have the support of the people or does he not have the support of the people? What I really mean to say is that it is the president of the republic, the legitimate president, who has the support of the people of Cuba, and that is Dr. Manuel Urrutia. Who wants Mr. Piedra as president? If no one wants Mr. Piedra as president, how are they going to impose Mr. Piedra on us now?

Since those are the instructions given by the people of Santiago de Cuba, and since they represent the feelings of all the people of Cuba, as soon as this meeting is over I will march with the veteran troops of the Sierra Maestra, with the tanks and the artillery, toward Havana in order to fulfill the will of the people. We are here entirely at the request of the people. The mandate of the people is the only legal mandate at present. The president is elected by the people and not by a council in Camp Columbia, meeting at 4:00 in the morning...

I am absolutely convinced that by tomorrow morning all the army commands throughout the country will have put themselves at the service of the president of the republic. The president will immediately appoint the chiefs of the army, the navy and the police. Because of the very valuable service rendered now to the revolution, and because he placed thousands of his people at the service of the revolution, we would recommend that Colonel Rego Rubido be made chief of the army. Similarly, the chief of the navy will be one of the two commanders who first placed their vessels at the orders of the revolution. And I would recommend to the president of the republic that Commander Efigenio Almeijeiras be appointed national chief of police. He lost three brothers in the revolution, was one of the *Granma* expeditionaries and one of the most capable combatants in the revolutionary army. Almeijeiras is on active duty in Guantánamo but will arrive here tomorrow.

All I ask for is time for us and for the civil power of the republic, so that we can do the things the people want; but they must be done gradually, little by little. I would only ask one thing of the people, and that is that you remain calm... Time is a highly important factor in everything. The revolution cannot be completed in a single day but you may be sure that we will carry the revolution through to the end. You may be sure that for the first time the republic will be truly and entirely free and the people will have their just reward. Power was not achieved through politics, but through the sacrifices of hundreds and thousands of our fellow Cubans. It is not a promise we make to ourselves but to the people, the whole Cuban nation; the man who has taken over power has no commitment to anyone other than the people.

Che Guevara has been ordered to march on the capital, not on the provisional capital of the republic, but on Havana. Commander Camilo Cienfuegos of Column Two — the Antonio Maceo column — was also ordered to march on Havana and to take over command of Camp Columbia. They will carry out the orders issued by the president of the republic and the mandate of the revolution.

We cannot be blamed for the excesses occurring in Havana. General Cantillo and his fellow dawn conspirators are to blame for those...

It is important to remember that the military forces are primarily at the service of law and authority, not improperly constituted authorities but legitimate authority. No reputable army man need fear anything from the revolution. In this struggle, there are no conquered ones because the only conqueror is the people. There are those who have fallen on one side and the other, but we have all joined together so that the victory may belong to the nation. We have all joined together, the reputable military and the revolutionaries. There will be no more bloodshed. I hope that no group puts up any resistance because, apart from being foolhardy, it would be overcome in short shrift...

There will be no privileges; there will be no privileges for anyone; and the members of the armed forces who are capable and deserving will be promoted. It will not be as it was in the past—that is, when friends and relatives were promoted, regardless of performance. This sort of thing is over in the military as it is over for laborers. There will be no more exploitation or compulsory contributions, which for the workers are the trade union payments and for the military is a peso here for the First Lady and two pesos elsewhere for something else, until all their pay dwindles away.

Naturally, the entire population has expectations and we are going to deliver. However, I have spoken of the military so that they, too, know they can count on the revolution for improvements in their situation; if the budgetary resources are not stolen, the military will be in a much better position than at the present. Moreover, the soldier will not be called on to act as a policeman because he will be busy with his own training in the barracks; the soldier will not be engaged in police work but will be busy being a soldier...

I am certain that as soon as the president of the republic takes office and assumes command, he will decree the restoration of all rights and freedoms, including the absolute freedom of the press, of all individual rights, of all trade union rights, and of the rights and demands of the campesinos and our own people. We will not forget our campesinos in the Sierra Maestra and those in Santiago de Cuba. We will not go and live in Havana and forget everyone, because I prefer to live in the Sierra Maestra, at least in that part for which I feel a very deep sense of gratitude. I will never forget those campesinos and as soon as I have a free moment we will see about building the first school city with places for 20,000 children. We will do it with the help of the people and the rebels will work with them there. We will ask each citizen for a bag of cement and a trowel. I know we will have the help of our citizens...

The country's economy will be reestablished immediately. This year we will take care of the sugarcane to prevent it being burnt, because this year the tax on sugar will not be used for the purchase of murderous weapons, or for planes and bombs with which to attack the people.

We will take care of communications and already from Jiguani to Palma Soriano the telephone lines have been reestablished, and the railroad is being rebuilt. There will be a harvest all over the country and there will be good wages because I know that this is the intention of the president of the republic. There will be good prices because the fear that there would be no harvest has raised prices on the world market. The campesinos can sell their coffee and the cattle breeders can sell their fat steers in Havana because fortunately we triumphed early enough to prevent any catastrophes. I am not just saying these things. You know that we keep our word, and what we promise we accomplish and we promise less than what we intend to accomplish; we promise not more but less and we intend to do more than we have told the people of Cuba.

We do not believe that all the problems can be solved easily; we know the road is strewn with obstacles, but we are people of good faith and we are always ready to face great difficulties. You can be certain of one thing, and that is that we might make one or even many mistakes. But the one thing that can never be said of us is that we have stolen, that we have profited from our position, that we have betrayed the movement. I know that the people can forgive mistakes but not dishonorable deeds, and what we have had in the past were dishonorable men.

In accepting the presidency, Dr. Manuel Urrutia, from the moment he was invested in office, became the highest authority in the country. Let no one think that I intend to exercise any power greater than that of the president of the republic. I will be the first to obey orders issued by the civil authority of the republic and I will be the first to set an example. We will carry out his orders, and within the scope of the authority granted to us, we will try to do the utmost for our people without personal ambition; fortunately we are immune to the temptations of such ambitions and such vanity. What greater glory could we have than the affection of our people? What greater reward could we envisage than the thousands of arms waving before us, full of hope, and faith in us and affection for us.

We will never succumb to vanity or ambition, because, in the words of the Apostle, "All the glory in the world can fit into a kernel of corn." There can be no greater reward or satisfaction than to fulfill one's duty, as we have been doing up to now and as we will continue to do. In saying this, I do not speak just for myself but in the name of the thousands and thousands of combatants who made the people's victory possible. I speak with the deepest sense of respect for our dead, who will not be forgotten, and whose faithful compañeros we will always remain. This time they will not say of us, as has been said of others in the past, that we betrayed the memory of those who died, because those who died will continue to guide us. Frank País is not physically among us, nor are many others, but they are all spiritually and morally present and the mere knowledge that their sacrifice was not in vain is partial compensation for the immense emptiness they left behind them.

Fresh flowers will continue to adorn their tombs; their children will not be forgotten and assistance will be given to the families of the fallen. We rebels will not ask for retrospective pay for the years during which we struggled because we feel proud not to be paid for the services rendered to Cuba…

I will repeat here what I have already said in *History Will Absolve Me,* that the children of the military who died fighting against us will be assured of maintenance, assistance and education because they cannot be blamed for the horrors of the war. We will be generous to everyone because, as I have said, here there are no vanquished, but only victors. Only war criminals will be punished because this is the irrevocable duty of the revolution, and the people can be certain that we will fulfill that duty. The people can also be sure that when justice reigns there will be no revenge. If tomorrow there are to be no assaults against anyone, justice must reign today. As there will be justice, there will be no revenge, neither will there be hatred.

Hatred will be exiled from the republic, hatred that is a damned and evil shadow bequeathed to us by ambition and tyranny. Unfortunately, the major criminals escaped. There are thousands of people who would pursue them, but we must respect the laws of other countries. It would be easy for us because we have more than enough volunteers to pursue those delinquents, ready and willing to risk their lives. However, we do not wish to appear as people who violate the laws of other peoples; we will respect these laws while ours are respected. Nonetheless, I will issue one warning: If in Santo Domingo they begin to conspire against the revolution, if [Dominican dictator] Trujillo… makes any mistake and directs any aggression against us, it will be a sorry day for him...

If Santo Domingo is converted into a counterrevolutionary arsenal, if Santo Domingo becomes a base for conspiracies against the Cuban revolution, and if these gentlemen over there devote themselves to conspiracies, it would be better for them to leave Santo Domingo immediately. They will not be very safe over there, not because we intend to meddle in Santo Domingo's problems, but because the citizens of the Dominican Republic have learned from Cuba's example and conditions there will become very serious indeed. The citizens of the Dominican Republic have learned that it is possible to struggle against tyranny and defeat it. And this is the lesson dictatorships fear the most. Yet, it is a lesson that is encouraging for the Americas; a lesson exemplified just now in our country.

All the Americas are watching the course and the fate of our revolution. All the Americas are watching us, following our actions with their best wishes for our triumph, supporting us in our difficult moments. Our happiness today in Cuba is shared throughout the Americas. As we rejoice at the overthrow of a dictator in Latin America, so do they rejoice with the Cuban people.

I really should conclude, although I do so with an overwhelming sense of emotion and so many ideas all mixed up in my mind. As I was saying, there will be justice, and it was a pity that the major criminals escaped...

If only one could see Mr. Batista now, if only one could see the arrogant, handsome Mr. Batista, who never spoke without calling others cowards, wretched villains, and so on. Here, we have called no one a "villain." Here, there is not a whisper of hatred, arrogance or disdain, which filled the speeches of the dictator—that man who claimed that he had a single bullet in his pistol when he entered Camp Columbia and who left on a plane in the early hours of the dawn, with that single bullet still in his pistol. Surely this shows these dictators are not so fearsome or so likely to commit suicide, because when they have lost the game, they immediately take flight like cowards. The sad part is that they escaped when they should have been taken prisoner. Had we caught Batista, we could have seized the 200 million pesos he stole. But we will claim that money, wherever he is hiding it, because they are not political exiles but common criminals. And we will see who turns up in the embassies, if Mr. Cantillo has not already given them safe-conduct passes. We will make a distinction between the political prisoners and the common criminals. They will have to go before the courts and prove that they are political delinquents. However, if they are proved to be common criminals, they will have to appear before the proper authorities...

At last, the people have been able to rid themselves of this rabble. Now anyone may speak out, whether they are for or against. Anyone who wishes to do so may speak out. That was not the case previously because until now, they were the only ones [allowed] to speak out; and they spoke against us. There will be freedom for those who speak in our favor and for those who speak against us and criticize us. There will be freedom for everyone because we have achieved freedom for everyone. We will never feel insulted; we will always defend ourselves and we will follow a single precept, that of respect for the rights and feelings of others.

Others have been mentioned here. Those people — wherever they might be, in whatever embassy, on whatever beach, in whatever boat they now find themselves — we are free of them. If they have some tiny shack, a small boat, or a little farm somewhere, we will naturally have to confiscate it; we must sound the warning that the hirelings of tyranny, the representatives, the senators, and so on, those who did not necessarily steal but who accepted their remuneration, will have to pay back, up to the last penny, what they received over these four years, because they received it illegally. They will have to pay back to the republic the money they received; and if they do not reimburse the national treasury, we will confiscate whatever property they have. That is quite separate from what they may have stolen. Those who robbed will not be allowed to retain any of the stolen goods. That is the law of the revolution. It is not fair to send a person to prison for stealing a chicken or a turkey, and at the same time to allow those who stole millions of pesos to have a wonderful lifestyle, traveling the world.

Let them beware! Let those thieves of yesterday and today beware! The revolution's laws may extend to the guilty in every period. The revolution has triumphed and its only obligation is to the people, to whom it owes its victory.

I am going to conclude for today. Remember that I have to leave right away. It is my duty. Moreover, you have been standing here for a good many hours. I see so much red and black on the clothing of our compañeras that it is really hard to leave this platform, where all of us have experienced the greatest emotions of our lives...

For the moment, the task that required rifles is done; so let us keep the rifles where they are, within reach of those who have to defend our sovereignty and our rights. So that when our people are threatened, it will not be only the 30,000 or 40,000 armed combatants who will fight, but the 300,000 or 400,000 or 500,000 Cubans, men and women, who will have arms. There will be arms for everyone who wishes to fight when the time comes to defend our freedom.

It has been proven that it is not only men who fight in Cuba but that women can also fight. The best evidence of this is the Mariana Grajales platoon [of the Rebel Army], which distinguished itself in numerous encounters. The women soldiers are as good as our best military men. I wanted to prove that women can be good soldiers. In the beginning, this gave me a lot of trouble because there was considerable prejudice. There were men who asked how on earth a woman could be given a rifle while there were still men without weapons. And why not? I wanted to show that women could be just as good soldiers. Women represent a sector of our country that must be redeemed; they still face discrimination in employment and many other aspects of their lives. So we organized the women's units and these proved that women could fight, and furthermore, when the men of a village fight and the women fight alongside them, that village is impregnable. We have organized the female combatants or militias and we will continue to train them as volunteers. All these young women I see here with their black and red clothing reminded me of July 26. And I hope all of you will learn how to handle firearms.

Compatriots, this revolution that was made with so much sacrifice, our revolution, the revolution of the people, is now a magnificent and indestructible reality. What a source of pride and great joy for all our people, who waited for this day! I know that it is not only here in Santiago de Cuba, it is everywhere, from Maisí to Cape San Antonio.

I long to see the people on our route to the capital, because I know I will encounter the same hope, the same faith, of an entire people that rose up, a people who patiently bore all the sacrifices, who cared little for hunger. When we gave them three days' leave to reestablish communications, in order to avoid hunger, everyone protested because what they wanted was victory at any price. Such a people deserves a better fate, and deserves the happiness it has not had in the last 56 years of the republic. It deserves to become one of the leading nations in the world by reason of its intelligence, its valor and its spirit.

Let no one think I am speaking as a demagogue. Let no one accuse me of seeking to deceive the people. I have given ample proof of my faith in the people; when I landed with 82 combatants on the beaches of Cuba, and people said we were mad and asked us why we thought we could win the war, we replied, "Because we have the people behind us!" When we were defeated for the first time, and only a handful of us remained, still we persisted in the struggle. We knew that this would be the outcome because we had faith in the people. When they dispersed us five times in 45 days and we met up together again and renewed the struggle, it was because we had faith in the people. And today is the most palpable demonstration of the fact that our faith was justified.

I have the greatest satisfaction in the knowledge that I believed so deeply in the people of Cuba, and in having inspired my compañeros with this same faith. This faith is more than faith — it is total confidence in our people. This same faith that we have in you is the faith we hope that you will always have in us.

The republic was not liberated in 1895 when the dream of the *mambises* was frustrated at the last minute. The revolution did not take place in 1933 when it was frustrated by its enemies. This time, however, we have a revolution of the entire people, supported by all the honorable military men. It is so vast and such an uncontainable force that this time victory is certain.

We can say with great joy that in the four centuries since our country was founded, this will be the first time that we are entirely free and that the work of the *mambises* is completed.

A few days ago, I could not resist the temptation to go and visit my mother whom I had not seen for several years. On my return, as I was traveling along the road that cuts through Mangos de Baraguá late at night, a sense of deep devotion among those of us in that vehicle made us stop at the monument erected to the memory of those involved in the protest at Baraguá and the beginning of the invasion. At that late hour, at that place, we thought about the daring feats involved in our wars of independence and the fact that those people fought for 30 years and never saw their dream come true, but saw only one more frustrated republic. Yet they had a presentiment that sooner or later the revolution of which they dreamed, the homeland of which they dreamed, would become a reality. This filled us with the greatest conceivable emotion. In my mind's eye, I saw these people relive their sacrifice, sacrifices which we also experienced. I conjured up their dreams and their aspirations, which were our dreams and our aspirations, and I ventured to think that the present generation in Cuba must render, and has rendered, homage, gratitude and loyalty as a fervent tribute to those heroes of our independence.

The efforts of those who fell in our three wars of independence are now united with those who fell in this war, and of all those who fell in the struggle for freedom. We can now tell them that their dreams are about to be fulfilled and that the time has finally come when you, our people, our good and noble people, our people who have so much enthusiasm and have so much faith, our people who demand nothing in return for their affection, who demand nothing in return for their confidence, who offer a kindness far beyond anything they might deserve, the time has come, I say, when you will have everything you need. There is nothing left for me to add, except, with modesty and sincerity, to say with the deepest emotion, that you will always have in us, the combatants of the revolution, loyal servants whose sole motto is service to you.

On this day, when Dr. Urrutia takes over the presidency of the republic — Dr. Manuel Urrutia Lleó, the leader who declared that this was a just revolution — on territory that has been liberated, which by now includes the whole country, I declare that I will assume only those duties assigned to me by him. The full authority of the republic is vested in him. And our arms now submit respectfully to the civil authority of the civil republic of Cuba.

All I have to say is that we hope he will fulfill his duty. Naturally, we are confident that he will know how to fulfill his duty. I surrender my authority to the provisional president of the Republic of Cuba and with it I surrender to him the right to address the people of Cuba.

CAMP COLUMBIA, HAVANA
JANUARY 8, 1959

After crossing the island of Cuba in a triumphal march, Fidel arrived in Havana, and in this speech at General Batista's former military fortress, Camp Columbia, on January 8, 1959, he presented the next tasks in the revolution.

I know that my speaking here this evening presents me with an obligation that may well be one of the most difficult in the long process of struggle that began in Santiago de Cuba on November 30, 1956.

The revolutionary combatants, the army soldiers, whose fate is in our hands, and all the rest of the people are listening.

I think that this is a decisive moment in our history. The dictatorship has been overthrown and there is tremendous joy, but there is still much to do. We shouldn't fool ourselves, thinking that everything will be easy from now on, because things may turn out to be more difficult.

The first duty of all revolutionaries is to tell the truth. Fooling the people, promoting illusions, always brings the worst consequences, and I believe that the people should be warned against excessive optimism.

How did the Rebel Army win the war? By telling the truth. How did the [Batista] dictatorship lose the war? By deceiving the soldiers.

When we were dealt a setback, we said so over Radio Rebelde; we criticized the mistakes of any officer who committed them; and we warned all the compañeros so the same thing wouldn't happen with another unit. That didn't happen with the army's companies. Several units made the same mistakes, because no one ever told the officers and soldiers the truth.

That's why I want to start — or, rather, continue — using the same system: that of always telling the people the truth.

We have advanced, perhaps quite a long way.

Here we are in the capital, at Camp Columbia. The revolutionary forces appear to be victorious. The government has been constituted and recognized by many countries. It seems that we have achieved peace, yet we shouldn't be too optimistic.

While the people laughed and celebrated today, I worried; the larger the crowd that came to welcome us and the greater the people's joy, the more worried I was, because the greater was our responsibility to history and to the Cuban people.

The revolution no longer has to confront an army ready for action. Who might be the enemies of the revolution now and in the future? Who, in the face of this victorious nation, might be the enemies of the Cuban revolution in the future? We ourselves, the revolutionaries.

As I always told the rebel combatants, when we aren't confronting the enemy, when the war is over, we ourselves will be the only enemies the revolution can have. That's why I always said and still say that we should be more rigorous and demanding with the rebel soldiers than with anyone else, because the success or failure of the revolution depends on them...

The first thing that those of us who have carried out this revolution have to ask ourselves is why we did it. Was it out of ambition, a lust for power or any other ignoble reason? Were any of the combatants for this revolution idealists who, while moved by idealism, also sought other ends? Did we carry out the revolution thinking that as soon as the dictatorship was overthrown we would benefit from being in power? Did any of us do what we did simply to jump on the bandwagon? Did any of us want to live like a king and have a mansion? Did any of us become revolutionaries and overthrow the dictatorship in order to make life easy for ourselves? Did we simply want to replace some ministers?

Or, did we do what we did out of a real spirit of selflessness? Did each of us have a true willingness to make sacrifices? Was each of us willing to give their all without any thought of personal gain? And, right from the start, were we ready to renounce everything that didn't mean continuing to carry out our duty as sincere revolutionaries?

Those are the questions we must ask ourselves, because the future of Cuba, ourselves and the people, is largely dependent on this examination of conscience.

When I hear talk of columns, battlefronts, and troops of whatever size, I always think, here is our firmest column, here are our best troops — the only troops that, alone, can win the war: the people!

No general or army can do more than the people. If you were to ask me what troops I preferred to command, I would say, I prefer to command the people, because the people are invincible. It was the people who won this war, because we didn't have any tanks, planes, cannon, military academies, recruiting and training centers, divisions, regiments, companies, platoons or even squads.

So, who won the war? The people. The people won the war.

It was the people who won this war — I'm saying this very clearly in case anyone thinks they won it or any troops think they won it. Therefore, the people come first.

But there is something else: The revolution isn't interested in me or in any other commander or captain as individuals; the revolution isn't interested in any particular column or company. What it is interested in is the people.

It was the people who won or lost. It was the people who suffered the horrors of the last seven years, the people who must ask themselves if, in 10, 15 or 20 years, they and their children and grandchildren are going to continue suffering the horrors they have suffered ever since the establishment of the Republic of Cuba, crowned with dictatorships such as those of Machado and Batista.

The people want to know if we're going to do a good job of carrying out this revolution or if we're going to make the same mistakes that previous revolutions made — and, as a result, make them suffer the consequences of our mistakes, for every mistake has terrible consequences for the people; sooner or later, every political mistake takes its toll.

Some circumstances aren't the same. For example, I think that this time there is a greater chance than ever before that the revolution will really fulfill its destiny. This may explain why the people are so very happy, losing sight a little of how much hard work lies ahead...

What do the people want? An honest government. Isn't that right? There you have it: an honorable judge as president of the republic. What do you want? That young people whose slates are clean be the ministers of the revolutionary government? There you have them: check out each of the ministers of the revolutionary government, and tell me if there are any thieves, criminals or scoundrels among them.

It's necessary to talk this way so there will be no demagogy, confusion or splits, and so the people will be immediately aware if anyone becomes ambitious. As for me, since I want the people to command, and I consider the people to be the best troops and prefer them to all the columns of armed men put together, the first thing I will always do, when I see the revolution in danger, is call on the people.

We can prevent bloodshed by speaking to the people. Before there is any shooting here, we must call on the people a thousand times and speak to the people so that, without any shooting, the people will solve the problem. I have faith in the people, and I have demonstrated this. I know what the people are capable of, and I think I have demonstrated this, too. If the people here want it, no more shots will be heard in this country. Public opinion has incredible strength and influence, especially when there is no dictatorship. In eras of dictatorship, public opinion is nothing, but in eras of freedom, public opinion is everything, and the military must bow to public opinion.

How am I doing, Camilo?

The important thing, what I still have to tell you, is that I believe that the actions of the people in Havana today, the mass meetings that were held today, the crowds that filled the streets for kilometers — all of that was amazing, and you saw it; it will be in the movies and photos — I sincerely think that the people went overboard, for it's much more than we deserve.

Moreover, I know that there never will be such a crowd again, except on one other occasion — the day I'm buried. I'm sure that there will be a large crowd then, too, to take me to my grave, because I will never defraud our people.

3. AT THE UNITED NATIONS GENERAL ASSEMBLY

NEW YORK, SEPTEMBER 26, 1960

Having visited the United States at the invitation of the Association of News-paper Editors only a few months after the revolution in 1959, Fidel Castro returned to address the United Nations General Assembly in New York in September 1960. He was greeted at the airport by thousands of supporters, but the US government immediately restricted the movements of the Cuban delegation to the island of Manhattan. After conflicts with the management of the downtown Shelburne Hotel, the Cubans moved to the Hotel Theresa on 125th Street in Harlem.

Mr. President;

Distinguished representatives:

Although it has been said that I speak at great length, you may rest assured that we will endeavor to be brief and to put before you what we consider our duty to say. I will speak slowly to assist the interpreters.

Some people may think that we are annoyed and upset by the treatment the Cuban delegation has received. This is not the case. We understand full well the reasons for the state of affairs and that is why we are not upset. Cuba will spare no effort to bring about an understanding in the world. But rest assured, we will speak frankly.

It is extremely expensive to send a delegation to the United Nations. We underdeveloped countries do not have many resources to squander, and when we do spend money in this fashion it is because we wish to address the representatives of virtually every country in the world.

The speakers who have preceded me here expressed their concern about problems that are of interest to the whole world. We, too, are concerned about those same problems. However, in the case of Cuba, a special circumstance exists. Cuba itself should be a world concern. As various speakers here have correctly pointed out, the problem of Cuba is an international issue.

Much has been said of the universal desire for peace. Everyone wants this, and this is also the desire of our people. But this peace the world wishes to preserve is something Cuba has not been able to enjoy for a long time. The dangers that other peoples of the world may now consider remote are, for us, very immediate concerns. It has not been easy to come here to this assembly to talk about the problems of Cuba.

I do not know whether you are privileged in this respect. Do we, the representatives of the Cuban delegation, represent the worst type of government in the world? Do we, the representatives of the Cuban delegation, deserve the treatment that we have received? Why has our delegation been singled out? Cuba has sent many delegations to the United Nations in the past. Cuba has been represented at the United Nations by many different people. Yet only we have been singled out for such extraordinary measures: confinement to the island of Manhattan; notice to all the hotels not to rent us rooms; hostility; and, under the pretext of security, isolation.

Perhaps none of you, fellow delegates, on your arrival in the city of New York, has had to suffer the personal mistreatment, the physically humiliating treatment, as that meted out to the president of the Cuban delegation.

I am not trying to stir up anyone in this assembly. I am merely stating the truth. Now it is our turn to take the floor and to speak. So much has been said about us. For so many days we have been a focus of attention, but we have held our peace since we cannot defend ourselves against attacks in this country. But the time to speak the truth has come, and rest assured, we will not hesitate to do so.

As I have said, we have put up with degrading and humiliating treatment, including eviction from the [Shelburne] Hotel where we were staying, along with efforts at extortion. We went to another hotel, doing everything possible to avoid difficulties. We refrained from leaving our hotel rooms, we went nowhere, except to this assembly hall, on the few times that we have come to the General Assembly. We also accepted an invitation to a reception at the Soviet embassy; but generally we restricted our movements in order to avoid problems. But, this was not enough for us to be left in peace.

There has been considerable Cuban immigration to this country. More than 100,000 Cubans have come to this country over the past 20 years because economic reasons forced them to leave their own land, where they would prefer to live and to which they would like to return. The Cubans who came to this country dedicated themselves to work. They respected and continue to respect the laws of this land, but still felt close to their own country and to the revolution.

One day a different type of visitor began to arrive in this country. War criminals began to arrive, individuals who, in some cases, had murdered hundreds of our compatriots. It did not take long for them to gain publicity. The authorities received them warmly and encouraged them. Naturally that encouragement is reflected in their conduct, and is also the reason for the frequent incidents with those Cubans who had arrived many years earlier and who are making an honest living in this country.

One such incident resulted in the death of a child and was provoked by those who support the systematic campaigns against Cuba, with the connivance of the authorities. It was a tragic event. The Cubans who live here were not guilty, and neither were we, who have come to represent Cuba. But you have all seen the newspaper headlines stating that pro-Castro groups had killed a 10-year-old girl. With the typical hypocrisy of those who meddle in relations between Cuba and this country, a White House spokesperson immediately accused us, blaming the Cuban delegation.

His Excellency, the US representative to this assembly, did not miss the opportunity to add his voice to the farce, sending telegrams to the Venezuelan embassy and to the family, as though the United Nations felt obligated to give some explanation for something for which the Cuban delegation was supposedly responsible.

But that was not the end of it. We were forced to leave our hotel, and so a modest hotel of this city, a hotel in the black community of Harlem, took us in.

The offer from this hotel came while we were speaking with the UN secretary general. Nevertheless, a State Department official did everything in his power to stop us from being given rooms there. At that moment, as if by magic, offers arrived from hotels all over New York, even hotels that had previously refused us, and some even for free. But out of elementary gratitude, we accepted the Hotel [Theresa] in Harlem. We felt we had earned the right to some peace and quiet. But no, we were not left in peace.

As soon as we arrived in Harlem, since no one could stop us from staying there, the defamation campaign began. The news was spread that the Cuban delegation had found accommodation in a brothel. For some, a humble hotel in Harlem, a hotel occupied by the black people of the United States must, by definition, be a brothel. So they heaped slander on the Cuban delegation, showing particular disrespect for the female members of our delegation.

If we were the type of individuals that we are constantly portrayed as, then imperialism would not have lost hope, as it did long ago, of buying us off or seducing us in some way. But, since imperialism has lost all hope of winning us over, they should recognize the fact that imperialist finance capital is itself a prostitute that cannot seduce us — and not necessarily Jean-Paul Sartre's "respectful prostitute."

So to return to the problem of Cuba: Some of you may be aware — others not, depending on the sources of your information — that as far as the world is concerned, the problem of Cuba has arisen in the last few years. Previously, there were few reasons to recognize that Cuba even existed. For many, especially for many citizens of this country, Cuba was an appendage of the United States, a virtual colony of the United States. Although the map showed something different — Cuba being represented with a different color from the United States — in reality, Cuba was a colony of the United States.

How did our country become a colony of the United States? It was not so by origin. The people who colonized the United States did not colonize Cuba; Cuba's ethnic and cultural roots were very different, and over centuries these roots have grown stronger.

Cuba was the last country of the Americas to shake off Spanish colonial rule, to cast off, with all due respect to the representative from Spain, the Spanish colonial yoke. Because it was the last, Cuba had to struggle: Spain had one last foothold in the Americas and defended it tooth and nail. Our people, few in numbers, scarcely a million inhabitants at that time, stood alone for nearly 30 years confronting an army considered one of the strongest in Europe. Against the tiny population of Cuba, the Spanish mobilized an enormous number of troops, as many as had been mobilized against the independence struggles of all the Latin American countries com-

bined. Half a million Spanish soldiers fought against the heroic and indomitable desire of our people to be free. For 30 years, the Cubans fought alone
for their independence, 30 years that laid the foundation of our love for independence and freedom.

But in the opinion of John Adams, US president at the beginning of the
last century, Cuba was a fruit, a ripe apple on the Spanish tree ready to fall
into the hands of the United States.

The Spanish power had exhausted itself in Cuba. Spain did not have the
soldiers or the economic resources left to continue the fight in Cuba. Spain
was defeated. Apparently the apple was ripe, and the US government held
out its hands. Cuba was not the only apple to fall. Puerto Rico fell—heroic
Puerto Rico which had begun its independence struggle at the same time as
Cuba. The Philippines fell, as did several other Spanish possessions.

But the measures required to dominate our country had to be different.
Cuba had struggled for independence and world opinion was in our favor.
Our country had to be seized in a different way.

The Cubans who had fought for our independence, the Cubans who at
that very moment were giving their blood and their lives, believed in good
faith in the joint resolution of the US Congress of April 20, 1898, which
declared, "Cuba is, and by right ought to be, free and independent." The
people of the United States were supposedly behind the Cubans in their
struggle for independence. The US Congress adopted the joint declaration
into law, by virtue of which, war was declared on Spain.

This illusion ended in a cruel deception. After two years of military occupation of our country, at the very moment when the people of Cuba,
through their constituent assembly, were drafting the constitution of the
republic, the US Congress passed a new law proposed by Senator Platt. This
stated that the Cuban constitution must stipulate that the United States had
the right to intervene in Cuba's political affairs and the right to lease certain
parts of the island for naval bases or coaling stations. In other words, Cuba's
constitution had to include those provisions passed by the legislative body
of a foreign country. The drafters of our constitution were clearly told that if
they did not accept this, the occupying forces would not be withdrawn. The
legislative body of a foreign country imposed on our country, by force, its
right to intervene and its right to lease bases or naval stations.

It would be worthwhile for those countries entering this organization, countries just beginning their independent life, to bear in mind our history. They may find similar experiences awaiting them along their own road, if not now, then maybe for those coming after them, for their children or their grandchildren—although it seems to us that it might not be that long.

Thus the recolonization of our country began: the acquisition of the best agricultural land by US firms, concessions of Cuban natural resources and mines, concessions of public utilities for purposes of exploitation, commercial concessions, concessions of all types that, when linked with the constitutional right of intervention in our country, transformed Cuba from a Spanish colony into a US colony.

Colonies do not speak. Colonies are not recognized in the world. Colonies are not allowed to express their opinions until they are granted permission to do so. That is why our colony and its problems were not known to the rest of the world. In geography books there appeared one more flag, one more coat of arms. There was another color on the map, but there was no independent republic. Let no one be deceived, because only fools allow themselves to be deceived. Let no one be mistaken. There was no independent republic. It was a colony where the US ambassador gave the orders.

We are not ashamed to proclaim this from the rooftops. On the contrary, we are proud that we can now say: Today no embassy rules our people; our people govern themselves!

Once again, the Cuban people had to return to fight for independence, and that independence was finally attained after seven bloody years of dictatorship. What dictatorship? The dictatorship of forces that were nothing but the cats' paws of those who dominated our country economically.

How can an unpopular regime, inimical to the interests of the people, stay in power unless by force? Do we have to explain to our sister republics of Latin America what military dictatorships are? Do we have to outline how these dictatorships have kept themselves in power? Do we have to explain to them the classic history of many of those dictatorships? Do we have to show what kept them in power? Do we have to explain what national and international interests kept them in power?

The military group that tyrannized our country was based on the most reactionary sectors of the nation and, above all, was based on the foreign interests that dominated the country's economy. Everyone here knows—and we understand that even the US government recognizes—that this type of government was preferred by the monopolies. Why? Because with force you can repress any demands made by the people. With force, you can repress strikes that seek better conditions of work and living standards. With force, you can quell the peasants' movement demanding land. With force, you can quash the most deeply felt aspirations of a nation.

That is why governments based on force are the governments preferred by the US policy makers. That is why governments based on force are able to stay in the saddle for so long. That is why governments based on force still rule in the Americas.

Naturally, it depends on the circumstances whether the support of the US government is forthcoming or not. For example, it is now said that the United States opposes one such government, that of Trujillo [in the Dominican Republic]. But they are not against other governments based on force — in Nicaragua or Paraguay, for example. In Nicaragua there is no longer just a government based on force; it is a monarchy that is almost as constitutional as that of the United Kingdom, where the mantle is passed down from father to son.

The same might have occurred in our own country. Fulgencio Batista's regime best suited the US monopolies in Cuba, but it was not the type of government that suited the Cuban people. The Cuban people, with great sacrifice, rose up and threw that government out.

When the revolution triumphed in Cuba, what did we find? What "marvels" lay spread out before the eyes of Cuba's victorious revolutionaries? First of all, the revolution found that 600,000 Cubans, ready and able to work, were unemployed — as many, proportionally, as were unemployed in the United States at the time of the Great Depression which shook this country, and which produced a catastrophe here. We found permanent unemployment in my country. Three million in a population of just over six million had no electricity and therefore none of its advantages and comforts. Three and a half million people lived in shacks or in slums, without even minimal sanitation. In the cities, rents took almost one-third of family incomes. Electricity rates and rents were among the highest in the world.

Thirty-seven and a half percent of our population was illiterate; 70 percent of rural children lacked teachers; 2 percent of our population suffered from tuberculosis, that is to say, 100,000 people, out of a total population of a little over six million, were suffering from the ravages of tuberculosis. Ninety-five percent of children in rural areas were suffering from parasites. Infant mortality was appallingly high. The standard of living was appallingly low. Eighty-five percent of the small farmers were paying rent on their land to the tune of almost 30 percent of their gross income, whilst 1.5 percent of all landowners controlled 46 percent of land in the countryside. The proportion of hospital beds to the number of inhabitants of the country was ludicrous when compared with countries that have even half-way decent medical services. Public utilities, electricity and telephone services all belonged to US monopolies. A major portion of the banking sector, importing businesses and the oil refineries; a greater part of the sugar production; the lion's share of arable land in Cuba and the most important industries in all sectors belonged to US companies.

The balance of payments in the last 10 years, from 1950 to 1960, has favored the United States vis-à-vis Cuba to the tune of $1 billion. This is without taking into account the hundreds of millions of dollars that were extracted from the country's treasury by corrupt officials of the dictatorship, which were later deposited in US or European banks. A poor and under-developed country in the Caribbean, with 600,000 unemployed, was contributing $1 billion over 10 years to the economic development of the most highly industrialized country in the world!

This was the situation that confronted us. Yet this should not surprise many of the countries represented in this assembly, because when all is said and done, what applies in Cuba is, one might say, a template that could be superimposed and applied to many of the countries represented here.

What alternative was there for the revolutionary government? To betray the people? As far as the US president is concerned, of course, we have betrayed our people. But would he have said the same if, instead of being true to the people, we had been true to the monopolies that were exploiting Cuba?

At the very least, let a note be taken of the "marvels" that were laid before our eyes when our revolution triumphed. These were no more and no less than the usual marvels of imperialism, which are themselves no more and no less than the marvels of the "free world," as far as we, the colonies, are concerned.

We cannot be blamed for the 600,000 unemployed in Cuba or the 37.5

percent of the population that was illiterate, for the 2 percent of the population that suffered from tuberculosis or for the 95 percent that suffered from parasites. Not in the least! Until that moment, none of us had any hand in the destiny of our country. Until that moment when the revolution was victorious, the only voices heard in our country were those of the monopolies. Did anyone object? No! Did this bother anyone? No! The monopolies went about their nefarious business, and these were the results.

What was the state of the national reserves? When the dictator Batista came to power there was $500 million in the treasury. A decent amount — had it been invested in the development, industrial or otherwise, of the country. But when the revolution triumphed, we found only $70 million. Was any concern ever shown for the economic and industrial development of our country? No, never! That is why we were astonished, and we are even more amazed to hear about the extraordinary concern of the US government for the fate of countries in Latin America, Africa and Asia. And it continues to amaze us, when we have seen the results of that concern over 50 years.

What has the revolutionary government done? What crime has been committed by the revolutionary government to warrant the treatment we have been given here? Why do we have such powerful enemies?

Did these problems with the United States arise at the very beginning? No, they did not. When we came to power, did we desire international difficulties? No. No revolutionary government achieving power wants international problems. What it wants to do is to devote itself to settling its own problems at home; like any government truly concerned with the progress of their country, it wants to improve things for the people.

The first unfriendly act perpetrated by the US government was to throw open its doors to a gang of murderers and bloodthirsty criminals — men who had murdered hundreds of defenseless peasants, who had tortured prisoners for years, who had killed right and left. These criminals were received by this country with open arms. We were deeply stunned at this unfriendly act by the US authorities. Why such hostility? At the time, we could not quite understand. Now we see the reasons clearly.

Was that policy in keeping with proper treatment of Cuba, with proper relations between the United States and Cuba? No! Cuba was the injured party. We were the injured party because Batista's government was maintained in power with the assistance of the US government. The Batista regime was maintained in power with the assistance of tanks, planes and weapons supplied by the US government. Batista's government was maintained in power thanks to the use of an army whose officers were instructed and trained by a US military mission. We hope no official of the United States will dare to deny this fact.

When the Rebel Army arrived in Havana at the most important military camp [Camp Columbia] in that city, it encountered the US military mission. We could easily have considered that these foreign officers were training enemies of the people; we could have considered them to be prisoners of war. But we did not. We merely asked the members of that military mission in Havana to go home. After all, we did not need their lessons and their pupils had been defeated.

I have a document here. Don't be surprised at its worn appearance. It is an ancient military pact, by virtue of which the Batista regime received generous assistance from the US government. It is interesting to note the contents of Article 2 of this agreement:

> The government of the Republic of Cuba commits itself to make efficient use of the assistance it receives from the US government in conformity and pursuant to the present agreement, in order to carry out the plans of defense accepted by both governments, pursuant to which the two governments would take part in important missions for the defense of the Western Hemisphere, and unless prior agreement is obtained from the US government...

I repeat:

> ...and unless *prior agreement* is obtained from the US government, such assistance will not be devoted to ends other than those for which such assistance has been given.

That assistance was used to fight the Cuban revolutionaries, and to do so, prior agreement from the US government was required. A few months before the war ended, after more than six years of military assistance, an arms embargo was declared on weapons sent to or intended for Batista. Nevertheless, even after this embargo was solemnly declared, the Rebel Army has documentary proof to show that Batista's forces were supplied with 300 rockets, to be fired from planes.

When Cuban immigrants in this country revealed these documents to the public, the US government simply argued that we were mistaken. They said the United States had not supplied *new* weapons to the dictatorship; they had merely exchanged some rockets that were the wrong size for their planes for new rockets of a different caliber that were the correct size. These rockets were, as a matter of fact, fired at us when we were in the mountains.

I must say that this is a novel way of explaining a contradiction that can be neither justified nor explained. According to the United States, this was not military assistance. What was it then—some type of "technical" aid?

Why did this make our people angry? After all, even the most naive, innocent, guileless person knows that in these modern times, given the revolution that has taken place in military equipment and technology, weapons from the last war have become obsolete for modern warfare; 50 tanks or armored cars and a few obsolete aircraft cannot defend a continent or a hemisphere. But they are useful to oppress people, especially if those people have no weapons. They are useful to intimidate people; they are useful to defend the outposts of monopoly. These hemispheric defense pacts might better be described as "pacts to defend US monopolies."

So the revolutionary government began to take its first steps. The first was a 50 percent reduction in rents paid by families—a very just measure since, as I said earlier, some families were paying up to one-third of their incomes on rent. People had been the victims of housing speculation; urban real estate had been the subject of speculation, to the detriment of the entire Cuban economy. When the revolutionary government reduced rents by 50 percent, there were some people who were very upset. Yes, a few people: Those who owned buildings and apartment houses were upset. But the people rushed into the streets rejoicing, as they would in any country, even here in New York, if rents were reduced by 50 percent for all families. But this caused no problems for the monopolies. Some US monopolies owned large buildings, but they were relatively few in number.

Then another law was passed, a law cancelling the concessions granted by Batista to the telephone company, a US monopoly. Due to the defense-lessness of the people, valuable concessions had been obtained. The revolutionary government cancelled those concessions and reestablished normal prices for telephone services. That is how the first conflict with the US monopolies arose.

The third measure was a reduction in the cost of electricity, which had been among the highest in the world. This led to the second conflict with the US monopolies. They were already painting us as "reds," simply because we had clashed with their interests.

Then came another law, an essential and inevitable law for our people and, sooner or later, for all the peoples of the world. This was the Agrarian Reform Law. Naturally, everyone agrees with agrarian reform — in theory. Nobody would dare deny it; nobody except an ignorant fool would deny that agrarian reform in the underdeveloped countries of the world is one of the essential conditions for economic development. In Cuba, even the landowners agreed with agrarian reform — only they wanted their own type of reform, like that defended by many theorists. They wanted an agrarian reform that was never actually carried out, as long as it could be avoided. Agrarian reform is something that is recognized by the economic bodies of the United Nations; it is something no one can argue with.

In our country such reform was indispensable. More than 200,000 peasant families lived in the countryside without land on which to plant essential foodstuffs. Without agrarian reform, our country could not have taken its first tottering steps toward development. So we took that step. We instituted an agrarian reform. Was it radical? Yes, it was a radical reform. Was it very radical? No, it was not very radical. We instituted an agrarian reform appropriate to our need for development, appropriate to the possibilities of agricultural development. In other words, it was an agrarian reform that would solve the problem of landless peasants; the problem of the lack of basic foodstuffs; the great unemployment problem on the land, and a reform that would end, once and for all, the appalling poverty of the countryside.

That is when the first major difficulty arose. In the neighboring republic of Guatemala the same thing happened. When agrarian reform occurred in Guatemala [in 1954], problems developed. Speaking quite frankly, I would like to draw to the attention of my colleagues from Latin America, Africa and Asia that when they plan a just and fair agrarian reform, they must be ready to confront a situation similar to that which confronted us, especially if the best and largest lands are held by the US monopolies, as was the case in Cuba.

It is possible we may later be accused of giving bad advice in this assembly. That is not our intention. It is not our intention to keep anyone awake at night. We merely want to express the facts, which are enough to give anyone insomnia.

So then the question of payments and indemnities arose. Notes from the US State Department rained down on Cuba. They never asked us about our problems, they never expressed any sympathy with our situation, despite their responsibility for the problems. They never asked us how many people died of starvation in our country, how many were suffering from tuberculosis or how many were unemployed. No. Did they express any solidarity regarding our needs? Never. Every conversation with the representatives of the US government concerned the telephone company, the electricity company or the problem of the lands owned by US companies. The first question they always asked was how we were going to pay, while the first question that should have been asked was not "How?" but "With what?"

Ours is a poor, underdeveloped country bearing the burden of 600,000 unemployed, with extremely high rates of disease and illiteracy, whose reserves have been sapped, and which has contributed to the economy of a powerful country to the tune of $1 billion in 10 years. How were we to pay for the lands affected by the agrarian reform, or at least pay for them under the conditions set by the US State Department as compensation?

What did the US State Department say? They demanded three things: "speedy, efficient and just payment." Do you understand that language? "Speedy, efficient and just payment." It means: "Pay up now, in dollars, and whatever we ask."

We were not 150 percent communists at that time. We were only slightly pink. We were not confiscating land. We simply proposed to pay compensation over 20 years, and the only way we could pay was through bonds, which would mature in 20 years, at 4.5 percent interest, amortized annually. How could we pay for the land in dollars? How could we pay cash, upfront, and how could we pay the price they asked? It was ludicrous.

Under those circumstances, we had to choose between proceeding with the agrarian reform or doing nothing. If we chose to do nothing, then the economic misery of our countryside would continue, and if we carried out agrarian reform we risked incurring the wrath of the government of our powerful neighbor of the north.

We went ahead with the agrarian reform. Clearly, the representative here from the Netherlands, for example, or a representative of any European country, would be surprised by the limits we set to land holdings and estates, because they were so big. The maximum amount of land established by the Agrarian Reform Law was 400 hectares. In Europe, 400 hectares is a true estate. In Cuba, where there were US monopolies that had up to 200,000 hectares — that is 200,000 hectares, in case anyone thinks they misheard — an agrarian reform that reduced the maximum to 400 hectares was outrageous to those monopolies and landowners.

The trouble was that in our country, not only the land was in the hands of the US monopolies, but also the best mines. For example, Cuba produces a lot of nickel, which was exploited by US interests. A US company, the Moa Bay company, had obtained such a juicy concession that in only five years — only five years! — it sought to amortize an investment of $120 million. That certainly was a juicy plum!

Who had given the Moa Bay company this concession — completely tax free — through the intercession of the US government? Quite simply, the Fulgencio Batista dictatorship, which was there to defend the interests of the monopolies. What were these enterprises going to leave for the Cubans? Empty, exhausted mines and impoverished land, without making the slightest contribution to the economic development of our country.

So the revolutionary government passed a mining law obliging these monopolies to pay a 25 percent tax on the export of minerals.

The attitude of the revolutionary government had already been too bold. It had clashed with the interests of the international electricity trust; it had clashed with the interests of the international telephone trust; it had clashed with the interests of the international mining trusts; it had clashed with the interests of the United Fruit Company; it had clashed, in effect, with the most powerful interests of the United States, which, as you know, are very closely linked with each other. This was more than the US government, that is, the representative of the US monopolies, could tolerate.

Then a new stage began in the harassment of our revolution. I pose the question to anyone who objectively analyzes the facts, who is ready to think for themselves and not parrot United Press International (UPI) and

Associated Press (AP), who thinks with their own brain and draws their own conclusions, who sees the facts without prejudice, sincerely and honestly: Is what the revolutionary government has done enough to justify the destruction of the Cuban revolution? Surely not.

But the interests adversely affected by the Cuban revolution were not particularly concerned about Cuba; they were not being ruined by the measures of the Cuban revolutionary government. That was not the problem. The problem lay in the fact that those same interests owned the natural wealth and resources of the majority of the peoples of the world. So the Cuban revolution had to be punished. Punitive actions of every type—including the destruction of those insolent Cubans—had to be carried out against the revolutionary government.

Honestly, to that moment, we had not had the opportunity to even exchange letters with the distinguished prime minister of the Soviet Union, Nikita Khrushchev. On our honor, we swear that is the truth. At a time when the US press and the international news agencies who supply information to the world described Cuba as a communist government, a "red menace" 90 miles from the United States, the revolutionary government had not yet had the opportunity of establishing diplomatic or commercial relations with the Soviet Union.

But hysteria knows no boundaries; hysteria can lead to the most unlikely and absurd claims. Yet no one should think for a moment that we are going to intone a *mea culpa*. There will be no *mea culpa*. We do not have to beg anyone's pardon. We have acted with our eyes wide open and, above all, fully convinced of our right to do so.

Threats began against our sugar quota. The cheap philosophy of imperialism revealed its nobility, its egotistical and exploitative nobility. They began to show kindness to Cuba, declaring they were paying us a preferential price for sugar, amounting to a subsidy for Cuban sugar (sugar which was not so sweet for Cubans since we did not own the best sugar producing lands or the largest sugar mills). In their threats lay hidden the true history of Cuban sugar, the sacrifices made by my country, the periods when it had been economically harmed.

Previously, it had not been a question of quotas, but of customs tariffs. By virtue of one of those agreements made between "a shark and a sardine," the United States, through a so-called reciprocity agreement, obtained a range of concessions for its products, enabling them to compete easily and displace from the Cuban market the products of its English and French friends. In exchange, certain tariff concessions were granted on our sugar which, on the other hand, could be altered unilaterally in accordance with the will of Congress or the US government. And that is what happened. When they deemed it to be in their interests, they raised the tariff, and our sugar was blocked. Or if it was allowed in, it faced a disadvantage in the US market.

As World War II approached, the tariffs were reduced, since Cuba was the source of sugar closest to home, and that source had to be assured. Thus, tariffs were lowered and production was encouraged. During the war years, when the price of sugar in the rest of the world was up in the stratosphere, we were selling our sugar to the United States at a low price, despite the fact that we were the only supplier. At the end of the war our economy collapsed.

We paid for these errors committed in the distribution of our raw material. At the end of World War I, for example, prices rose dramatically. There was tremendous encouragement to production. Then, a sudden reduction of prices ruined the Cuban sugar refineries, which fell conveniently into the hands of—I'll give you one guess—US banks, because when the Cuban nationals went bankrupt, the US banks in Cuba became wealthy. This situation continued until the 1930s.

The US government, searching for a formula that would reconcile its need for supplies with the interests of its domestic producers, established a quota system. This was supposed to be based on the historical participation of the different sources of supply in the market. The historical participation of my country's supply would have been almost 50 percent of the US market. When the quota was set up, however, our participation was reduced to 28 percent and the few advantages granted to us by those laws were gradually taken away in successive laws.

Naturally the colony depended on the colonial power. The economy of the colony had been organized by the colonial power. The colony was subordinated to the colonial power, and if the colony took measures to declare itself free, the colonial power would take measures to crush it. The US government was conscious of the importance of our economy to the US market, so it began to issue a series of warnings that our quota would be reduced further.

Meanwhile, other events were taking place in the United States: the activities of the counterrevolutionaries. One afternoon, an airplane coming from the north flew over one of the sugar refineries and dropped a bomb. This was an unprecedented event, but we knew full well where that plane came from. On another afternoon, another plane flew over some sugarcane fields and dropped a few incendiary bombs. These events, which began sporadically at first, continued systematically.

One afternoon, when a number of US tourist agencies were visiting Cuba as a result of the revolutionary government's effort to promote tourism as one of the sources of national income—a US plane flew over Havana, dropping pamphlets and a few hand grenades. Naturally, antiaircraft guns went into action. There were more than 40 victims, between the grenades dropped by the plane and the antiaircraft fire, because as you know, some of the shells explode on contact. Among the victims were children with their entrails torn out, old men and old women.

This was not the first time, either. Young girls and boys, old men and women, had often been killed, murdered in the villages of Cuba by US bombs supplied to the Batista dictatorship. On one occasion, 80 workers were killed when a mysterious explosion—too mysterious—took place on a ship [*La Coubre*, in March 1960] carrying Belgian weapons to our country, after the US government made a great effort to prevent the Belgian government from selling weapons to us.

There have been dozens of victims in the war: 80 families were destroyed with that explosion; there were another 40 victims caused by an airplane "peacefully" flying over our territory. The US authorities denied that these planes came from US territory. Moreover, they said that the plane was safely in its hangar. But when one of our magazines published a photograph of this plane in Cuba, the US authorities seized the plane. As expected, an account of the affair was issued to the effect that this was not particularly significant and that these victims had not died because of the bombs but because of antiaircraft fire. Meanwhile, those who were to blame for this crime were wandering about peacefully in the United States, where they were not prevented from continuing these acts of aggression.

I would like to take this opportunity to tell His Excellency, the representative of the United States, that there are many mothers in Cuba who are still hoping to receive a telegram of condolence from the US government for their children murdered by US bombs.

The planes came and went. There was no proof, unless you define what you mean by proof. The plane was right there, photographed and seized. Yet we were told that this plane had not dropped any bombs. It is not known how the US authorities were so well informed. These pirate planes continued to fly over our territory dropping incendiary bombs. Millions upon millions of pesos were lost with the burning of sugarcane fields. Many working people, the humble people of Cuba, who saw this wealth in flames, a wealth that was now theirs, were themselves burned or wounded in the struggle against these persistent and tenacious bombings by pirate aircraft.

Then one day, while flying over one of the sugar refineries, a plane exploded and the revolutionary government had the opportunity of gathering the remains of the pilot. It was, in fact, a US pilot, whose papers were found, identifying the plane as from the United States, with proof about the airfield from which he had taken off. The plane had actually flown over two bases in the United States.

Now it could not be denied that this plane had come from the United States. In view of such irrefutable proof, the US government gave an explanation to the Cuban government. Its response in this case was not the same as it was later in the case of the U-2 [in the Soviet Union]. When it was proven that the planes were coming from the United States, the US government did not proclaim its right to burn our cane fields. Instead, they apologized. We were lucky, after all, considering that after the U-2 incident the US government never even apologized, but proclaimed its right to fly over Soviet territory. Too bad for the Soviets!

At any rate, we do not have many antiaircraft batteries and planes continued to come until the sugarcane was harvested. When there was no cane left in the fields, the bombings stopped. We thought we were the only country in the world where this had happened, although I do recall that at the time of his visit to Cuba, [Indonesian] President Sukarno told us that they, too, had suffered problems with certain US planes flying over their territory. I don't know whether I have committed an indiscretion in mentioning this; I hope not.

The fact of the matter is that at least in this peaceful hemisphere, our country, while not being at war with anyone, had to withstand the constant attacks of pirate aircraft. Were those planes able to leave and enter US territory with impunity? We invite you to think about this for a moment and we also invite the people of the United States, if by chance the US people have the opportunity to hear about the matters we are discussing here, to meditate on this matter.

According to the statements of the US government itself, the territory of the United States is completely protected against any air incursion and the defense measures protecting US territory are infallible. It is stated that the defense of the "free" world—although, as far as we are concerned, we were not free, at least, not until January 1, 1959—is complete and impregnable. If that is so, how could these little propeller planes that can barely fly 150 miles an hour—I am not talking about supersonic jets—fly in and out of US national territory undetected? How could they pass over two bases, and back over these same two bases, without the US government ever being aware of the fact that these planes were flying in and out?

This means one of two things. Either the US government is lying to the US people and the United States is not impregnable against aerial incursions, or the US government was an accomplice in these aerial incursions.

The aerial incursions finally ceased, and then came economic aggression. What was the argument against our agrarian reform? The enemies of our agrarian reform said that it would cause chaos in agricultural production; that production would diminish considerably and that the US government was concerned because Cuba might not be able to fulfill its commitments to the US market.

That was the first argument, and I think that the new delegations here in the General Assembly should at least become familiar with some of these arguments, because at some time they may have to answer similar accusations, that agrarian reform might bring about the ruin of their countries.

In Cuba, that was not the case. Had agrarian reform brought about the ruin of our country, had agricultural production been reduced drastically, then the US government would not have had to carry out its economic aggression. Did they sincerely believe what they said when they asserted that the agrarian reform would bring about a decline in production? Perhaps. Everyone believes what they want to believe. It is possible they imagined that without the all-powerful monopolies, we Cubans would be incapable of producing sugar. It is possible they even believed that we would destroy our own country. It is clear that if the revolution was ruining the country, the United States would not have had to attack us. They would have left us alone, so that the US government would have appeared as a good and honorable government, while we revolutionaries proceeded to destroy our own country. This would demonstrate that revolutions should not be carried out because revolutions destroy countries.

Fortunately, that is not the case. There is living proof that revolutions do not destroy countries, and this proof has just been supplied by the US government. It has proved many things, in particular, that revolutions do not destroy countries, while imperialist governments do destroy countries.

Cuba was far from being ruined and, therefore, it had to be ruined. Cuba needed new markets for its products. We honestly and frankly ask any delegate present: Which country does not want to sell what it produces? Which country does not want its exports to increase? We wanted what every country wants: to increase our exports. This is a universal law; only selfish interests can oppose the universal interest in commercial exchange, which surely is one of the most ancient aspirations and needs of humankind.

We wanted to sell our products and we went to seek new markets. We signed a trade agreement with the Soviet Union, according to which we would sell one million tons of sugar and we would purchase a certain amount of Soviet products. Surely no one can say that this was wrong. We did not have to ask permission of the State Department in order to sign a trade agreement with the Soviet Union, because we considered ourselves, and we continue to consider ourselves, a truly independent and free country.

When more of our sugar began to be sold, we received a major blow. By request of the executive branch of the United States, Congress approved an act according to which the US president or the executive power could set the appropriate limits for the quota of sugar imports from Cuba. This economic weapon was wielded against our revolution. The justification for this measure had been prepared in advance in the media. A campaign had been conducted over a long period of time, because you know perfectly well that here in the United States, the monopolies and the mass media are completely intertwined.

The economic weapon was used and in one fell swoop our sugar quota was cut by about one million tons — sugar that had already been produced for the US market. The goal was to deprive our country of the resources it needed for development and to reduce our country to impotence in order to obtain a political objective.

Such a measure had been expressly prohibited by regional international law. As all representatives of Latin America here know, economic aggression is expressly condemned by regional international law. Nevertheless, the US government violated that law, wielded their economic weapon and cut our sugar quota by almost a million tons — and that was that. They could do it.

What could Cuba do when confronted by that reality? Turn to the United Nations. Go to the United Nations to denounce the political and economic aggression, to denounce the incursions by pirate aircraft, to denounce the constant interference of the US government in our country's political affairs and the subversive campaigns against the revolutionary government of Cuba.

So we turn to the United Nations. The United Nations has the power to deal with these matters. The United Nations, in the hierarchy of international organizations, stands at the head. It has authority even above the Organization of American States (OAS). We wanted the problem aired in the United Nations, because we fully understand Latin America's economic dependency on the United States.

The United Nations took up the question. It sought an investigation to be carried out by the OAS. The OAS met. What was to be expected? That the OAS would protect the attacked country? That the OAS would condemn the political aggression against Cuba, or that it would condemn, in particular, the economic aggression of which we were the victims? We expected this, and had a right to expect it. After all, we are a small nation, a member of the Latin American community. And besides, we were just one more victim — not the first and we will not be the last. Mexico has been attacked more than once militarily. A great part of Mexico's territory was stolen in a war, during which the heroic sons of Mexico, draped in the Mexican flag, threw themselves from Chapultepec castle rather than surrender. Such were the heroic sons of Mexico!

And that was not the only aggression. That was not the only time that US infantry forces plowed their way into Mexican territory. Nicaragua was invaded, and for seven long years was heroically defended by César Augusto Sandino. Cuba was attacked more than once, as were Haiti and the Dominican Republic. Guatemala was attacked. Who here can honestly deny the role of the United Fruit Company and the US State Department in the overthrow of the legitimate government of [President Árbenz in] Guatemala? I understand there are some who consider it their official duty to be discreet about such matters, and who may even be willing to come here and deny this. But in their consciences they know I am speaking the truth.

Cuba was not the first victim of aggression. Cuba was not the first country threatened by aggression. In this hemisphere everyone knows that the US government has always imposed its own law, the law of the mightiest. In accordance with this law, it has destroyed Puerto Rican nationhood and maintained its control over that island. In accordance with this law, it seized and still holds the Panama Canal.

So this was nothing new. The OAS should have defended us, but it didn't. Why not? Let us now go to the heart of this matter and not merely consider the surface. If we stick to the letter of the law, then we have guarantees. If we stick to reality, however, there are no guarantees whatsoever because reality imposes itself over and above the law outlined in international codes. And this reality is that a small country attacked by a powerful country was not defended and could not be defended.

What happened [at the OAS meeting] in Costa Rica? Lo and behold, by an ingenious miracle there was no condemnation of the United States or the US government in Costa Rica! (I wish to avoid any misunderstanding here that we are confusing the government of the United States with the US people. We regard them as two completely different entities.) The US government was not condemned in Costa Rica for the 60 incursions by pirate aircraft. The US government was not condemned for the economic and other aggressions of which we have been victim. No! The Soviet Union was condemned! It was really quite bizarre. We had not been attacked by the Soviet Union. We had not been the victims of aggression by the Soviet Union. No Soviet aircraft had flown over our territory. Yet in Costa Rica it was the Soviet Union that was condemned for interference.

The Soviet Union had only said, theoretically speaking, that if there was a military aggression against our country, they could, figuratively speaking, support us with rockets. Since when is support for a weak country under attack from a powerful country regarded as interference? In legal terms, there is something called an impossible condition. If a country considers that it is incapable of committing a certain crime, it can simply say: "Because there is no possibility that we [ie. the United States] will attack Cuba, there is no possibility that the Soviet Union will support Cuba." But that principle was not followed. Instead, it was established by the OAS that the intervention of the Soviet Union had to be condemned.

And what about the bombing of Cuba? Not a word. And what about the aggressions against Cuba? Not a word.

Of course, there is something that we should remember, which should concern us all to some extent. We are all, without exception, actors and participants in a crucial moment in the history of humanity. At times, criticism apparently does not reach us; we may not be aware of the condemnation and censure of our deeds. This is especially the case when we forget that just as we have the privilege of playing a part in this all-important historic moment, some day history itself will judge us for our acts.

In the face of the refusal of the Costa Rica meeting to defend our country, we can only smile, because history will judge that episode. I say this without bitterness. It is difficult to condemn individuals, who are often just the playthings of circumstance. And we, who know the history of our country and who are also exceptional witnesses to what our country is experiencing today, understand how terrible it is for a nation's economy and its very life to be subjected to the economic might of a foreign country.

I need only note that my country was not defended at the OAS in Costa Rica. Furthermore, there was a desire to avoid bringing this matter to the United Nations, perhaps because it was felt it would be easier to obtain a mechanical majority in the OAS. That fear is not easy to explain, since we have seen that mechanical majorities also often operate in the United Nations.

With all due respect to this organization, we must say that our people have learned so much in the school of these recent international events, a people equal to the role they are now playing and to their heroic struggle. They know that in the end, when their rights have been denied or are not safeguarded by either the OAS or the United Nations, and when aggressive forces fall upon them, they have the supreme and heroic right to resist.

That is why we, the small countries, still do not feel confident that our rights will be protected. That is why, when we small countries want to be free, we know that we are doing so on our own account and at our own risk. Because, in truth, when the peoples are united, defending a just cause, they can rely only on their own energies. It is not a matter of a few individuals ruling a country, as they have tried to make us appear. It is a matter of a whole people ruling a country, firmly united and with a great revolutionary consciousness, defending their rights. The enemies of the Cuban revolution should know this; and if they don't know it they are making a big mistake.

These are the circumstances in which the revolutionary process in Cuba has taken place. This is how we found the country and this is why difficulties have arisen. Nevertheless, the Cuban revolution is changing things. What was yesterday a land without hope, a land of misery, a land of illiteracy, is gradually becoming one of the most enlightened, advanced and developed nations of this continent.

The revolutionary government, in just 20 months, has created 10,000 new schools. In this brief period of time, we have doubled the number of rural schools that had been established in 50 years, and Cuba today is the first country of the Americas that has met all its educational needs, having teachers in even the most remote corners of the mountains.

In this brief period of time, the revolutionary government has built 25,000 houses in the countryside and the urban areas. Fifty new townships are at this moment being built in our country. What were previously the most important military fortresses, today house tens of thousands of students.

In the coming year, our country plans to commence its great battle against illiteracy, with the ambitious goal of teaching every single illiterate person in our country to read and write. To that end, organizations of teachers, students, workers—that is, the entire people—are preparing themselves for an intensive campaign to wipe out illiteracy. Cuba will be the first country in the Americas that, after a few months, will be able to say it does not have a single illiterate person in the country.

Today our people are receiving the assistance of hundreds of doctors who have been sent out into the rural areas to fight against the endemic sicknesses, the parasitic diseases, and to improve the sanitary conditions of the nation.

With regard to the preservation of our natural resources, we point with pride to the fact that in one year, in the most ambitious conservation plan for natural resources being carried out in this hemisphere—including the United States and Canada—we have planted close to 50 million timber-yielding trees.

Young people who were unemployed, or who had no schools, have been organized by the revolutionary government and today are gainfully and usefully employed. Agricultural production in our country has registered something almost unique: an increase in production from the very start. Why did this happen? First of all, the revolutionary government transformed more than 100,000 agricultural workers into landowners. At the same time, large-scale production was maintained through agricultural cooperatives, thanks to which we have been able to apply the most modern techniques and processes to our agricultural production. Since the very beginning we have seen an increase in production.

All of these social programs—teachers, houses, hospitals—have been carried out without sacrificing the resources needed for development. At this moment, the revolutionary government is carrying out a program of industrialization, and the first factories are already being built in Cuba.

We have utilized the resources of our country rationally. Previously, for example, cars were imported into Cuba to the value of $35 million and just $5 million was spent on tractors. A primarily agricultural country imported seven times more automobiles than tractors. We have reversed this figure, and we are now importing seven times more tractors than automobiles.

Close to $500 million was recovered in cash and assets from the corrupt politicians who had enriched themselves during the dictatorship. The proper investment of this wealth and these resources is allowing the revolutionary government to carry out its plans of industrialization and increasing agricultural production, to build houses and schools, to send teachers to the farthest corners of the country, and to provide everyone with medical attention. In other words, it is carrying out a real program of social development.

At the recent Bogotá meeting, the US government proposed another plan. Was it a plan for economic development? No, it was a plan for "social development." What did this mean? Well, it was a plan for building houses, schools and roads. Does this solve the problem? How can there be a solution for social problems without a plan for economic development? Is this how they try to deceive the peoples of Latin America? What will the families live on when they occupy those houses, if those houses are actually built? What shoes or clothes are they going to wear, and what food are they going to eat, when they go to those schools, if those schools are actually built? Perhaps they do not understand that when a family doesn't have clothes or shoes for the children, the children are not sent to school. With what resources are they going to pay the teachers? With what resources are they going to pay the doctors, or pay for the medicines? If they want a good way of saving on medicines, they should increase the people's nutritional level so that what is spent in feeding the people will not have to be spent on hospitals.

In view of the tremendous reality of underdevelopment, the US government now comes out with a plan for social development. Naturally it is significant that the US government is now concerned about the problems of Latin America, as up to now, it has not cared at all. Isn't it a coincidence that they are now concerned with these problems? And the fact that this concern has arisen after the Cuban revolution — they might say this is purely coincidental.

Until now the monopolies have only been concerned with exploiting the underdeveloped countries. But as soon as the Cuban revolution rears its head, the monopolies start concerning themselves with the underdeveloped countries. While they attack our economy and try to crush us, at the same time the US government offers charity to the peoples of Latin America. Not the resources for economic development, of course, which is what Latin America wants, but resources for social development. They offer resources for houses for people without work, for schools that children cannot attend, and for hospitals that would not be necessary if there were adequate levels of nutrition in Latin America.

Although some of my Latin American colleagues may feel it is their duty to be discreet here, they should welcome a revolution like the Cuban revolution, which has forced the monopolies to return at least a small part of their profits from the natural resources and the sweat of the peoples of Latin America.

As you know, we are not included in any of that assistance, and this does not bother us. We do not get angry about such things. We have been solving our own problems for a long time—problems of schools and housing and so on. Some people may feel, however, that we are using this forum for propaganda purposes—the US president said that some people might use this rostrum to make propaganda.

Well, all of my colleagues in the United Nations have a standing invitation to visit Cuba. We do not close our doors to anyone, and we do not restrict anyone's movements. All of my colleagues in this assembly are welcome to visit Cuba whenever they wish and see with their own eyes what is going on. There is that chapter of the Bible that speaks of St. Thomas—who had to see before he would believe. Well, we invite any newspaper correspondent, any member of any delegation, to visit Cuba and see what a people can do with its own resources when it invests those resources honestly and rationally.

We are not only solving our problems of houses and schools. We are solving our problems of development, because without solving the problems of development there can be no solution to social problems. So what is happening? Why does the US government not wish to speak of economic development? The answer is obvious: Because the US government does not want to quarrel with the monopolies, and the monopolies need natural resources and investment markets for their capital. That is the paradox, that is where the contradiction lies. That is why a real solution for this problem is avoided. That is why there is no development plan for the underdeveloped countries using public monies.

This should be stated frankly, because when all is said and done, we, the underdeveloped countries, are a majority here—just in case anyone was unaware of this fact. And we are witnesses to what is going on in the underdeveloped world. There is so much talk about the contribution of private capital, yet the true solution is not sought. Naturally, this means markets for the investment of surplus capital, such as investments that amortize in five years.

The US government cannot propose a plan for public investment, because this would go against its very reason for existence, which is the US monopolies. There is no need to beat about the bush—that is why no real program of economic development is planned. The goal is to preserve the lands of Latin America, Africa and Asia for the investment of surplus capital.

So far, we have referred to the problems of our own country. Why haven't those problems been solved? Is it because we don't want them solved? No, the government of Cuba has always been ready to discuss its problems with the US government, but the US government has not been ready to discuss its problems with Cuba. It must have its reasons for not wanting to discuss these problems with Cuba.

I have here the note sent by the revolutionary government of Cuba to the US government on January 27, 1960. It says:

> The differences of opinion between our two governments that are subject to diplomatic negotiation can be settled by such negotiation. The government of Cuba is ready and willing to discuss these problems without reservation and in depth, and declares itself as being unaware of any obstacles in the path of such negotiations through any of the traditional channels, on the basis of mutual respect and reciprocal benefit. The government of Cuba wishes to maintain and increase diplomatic relations as well as economic relations between our two countries, and understands that on this basis the traditional friendship between the peoples of Cuba and the United States is indestructible.

On February 22 of this year the revolutionary government of Cuba wrote:

> In accordance with its desire to renew through diplomatic channels the negotiations already begun on issues outstanding between the United States and Cuba, the revolutionary government has decided to set up a commission with the necessary powers to carry out negotiations and discussions in Washington on a mutually agreed date.
>
> The revolutionary government of Cuba wishes to clarify, however, that the renewal and continuance of such negotiations must obviously be subject to the proviso that the government or Congress of your country take no unilateral measures prejudging the results of the above-mentioned negotiations or prejudicial to the economy or the people of Cuba.
>
> It seems obvious that the adherence of your government to this point of view would not only contribute to the improvement of relations between our respective countries but would also reaffirm the spirit of

close friendship that has traditionally linked and still links our peoples.

It would also allow both governments, in an atmosphere of calm and with the widest scope possible, to examine the questions that have affected the traditional relations between Cuba and the United States of America.

What was the reply of the US government?

The government of the United States cannot accept the conditions for negotiations expressed in Your Excellency's note, to the effect that measures not be taken of a unilateral nature on the part of the government of the United States that might affect the Cuban economy or the people of Cuba, be it through the legislative or the executive branches. As President Eisenhower stated on January 26, the government of the United States, in the exercise of its own sovereignty, must remain free to take whatever measures it deems necessary, conscious of its international commitments and obligations to defend the legitimate rights and interests of its people.

In other words, the US government does not deign to discuss matters with the small country of Cuba.

What hope can the people of Cuba have for the solution of these problems? All the facts that we ourselves have noted here conspire against the resolution of these problems. Surely the United Nations should take this very much into account, because the government of Cuba, and the people of Cuba, too, are justifiably concerned at the aggressive turn in US policy regarding Cuba. It is important that the United Nations should be up-to-date and well informed.

First of all, the US government considers it has the right to promote and encourage subversion in our country. The US government is promoting the organization of subversive movements against the revolutionary government of Cuba, and we denounce this here in the General Assembly. Concretely, we wish to denounce that Caribbean islands belonging to Honduras, known as the Swan Islands, have been taken over militarily by the US government. The US marines are there, despite the fact that this is Honduran territory; and in violation of international law, in violation of the international conventions that govern radio broadcasting, it has set up a powerful transmitter, which it has put at the disposal of the war criminals and subversive groups that are sheltered in this country. Furthermore, military training is taking place there to promote subversion and the landing of armed forces on our island.

It would be good for the representative of Honduras here to assert Honduras's right to that piece of its territory, but that is incumbent on the representative of Honduras. What does concern us is that a piece of territory belonging to a sister country, seized in a pirate-like fashion by the US government, should be used as a base for subversion and attacks against our territory.

I want careful note taken of this denunciation that we make on behalf of the people of Cuba.

Does the US government feel that it has the right to promote subversion in our country, violating all international agreements, invading our airwaves to the detriment of our own radio stations? Does this mean that the Cuban government has a similar right to promote subversion in the United States; that we have the right to violate the airwaves of the United States?

What right does the US government have over us or over our island that it denies to others? Let the United States return the Swan Islands to Honduras; it has never had jurisdiction over these islands.

There are even more alarming circumstances for our people. We know that through the Platt Amendment, the US government took upon itself the right to establish naval bases in our territory, a right imposed on us by force and which has been maintained by force.

A naval base in the territory of any country is surely a just cause for concern. In our case, first of all, because a country that has followed an aggressive and warlike policy possesses a base [Guantánamo] in the very heart of our island. It leaves our island vulnerable in any international conflict or even a nuclear conflict, despite us having no involvement whatsoever. We have nothing to do with the problems of the US government, or the crises that the US government provokes. And yet there is a base in the heart of our island that poses a great danger for us in the event of an armed conflict.

But is that the only danger? By no means! There is an even greater danger closer to home. The revolutionary government of Cuba has repeatedly expressed its concern at the fact that the imperialist US government may use that base in the heart of our national territory to stage an attack against its own forces as a pretext for an attack on our country.

Our concern about this is increasing, because the aggressiveness and the attacks are increasing and the signs are becoming more alarming. For instance, I have here an AP cable, which reads as follows:

> Admiral Arleigh Burke, US chief of naval operations, says that if Cuba should attempt to take the Guantánamo Naval Base by force, "we would fight back."
>
> In a copyrighted interview published today in the magazine *US News & World Report* Admiral Burke was asked if the navy is concerned about the situation in Cuba under Premier Fidel Castro.
>
> "Yes, our navy is concerned — not just about our base at Guantánamo, but about the whole Cuban situation," Admiral Burke said. He added that all the military services were concerned. "Is that because of Cuba's strategic position in the Caribbean?" he was asked.
>
> "Not necessarily," Admiral Burke said. "Here is a country with a people normally very friendly to the United States, people who have liked the people of this country, and we have liked them. Yet, here comes a man with a small, hard core of communists determined to change all of that. Castro has taught hatred of the United States and he has gone a long way toward wrecking his country."
>
> Admiral Burke said, "we would react very fast" if Castro moved against the Guantánamo base.
>
> "If they would try to take the place by force, we would fight back," he added.
>
> To a question whether Soviet Premier Khrushchev's threat about retaliatory rockets gives Admiral Burke "second thoughts about fighting in Cuba," the admiral said, "No. Because he's not going to launch his rockets. [Khrushchev] knows he will be destroyed if he does — I mean Russia will be destroyed."

First of all, I must emphasize that for this gentleman, the fact that industrial production in my country has increased by 35 percent, the fact that we have given jobs to more than 200,000 Cubans, the fact that we have solved many of the social problems of our country, constitutes the wrecking of our country. Therefore, they take upon themselves the right to set the stage for aggression.

See how they make their calculations. And their calculations are very dangerous, since this gentleman intimates that if there was an attack against us we would be alone. Maybe Admiral Burke thought this up for himself.

But let's imagine that Mr. Burke is mistaken. Let's suppose for a moment that Mr. Burke, even though he is an admiral, is mistaken. Then in that event, Admiral Burke is playing irresponsibly with the fate of the world. Admiral Burke and that whole group of aggressive militarists are playing with the fate of the world.

The fate of each of us as individuals is really of no concern. Yet we, who represent the peoples of the world, are duty bound to concern ourselves with the fate of the world, and it is our duty to condemn all those who play irresponsibly with it. They are not only playing with the fate of the people in my country; they are also playing with the fate of their own people, and that of all of the peoples on the entire planet.

Or does this Admiral Burke think that we are still living in the time of the blunderbuss? Does he not realize that we are living in the nuclear age, with disastrous and cataclysmic destructive forces beyond what even Dante or Leonardo da Vinci could have imagined, because they surpass what humankind has been able to imagine in our worst nightmares. And yet, he makes this calculation, which AP then spreads around the world. The magazine has just come out and already the campaign has begun, fanning the hysteria about the imaginary danger of a Cuban attack against the Guantánamo base.

But that is not all. Yesterday, a UPI dispatch was released with a declaration by US Senator Styles Bridges, who, I understand, is a member of the Senate Armed Services Committee. He said, "the United States must defend at all costs its naval base at Guantánamo in Cuba." He explained:

> We must go as far as necessary to preserve that base and to defend that gigantic installation of the United States. We have naval forces there, we have military forces and we have the marines, and if we were attacked we should defend it, for I consider it to be the most important base in the Caribbean area.

This member of the Senate Armed Services Committee did not entirely discount the use of nuclear weapons in the case of an attack against the Guantánamo base. What does this mean? This means it is not only a matter of whipping up hysteria and the systematic preparation of the right climate, but even of threatening the actual use of nuclear weapons. Among the many questions we should ask this Mr. Bridges is whether he is ashamed of himself to threaten a small country like Cuba with nuclear weapons.

As far as we are concerned, and with all due respect, I must say that the world's problems are never settled by threats or by sowing fear. And what about our small and humble nation? We exist, whether they like it or not. And the revolution will go forward, whether they like it or not. Our people are not afraid. Our small and humble country must resign itself to its fate. It will not be shaken by this threat to use nuclear weapons.

What does this mean? Many countries have US military bases, but those bases, naturally, are not directed against the governments that granted the concessions — at least, not as far as we know. In our case, we are in the tragic position of having a base within our own territory, directed at the heart of Cuba and the heart of the revolutionary government of Cuba, in the hands of the declared enemies of our country, our revolution and our people.

In the entire history of bases set up around the world, the most tragic case is that of Cuba. This base was thrust upon us by force, in a territory that is unquestionably ours, that is a good many miles from the coast of the United States. It is a base that was imposed by force, that is directed against Cuba and its people, that is a constant threat and a constant cause for concern for our people.

For these reasons, we must state here that all this talk of attacks is intended primarily to create a climate of hysteria and to set the stage for attacks against our country. We have never spoken a single word that could imply any type of attack on the Guantánamo base, because it is clearly in our interest not to give imperialism the slightest pretext to attack us.

We state this here categorically. We have always stated this since the base became a threat to the peace and security of our country and our people. The revolutionary government of Cuba is seriously considering requesting, within the framework of international law, that the naval and military forces of the United States be withdrawn from the Guantánamo base, from that part of our national territory. There will be no option for the imperialist US government but to withdraw its forces. How will it be able to justify before the world its right to install in our national territory a nuclear base or a base that threatens our people?

How can they justify to the world any right to retain a hold over a part of our territory? How can they stand before the world and justify something so arbitrary? And since they will be unable to justify this to the world when our government requests it, then within the framework of international law, the US government will have no option but to abide by the canons of international law.

This assembly has to be kept informed regarding the problems of Cuba and must be alert to attempts to confuse or deceive. We have to explain these problems very clearly because with them lies the security and the fate of our country. That is why we want these matters clearly understood — especially since there seems to be little chance of correcting the opinion, or the erroneous impression, the politicians of this country have regarding Cuba.

Here, for example, I have Mr. Kennedy's declarations that are enough to astound anyone. On Cuba he says: "We must use all the power of the OAS to avoid Castro interfering in other Latin American countries and force him to return freedom to Cuba." They are going to return freedom to Cuba!

"We must state our intention," he says, "of not allowing the Soviet Union to turn Cuba into its Caribbean base, and to apply the Monroe Doctrine." More than halfway through the 20th century, and this [presidential] candidate speaks of the Monroe Doctrine! "We must force Prime Minister Castro to understand that we intend to defend our right to the naval base of Guantánamo." He is the third person to speak of this problem. "And we must show the Cuban people that we sympathize with their legitimate economic aspirations..." So why did they not sympathize before? "We recognize their love of freedom, and we will never be satisfied until democracy returns to Cuba." What democracy is he speaking about? The democracy made by the monopolies of the United States?

To explain why planes from US territory fly over Cuba, pay attention to what this gentleman says:

> The forces that are struggling for freedom in exile and in the mountains of Cuba must be supplied and assisted, and in other countries of Latin America, communism must be confined and not allowed to expand or spread.

If Kennedy were not an illiterate, ignorant millionaire, he would understand that it is not possible to carry out a revolution against the wishes of the peasants in the mountains and with the support of the landowners. Every time imperialism has tried to stir up counterrevolutionary groups, the peasant militia has put them out of action within a few days. But it seems he has been reading too much fiction or watching too many Hollywood films—stories about guerrilla warfare—and believes that the social forces exist in Cuba today to conduct [counterrevolutionary] guerrilla warfare.

In any case, this is not encouraging. Nevertheless, no one should think that our comments on Kennedy indicate that we feel any sympathy for the other candidate, Mr. Nixon, who has, in actual fact, made similar statements. As far as we are concerned, both of them lack political brains.

General Assembly President Boland: I am sorry to have to interrupt the prime minister of Cuba, but I am sure that I am faithfully reflecting the feelings of the assembly as a whole when I ask him to consider whether it is right and proper that the candidates in the current election in this country be discussed at the rostrum of the assembly of the United Nations.

I am sure that in this matter the distinguished prime minister of Cuba will, on reflection, see my point of view, and I feel that I can rely with confidence on his goodwill and cooperation. On that basis I would ask him kindly to continue with his remarks.

Fidel Castro: It is not our intention in the least to infringe upon the rules that determine behavior in the United Nations, and the president can depend fully on my cooperation to avoid having my words misunderstood. I have no intention of offending anyone. It is somewhat a question of style and, above all, a question of confidence in the assembly. In any case, I will try to avoid giving the wrong impression.

Up to this point we have been dealing with the problems of our country, the fundamental reason for us attending this session of the United Nations. We understand perfectly that we would be somewhat selfish if we limited our concerns to our specific case alone. It is also true that we have used the greater part of our time informing the assembly about the case of Cuba, and in the little time left, we would like to deal with the remaining questions, to which we will briefly refer.

The case of Cuba is not an isolated one. It would be an error to think of it only as the case of Cuba. The case of Cuba is that of all underdeveloped nations. It is the case of the Congo, it is the case of Egypt, it is the case of Algeria, it is the case of Iran, and finally, it is the case of Panama, which wants its canal back. It is the case of Puerto Rico, whose national spirit they are destroying. It is the case of Honduras, a portion of whose territory has been seized. In short, without specifically referring to other countries, the case of Cuba is the case of all the underdeveloped and colonized countries.

The problems we have outlined in relation to Cuba apply to all of Latin America. The control of Latin America's economic resources is exercised by the monopolies which, when they do not directly own the mines, control them in other ways, as is the case with copper in Chile, Peru and Mexico; with zinc in Peru and Mexico; and with oil in Venezuela. They are the owners of the public utility companies, such as is the case with the electricity services in Argentina, Brazil, Chile, Peru, Ecuador and Colombia, or with the telephone services in Chile, Brazil, Peru, Venezuela, Paraguay and Bolivia. Or, they commercially exploit our products, as is the case with coffee in Brazil, Colombia, El Salvador, Costa Rica and Guatemala; with cotton in Mexico and Brazil; or with the exploitation, marketing and transportation of bananas by the United Fruit Company in Guatemala, Costa Rica and Honduras. Economic control of the most important industries of our countries is exercised by US monopolies. These countries are completely dependent on those monopolies.

Woe to any countries in Latin America, if they too wish to carry out agrarian reform! They will be asked for "speedy, efficient and just payment." And if, in spite of everything, a sister nation carries out agrarian reform, any representatives coming here to the United Nations will be confined to Manhattan; they will have hotel rooms denied to them; they will have insults poured on them and they may, possibly, be mistreated by the police themselves.

The problem of Cuba is only an example of the problem of Latin America. How long must Latin America wait for its development? As far as the monopolies are concerned, it will have to wait *ad calendas Graecas* [forever]. Who will industrialize Latin America? It will certainly not be the monopolies. No way!

There is a UN Economic Commission report that explains how even private capital, instead of going to the countries that need it most for the establishment of basic industries, is being channeled to the more industrialized countries, where private capital finds greater security. Naturally, even the UN Economic Commission has had to recognize the fact that there is no possibility of development through the investment of private capital — in other words, through the monopolies.

The development of Latin America will have to be achieved through public investment planned and granted unconditionally with no political strings attached. Obviously, we all want to be representatives of free countries. No one wants to represent a country that does not feel itself to be completely free. No one wants the independence of one's country to be subject to any interests other than its own. Any assistance must therefore have no political strings attached.

The fact that Cuba has been denied assistance does not matter. We never asked for it. However, in the interests of and for the benefit of the peoples of Latin America we feel bound, out of solidarity, to stress that assistance must be given without any political conditions whatsoever. Public investment must be for economic development, not for "social development," which is the latest invention to hide the genuine need for economic development.

The problems of Latin America are like the problems of the rest of the underdeveloped world, in Africa and Asia. The world is divided up among the monopolies, and those same monopolies that we find in Latin America are also found in the Middle East. Oil in Iran, Iraq, Saudi Arabia, Kuwait, Qatar and in every corner of the earth is in the hands of monopolistic companies that are controlled by the financial interests of the United States, the United Kingdom, the Netherlands and France. The same situation exists in the Philippines. The same situation exists in Africa.

The world has been divided among the monopolistic interests. Who would dare deny this historical truth? The monopolistic interests are not concerned with the development of the peoples. What they want is to exploit the natural resources of our countries and to exploit the peoples. And they want to amortize their investments or get them back as quickly as possible.

The problems experienced by the Cuban people with the imperialist US government are the same problems that Saudi Arabia, Iran or Iraq would face if they decided to nationalize their oil fields; the same problems that Egypt had when it justifiably and correctly nationalized the Suez Canal; the very same problems Indonesia had when it wanted to become independent. They would face the same surprise attacks that were made against Egypt and the Congo.

Have the colonialists or the imperialists ever lacked a pretext when they wanted to invade a country? Never! Somehow they always manage to find the necessary pretext. Which are the colonialist countries? Which are the imperialist countries? There are not four or five countries but four or five groups of monopolies that possess the world's wealth.

Let us imagine someone from outer space were to come to this assembly, someone who had read neither Karl Marx's *Communist Manifesto* nor the UPI and AP cables, nor any other publication controlled by the monopolies. That person might ask how the world was divided, and would see on a map how wealth was divided among the monopolies of four or five countries. They would say: "The world has been divided up badly, the world has been exploited." Here in this assembly, where there is a majority of under-developed countries, they might comment: "The great majority of the peoples, who are represented here, have been exploited for a long time. The forms of that exploitation may have varied, but the peoples are still being exploited." That would be the verdict.

In the statement made by Premier Khrushchev, a particular remark attracted our attention because of the value that it holds. He said that the Soviet Union has neither colonies nor investments in any country. How great would it be for our world, a world threatened with catastrophe, if all the representatives of all countries could make the same statement: Our country has neither colonies nor investments in any foreign country!

Why labor the matter further? Because this is the crux of the matter. This is the crux of the question of peace and war. This is the crux of the arms race and disarmament. Since the beginning of humankind, wars have emerged for one reason, and one reason alone: the desire of some to plunder the wealth of others.

End the philosophy of plunder and the philosophy of war will end. End the existence of colonies and the exploitation of countries by monopolies, and humankind will achieve a true era of progress.

Until that step is taken, until that stage is reached, the world will live in constant terror of being dragged into crisis and wiped out by a nuclear conflagration. Why? There are those who wish to perpetuate this plunder and there are those who wish to maintain this exploitation.

We have spoken here about Cuba. Because of the problems we have had to confront with imperialism, we have learned that imperialism is always the same, and that all imperialisms are allied. A country exploiting the peoples of Latin America or elsewhere is the ally of others who are doing the same in other parts of the world.

One thing alarmed us considerably in the statement made by the US president:

> In the developing areas, we must seek to promote peaceful change, as well as to assist economic and social progress. To do this—to assist peaceful change—the international community must be able to manifest its presence in emergencies through United Nations observers or forces.
>
> I would like to see member countries take positive action on the suggestion in the secretary general's report looking to create a qualified staff within the secretariat to assist him in meeting future needs for UN forces.

In other words, after considering Latin America, Africa, Asia and the Pacific as "developing areas," he recommends "peaceful change," and proposes that in order to bring this about, UN "observers" or "forces" should be used.

The United States itself came into being as the result of a revolution against colonial rule. The right of a people to self-determination, by means of revolution if necessary, to throw off colonialism or any type of oppression, was recognized in Philadelphia with the declaration of July 4, 1776. And yet today the United States proposes to use UN forces to block revolutionary change. President Eisenhower continued:

> The secretary general has now suggested that members should maintain a readiness to meet possible future requests from the United Nations for contributions to such forces. All countries represented here should respond to this need by earmarking national contingents that could take part in UN forces in case of need. The time to do it is now—at this assembly.

I assure countries that now receive assistance from the United States that we favor use of that assistance to help them maintain such contingents in a state of readiness suggested by the secretary general.

In other words, he proposes to the countries that have bases and that are receiving assistance that he is ready to give them more assistance for the formation of this UN emergency force. He continued:

To assist the secretary general's efforts, the United States is prepared to earmark substantial air and sea transport facilities on a standby basis to help move contingents requested by the United Nations in any future emergency."

In other words, the United States also offers its planes and ships for the use of such emergency forces. We wish to state here that the Cuban delegation does not agree with this emergency force until all the peoples of the world can feel sure that these forces will not be at the disposal of colonialism and imperialism. This is especially the case as any of our countries might, at any moment, become the victim of the use of such forces against our people.

There are a number of inherent problems here, and much has been said on this by various delegations. For reasons of time, we would merely like to express our views on the problem of the Congo.

Naturally, since we oppose colonialism and the exploitation of the under-developed world, we condemn the way in which the intervention by UN forces was carried out in the Congo. First of all, these forces did not go there to counter the invading forces, the original reason why they were to be sent. All the time necessary was given to bring about the first dissension, and when this did not suffice, further time was allowed to enable the second division to occur in the Congo.

And finally, while the radio stations and the airfields were occupied, further time was given for the emergence of the "third man," as they call those saviors who emerge in such circumstances. We know them only too well. In 1934, one of these saviors appeared in our country; his name was Fulgencio Batista. In the Congo his name is Mobutu. In Cuba this savior paid a daily visit to the US embassy, and it seems the same thing happens in the Congo. Don't just take my word on this. This was published in none other than *Time* magazine, a major defender of the monopolies, which therefore cannot be considered biased against them. In no way can they be considered to be in favor of [Patrice] Lumumba; they are against him and in favor of Mobutu. *Time* magazine explains who Mobutu is, how devoted he is to his work, and concludes:

> Mobutu became a frequent visitor to the US embassy and held long talks with officials there… One afternoon last week, Mobutu conferred with officers at Camp Leopold, and got their enthusiastic support. That night he went to Radio Congo—

the same radio Lumumba had not been allowed to use

> —and abruptly announced that the army was assuming power.

In other words, all this occurred after frequent visits and lengthy conversations with the officials of the US embassy. This is what *Time* magazine says, as the champion of the monopolies.

The hand of the colonialists has been clearly visible in the Congo and therefore, in our view, bad faith has been evident in the Congo and favoritism shown to the colonial interests. The people of the Congo (and this is the reason for the problems in the Congo) support the only leader who remained there defending the interests of his country, and that leader is Lumumba.

This mysterious third man in the Congo was called upon to overthrow the legitimate government and trample the legitimate interests of the Congolese people. In spite of this, if the Afro-Asian countries manage to reconcile all these interests to the benefit of the Congo, so much the better. But if this conciliation fails, then justice and the law will be on the side of the person who not only has the support of the people and the parliament but who stood firm against the interests of the monopolies and shoulder to shoulder with his people.

Regarding the problem of Algeria, I hardly need to say that we support 100 percent the right of the Algerian people to independence. It is ridiculous to pretend—as many vested interests do—that Algeria is part of the French nation. At other times, other countries have made similar efforts to keep hold of their colonies. Such a stance, known as integralism, has been a historic failure. Let's look at the question in reverse: Suppose Algeria was the metropolis and declared that part of Europe formed an integral part of its territory. This is obviously a ludicrous idea that makes no sense whatsoever. Algeria belongs to Africa, gentlemen, just as France belongs to Europe.

For a number of years this African people has been struggling heroically against the metropolis. While we are calmly discussing matters here, French army bombs and shells are falling over the villages and hamlets of Algeria. And people are dying in this struggle where there can be no possible doubt which side is right. This fight could be settled, even taking into account the interests of the minority living there, which has been used as a pretext to deny the right of independence to nine-tenths of the population of Algeria. Yet we do nothing. We were so quick to go to the Congo, but so half-hearted about Algeria. If the Algerian government—which is a government because it represents millions of Algerians who are fighting and struggling—asks for UN forces, would we go there? And with the same enthusiasm? I wish this were the case, but we would go with a very different purpose: to defend the interests of the Algerians, and not the interests of the colonizers.

We are on the side of the Algerian people, just as we are on the side of the other countries of Africa that are still colonies. We are on the side of the blacks who are discriminated against in the Union of South Africa. We are on the side of the peoples who wish not only to be politically free—because it is very easy to raise a flag, choose a coat of arms, sing an anthem and put another color on the map—but also to be economically free. There is a truth we should bear in mind above all others: There can be no political independence unless there is economic independence. Political independence is a fiction unless there is economic independence, and therefore we defend the aspiration to be economically and politically free, not just the right to have a flag, a coat of arms and representation in the United Nations.

Here, we want to mention another right, a right that was proclaimed by our people at a gigantic public meeting a few days ago. I refer to the right of the underdeveloped countries to nationalize, without compensation, their natural resources and the monopoly investments in their countries. In other words, we support the right to nationalize the natural resources of any foreign investments in the underdeveloped countries. If the highly industrialized countries wish to do likewise, we will not oppose them.

For countries to be truly free politically, they must be truly free economically. And they must be assisted in this aim. We may be asked: What about the value of the investments? We would ask in return: What about the value of the profits that have been extracted from the colonies and the under-developed countries for decades, if not centuries?

We would like to support a proposal made by the head of the delegation from Ghana to rid African territory of military bases, and therefore of nu-clear weapons bases. The proposal aims to keep Africa free from the dangers of nuclear war. This has already been done in relation to Antarctica. Why, as we advance on the road to disarmament, do we not also advance on the road to freeing certain regions of the earth from the danger of nuclear war? If Africa is to be reborn, it will be the Africa we are learning about today, not the Africa we are shown on the maps, in Hollywood films and about which we read in novels; not the Africa of semi-naked tribes carrying spears, ready to run away at their first encounter with the white hero (whose heroism increases in proportion to the number of Africans he kills); not that Africa, but the Africa which stands here today represented by such leaders as Sékou Touré and Kwame Nkrumah; the Africa of the Arab world, of Nasser. That is the true Africa, the oppressed continent, the exploited continent, the continent from which millions of slaves came, the Africa that has suffered so greatly throughout its history. Toward that Africa we have a duty: to preserve it from the danger of destruction.

Let other nations of the world compensate Africa! Let the West somehow compensate it for everything Africa has suffered, by preserving it from the danger of nuclear war, by declaring it a zone free from that danger. Let no nuclear bases be established there. If we can do nothing else, let that continent become a sanctuary where human life is preserved.

So we warmly support Ghana's proposal.

On the question of disarmament, we entirely support the Soviet proposal. We do not blush when we say we openly and warmly support the Soviet proposal. We believe it is a correct proposal, with clear and precise terms.

We have very carefully read the speech delivered here by President Eisenhower. He did not speak of disarmament; neither did he speak of the development of the underdeveloped countries; he did not speak of the problem of colonies. It would be worthwhile for US citizens, who are so influenced by false propaganda, to carefully and objectively read the US president's speech and the speech of the Soviet prime minister in order to see who is truly concerned about the problems of the world; they could then see who uses clear and sincere language; they could then see who wants disarmament and who does not want disarmament, and why.

The Soviet proposal could not be clearer; it leaves nothing to be desired. Why are there reservations when this tremendous problem has never before been so clearly presented?

The history of the world has shown, tragically, that arms races always lead to war. Yet at no time has war entailed such a dreadful holocaust for humanity as at the present time; it follows, therefore, that the responsibility has never been greater. What has the Soviet delegation proposed on this question that is so crucial for humankind? The Soviet delegation has presented a proposal for total and complete disarmament. Can anything more be asked? If so, then ask for it! If further guarantees are required, then ask for them! The Soviet proposal could not be clearer or more precise. It cannot be rejected without taking on the dreadful responsibility for war and everything war entails.

Why should responsibility for this problem be removed from the General Assembly? Why doesn't the US delegation want this problem to be discussed here, among all of us? Have we in the General Assembly no judgment? Should we remain uninformed about this problem? Does a commission have to meet? Why shouldn't the problem be discussed in the most democratic way possible? Why shouldn't all the delegates in the General Assembly discuss the problem of disarmament? Let everyone lay their cards on the table so that we may know who stands for disarmament and who does not, who wants to play at war and who does not. We should know who is betraying humanity's aspiration for peace and who is not. Humankind must never be dragged into a holocaust because of egotistical and illegitimate interests. Humankind, our peoples — not just ourselves — must be safeguarded from that holocaust, so that everything human knowledge and intelligence has created does not serve to destroy humanity itself.

The Soviet delegation spoke in clear terms, and I am speaking objectively here. I invite you all to study those proposals and to place your cards on the table. This is not simply a question of delegations now; this is, above all, a question of world public opinion. The warmongers and the militarists must be exposed and condemned by world public opinion. This is not just the duty of a minority; this is the duty of the world itself. The warmongers and the militarists must be unmasked. That is the task for world public opinion.

Not only must this be discussed in the plenary of the General Assembly, but it must be discussed before the eyes of the entire world. It must be discussed in the great assembly of the world itself. Remember, in the event of a war, those responsible will not be the only ones exterminated; hundreds of millions of totally innocent people will be exterminated. That is why we are meeting here as representatives of the world, or at least part of it, because the world is not completely represented here because the People's Republic of China is not represented—a quarter of the world is absent from this assembly. But those of us who are present here have a duty to speak frankly and not beat around the bush.

This is an extremely serious problem—a more important problem than economic assistance and all other commitments; this is the commitment to preserve human life. Everyone has to discuss the problem, we all have to speak about it, and we all have to struggle so that peace will prevail in the world.

Above all, if we of the underdeveloped countries want to have some hope of progress; if we want to have some hope that our peoples will enjoy a better standard of living, then we must struggle for peace, we must struggle for disarmament. With one-fifth of what the world spends on arms, we could stimulate development in the underdeveloped countries at a growth rate of 10 percent per annum. With one-fifth! And of course the standard of living of the people in those countries spending their resources on arms would be raised as well.

So what are the difficulties of disarmament? Who is interested in being armed? Those interested in being armed to the teeth are those wanting to hold on to their colonies or their monopolies, those wanting to hold on to the oil of the Middle East and the natural resources of Latin America, Asia and Africa. And in order to defend those interests, they need force. You know full well that these territories were occupied and colonized through force. It was through force that millions of human beings became slaves. And it is with force that this exploitation is maintained throughout the world. Clearly, those who do not want disarmament are those who wish to maintain the use of force, to maintain their control over the resources and the cheap labor of the underdeveloped countries.

I said I would speak frankly, and things must be called by their right names.

The colonialists, therefore, are those opposed to disarmament. We will have to fight, with world opinion on our side, to impose disarmament on them, just as we will have to fight to impose on them the rights of the peoples to political and economic liberation.

Another reason why the monopolies are against disarmament, besides the fact that they need arms to defend their interests, is the fact that the arms race has always been good business. Everyone knows, for example, that the great monopolies in this country doubled their capital during World War II. Like vultures, the monopolies feed on the corpses of the wars. And war is good business. Let's unmask those for whom war is a business, those who enrich themselves through war. Let's open the eyes of the world and expose those warmongers who make a business out of the fate of humanity, who trade on the dangers of war, even when war can be so terrifying as to leave no hope of escape for anyone.

To do this, we, a small, underdeveloped country, invite other small, underdeveloped countries, as well as this whole assembly, to fight to bring the problem here for discussion. We would never forgive ourselves if, through neglect or weakness on our part, the world were to find itself increasingly confronting the dangers of war.

There is one remaining point which, as I have read in some newspapers, was one of the points that the Cuban delegation wanted to raise. That is the question of the People's Republic of China. A number of delegations have already spoken about this. We merely wish to say that the fact that this question has not even been discussed here is a negation of the raison d'être of the United Nations. Why hasn't it been discussed? Because the US government does not wish to discuss the matter? Why should the UN General Assembly renounce its right to discuss the question?

In recent years, various countries have joined our organization. It is a denial of historical reality and a denial of life itself to oppose discussing the right of the People's Republic of China—one of the most populous countries of the world—to be represented here. It is simply preposterous and absurd that this matter cannot even be discussed. How long must we play this pathetic game of avoiding this problem in the United Nations, even when there are representatives here, for example, of Franco's Spain? Mr. President, will you allow me to express my opinion, with all due respect, on this specific point, without offense to anyone?

General Assembly President Boland: I think it is only fair to the prime minister to make clear the position of the chair. The chair does not think it is in keeping with the dignity of the assembly or the decorum that we like to preserve in our debates that references of a personal nature should be made to the heads of state or government of member states of the United Nations, whether or not they are present. I hope that the prime minister will consider that a fair and reasonable rule.

Fidel Castro: I merely wanted to make some comments, sir, on how the United Nations arose. The United Nations emerged after the struggle against fascism, after tens of millions died on the battlefield. From that struggle, which took so many lives, this organization arose as a hope. But there are some extraordinary paradoxes. While US soldiers were falling in Guam, Guadalcanal, Okinawa and many other islands in the Pacific, they were also dying on the Chinese mainland, fighting on the same side as those to whom today we deny even the right to discuss their entry into the United Nations. At the same time, the soldiers of the Blue Division [from Spain] were fighting in the Soviet Union to defend fascism. While the People's Republic of China is denied the right to put its case to the United Nations, the regime born of Italian fascism and German Nazism, which took power thanks to Hitler's armies and Mussolini's Blackshirts, has received the generous accolade of membership in the United Nations.

China represents one-fourth of the world, and is truly represented by the government of the People's Republic of China. And yet another regime [Taiwan] sits in its place, a regime maintained in power by the interference of the US Seventh Fleet dispatched in the midst of a civil war.

Can we ask here by what right the fleet of one country, and an extra-continental country at that—and let us emphasize the word "extra-continental" because there has been so much talk here about extra-continental interference—can interfere in the purely domestic affairs of China. It would be interesting to hear an explanation for this. It was done with the sole purpose of maintaining a group of US allies and preventing the total liberation of China. And since this is an absurd and illegitimate position, from any point of view, the US government wants to avoid a discussion on the problem of the representation of the People's Republic to China.

We want it to be clearly noted that we support a discussion of this problem here. We believe the UN General Assembly should seat the legitimate representatives of the Chinese people, the government of the People's Republic of China.

I understand very well that it is somewhat difficult for anyone here not to be judged according to certain stereotypes. But let me state that we came here free of all prejudice, to analyze the problems objectively, without fear of what others might think of us, and without fear of the consequences of our conduct or our position. We have been honest and frank without being Francoist, because we do not want to be accomplices to the injustice perpetrated against many Spaniards who, for more than 20 years, have been imprisoned in Spain, who fought together with the North Americans in the Lincoln Brigade that went to Spain to raise the name of that great man Abraham Lincoln.

We would like now to sum up our views on certain aspects of world affairs about which there can be no doubt. In doing this, we place our trust in reason and honesty.

We have explained the problem of Cuba, which is part of the world's problems. Those who attack us today are those who attack others elsewhere in the world.

The US government cannot be on the side of the Algerian people, because the United States is an ally of France. It cannot be on the side of the Congolese people, because the United States is an ally of Belgium. It cannot be on the side of the Spanish people, because it is an ally of Franco. It cannot be on the side of the Puerto Rican people, whose nationhood it has been destroying for 50 years. It cannot be on the side of the Panamanian people, who are demanding their canal. It cannot allow the expansion of civilian rule in Latin America, or in Germany or Japan.

The US government cannot be on the side of the peasants who want land because it is an ally of the landowners. It cannot be on the side of workers seeking better living conditions, in any part of the world, because it is an ally of the monopolies. It cannot be on the side of the colonies seeking liberation, because it is an ally of the colonizers.

In other words, the US government is on Franco's side. It is on the side of the colonizers of Algeria. It is on the side of the colonizers of the Congo. It is on the side of maintaining its own privileges and interests in the Panama Canal. It is on the side of colonialism all over the world.

The US government is on the side of German militarism and its resurgence. It is on the side of Japanese militarism and its resurgence.

The US government forgets the millions of Jews who died in the concentration camps of Europe at the hands of the Nazis, who are today recovering their influence in the German army. It forgets the French who were slaughtered in their heroic struggle against the German occupation. It forgets the US soldiers who died at the Siegfried Line, in the Ruhr, on the Rhine and on all the battlefields of Asia.

The US government cannot be on the side of the unity and the sovereignty of the peoples. Why not? Because it must suppress the sovereignty of the peoples in order to maintain its military bases. Each military base is a dagger stuck into the sovereignty of a nation; each base is a sovereignty suppressed. That is why the US government must oppose the sovereignty of the peoples. It must constantly suppress this sovereignty in order to maintain its policy of bases around the Soviet Union.

We understand that these issues have not been clearly explained to the people of the United States, but they should try to imagine what would happen if the Soviet Union were to begin to set up a string of nuclear bases in Cuba, Mexico or Canada. They would certainly not feel calm or secure.

World opinion, including public opinion in the United States, has to be taught to understand these problems from another point of view, from other nations' points of view. The underdeveloped countries cannot always be presented as aggressors; revolutionaries cannot always be presented as aggressors, as enemies of the US people.

We can't be enemies of the US people because we have seen North Americans like Carleton Beals and Waldo Frank, and other illustrious and distinguished intellectuals like them, who weep at the thought of the errors that are committed, at the lack of hospitality toward us, in particular. There are many humane North Americans, intellectuals, progressive and courageous writers, in whom I see the nobility of the early leaders of this country, such as Washington, Jefferson and Lincoln.

I am not speaking demagogically. I am speaking with the sincere admiration that we feel for those who fought to free their people from colonialism, so that their country would always defend noble and just ideals. They did not fight so that this country would become, as it is today, the ally of all the reactionaries, gangsters, big landowners, monopolies, militarists and fascists in the world. They did not fight so that their country would become the ally of the most backward and reactionary forces in the world.

We know full well what the people of the United States will be told about us today, tomorrow and always, to deceive them. It makes no difference. We are fulfilling our duty by expressing our views and stating these true facts in this historic assembly.

We proclaim the right of the peoples to their territorial integrity and to their nationhood. Those who conspire against nationalism do so because they know it means the desire of the peoples to recover what belongs to them, their wealth and their natural resources.

In short, we support all the noble aspirations of all peoples. That is our position; that is where we stand. We are, and always will be, on the side of the just. We are, and always will be, against colonialism, against exploitation, against the monopolies, against warmongering, against the arms race and against the playing at war. That is, and always will be, our position.

In conclusion, we consider it our duty to bring to the attention of this assembly the essential part of the Declaration of Havana. The Declaration of Havana was the response of the Cuban people to the Declaration of San José [at the OAS meeting in Costa Rica]. It was not made by 10 people, or 100, or 100,000. An assembly of more than a million Cubans made this declaration [on September 2]. Anyone who doubts this can come and count them at the next mass rally or general assembly that we hold in Cuba. You will certainly see the spectacle of a fervent and conscious people, a sight difficult to encounter except when people are passionately defending their most sacred interests.

At this assembly, in answer to the Declaration of San José, the people were consulted and proclaimed by acclamation the following principles of the Cuban revolution:

The National General Assembly of the people of Cuba:

Condemns the latifundium as the source of misery and poverty for the peasants and as a backward and inhuman agricultural system. It condemns starvation wages and the iniquitous exploitation of human labor by illegitimate and privileged interests. It condemns illiteracy and the lack of teachers, schools, doctors and hospitals, and the lack of care of the elderly that prevails in Latin America. It condemns the inequality and exploitation of women. It condemns discrimination against blacks and Indians. It condemns the military and political oligarchies that keep our peoples in abject poverty and block the development toward democracy and the full exercise of their sovereignty. It condemns the handing over of our countries' natural resources to foreign monopolies in a submissive policy that betrays the interests of the peoples. It condemns the governments that ignore the feelings of their people and yield to foreign dictates. It condemns the systematic deception of the people by the information media that serve the interests of the oligarchies and the imperialist oppressors. It condemns the news monopoly by the instruments of the monopoly trusts and their agents. It condemns the repressive laws that prevent workers, peasants, students and intellectuals, who form the great majority of each country, from organizing themselves to fight for their social demands and patriotic aspirations. It condemns the monopolies and imperialist companies that continuously plunder our wealth, exploit our workers and peasants, bleed and keep in backwardness our economies, and force the political life of Latin America to submit to their own designs and interests.

In summary, the National General Assembly of the people of Cuba condemns both the exploitation of one human being by another and the exploitation of underdeveloped countries by imperialist finance capital.

Therefore, the National General Assembly of the people of Cuba proclaims before the Americas —

and we do so here before the world:

The right of the peasants to the land; the right of the workers to the fruits of their labor; the right of children to education; the right of the sick to medical treatment and hospital attention; the right of youth to work; the right of students to free education that is both practical and scientific; the right of blacks and Indians to full dignity as human beings; the right of women to civil, social and political equality; the right of the elderly to a secure old age; the right of intellectuals, artists and scientists to fight, with their work, for a better world; the right of nations to nationalize the imperialist monopolies, thereby recovering their national wealth and resources; the right of countries to engage freely in trade with all the peoples of the world; the right of nations to their full sovereignty; the right of peoples to turn fortresses into schools and to arm their workers —

because on this question we must indeed engage in an arms buildup. We must arm our people to defend ourselves from imperialist attack

> —and to arm their workers, peasants, students, intellectuals, blacks, Indians, women, the young and the old, and all the oppressed and exploited people, so they themselves can defend their rights and their destiny.

Some of you wanted to know what line the revolutionary government in Cuba was following. There it is!

4. THE BAY OF PIGS INVASION AND THE PROCLAMATION OF THE SOCIALIST CHARACTER OF THE REVOLUTION

On April 15, 1961, simultaneous air attacks were launched on three airfields in Cuba with the aim of eliminating the possibility of an effective Cuban defense against the invasion scheduled to take place the following day. The invasion was defeated within 72 hours and over 1,179 members of the invading mercenary Brigade 2506 were captured.

COLÓN CEMETERY, HAVANA
APRIL 16, 1961

In a speech outside the main cemetery in Havana where the victims of the bombing raids were buried, Fidel Castro compared the attack to the Japanese attack on Pearl Harbor in 1941, and went on to proclaim, for the first time, the socialist character of the Cuban revolution.

When, in the midst of [World War II], the imperialist government of Japan wanted to join in, it made no declaration of war and issued no warning. One Sunday morning, at dawn — December 7, 1941 — Japanese planes and ships made a surprise attack on the naval base at Pearl Harbor and destroyed nearly all of the ships and planes of the US naval force in the Pacific.

Everyone remembers what happened there. Everyone remembers the wave of indignation it caused among the people of the United States; everyone remembers the irritation which that underhanded, surprise attack produced in that country and the indignation it caused in the rest of the world. The people of the United States mobilized in the face of that act of aggression, and they will never forget the treacherous, cowardly way in which their ships and planes were attacked that December dawn in 1941.

That attack stands as a symbol of treachery; it has gone down in the history of the United States as a symbol of perfidy, wickedness and cowardice. The United States and US public opinion have condemned it as a despicable, treacherous, cowardly act.

I'm not trying to establish comparisons, because when the Japanese were fighting against the United States, it was a struggle between two imperialist countries; two capitalist countries; two exploiting governments; two colonialist governments; two governments that were trying to control the markets, raw materials and economies of a large part of the world... Here, it isn't a struggle between two exploiting forces; it isn't a struggle between two imperialisms...

Cuba is very different from the United States. The United States exploits other nations, has appropriated a large part of the world's natural resources and is making tens of millions of workers all over the world labor in the service of its caste of millionaires. Cuba doesn't exploit other nations; Cuba hasn't appropriated, and is not struggling to appropriate, the natural resources of other nations; Cuba isn't trying to make the workers in other nations labor in its service...

With our revolution, we are eradicating not only the exploitation of one nation by another but also the exploitation of one human being by another. We have stated in a history-making general assembly [the Declaration of Havana in September 1960] that we oppose the exploitation of human beings; we have denounced the exploitation of human beings, and we will put an end to the exploitation of human beings in our homeland...

The people of the United States consider the attack on Pearl Harbor to have been a crime and a treacherous, cowardly act. Our people, therefore, are fully entitled to consider the imperialist attack that took place yesterday as a doubly criminal, doubly underhanded, doubly treacherous and thousand-times more cowardly act...

Without a doubt, the imperialist US government is treating us this way because Cuba isn't a powerful country; unquestionably, it is treating us this way because it knows that we can't give the criminal, cowardly actions it carries out against us the response they deserve. Without a doubt, if Cuba were a military power, the imperialist US government would never dare to perpetrate any such acts against us...

When the imperialist government of Japan took that action, it didn't try to hide its responsibility. In contrast, the president of the United States is acting like Pontius Pilate. President Kennedy is acting exactly like Pontius Pilate—which sums up the US government's policy.

How well those facts help us to understand! How well they show us what our world is really like and help us to educate our people. Those lessons come at a high price; they are painful and bloody. But how much the people learn from these things! How well our people have learned and have grown!...

Yesterday, as everyone knows, three groups of bombers, coming from outside the country, entered our national territory at 6:00 in the morning and attacked three different targets in our national territory. In each of these places, our people defended themselves heroically; in each of these places the valuable blood of our defenders was shed; in each of these places there were thousands and, where there were not thousands, hundreds and hundreds, of witnesses to what happened. Moreover, this was something we expected; it was something that was expected every day; it was the logical culmination of the burning of the sugarcane fields, of the hundreds of violations of our air space, of the pirate air raids, of the pirate attacks on our refineries from vessels that enter our waters before the sun is up. It was the consequence of what everyone knows; it was the consequence of the plans to attack us that were hatched by the United States in complicity with its lackey governments in Central America; it was the consequence of the air bases that everyone knows about only too well, because even the US newspapers and news agencies have published this information, and even their own news agencies and newspapers are tired of talking about the mercenary armies that are being organized, about the air fields that they have made ready, about the planes that the US government has given to them, about the Yankee instructors, about the air bases they have established in Guatemalan territory...

Imperialism plans the crime, organizes the crime, arms the criminals, trains the criminals, pays the criminals and the criminals come here and kill seven working people and then calmly go back and land in the United States. Even when the whole world knows about their deeds, they then say it was Cuban pilots who did it and they make up a fantastic tale, spread it all around the world, publish it in all the newspapers, propagate it from all the radio and television stations of the Miami reactionaries throughout the world, and then along come the archbishops to bless and sanctify the lie. Thus the whole throng of mercenaries, exploiters and phonies from all around the world come together in crime...

This is because what these imperialists can't forgive is that we are here, and what these imperialists can't forgive is the dignity, the firmness, the courage, the ideological integrity, the spirit of sacrifice and the revolutionary spirit of the Cuban people.

This is what they can't forgive, the fact that we are here right under their very noses, and that we have brought about a socialist revolution right under the nose of the United States!

And we are defending this socialist revolution with these guns! We are defending this socialist revolution with the same courage that our anti-aircraft artillery showed yesterday in riddling the attacking planes with bullets!...

We are not defending this revolution with mercenaries; we are defending this revolution with the men and women of our people.

Who has the arms here? Perhaps it is the mercenary who has the arms? Perhaps it is the millionaire who has the arms? Perhaps the mercenary and the millionaire are one and the same thing. Perhaps the little boys with rich daddies have the arms? Perhaps the overseers have the arms?

Whose hands hold the arms here? Are they the hands of playboys? Are they the hands of the rich? Are they the hands of the exploiters? Whose hands hold the arms here? Aren't they workers' hands, peasants' hands? Aren't they hands that have been hardened by work? Aren't they hands that create? Aren't they the hands of our humble people? And who are the majority of our people? Millionaires or workers? Exploiters or exploited? The privileged or the humble? Do the privileged have arms? Or do the humble have arms? Aren't the privileged a minority? Aren't the humble a majority? Isn't a revolution where the humble bear arms democratic?

Compañeros, workers and peasants: This is a socialist and democratic revolution of the humble, by the humble and for the humble. And for this revolution of the humble, by the humble, for the humble, we are ready to give our lives.

Workers and peasants, humble men and women of our country: Do you swear to defend this revolution of the humble, by the humble, for the humble, to the last drop of your blood?

Compañeros, workers and peasants of our country, yesterday's attack was a prelude to a mercenary aggression. Yesterday's attack, which cost seven heroic lives, aimed to destroy our planes on the ground. But it failed. They only destroyed two planes while most of the enemy planes were damaged or shot down. Here, before the tomb of our fallen compañeros; here, next to the remains of these heroic young people, children of workers, children of the humble, we reaffirm our resolve that just as they exposed themselves to the bullets, just as they gave their lives, we, too, all of us, proud of our revolution, proud of defending this revolution of the humble, by the humble and for the humble, shall not hesitate, whenever the mercenaries come, no matter who is against us, to defend it to our last drop of blood.

Long live the working class! Long live the peasants! Long live the humble! Long live the martyrs of our country! May the martyrs of our country live forever! Long live the socialist revolution! Long live a free Cuba!

Patria o muerte! [Homeland or death!]
Venceremos! [We will win!]

MAY DAY
HAVANA, MAY 1, 1961

A few weeks after the Bay of Pigs at a mass rally in Havana celebrating May Day, Fidel summed up the lessons of the invasion, reviewing the unfolding revolutionary process and the next steps forward.

Distinguished visitors from Latin America and the entire world; Combatants of the armed forces of the people, workers:

We have had 14 and a half hours of marching. I think that only a people imbued with infinite enthusiasm is capable of such an endurance test. Nevertheless, I will try to be as brief as possible...

I believe that today we should outline the course we should follow, analyze a little what we have done up to now, consider what point in our history we have reached, and what lies ahead...

This May Day says a lot. It says a lot about what the revolution has been so far, and what it has achieved so far. Maybe it tells our visitors more than it tells us.

All we Cubans have been witnesses to every step taken by the revolution, so maybe we don't realize how much we have advanced as fully as our visitors do, particularly those visitors from Latin America, where today they still live in a world very similar to the one we lived in yesterday. It is as if they were suddenly transported from the past and parachuted into this moment of our revolution to see all the incredible progress. We do not intend tonight to stress the merits of what we have done. We merely want to identify for ourselves the point we have currently reached and assess the revolution's genuine results.

This May Day is so different from those of the past. Previously, this date was the occasion for each sector of labor to raise its demands, its aspirations for improvement, to those who were totally deaf to working-class interests, to those who would not grant even the most basic demands because they did not govern for the people, for the workers, for the peasants, for the humble. They governed solely for the privileged, for the dominant economic interests. Doing anything for the people would have meant harming the interests they represented. So they could not accede to any just demand from the people. The May Day marches of those years registered the complaints and protests of the workers.

How different today's march has been! How different even from the first marches after the triumph of the revolution. Today's march shows us how much progress we have made. The workers no longer have to submit themselves to those ordeals; the workers no longer have to implore rulers deaf to their appeals; the workers are no longer subject to the domination of any exploiting class; the workers no longer live in a country run by those serving exploiting interests. The workers know now that everything the revolution does, everything the government does or can do, has one goal: helping the workers, helping the people.

Otherwise, there would be no explanation for this spontaneous show of support for the revolutionary government, this flood of goodwill that every man and woman has expressed here today.

The fruits of the revolution can be seen everywhere. The first to parade today were the children of the Camilo Cienfuegos school complex. We saw the Pioneers march by with smiles of hope, confidence and affection. We saw the Young Rebels march by. We saw the women of the Federation [of Cuban Women (FMC)] go by. We saw children from countless schools created by the revolution. We saw 1,000 students from the 600 sugarcane cooperatives who are studying artificial insemination here in the capital. We saw young people, humble people, parade in the uniforms of the schools where they are learning to be the diplomatic representatives of the future.

We saw the pupils of the schools for young peasants of the Zapata swamps, where the mercenaries chose to launch their [Bay of Pigs] attack. We saw thousands and thousands of peasants who are studying in the capital and who come from remote mountain areas, from sugarcane cooperatives or from people's farms. We saw the young women studying to be workers in child-care centers.

Each of these groups created a wonderful display. We have seen not only those who came from the rural areas but also those who are going to the countryside, such as the volunteer teachers and some of the 100,000 young people on their way to the interior of the country to wipe out illiteracy.

Where does this strength come from? It comes from the people, and it extends toward the people in return. These young people are truly children of the people. When we saw them today spelling out "Long live our socialist revolution," we realized how difficult it would have been to have all this without a revolution; how difficult for any of these children from the mountains to have marched here today, or for any of them to have the chance to get to know the capital, or to study in any of these schools, or to march with the joy and pride shown here today, or to march with the faith in the future shown today. Schools, university careers, art, culture and honors were never for the children of poor families, in the towns or in the countryside. They were never meant for peasants in the remote rural areas; they were never meant for the poor youth, black or white, from the countryside or the cities.

Art, culture, university careers, opportunities, honors, elegant clothes — all these were the privileges of a small minority, a minority represented today with that grace and humor shown by some workers' federations in their mimicry of the rich. It is truly astounding to think that today more than 20,000 athletes and gymnasts marched, bearing in mind we are only just beginning.

And all this, without mentioning the most marvelous thing we have seen today: this armed nation, this united people, which has been a highlight of these ceremonies.

How would this be possible without a revolution? How can one compare the present with the past? How can one not feel emotion on seeing the endless lines of workers, athletes and militia march by. At times all became intermingled. After all, workers, athletes and soldiers are the same thing.

Everyone can see why our people must emerge victorious from any battle. We noted the many women in the ranks of the union federations. The men were in the artillery units, mortar units, anti-aircraft units or militia battalions. The women were the wives and sisters and sweethearts of the militiamen who marched by later.

And those secondary school students, the Pioneers who marched by first or with the athletes — these too are the children of the militia members.

In this way, we can appreciate the working people as a whole. Workers of every profession, all marching together; manual laborers and intellectual workers; the writers, artists, actors, radio announcers, doctors, nurses, health care workers — all marching together in massive numbers. Under the banner of the National Education Workers Union were teachers and employees of the Ministry of Education.

Today we have had a chance to see everything that is worthwhile in our country, everything produced by our country. We can understand better than ever that there are two classes of citizens — or rather, there used to be two classes of citizens — those who worked, who produced and who created; and those who lived without working or producing, those who were simply parasites.

In this young, combative nation, who did not march today? The parasites! Today it was the working people who marched, everyone who produces with their hands or their brain...

This truly is the people. Someone living as a parasite or who wants to live as a parasite does not belong to the people. Only invalids, the sick, the elderly and children are entitled to live without working and are entitled to have us work for them and care for them. We have a duty to work for the children, the elderly and the sick. No moral law can ever justify that the people must work for the parasites.

Those marching today were the working people who will never again resign themselves to work for the parasites. This is the way our nation has come to understand what the revolution is, and how a nation can rid itself of foreign and domestic parasites.

We recall that when the largest industries were nationalized, in the same way that we nationalized the US factories, some people asked: "But wasn't this factory a Cuban factory? Why should a Cuban factory be nationalized?" Well, that factory did not belong to the people, it belonged to some gentleman. It did not belong to the people; it did not belong to the nation...

Certain gentlemen used to talk a lot about the homeland and the need to defend the homeland. They had quite a distorted idea of the homeland. What homeland were they referring to? The homeland of the few? The homeland of the privileged? The homeland of the gentleman with 1,000 *caballerías* of land and three houses, while others live in hovels?

What homeland did you have in mind, sir? A homeland where a small group has all the opportunities and lives off the labor of others? A homeland of the unemployed? The homeland of a family living in a slum? The homeland of the hungry, barefoot child begging for alms on the street?

What homeland are you referring to? The homeland that belonged to a small minority? Or the homeland of today, where we have won the right to chart our own destiny, where we have won the right to construct a better future. A homeland that will be, now and forever — as Martí wanted it — for the good of all, and not a homeland for the few!

The homeland will be a place where injustice is eliminated. This is our concept of the homeland. We will defend and are willing to die for a homeland that belongs to all Cubans, not just the few...

When a Yankee monopolist or a member of the US ruling circles talks about the homeland, they are referring to the homeland of the monopolies, of the large banking monopolies. They are thinking of sending the blacks of the South and the workers to be killed to defend the homeland of the monopolies.

What kind of morality and what right or reason do they have to make a black person die defending the monopolies, or the factories and the mines of the ruling class? What right do they have to send a Puerto Rican of Latin blood, of Latin tradition, to the battlefields to defend the policy of large capitalists and monopolies? The only threat to security is the threat to the monopolies. What concept of morality, law and rights is it to send the blacks from the South and Puerto Ricans to fight for them? This is their concept of homeland. A real homeland is one where the interests of the privileged classes have been eliminated, and where the nation and its wealth belong to everyone, the wealth is for everyone, and opportunity and happiness are for everyone...

Let's not talk about what might have happened to the people's hopes and aspirations if the imperialists had succeeded [in the Bay of Pigs invasion]. There can be no more tragic spectacle in the history of humanity than that of a defeated revolution. When the revolt of the slaves in Rome was defeated, thousands were nailed to crosses on the roadside. This should give us an idea of what a defeated revolution is.

There was also the dreadful slaughter of workers after the defeat of the Paris Commune [in 1871]. This, too, should give us an idea of what a defeated revolution is.

History teaches us that a defeated revolution has to pay an extraordinary toll in blood. The victorious ruling class demands payment for the anxiety it experienced, for all the interests that were affected, or that were threatened.

But it not only demands payment for present debts; it also seeks to collect, in blood, payment for future debts. It tries to annihilate the revolution down to its very roots.

Of course, under certain circumstances it is impossible to smash a revolution. I've spoken of revolutions that were defeated before the people had conquered power. What has never happened before in history is the defeat of a revolutionary people that has truly conquered power.

I am only trying to point out what the situation of this country might have been had imperialism got what it wanted. I am trying to point out the kind of May Day our workers would be having had imperialism got what it wanted!

For this reason, we think about everything we owe to those who fell. This is why we consider that every smile today is a tribute to those who made possible this happy and optimistic day.

The blood that was shed in battle was the blood of workers and peasants. It was the blood of children from poor working families. It was not the blood of plantation owners, millionaires, thieves, criminals or exploiters. The blood that was shed was of those who were exploited yesterday but today are free. It was humble blood, honest blood, working-class blood, creative blood. It was the blood of patriots, not mercenaries. It was the blood of workers who voluntarily and spontaneously enlisted in the army of the homeland. It was not the blood of conscripts forced into service by some law. It was the blood of those who spontaneously and generously offered to confront all the risks of battle to defend an ideal, a true ideal they felt deeply — not the false and hypocritical ideal that the Yankees inculcated in their mercenaries, as if they were parrots repeating the word "ideal."

Theirs was not an ideal of parrots, not an ideal to which you pay lip service, but an ideal from the heart. Not an ideal of those coming to recover their lost privileges, their lost lands, their lost banks, their lost factories, their lost riches. Not an ideal of those who came to recover the easy life, by those who never had a drop of sweat on their brow while they lived off the sweat and blood of everyone else. Not the ideal of the mercenary who sells his soul for the mighty empire's gold.

Rather, it is the ideal of the worker who does not want to continue being exploited. The ideal of the peasants who do not want to lose their land again. The ideal of the young person who does not want to lose his or her teacher.

The ideal of the black person who does not want to be discriminated against anymore. The ideal of the woman who wants to live with rights and dignity. The ideal of working people, those who never lived off the sweat of others. The ideal of those who never considered life as a gift, but as work. The ideal of those who never stole anything from anyone, or killed anyone in defense of illegitimate interests.

It is the ideal of a working person who defends the revolution because the revolution is everything. Previously that worker was nothing, lowly and downtrodden, subject to humiliation, discriminated against and mistreated. A person whom the ruling and exploiting class considered to be a nobody. Today that worker is a somebody, one among millions of people. And that worker defends the revolution because the revolution is their life, and because identified with the revolution is that person's life, future and hopes.

Before sacrificing these hopes, those workers would rather lose their lives a thousand times. Because they are not thinking selfishly about themselves. They are thinking that while an individual may fall, it would not be in vain, because the cause for which they fall will bring happiness to millions of their brothers and sisters.

Working-class blood, peasant blood, the blood of the poor was shed by the homeland in the battle against imperialism's mercenaries. What kind of blood and what kind of people did imperialism send here to establish a beachhead? A beachhead from which they could plunge our people into a war of attrition, systematically burning our cane fields with incendiary bombs—as they have been doing without holding a piece of the national territory with which to try to give some legitimacy for launching their planes. Launching a war of destruction against our factories and our people, as they have been doing when they didn't even have a base here, sending their planes from abroad, at the same time as they were deceiving the world in the most cynical manner.

We have a right to say to the people, above all to our visitors, that at the same time that three of our airports were being bombed by US-made planes, with Yankee bombs and bullets, US news agencies were telling the world that our airports had been attacked by planes from our own air force, with pilots who had deserted that same day...

So, who were the people that fought against those workers and peasants? I'm going to tell you.

There are close to 1,100 mercenary prisoners captured by the revolutionary forces at the present moment, not counting the ship's crews. We analyzed the social composition of these prisoners with the following results: approximately 800 are from wealthy families, whose property collectively amounts to 27,566 *caballerías* of land taken over by the revolution; 9,666 houses, 70 factories, 10 sugar mills, two banks, five mines, and two newspapers. In addition, more than 200 of these 800 belonged to the most exclusive and aristocratic clubs in Havana. Of the remaining 200, 135 were former members of Batista's army, and the other 65 were lumpen or declassed individuals.

You will remember that during a discussion with the prisoners, I asked if any of them had cut sugarcane and no one came forward. Finally, one person raised his hand and said that he had once been a sugarcane cutter. If instead of this question, I had asked how many owned large landed estates, 77 would have raised their hands. So this is the social composition of the invaders: 27,556 *caballerías* of land, 9,666 buildings and houses, 70 factories, 10 sugar mills, two banks, five mines and two newspapers.

We are sure that if we were to ask everyone here how many own sugar mills, or how many own banks, or how many own large landed estates, there would not be one. Had we asked the combatants who were killed, members of the militias or soldiers of the Revolutionary National Police or Rebel Army; had we asked about the wealth of those who were killed or who fought, you can be sure there would not have been a single bank, a single mine, a single sugar mill, a single apartment building, a single factory, a single plantation, nor would there be a single member of any of the aristocratic clubs that used to exist in this city.

And some of those shameless individuals said they came here to fight for ideals, for free enterprise! Let some idiot come here today to say he was fighting for free enterprise! As if our people did not know more than enough about what free enterprise is. Free enterprise was the slums of Las Yaguas, Llega y Pon, Cueva del Humo and dozens of other places around this city. Free enterprise was unemployment for 500,000 Cubans. Free enterprise was hundreds or thousands of families living in *guardarrayas*.

Free enterprise was more than 100,000 peasant families working the land in order to pay a considerable part of their produce to absentee landlords who had never even seen a single seed being planted. Free enterprise was discrimination, arbitrary acts, abuse against workers and peasants, beatings by police, murders of workers' leaders, Mujalism [yellow unionism], contraband, gambling casinos, vice, exploitation, lack of education, illiteracy and poverty.

How are they going to talk about free enterprise to a people that had almost half a million unemployed, a million and a half illiterates, half a million children without schools, who had to stand in line to get into a hospital—in addition to finding some politician to help, in exchange for selling him your vote! How can they come and talk about free enterprise to a people that knows what free enterprise is: aristocratic clubs for a few thousand families while there are beggars in the streets, while hungry children go swimming at El Morro, next to sewage because they could not afford to go to a beach, because the beaches were off-limits and for the aristocrats only; the beaches were for the fortunate beneficiaries of free enterprise.

They could not even dream of going to Varadero beach, because Varadero was for a few wealthy families. They could not even dream that the child of a poor person could go to a university, because the universities were only for the privileged of free enterprise. They could not dream that their child would go and study languages in Europe, because the only ones who went to Europe were the privileged of free enterprise. They could not dream that the child of a construction worker or any low-paid worker could attend high school. A sugar worker could not dream that their child could graduate from high school, not to mention become a doctor or engineer. The child of a worker could only go to school if the worker lived in the capital and could afford to send that child—even then the possibilities were few—but 75 or 90 percent of the workers' children lived in areas where there were no secondary schools and they lacked the resources to pay for room and board in the city; so there was no opportunity to go to school. That opportunity was exclusively for the children of the beneficiaries of free enterprise. A cart driver or a sugarcane cutter could not even dream that his daughter would march in a parade, or do a tap dance and wear elegant clothing. A peasant could not even dream that his son could go and study agriculture in the Soviet Union. Nor could working families dream that their children would have the opportunity to study diplomatic law, mechanics, or any other profession, because these opportunities, with only a few exceptions, were for the children of wealthy families.

Some little rich kid, who doesn't know what it means to work, to sweat, or to suffer, and who came to murder peasants and workers — how can he tell us that he shed the people's blood in order to defend free enterprise? And not just his daddy's free enterprise, but the free enterprise of the United Fruit Company, the free enterprise of the Yankee electricity monopoly, the free enterprise of the company that used to control the telephones, the free enterprise of the companies that used to control the oil refineries. These were not free enterprises, they were monopolies that as such virtually eliminated competition.

When these gentlemen who came here, armed by imperialism, say they were defending free enterprise, what they were really defending were the monopolies. Monopolies in fact are against free enterprise, because they control the entire industry, its prices and its resources. Its method consists precisely in ruining everyone else. So, they were not even defending free enterprise, technically speaking. These very ignorant or very stupid people were defending the Yankee monopoly interests here and abroad. How can they tell the Cuban people that they came to defend the interests of free enterprise?

They also say they came to defend the 1940 constitution. It is curious that they did nothing to defend the 1940 constitution when it was torn up by the Batista dictatorship. They did nothing to defend the constitution when it was destroyed in the March 10 military coup with the complicity of first, the US embassy; second, the reactionary clergy; and third — or rather first, together with the others — the dominant economic classes, the monopolies, and the rich of our country, with the complicity of a judiciary corrupted down to the marrow of its bones, and of a whole series of corrupt politicians. It is truly cynical to see a little rich kid together with mayors, representatives and politicians of all types from the Batista years saying they were coming to defend the 1940 constitution. It was Batista himself who trampled on and destroyed that constitution, with the complicity of imperialism and the ruling classes. Also accompanying these little rich kids were hundreds of former members of Batista's army, and along with them a bunch of criminals and torturers, as well as a bunch of corrupt politicians — all saying they were coming to defend the 1940 constitution.

In point of fact, insofar as there were any advanced or revolutionary aspects of the 1940 constitution, the only government that has respected it, abided by it and moved it forward is precisely the revolutionary government.

That constitution said, "The system of large landed estates is prohibited," and that "to bring about its disappearance" — the constitution spoke of "its disappearance" — "the law will establish the maximum amount of landed property that any agricultural or industrial enterprise can possess." Obviously that provision was never carried out. Why not? Because there needed to be a subsequent law brought into Congress. And who was in Congress? The politicians, the lawyers for the Yankee monopolies, the owners of the large landed estates, the millionaires, the rich. Only a tiny handful of workers' leaders made it to the House of Representatives or the Senate, where they were condemned to remain in the minority, because all the newspapers, all the radio and television stations belonged to the same ruling economic sectors who owned and had a monopoly over the means of disseminating ideas. Any attempt to do something on behalf of the peasants was drowned in lies.

Back then it was very difficult for the people to learn about the evictions of peasants, about the frightful misery of the peasants, about the extremely high infant mortality rate. Tens of thousands of children of all ages died without a single doctor. The fact that tens of thousands of children died for lack of doctors and medicine was not a crime as far as the ruling class was concerned. It was not a crime as far as the beneficiaries of free enterprise were concerned. This did not pain them. This was not important to them. Society hardly even knew of these things!

The members of that Congress who had to decide on the supplementary provisions of the constitution were none other than the owners of large landed estates, the millionaires and the lawyers for the Yankee monopolies. There was no Agrarian Reform Law then. Despite the fact that the law said, "The system of large landed estates is prohibited," a single Yankee company owned 17,000 *caballerías* of land. And despite the fact that another provision of the 1940 constitution said, "the law will determine the appropriate norms so that the land returns to Cuban hands," in 19 years after the 1940 constitution was approved and went into effect, there was not a single law that took even a single *caballería* from a Yankee monopoly that owned 17,000.

Another monopoly had 15,000 *caballerías*, another had 10,000, which is almost 140,000 hectares. There were companies here with more than 200,000 hectares of the best land in Cuba.

The constitution also stated that "the state shall exhaust all means at its disposal to give work to every worker, manual or intellectual." Does this refer to teachers? The revolution discovered over 10,000 teachers without a classroom, without work, and it immediately gave them jobs, because there were also half a million children who needed schools. Let me repeat: "The state shall exhaust all the means at its disposal to give work to every worker, manual or intellectual, in order to provide them a decent existence." This is what the revolution did. It exhausted all the means at its disposal for this. And if it didn't exhaust all the means at its disposal, it was prepared to exhaust all the necessary means to give them jobs. Yes, jobs, because that's what the constitution ordered.

Those basic principles, which would have resolved the problem of hundreds of thousands of peasants, hundreds of thousands of unemployed, were set forth in the constitution but not complied with...

Those who follow the instructions of the US State Department, promoting the policy of isolating Cuba, those complying with imperialism's orders and breaking relations with a Latin American country under attack by imperialism, are miserable traitors to the interests and feelings of the Americas.

These facts show us the rotten and corrupt politicking that prevails in many Latin American countries. It shows how the Cuban revolution has turned those business-as-usual and corrupt ways upside down in order to establish completely new ways of life in our country.

To those who talk to us about the 1940 constitution, we say that the 1940 constitution is already too outdated for us. We are way beyond it; we have outgrown the 1940 constitution like an old jacket. That constitution was good for its time although it was never carried out. That constitution has been bypassed by this revolution, which as we have said is a socialist revolution.

We must talk of a new constitution. Yes, a new constitution, but not a bourgeois constitution, not a constitution corresponding to the rule of an exploiting class over other classes. What we need is a constitution corresponding to a new social system, one without the exploitation of one human being by another. That new social system is called socialism, and this constitution will therefore be a socialist constitution.

If Mr. Kennedy does not like socialism, well, we do not like imperialism! We do not like capitalism!

We have as much right to protest the existence of an imperialist and capitalist system 90 miles from our shore as he feels he has the right to protest over the existence of a socialist system 90 miles from his shore.

Rights do not come from size. Right does not come from one country being bigger than another; that does not matter. We have only a limited territory, a small nation, but our right is as respectable as that of any country, regardless of its size. It does not occur to us to tell the people of the United States what system of government they must have. Therefore, it is absurd for Mr. Kennedy to take it into his head to tell us what kind of government we should have here. That is absurd! It occurs to Mr. Kennedy to do that only because he does not have a clear concept of international law or sovereignty. Who had those ideas before Kennedy? Hitler and Mussolini!

They spoke the same language of force; it is the language of fascists. We heard it in the years before Germany's attack on Czechoslovakia. Hitler split it up because it was governed by a reactionary government. The reactionary and pro-fascist bourgeoisie were afraid of the advance of a socialist system, and even preferred domination by Hitler. We heard that language on the eve of the invasion of Denmark, Belgium, Poland and so forth. It is the right of might. This is the only right Kennedy advances in claiming the right to interfere in our country.

This is a socialist regime, yes! Yes, this is a socialist regime. It is here, but the fault is not ours, the blame belongs to Columbus, the English colonizers, the Spanish colonizers. The people of the United States, too, will someday get tired [of capitalism].

The US government says that a socialist regime here threatens US security. But what threatens the security of the US people is the aggressive policy of the warmongers of the United States. What threatens the security of the North American family and the US people is the violent, aggressive policy that ignores the sovereignty and the rights of other peoples. It is Kennedy's aggressive policy that is threatening the security of the United States. That aggressive policy could lead to a world war; and that world war might cost the lives of tens of millions of North Americans. Therefore, it is not the Cuban revolutionary government threatening the security of the United States, but the aggressive government of the United States itself.

We do not endanger the security of a single North American. We do not endanger the life or security of a single US family. We are making cooperatives, agrarian reform, people's farms, houses, schools, literacy campaigns, and sending thousands and thousands of teachers to the interior [of Cuba], building hospitals, sending doctors, giving scholarships, building factories, increasing the productive capacity of our country, creating public beaches, converting fortresses into schools, and giving the people the right to a better future. We are not endangering a single US family or a single US citizen.

The lives of millions of families, of tens of millions of North Americans are being endangered by those who are playing with nuclear war. Those who, as General Cardenas said, are playing with the possibility that New York becomes a new Hiroshima. Those playing with nuclear war, along with their aggressive war and their policy violating the rights of people, are the ones endangering the security of the US nation and the lives of untold millions of North Americans.

What do the monopolists fear? Why do they say that they are not secure with the socialist revolution nearby? As Khrushchev says, they are proving that they know their system is inferior. They don't even believe in their own system. Why don't they leave us alone when all our government wants is peace?

Our government recently issued a statement saying we were willing to negotiate. Why? Because we are afraid? No! We are convinced that they fear the revolution more than we fear them. They have a mentality that does not permit them to sleep when they know that there is a revolution nearby.

Fear? No one is afraid here. The people struggling for their liberty are never frightened. Those frightened are the wealthy, those who have been wealthy. We are not interested in having imperialism commit suicide at our expense. They do not care about the death of blacks, Puerto Ricans or Americans. But we do care about every Cuban life. We want peace.

We are ready to negotiate. They say that economic conditions can be discussed, but not communism. Well, where did they get the idea we would discuss that? We would discuss economic problems. But we are not ready to admit that these talks so much as brush a petal of a rose here. The Cuban people are capable of establishing their own government. We have never considered the possibility of discussing this. We will discuss only matters that do not affect our sovereignty. But we do want to discuss peace.

Those who are not concerned about taking the US people to war are being led by their emotions. We have no fear. If they think that is the case, they should forget it. No Cuban is afraid. If they think we will discuss our internal politics, they should forget that, too. They can discuss anything they want to discuss. We discussed things with invaders, didn't we? Well, we will debate with anyone. We are willing to talk. We are willing to debate. But does that mean we are desperate to negotiate? No way! We are just acting rationally. Does this mean the revolution will slow down? No way! We will continue, picking up speed as we can...

We announce here that in the next few days the revolutionary government will pass a law nationalizing the private schools. This law cannot be a law for one sector; it will be general. That means the private schools will be nationalized—of course, not a little school where one teacher gives classes, but private schools with several teachers.

The conduct of the directors of private schools has varied. Many private school directors have not been instilling counterrevolutionary poison. The revolution feels it is its duty to organize and establish the principle of free education for all citizens. The people feel they have the duty of training future generations in a spirit of love for the country, for justice, for the revolution.

What will happen to the private schools that have not supported the counterrevolution? The revolutionary government will indemnify those directors or owners of schools whose attitude has not been counterrevolution-ary, whose attitude has been favorable to the revolution; but the revolution will not indemnify any school whose directors have been waging a counter-revolutionary campaign, who have been against the revolution. In other words, there will be indemnity for those schools that have displayed a patriotic, decent attitude toward the revolution and their directors will be invited to work with the revolutionary government in directing that school or another school...

The teachers and employees of all these schools, of a lay nature, will be given work; they will have their jobs guaranteed. The pupils of these schools can go on attending, the educational standards will be maintained and even improved, and furthermore, now they will have to pay absolutely nothing to attend these schools...

Religion is one thing, politics is another. If those gentlemen [the Catholic bishops] were not against the political interests of the people, we would not care at all about their pastorals, their discussions about religious matters. The churches can remain open; religion can be taught there. Wouldn't it be much better if they had stuck to their religious teaching? Wouldn't it be much better to have peace? They can have peace, within strict limits of the respect due to the revolutionary people and government. But they cannot make war on the people on behalf of the exploiters. That has nothing to do with religion; it concerns blood, gold and material interests. They can have the consideration of the people, within a mutual respect for rights.

Christianity arose as a religion of the poor, the slaves and the oppressed of Rome; it was the religion that flourished in the catacombs. It was the religion of the poor, and it won respect. It coexisted with the Roman empire. Then came feudalism. The church coexisted with feudalism, later with absolute monarchies, and later still with bourgeois republics. With the disappearance of the bourgeois republic, why shouldn't the church continue to coexist with a system of social justice that is far superior to those previous forms of government? This system is much more like Christianity than Yankee imperialism, the bourgeois republic or the Roman empire.

We believe coexistence is perfectly possible, because the revolution does not oppose religion. Religion has been used as a pretext to combat the poor, forgetting that Christ said it was easier for a camel to pass through the eye of a needle than for a rich man to get into heaven.

These are the facts. We have spoken clearly as always. It means simply that we are prepared to defend the revolution and continue to move forward, convinced of the justice of our cause.

We have spoken about our socialist revolution. It doesn't mean the small business owner or small industrialist need worry. Mines, fuel, banking, sugar mills, export and import trade — the bulk of the economy — is in the hands of the people. That way the people can develop our economy. The small industrialist and small business owner can coexist with the revolution. The revolution has always cared for the interests of small business.

Our urban reform is a proof of this; this month small landlords will be collecting around 105,000 pesos. Formerly, if tenants did not pay their rent the landlord lost out; now a fund has been established to ensure that the small landlord will be paid. The revolution will have some 80 million pesos a year for construction from the urban reform. And when rent is the only income of these landlords, the revolution has decided that after the house is all paid for, the landlord will receive a pension.

A socialist revolution does not mean that interests of certain sectors are eliminated without consideration. The interests of the big landholders, bankers and industrialists were eliminated... but no middle interests will be affected without due consideration.

Small business owners and industrialists have credit today and the revolution has no interest in nationalizing them. The revolution has enough to do developing the sources of wealth it now has at its disposal... Counter-revolutionaries have claimed that barber shops will be nationalized, and even food stands. That is not the aim of the revolution. The solution to those issues will be found over time. There are some problems related to a small plague of middlepeople that results in tomatoes and pineapples being sold in the city at far higher prices than in the country. The revolution must still take measures to eliminate such abuses, to improve the consumption levels of the people. But I don't want anyone to be confused. Everyone should know what to expect...

Why are some Cubans so incapable of understanding that this happiness can also be theirs? Why do they not adapt to the revolution?...

This is the time to ask them to join us... The revolution does not want to use its force against a minority. The revolution wants all Cubans to understand. We do not want to keep all this happiness and emotion to ourselves. It is the glory of the people.

We say this to those who have lied in the past or those who have not understood. In all honesty, we say that our revolution should not be diminished by severe sanctions against the mercenaries. It might serve as a weapon for our enemies. We have had a moral victory and it will be all the greater if we do not besmirch our victory.

The lives lost hurt us as much as they do others. But we must overcome that hurt and focus on our prestige and our cause. What lies ahead of us?

The risk of imperialist aggression! Big tasks! We should realize that the time has come to make the greatest effort. The coming months are very important; they will be months in which we must make greater efforts in every field. We all have the duty to do the utmost. No one has a right to rest. With everything we have seen today we must learn that with effort and courage we can harvest wonderful fruit. And today's fruits are nothing compared to what can be done if we apply ourselves to the maximum.

Before concluding, I want to recall what I said during the Moncada trial. Here is part of that statement: "The country cannot remain on its knees imploring miracles from the golden calf. No social problem is resolved spontaneously." At that time we expressed our views. The revolution has followed the revolutionary ideas of those who had an important role in this struggle.

That is why when one million Cubans met to proclaim the Declaration of Havana [in September 1960], the document expressed the essence of our revolution, our socialist revolution. It condemned landed estates, starvation wages, illiteracy, shortage of teachers, doctors and hospitals, discrimination, exploitation of women, oligarchies that hold our countries back, governments that ignore the will of their people by obeying US orders, monopoly of the news media by Yankee agencies, laws that prevent the masses from organizing, and imperialist monopolies that exploit our wealth. The general assembly of the people condemned the exploitation of human beings.

The general assembly proclaimed the following: the right to work, education, the dignity of human beings, civil rights for women, secure old age, artistic freedom, nationalization of monopolies, and the necessities of life.

This is the program of our socialist revolution.

Long live the Cuban working class!
Long live the Latin American sister nations!
Long live the homeland!
Patria o muerte! [Homeland or death!]
Venceremos! [We will win!]

Raúl Castro, Juan Almeida and Fidel Castro leaving prison, May 15, 1955. Behind them is Armando Mestre. Imprisoned after the July 26, 1953, assault on the Moncada military garrison, Fidel Castro was released in 1955 as the result of a popular amnesty campaign.

Celia Sánchez, Fidel Castro and Haydée Santamaría in the Sierra Maestra (1956–58).

Fidel Castro in the Sierra Maestra during the Cuban revolutionary war (1956–58).

Fidel Castro during the Cuban revolutionary war (1956–58).

Sierra Maestra, 1957: Che Guevara (second from left), Fidel Castro (fourth from left, standing), Raúl Castro (kneeling, front), and Juan Almeida (first on the right).

Fidel Castro speaking at Camp Columbia, Havana, January 8, 1959. Camilo Cienfuegos is on Fidel's right.

Camilo Cienfuegos and Fidel Castro, January 1959. Photograph by Alberto Korda.

Fidel Castro addressing a rally in front of the presidential palace in Havana, January 21, 1959.

Havana, January 1959.

Havana, January 1959. Fidel Castro and Camilo Cienfuegos playing baseball for the "Barbudos" (The Bearded Ones).

Fidel Castro, 1960s.

Fidel Castro and Che Guevara, January 1959.

Drafting the agrarian reform law, 1959. Photograph by Alberto Korda.

Fidel Castro in Washington, DC, April 1959. Photograph by Alberto Korda.

Fidel Castro at the Bay of Pigs, April 1961.

Fidel Castro during voluntary work.

Fidel Castro doing voluntary work in the sugarcane fields.

Fidel Castro and Che Guevara at a rally.

Daniel Ortega of Nicaragua, Maurice Bishop of Grenada and Fidel Castro, May 1, 1980, Havana.

Nelson Mandela and Fidel Castro, July 26, 1991, Cuba.

Hugo Chávez and Fidel Castro.

Raúl Castro and Fidel Castro.

5. WORDS TO INTELLECTUALS

HAVANA, JUNE 30, 1961

On June 16, 23 and 30, 1961, broadly representative meetings of Cuba's intellectuals and cultural figures were held in the auditorium of the National Library in Havana. Artists and writers had the opportunity to discuss at length different aspects of cultural work and problems related to creative activity. Present at these meetings were President Osvaldo Dorticós, Prime Minister Fidel Castro, Minister of Education Armando Hart, members of the National Council of Culture and other representatives of the revolutionary government. At the last session, Fidel argued "within the revolution, everything; against the revolution, nothing."

Compañeros;
Compañeras:

Over the course of three sessions, various issues relating to culture and creative work have been discussed. Many interesting questions have been raised and different points of view expressed. Now it is our turn. I am not speaking because I'm the best-qualified person to deal with this matter, but because this is a meeting between you and us, we feel it is necessary to express our point of view.

We have been very interested in these discussions, and I believe we have shown what might be called "great patience." Actually no heroic effort was necessary; for us it has been an enlightening discussion and, in all sincerity, a pleasant experience. Of course, in this type of discussion we, the members of the government, are not the most qualified people to be expressing opinions on issues you specialize in. At least, that is true for me...

We have been active participants in this revolution, the social and economic revolution taking place in Cuba. At the same time, this social and economic revolution will inevitably produce a cultural revolution in our country.

We have tried to do something in this field (although perhaps there were more pressing problems to deal with at the beginning of the revolution). If we were to review our efforts with a critical eye, it could be said we have somewhat neglected a discussion as important as this one. Not that it was forgotten completely. The government was already considering a discussion like this, and perhaps the incident referred to repeatedly here helped speed things up. Months ago we intended to call a meeting like this one to review and discuss the question of culture. But important events kept taking place, one after the other, and the latest ones especially prevented this from taking place earlier. The revolutionary government has adopted a few measures that express our concern over this question. A few things have been done, and several members of the government have brought the question up more than once. In any case, it can be said that the revolution itself has already brought about changes in the cultural sector, and that the artists' conditions of work have changed.

I believe that a pessimistic perspective has been somewhat overemphasized here. Concerns have been expressed that go far beyond what can really be justified. The reality of the changes that have occurred in this sector and in the actual conditions for artists and writers has been almost ignored in the discussion. It is unquestionable that things are better for Cuban artists and writers than in the past, when their conditions were truly depressing. If the revolution started off by bringing about profound changes in the environment and conditions of work, why should we fear that the same revolution would seek to destroy those changes? Why should we fear that the revolution would destroy the very conditions it created?

What we are discussing here is not a simple problem. All of us here have the responsibility to analyze it carefully. It is not a simple problem, it has arisen many times in all revolutions. It is a knotty problem, we might say, and it is not easy to untangle. Nor is it one we are going to solve easily.

The various compañeros who have spoken here expressed a great variety of points of view, and they gave their reasons for them. The first day, people were a little timid, and for this reason, we had to ask the compañeros to tackle the subject directly, to have everyone state their concerns openly.

If we are not mistaken, the fundamental question raised here is that of freedom of artistic creation. When writers from abroad have visited our country, political writers in particular, this question has been brought up more than once. It has undoubtedly been a subject of discussion in every country where a profound revolution like ours has taken place.

By chance, shortly before we returned to this hall, a compañero brought us a pamphlet containing a brief conversation on this subject between [Jean-Paul] Sartre and myself that Lisandro Otero included in the book entitled *Conversations at the Lake* [*Revolución*, Tuesday, March 8, 1960]. I was asked a similar question on another occasion by C. Wright Mills, the US writer.

I must confess that in a certain way these questions caught us a little unprepared. We did not have our "Yenan conference" with Cuban artists and writers during the revolution. In reality, this is a revolution that arose and came to power in what might be called record time. Unlike other revolutions, it did not have the main problems resolved.

Therefore, one of the revolution's characteristics has been its need to confront many problems under the pressure of time. We are just like the revolution, that is, we have improvised quite a bit. This revolution has not had the period of preparation that other revolutions have had, and the leaders of this revolution have not had the intellectual maturity that leaders of other revolutions have had. Yet I believe that we have contributed to current developments in our country as much as has been in our power. I believe that through everyone's efforts, we are carrying out a true revolution, and that this revolution is developing and seems destined to become one of the important events of the century.

We have had an important part in these events, however we do not consider ourselves revolutionary theoreticians or revolutionary intellectuals. If people are judged by their deeds, perhaps we might have the right to consider the revolution itself to be our merit. But we do not think so, and I believe that we should all adopt a similar attitude, regardless of the work we might have done. Whatever merits our work may appear to have, we should begin by honestly placing ourselves in the position of not presuming that we know more than anyone else; that we know all there is to know; that our viewpoints are infallible; and that everyone who does not think exactly as we do is mistaken. We should honestly evaluate—although not with false modesty—what we know. I believe it will be easier to progress in this way and with confidence. If all of us adopt that attitude—you as well as us—subjective attitudes will disappear, and the element of subjectivity in analyzing problems will disappear too. What do we really know, in fact? We are all learning and we all have much to learn. We have not come here to teach; we have also come to learn.

There have been certain fears floating about, expressed by some compañeros. Listening to them, we felt at times that we were dreaming. We had the impression that our feet were not firmly planted on the ground—because if we have any fears or concerns today, they are connected with the revolution itself. The great concern, for all of us, should be the revolution. Or do we believe that the revolution has already won all its battles? Do we believe that the revolution is not in danger? What should be the first concern of every citizen today? Should it be concern that the revolution is going to commit excesses; that the revolution is going to stifle art or that the revolution is going to stifle the creativity of our citizens—or should it be the revolution itself? Should our first concern be the dangers, real or imaginary, that might threaten that creative spirit, or should it be the dangers that might threaten the revolution?

We are not invoking this danger as a simple point of argument. We are saying that the concern of the country's citizens and of all revolutionary writers and artists—or of all writers and artists who understand the revolution and consider it just—should be: What dangers threaten the revolution and what can we do to help the revolution? We believe that the revolution still has many battles to fight, and that our first thoughts and our first concerns should be: What can we do to assure the victory of the revolution? That comes first. The first thing is the revolution itself, and then, afterwards, we can concern ourselves with other questions. This does not mean that other questions should not concern us, but that the fundamental concern in our minds—as it is with me—has to be the revolution.

The question under discussion here and that we will tackle is the question of the freedom of writers and artists to express themselves.

The fear in people's minds is that the revolution might choke this freedom, that the revolution might stifle the creative spirit of writers and artists.

Freedom of form has been spoken of. Everyone agrees that freedom of form must be respected; I believe there is no doubt on this point.

The question becomes more delicate, and we get to the real heart of the matter, when dealing with freedom of content. This is a much more delicate issue, and it is open to the most diverse interpretations. The most controversial aspect of this question is: Should we or should we not have absolute freedom of content in artistic expression? It seems to us that some compañeros defend the affirmative. Perhaps it is because they fear that the question will be decided by prohibitions, regulations, limitations, rules and the authorities.

Permit me to tell you in the first place that the revolution defends freedom. The revolution has brought the country a very high degree of freedom. By its very nature, the revolution cannot be an enemy of freedom. If some are worried that the revolution might stifle their creativity, that worry is unnecessary, there is no basis for it whatsoever.

What could be the basis for such a concern? Only those who are unsure of their revolutionary convictions can be truly worried about such a problem. Someone who lacks confidence in their own art, who lacks confidence in their ability to create, might be worried about this matter. Should a true revolutionary, an artist or an intellectual who feels the revolution is just and is sure that they are capable of serving the revolution, worry about this problem? Should truly revolutionary writers and artists hold any doubts? My opinion is no—the only ones who could hold any doubts are those writers and artists who, without being counterrevolutionaries, are not revolutionaries either.

It is correct for writers or artists who do not feel themselves to be true revolutionaries to pose this question. An honest writer or artist, who is capable of grasping the revolution's purpose and sense of justice without being part of it, should consider this question.

A revolutionary puts one thing above all else. A revolutionary puts one thing above even their own creativity; they put the revolution above everything else. And the most revolutionary artist is one who is ready to sacrifice even their own artistic calling for the revolution.

No one has ever assumed that every person, every writer or every artist has to be a revolutionary, just as no one should ever assume that every person or every revolutionary has to be an artist, or that every honest person, just because they are honest, has to be a revolutionary. Being a revolutionary is to have a certain attitude toward life. Being a revolutionary is to have a certain attitude toward existing reality. There are some who resign themselves and adapt to this reality, and there are others who cannot resign or adapt themselves to that reality but who try to change it. That's why they are revolutionaries.

There can also be some who adapt themselves to reality who are honest people—it is just that their spirit is not a revolutionary spirit; their attitude toward reality is not a revolutionary attitude. Of course, there can be artists, and good artists, who do not have a revolutionary attitude toward life, and it is precisely this group of artists and intellectuals for whom the revolution constitutes something unforeseen, something that might deeply affect their state of mind. It is precisely this group of artists and intellectuals for whom the revolution constitutes a problem.

For a mercenary artist or intellectual, for a dishonest artist or intellectual, this would never be a problem. They know what they have to do, they know what is in their interest, they know where they are going.

The real problem exists for the artist or intellectual who does not have a revolutionary attitude but who is an honest person. Obviously, a person who has such an attitude toward life, whether or not they are a revolutionary, whether or not they are an artist, has their own goals and objectives. We should all ask ourselves about such goals and objectives.

For the revolutionary, those goals and objectives are directed toward changing reality and toward the redemption of humanity. It is humanity itself, one's fellow human being, the redemption of one's fellow human being that constitutes the revolutionary's objective. If we revolutionaries are asked what matters most to us, we will say: The people, and we will always say the people. The people in their true sense, that is, the majority of those who have had to live under exploitation and the cruelest neglect. Our fundamental concern will always be with the great majority of the people, the oppressed and exploited classes. We view everything from this standpoint: Whatever is good for them will be good for us; whatever is noble, useful and beautiful for them, will be noble, useful and beautiful for us. If one does not think in this manner, if one does not think of the people and for the people, if one does not think and act for the great exploited mass of the people, for the great masses we seek to redeem, then one simply does not have a revolutionary attitude.

From this standpoint we analyze what is good, what is useful and what is beautiful.

We understand that it must be a tragedy when someone understands this and nevertheless has to confess that he or she is incapable of fighting for it.

We are, or believe ourselves to be, revolutionaries. Whoever is more an artist than a revolutionary cannot think in exactly the same way that we do. We suffer no inner conflict, because we fight for the people and we know that we can achieve the objectives of our struggle. The principal goal is the people. We have to think about the people before we think about ourselves — that is the only attitude that can be defined as truly revolutionary. It is for those who cannot or do not have such an attitude, but who are honest people, that this problem exists. And just as the revolution constitutes a problem for them, they constitute a problem the revolution should be concerned about.

The case was well made here that there are many writers and artists who are not revolutionaries, but who are nevertheless sincere writers and artists. It was stated that they wanted to help the revolution, and that the revolution is interested in their help; that they wanted to work for the revolution and that for its part, the revolution had an interest in them contributing their knowledge and efforts on its behalf.

It is easier to appreciate this by analyzing specific cases, and some of these are difficult. A Catholic writer spoke here, raising problems that concerned him and he spoke with great clarity. He asked if he would be able to write on a particular question from his ideological point of view, or if he would be able to write a work defending that point of view. He asked quite frankly if, within a revolutionary system, he could express himself in accordance with his beliefs. He thus posed the problem in a way that might be considered symptomatic.

He wanted to know if he could write in accordance with those beliefs or that ideology, which is not exactly the ideology of the revolution. He was in agreement with the revolution on economic and social questions, but his philosophical position was different from that of the revolution. It is worth keeping this case in mind, because it is representative of the type of writers and artists who demonstrate a favorable attitude toward the revolution, and wish to know what degree of freedom they have within the revolution to express themselves in accordance with their beliefs.

This is the sector that constitutes a problem for the revolution, just as the revolution constitutes a problem for them. It is the duty of the revolution to concern itself with these cases. It is the duty of the revolution to concern itself with the situation of these artists and writers, because the revolution should strive to have more than just the revolutionaries march alongside it, and more than just the revolutionary artists and intellectuals.

It is possible that women and men who have a truly revolutionary attitude toward reality are not the majority of the population. Revolutionaries are the vanguard of the people, but revolutionaries should strive to have all the people march alongside them. The revolution cannot renounce the goal of having all honest men and women, whether or not they are writers and artists, march alongside it. The revolution should strive to convert everyone who has doubts into revolutionaries. The revolution should try to win over the majority of the people to its ideas. The revolution should never give up relying on the majority of the people. It must rely not only on the revolutionaries, but on all honest citizens who, although they may not be revolutionaries—who may not have a revolutionary attitude toward life—are with the revolution. The revolution should turn its back only on those who are incorrigible reactionaries, who are incorrigible counter-revolutionaries.

The revolution must have a policy and a stance toward this sector of the population, this sector of intellectuals and writers. The revolution has to understand this reality and should act in such a way that these artists and intellectuals who are not genuine revolutionaries can find a space within the revolution where they can work and create. Even though they are not revolutionary writers and artists, they should have the opportunity and freedom to express their creative spirit within the revolution.

In other words: Within the revolution, everything; against the revolution, nothing. Against the revolution, nothing, because the revolution also has its rights, and the first right of the revolution is the right to exist, and no one can oppose the revolution's right to exist. Inasmuch as the revolution embodies the interests of the people, inasmuch as the revolution symbolizes the interests of the whole nation, no one can justly claim a right to oppose it.

I believe that this is quite clear. What are the rights of writers and artists, revolutionary or nonrevolutionary? Within the revolution, everything; against the revolution, there are no rights.

This is not some special law or guideline for artists and writers. It is a general principle for all citizens. It is a fundamental principle of the revolution. Counterrevolutionaries, that is, the enemies of the revolution, have no rights against the revolution, because the revolution has one right: the right to exist, the right to develop, and the right to be victorious. Who can cast doubt on that right, the right of a people who have said, "*Patria o muerte!*" [Homeland or death!], that is, revolution or death.

The existence of the revolution, or nothing. This is a revolution that has said, "*Venceremos!*" [We will win!]. It has very seriously stated its intention. And as much as one may respect the personal reasons of an enemy of the revolution, the rights and the welfare of a revolution must be respected more. This is even more true in light of the revolution being a historical process, inasmuch as a revolution is not and cannot be the product of a whim or of the will of a single individual. A revolution can only be the product of the needs and the will of the people. In the face of the rights of an entire people, the rights of the enemies of the people do not count.

We speak of extreme cases only in order to express our ideas more clearly. I have already said that among those extreme cases there is a great variety of attitudes and there is also a great variety of concerns. To hold a particular concern does not necessarily signify that one is not a revolutionary. We have tried to define basic attitudes.

The revolution cannot seek to stifle art or culture since one of the goals and fundamental aims of the revolution is to develop art and culture, precisely so that art and culture truly become the patrimony of the people. Just as we want a better life for the people in the material sense, so too do we want a better life for the people in a spiritual and cultural sense. Just as the revolution is concerned with the development of conditions that will let the people satisfy all their material needs, so too do we want to develop conditions that will permit the people to satisfy all their cultural needs.

Do our people have a low cultural level? Do a high percentage of the people not know how to read and write? A high percentage of our people have also known hunger, or live or have lived in very difficult conditions, in conditions of extreme poverty. A section of the population lacks a great many of the material goods they need, and we are trying to bring about conditions that will give those people access to all these material goods.

In the same way, we should bring about the necessary conditions so that works of culture reach the people. This does not mean that an artist has to sacrifice the artistic value of their creations, or the quality. It means that we all have to struggle so that the artist creates for the people, so that, in turn, the people's cultural level is raised and they draw nearer to the artist.

We cannot establish a general rule. All artistic expressions are not exactly the same, and at times we have spoken here as if that were the case. There are expressions of the creative spirit that by their very nature are much more accessible to the people than other manifestations of the creative spirit. Therefore it is impossible to establish a general rule. What type of expression should the artist follow in an effort to reach the people, and in what ways will the people draw nearer to the artist? Can we make a general statement about this? No, it would be an oversimplification. It is necessary to strive to reach the people with all creative expressions, but at the same time it is necessary to do everything we can to enable the people to understand more and to understand better. I believe that this principle does not conflict with the aspirations of any artist — and much less so if it is kept in mind that people should create for their contemporaries.

Don't say that there are artists who create only for posterity, because without considering our judgment infallible, I believe that anyone proceeding on this assumption is deluding themselves. That is not to say that artists who work for their contemporaries have to renounce posterity, because it is precisely by creating for one's contemporaries — whether or not one's contemporaries understand them — that works acquire historic and universal value. We are not making a revolution for the generations to come, we are making a revolution with this generation and for this generation, independently of the fact that it benefits future generations and may become a historic event. We are not making a revolution for posterity; this revolution will be important to posterity because it is a revolution for today, and for the men and women of today.

Who would support us if we were making a revolution for future generations? We are working and creating for our contemporaries, without depriving any artistic endeavor of its aspiration to eternal fame.

These are truths that we should all analyze with honesty. And I believe it is necessary to start from certain basic truths in order to avoid false conclusions. We do not see how any honest artist or writer has reason for concern.

We are not enemies of freedom. No one here is an enemy of freedom. Whom do we fear? What authority do we fear will stifle our creativity? Do we fear our compañeros in the National Council of Culture? In talks we have held with members of the National Council of Culture we have observed feelings and viewpoints that are far removed from the concerns expressed here about limitations, straitjackets and so on, imposed on creativity.

Our conclusion is that the compañeros of the National Council of Culture are as concerned as all of you are about achieving the best conditions for the development of creative work by artists and intellectuals. It is the duty of the revolution and the revolutionary government to see that there is a highly qualified agency that can be relied upon to stimulate, encourage, develop and guide—yes, guide—that creative spirit; we consider it a duty. Does this perhaps constitute an infringement on the rights of writers and artists? Does this constitute a threat to the rights of writers and artists, implying that there will be arbitrary measures or an excess of authority? It would be the same as being afraid that the police will attack us when we pass a traffic light. It would be the same as being afraid that a judge will condemn or sentence us, the same as being afraid that the forces of the revolutionary power will commit some act of violence against us.

In other words, we would then have to worry about all these things. And yet our citizens do not believe that the militia is going to fire at them, that the judge is going to punish them, that the state power is going to use violence against them.

The existence of an authority in the cultural sector does not mean that there is any reason to worry about that authority being abused. Does anyone think that such a cultural authority should not exist? By the same token, one could think that the militia should not exist, that the police should not exist, that the state power should not exist, and even that the state should not exist. And if anyone is so anxious for the disappearance of the slightest trace of state authority, then let them stop worrying, be patient, for the day will come when the state will not exist either.

There has to be a council that guides, that stimulates, that develops, that works to create the best conditions for the work of the artists and intellectuals. What organization is the best defender of the interests of the artists and intellectuals if not this very council? What organization has proposed laws and suggested various measures to improve those conditions, if not the National Council of Culture? What organization proposed a law to create the National Printing House to remedy the deficiencies that have been pointed out here? What organization proposed the creation of the Institute of Ethnology and Folklore, if not the National Council of Culture? What organization has advocated the allocation of the funds and the foreign currency necessary for importing books that had not entered the country in many months; for buying material so that painters and plastic artists can work? What organization has concerned itself with the economic problems, that is, with the material conditions of the artists? What organization has concerned itself with a whole range of current needs of writers and artists? What organization has defended within the government the budgets, the buildings and the projects directed at improving your working conditions? That organization is none other than the National Council of Culture.

Why should anyone view that council with suspicion? Why should anyone fear that it will use its authority to do exactly the opposite: limit our conditions, stifle our creativity?

It is conceivable that some people who have had no problems at all are concerned about that authority. But those who appreciate the necessity of all the steps the council has had to take, and all the work it has to do, can never look at it with suspicion, because the council also has an obligation to the people and it has an obligation to the revolution and to the revolutionary government. And that obligation is to fulfill the objectives for which it was created, and it has as much interest in the success of its work as each artist has in their own success.

I don't know if I have failed to touch on some of the fundamental questions that were raised here. There was much discussion on the question of the film ["Pasado Meridiano" or "PM" by Cuban filmmakers Orlando Jiménez and Sabá Cabrera]. I have not seen the film, although I want to see it. I am curious to see it. Was the film dealt with unfairly? In fact, I believe that no film has received so many honors or been discussed so much.

Although I have not seen that movie, I have heard the opinions of compañeros who have seen it, including the president and various members of the National Council of Culture. At the very least, their opinion, their judgment, merits respect from us all. But there is one thing I believe cannot be disputed, and that is the right established by law to exercise the function that was exercised in this case by the Film Institute or the Review Board. Perhaps that right of the government is being disputed? Does the government have the right to exercise that function or not? For us, what is fundamental in this case is, above all, to determine if the government did or did not have that right. The question of procedure could be discussed, as it was, to determine if it was fair or not, if another, more amicable procedure would have been better, if the decision was just or not. But there is one thing I believe no one can dispute, and that is the government's right to exercise that function. For if we challenge that right, then it would mean that the government does not have the right to review the films that are going to be shown to the people.

I believe this is a right that cannot be disputed. There is, in addition, something that we all understand perfectly, and this is that some intellectual or artistic creations are more important than others as far as the education or the ideological development of the people is concerned. I don't believe anyone can disagree that among the most fundamental and highly important media is the cinema, as well as television. Now, in the midst of the revolution, can anyone challenge the government's right to regulate, review and supervise the films that are shown to the people? Is this, perhaps, what is being disputed?

Can the revolutionary government's right to supervise the mass media that influence the people so much be considered a limitation or a prohibition? If we were to challenge that right of the revolutionary government, we would be faced with a problem of principle, because to deny that right to the revolutionary government would be to deny the government's function and responsibility, especially in the midst of a revolutionary struggle, in leading the people and leading the revolution. At times, it has seemed that this right of the government was being challenged; and in response, we state our opinion that the government does have such a right. And if it has that right, it can make use of that right. It can make mistakes; we are not pretending that the government is infallible. The government, in exercising its right or its functions, is not required to be infallible. But can anyone be so skeptical, so suspicious, and so distrustful toward the revolutionary government that in believing one decision is wrong, they are terror-stricken that the government might always be wrong?

I am not suggesting the government was mistaken in that decision. What I am saying is that the government exercised its right. I am trying to put myself in the place of those who worked on that film. I am trying to put myself in their state of mind, and I am even trying to understand their sorrow, unhappiness and pain when the film was not shown. That is perfectly understandable. But one must understand that the government acted within its rights. This judgment had the support of competent and responsible members of the government, and there is no reason for distrusting the spirit of justice and fairness of the members of the revolutionary government, because the revolutionary government has given no cause for anyone to doubt its spirit of justice and fairness.

We should not think that we are perfect, we should not even think that we are free of subjectivity. Some people might point out that certain compañeros in the government are subjective, or not free of subjectivity. Can those who believe this assure us that they themselves are completely free of subjectivity?

Can they accuse some compañeros of holding subjective views without accepting the fact that their own opinions might also be influenced by subjective factors? Let us state here that whoever feels themselves perfect or free from subjectivity should cast the first stone.

I believe there has been a personal and emotional element in the discussion. Hasn't there been a personal and emotional element in the discussion? Did absolutely everyone come here free of emotionalism and subjectivity? Did absolutely everyone come here free of any group spirit? Are there no currents and tendencies within this discussion? There undoubtedly are. If a six-year-old child had been seated here, he or she too would have noticed the different currents and viewpoints, the different emotions that were confronting one another.

People here have said many things. They have said interesting things. Some have said brilliant things. Everyone has been very "erudite." But, above all, there has been a reality, the reality of the discussion itself and the freedom with which everyone has been able to express themselves and defend their point of view. The freedom with which everyone has been able to speak and explain their views in the midst of a large meeting, which has grown larger by the day, a meeting that we consider positive, where we have been able to dispel a whole series of doubts and worries. Have there been quarrels? Undoubtedly. Have there been battles and skirmishes here among the writers and artists? Undoubtedly. Has there been criticism and supercriticism? Undoubtedly. Have some compañeros tried out their weapons at the expense of other compañeros? Undoubtedly.

The wounded have spoken here, expressing their complaints at what they consider unjust attacks. Fortunately, we've had no dead, only wounded, including compañeros who are still convalescing from their wounds. And some of them presented as a clear case of injustice the fact that they had been attacked with high-caliber artillery without ever having had the chance to return fire. Have harsh criticisms been made? Undoubtedly!

In a certain sense a problem has been raised here that we are not going to pretend to be able to address in a few words. But I believe that among the things said here, one of the most correct is that the spirit of criticism should be constructive; it should be positive and not destructive. That's what we believe. But, in general, that is not kept in mind. For some, the word "criticism" has become a synonym for "attack," when it really means nothing of the sort. When they tell someone, "So-and-so criticized you," the person gets angry before even asking what was really said. In other words, he or she assumes they were torn apart.

If those of us who have been somewhat removed from these problems or struggles — these skirmishes and weapons tests — were told about the cases of certain compañeros who have almost been on the verge of deep depression because of devastating criticism leveled against them, it is quite possible that we would sympathize with the victims, because we have a tendency to sympathize with victims. We who sincerely want only to contribute to an understanding and unity among everyone have tried to avoid words that could wound or discourage anyone.

One thing is unquestionable, however: There may have been struggles or controversies in which conditions have not been equal for everyone. From the point of view of the revolution, this cannot be fair. The revolution should not give weapons to some to be used against others. We believe that writers and artists should have every opportunity to express themselves. We believe that writers and artists, through their association, should have a broad cultural magazine open to all. Doesn't it seem to you this would be a fair solution? But the revolution cannot put those resources in the hands of one particular group. The revolution can and should marshal those resources in such a manner that they can be widely utilized by all writers and artists.

You will shortly constitute an association of writers and artists [UNEAC] at the congress you will attend. That congress should be held in a truly constructive spirit, and we are confident that you are capable of holding it in that spirit. From that congress will emerge a strong association of writers and artists where everyone who has a truly constructive spirit can take part. If anyone thinks we wish to eliminate them, if anyone thinks we want to stifle them, we can give assurances that they are absolutely mistaken.

Now is the time for you to contribute in an organized way and with all your enthusiasm to the tasks corresponding to you in the revolution, and to constitute a broad organization of all writers and artists. I don't know if the questions that have been raised here will be discussed at the congress, but we know that the congress is going to meet, and that its work — as well as the work to be done by the association of writers and artists — will be good topics for discussion at our next meeting.

We believe that we should meet again; at least, we don't want to deprive ourselves of the pleasure and usefulness of these meetings, which have served to focus our attention on all these questions. We have to meet again. What does that mean? That we have to continue discussing these questions. In other words, everyone can rest assured that the government is greatly interested in these questions, and that the future will hold ample opportunity for discussing all these questions at large meetings. It seems to us that this should be a source of satisfaction for writers and artists, and we, too, look forward to acquiring more information and knowledge.

The National Council of Culture should also have an information agency. I think that this is putting things in their proper place. It cannot be called cultural imposition or a stifling of artistic creativity. What true artist with all his or her senses could think that this constitutes a stifling of creativity? The revolution wants artists to exert the maximum effort on behalf of the people. It wants them to put the maximum interest and effort into revolutionary work. We believe this is a just aspiration of the revolution.

Does this mean that we are going to tell the people here what they have to write? No. Everyone should write what they want, and if what they write is no good, that's their problem. If what they paint is no good, that's their problem. We do not prohibit anyone from writing on the topic they prefer. On the contrary, everyone should express themselves in the form they consider best, and they should express freely the idea they want to express. We will always evaluate a person's creation from the revolutionary point of view. That is also the right of the revolutionary government, which should be respected in the same way that the right of each person to express what he or she wants to express should be respected.

A series of measures are being taken, some of which we have mentioned. We wish to inform those who were concerned about the question of the National Printing House that a law is under consideration to regulate its functions, to create various editorial divisions in line with different publishing needs and to overcome the deficiencies existing at present. The National Printing House is a recently created organization that has emerged under difficult conditions. It had to begin working in the offices of a newspaper that was closed suddenly (we were present the day that newspaper plant became the largest print shop in the country, with all its workers and editors), and it had to carry out the publication of urgently needed works, including many of a military nature. The National Printing House does have deficiencies, but these will be remedied. There will be no grounds for complaints such as those expressed here, in this meeting, about the National Printing House. Measures are also being taken to acquire books, to acquire work materials, that is, to resolve all the problems that have concerned writers and artists and which the National Council of Culture has repeatedly pointed to. For as you know, the state has different departments and different institutions and, within the state, each body seeks to have the resources necessary for doing its job well. We want to point to some areas where we have already advanced, areas that should be sources of encouragement for all of us.

One example is the success achieved by the Symphony Orchestra, which has been completely reorganized. Not only has it reached a high level in the artistic sense, but also in the revolutionary sense, for there are now 50 members of the Symphony Orchestra who belong to the militia.

The Cuban Ballet has also been rebuilt and has just made a tour abroad, where it won admiration and recognition in all the countries it visited.

The Modern Dance Group has also been quite successful, and has been highly praised in Europe.

The National Library, for its part, is working hard on behalf of culture. It is engaged in awakening the interest of the people in music and painting. It has set up an art department with the objective of making fine paintings known to the people. It has a music department, a young people's department, and a children's section.

Shortly before coming here, we visited the children's department of the National Library. We saw the number of children who were there, the work that is being done there. The progress made by the National Library is a motivation for the government to provide it with the means necessary for continuing this work.

The National Printing House is now a reality, and with its new form of organization, it is also a victory for the revolution that will contribute mightily to the education of the people.

The Cuban Film Institute [ICAIC] is also a reality. The first stage has consisted chiefly in supplying it with necessary equipment and materials. The revolution has established at least the foundation of a film industry. This has required a great effort, if it is kept in mind that ours is not an industrialized country and that the acquisition of all this equipment has meant sacrifices. Any lack of facilities for the cinema is not due to a restrictive government policy, but simply to the scarcity of economic resources at present for creating a movement of film enthusiasts that would permit the development of all cinematic talent when the resources are available. For its part the Cuban Film Institute's policy will be the object of discussion, and of emulation among the various work teams. It is not yet possible to assess the work of ICAIC itself. The film institute has not yet had time to do enough work to be judged, but it has been working hard, and we know that a number of its documentaries have contributed greatly to making the revolution known abroad. But what we should emphasize is that the foundation for the film industry has already been laid.

There has also been cultural work done in the form of publicity, lectures, and so on, sponsored by different agencies. However, this is nothing compared to what can be done and what the revolution aims to do.

There are still many questions to resolve that are of interest to writers and artists. There are problems of a material nature, in other words, of an economic order. Yesterday's conditions do not exist now. Today there is no longer a small privileged class to buy the works of artists—although at miserable prices, to be sure, since more than one artist died in poverty and neglect. These problems remain to be confronted and solved, and the revolutionary government should solve them. The National Council of Culture should be concerned with them, too, as well as with the problem of artists who no longer produce and are left completely abandoned. Artists should be guaranteed not only adequate material conditions for the present, but security for the future. In a certain sense, now, with the reorganization of the Institute of Royalty Payments, the living conditions of a great number of authors, who were miserably exploited and whose rights were scorned, have improved considerably. Today, authors, many of whom used to live in extreme poverty, have incomes that permit them to escape from that situation.

These are steps that the revolution has taken; but they are only preliminary steps. They will be followed by other steps that will create still better conditions.

There is also the idea of organizing a place where artists and writers can rest and work. Once, when we were traveling throughout the whole national territory, the idea occurred to us in a very beautiful place, on the Isle of Pines, to build a community in the middle of a pine forest, where we could send prize-winning writers and artists (at that time we were thinking about establishing some sort of prize for the best progressive writers and artists of the world). That project did not materialize, but it can be revived and a place can be created in some peaceful haven that facilitates rest, that facilitates writing. I believe that it is worthwhile for artists, and architects as well, to begin thinking of and planning the ideal retreat for writers and artists, and to see if they can agree. The revolutionary government is ready to contribute its share to the budget, now that everything is planned.

Will such planning be a limitation imposed by us revolutionaries on the creative spirit? Don't forget that we revolutionaries have been improvising a bit, and are now faced with the reality of planning. That presents a problem to us too, because until now we have had a creative spirit toward revolutionary initiatives and revolutionary investments, which are now part of a plan. So don't think we are exempt from the problem, for we could protest too. In other words, now that we know what is going to be done next year, the following year, and the year after that, who is going to dispute the fact that economic planning is necessary? But the construction of a retreat for writers and artists fits in with that plan. Truly, it would be a source of satisfaction for the revolution to accomplish this project.

We have been concerned here with the present situation of writers and artists. We have overlooked future perspectives to some degree. And we, who have no reason to grumble about you, have also spent a moment thinking about the artists and writers of the future. We wondered what it would be like if the members of the government—not us necessarily—and the artists and the writers were to meet again, as they should, in the future, in five or 10 years, when culture has achieved the extraordinary development we hope it will achieve, when the first fruits of the present educational and training programs begin to appear.

Long before these questions were raised, the revolutionary government was already concerned about the extension of culture to the people. We have always been very optimistic. I believe that it is not possible to be a revolutionary without being an optimist, because the difficulties that a revolution has to surmount are very serious, and one has to be an optimist. A pessimist can never be a revolutionary.

The revolution has had various stages. There was a stage when different agencies took the initiative in the field of culture. Even INRA [National Institute of Agrarian Reform] was conducting activities of a cultural nature. There was even a clash with the National Theater, because certain work was being done there and suddenly we were off doing other work on our own. Now all that is within one organization.

In connection with our plans for the peasants in the cooperatives and state farms, the idea arose of extending culture into the countryside, to the state farms and cooperatives. How? By training music, dance and drama instructors. Only optimists can take initiatives like that. So how were we to awaken love for the theater, for example, among the peasants? Where were the instructors? Where would we get instructors to send to 3,000 state farms and 600 cooperatives, for example? All this presents difficulties, but I am certain that you will all agree that if this is achieved it will be a positive accomplishment. Above all, it will be a start in discovering talents among the people and transforming the people from participants into creators, for ultimately it is the people who are the great creators. We should not forget this, and neither should we forget the thousands and thousands of creative talents lost in our countryside and cities due to lack of conditions and lack of opportunity to develop. Many talents have been lost in our countryside — of that we are sure — unless we presume ourselves to be the most intelligent people ever born in this country, and I want to say that I presume no such thing.

I have often given as an example the fact that of several thousand children in the place where I was born, I was the only one who was able to study at the university — study poorly to be sure. And I first had to attend a number of schools run by priests, and so on. I don't want to anathematize anyone, although I do want to say that I have the same right as anyone here to say what I please, to complain. I have the right to complain. Someone spoke of the fact that he was molded by bourgeois society. I can say that I was molded by something even worse, that I was molded by the worst reactionaries, and that a good many years of my life were lost in obscurantism, superstition and lies.

That was the time when you were not taught how to think, but forced to believe. I am of the opinion that when a human being's ability to think and reason is impaired, that human being is transformed into a domesticated animal. I am not challenging anyone's religious beliefs; we respect those beliefs, we respect the right to freedom of belief and religion. But they did not respect my right to this freedom. I had no freedom of belief or religion. On the contrary, they imposed a belief and a religion on me and domesticated me for 12 years.

Naturally I have to speak with an element of grievance about those years, the years when young people have the greatest interest and curiosity about everything, years I could have employed in systematic study that would have enabled me to acquire the culture that the children of Cuba today are going to have every opportunity to acquire.

With all that, only one in a thousand could get a university degree and that person had to bear that millstone where only by a miracle was his mind not crushed forever. The one person in a thousand had to go through all that. Why? Because he was the only one of a thousand who could afford to study at a private school. Now, am I to believe that I was the most capable and intelligent of the thousand? I believe that we are a product of selection, but not natural selection so much as social. I was selected to go to the university by a process of social selection, not natural selection. Who knows how many tens of thousands of young people, superior to us all, have been left in ignorance by social selection. That is the truth. And whoever thinks of themselves as an artist should remember that there are many people, better than they are, who were unable to become artists. If we do not admit this, we are avoiding reality. We are privileged, among other things, because our fathers were not wagon drivers. What I have said shows the enormous number of talented minds that have been lost simply through lack of opportunity.

We are going to bring opportunity to all those minds; we are going to create the conditions that permit all talent — artistic, literary, scientific or otherwise — to develop. Think about the significance of a revolution that permits such a thing. As of right now, we have already begun teaching everyone to read and write, and we will have accomplished this by the next school term. Add to this the creation of schools everywhere in Cuba, educational advancement campaigns, and the training of teachers, and we will be able to discover and bring to light every talent.

And this is only the beginning. All the teachers in the country will learn to recognize which child has a special talent, and will recommend which child should be given a scholarship to the National Academy of Art, and at the same time they will awaken artistic taste and love for culture among adults. Some trials have been made to demonstrate the capacity of peasants and common people to assimilate artistic questions, to assimilate culture and immediately begin to produce it. There are compañeros who have been at some cooperatives that now have their own theater groups. Recent performances in various parts of the republic, and the artistic works of ordinary men and women, demonstrate the interest of the people of the countryside in all these things. Imagine, then, what it will mean when we have drama, music and dance instructors at each cooperative and each state farm.

In the course of only two years, we will be able to send 1,000 instructors, from each one of these fields, more than 1,000 in drama, dance and music.

The schools have been organized. They are already functioning. Imagine when there will be 1,000 dance, music and drama groups throughout the island, in the countryside — we are not speaking of the city, it is somewhat easier in the city. Imagine what that will mean for cultural advancement, because some have spoken here of the need to raise the level of the people.

But how? The revolutionary government is concerned about this question, and it is creating conditions so that within a few years the people's level of culture will have been raised tremendously.

We have selected those three branches, but we can continue selecting other branches and we can continue working to develop all aspects of culture.

The school of art instructors is already functioning, and the compañeros who work there are satisfied with the progress of that group of future instructors. In addition, we have already begun to construct the National Academy of Art, separate from the National Academy of Manual Arts. Cuba is certainly going to have the most beautiful Academy of Art in the world. Why? Because that academy is going to be located in one of the most beautiful residential districts of the world, where the section of the bourgeoisie of Cuba living in the greatest luxury used to reside, in the best district of that section of the bourgeoisie that was the most ostentatious, the most luxurious, and the most uncultured—let me say this in passing, because none of those houses lacked a bar, but with few exceptions their inhabitants did not concern themselves with cultural questions. They lived in an incredibly luxurious manner, and it is worthwhile to take a trip there to see how these people lived. But they didn't know that one day an extraordinary Academy of Art would be built there, and this is what will remain of what they built, because the students are going to live in their homes, the homes of millionaires. They will not live sheltered lives, they will live in a home-like atmosphere, and they will attend classes in the academy. The academy is going to be located in the middle of the Country Club district, and it will be designed by a group of architects and artists. They have already begun work, and they are committed to finishing by December. We already have 300,000 feet of mahogany. The schools of music, ballet, theater and plastic arts will be in the middle of a golf course, in a dreamlike setting. This is where the Academy of Art will be located, with 60 houses surrounding it, with a social center, dining rooms, lounges, swimming pools, and also a building for visitors, where the foreign teachers who are coming to assist us can live. This academy will have a capacity of up to 3,000 children, that is, 3,000 scholarship students. We expect it to start operating in the next school year.

The National Academy of Manual Arts will also begin functioning soon.

It, too, has another group of houses for students to live in, another golf course, and a type of construction similar to the others. These academies will be national in character. This does not mean in any way that they are the only schools, but that the young people who show the greatest ability will receive scholarships to go there, costing their families absolutely nothing. These youth and children are going to have ideal conditions for developing their abilities. Anybody would want to be a child now, to attend one of those academies. Isn't that so? We spoke here of painters who used to live off *café con leche* alone. Just imagine how different conditions will be now, and we will see if the ideal conditions for developing the creative spirit are not found. Instruction, housing, food, general education... There will be children who will begin to study in those schools at the age of eight, and along with artistic training, they will receive a general education. They will be able to fully develop their talents and their personalities.

These are more than ideas or dreams; these are the realities of the revolution. The instructors are being trained, the national schools are being organized, the schools for art appreciation are also being founded. This is what the revolution means. This is why the revolution is important for culture. How could we do this without a revolution? Let's suppose that we are afraid that "our creative spirit is going to whither or be crushed by the despotic hands of the Stalinist revolution."

Wouldn't it be better, ladies and gentlemen, to think about the future? Are we going to think about our flowers withering when we are planting flowers everywhere? When we are forging those creative spirits of the future? Who would not exchange the present, who would not exchange even their own present existence for that future? Who would not exchange what they have now? Who would not sacrifice what they have now for that future?

Doesn't someone with artistic sensibility also possess the spirit of the fighter who dies in battle, understanding that they are dying, that they are ceasing to exist physically, in order to enrich with their blood the triumph of their fellow beings, of their people? Think about the combatant who dies fighting, who sacrifices everything: life, family, wife, children. Why? So that we can do all these things. And what person with human sensibility, artistic sensibility, does not think that to do all that the sacrifice must be worthwhile? But the revolution is not asking sacrifices from those with creative genius; on the contrary, it says: Put that creative spirit at the service of the revolution, without fear that your work will be impaired. But if, some day, you think that your personal work may be impaired, then say: It is well worth it for my work to be impaired if it contributes to the great work before us.

We ask artists to develop their creative efforts to the fullest. We want to bring about the ideal conditions for artists and intellectuals to create, because if we are creating for the future, how can we not want the best for the artists and intellectuals of today? We are asking for maximum development on behalf of culture and, to be very precise, on behalf of the revolution, because the revolution means precisely more culture and more art.

We ask intellectuals and artists to do their share in the work that is, after all, the work of this generation. The coming generation will be better than ours, but we will be the ones who will have made that better generation possible. We will be the ones to shape that future generation. We, the members of this generation, whether young or old, beardless or bearded, with an abundant head of hair, or no hair, or with white hair. This is the work of us all. We are going to wage a war against ignorance. We are going to wage a great battle against ignorance. We are going to unleash a merciless fight against ignorance, and we are going to test our weapons.

Is there anyone who doesn't want to collaborate? What greater punishment is there than to deprive oneself of the satisfaction that others are getting? We spoke of the fact that we were privileged. We learned to read and write in a primary school, went to secondary school, to university, to acquire at least the rudiments of education, enough to enable us to do something. Shouldn't we consider ourselves privileged to be living in the midst of a revolution? Haven't we read about other revolutions with great interest. Who has not avidly read the histories of the French revolution, of the Russian revolution? Who has never dreamed of witnessing those revolutions personally? In my own case, for example, when I read about the Cuban War of Independence, I regretted that I had not been born in that period and that I had not been a fighter for independence and had not lived through that epic time. All of us have read the chronicles of our War of Independence with deep-felt emotion, and we envied the intellectuals and artists and fighters and leaders of that time.

However, we have the privilege of living now and being eyewitnesses to a genuine revolution, to a revolution whose strength is now developing beyond the borders of our country, whose political and moral influence is making imperialism on this continent tremble and stagger. The Cuban revolution has become the most important event of this century for Latin America, the most important event since the wars of independence of the 19th century. In truth, the redemption of humanity is something new, for what were those wars of independence but the replacement of colonial domination by the domination of ruling and exploiting classes in all those countries?

It has fallen to us to live during a great, historic event. It can be said that this is the second great, historic event that has occurred in the last three centuries in Latin America. And we Cubans are active participants, knowing that the more we work, the more the revolution will become an inextinguishable flame, the more it will be called upon to play a transcendental role in history. You writers and artists have had the privilege of being living witnesses to this revolution. And a revolution is such an important event in human history that it is well worth living through, if only as a witness. That, too, is a privilege.

Therefore, those who are incapable of understanding these things, those who let themselves be tricked, let themselves be confused, those who let themselves become perplexed by lies, are renouncing the revolution. What can we say about those who have renounced it? How can we think of them but with sorrow? They have abandoned this country, in full revolutionary effervescence, to crawl into the belly of the imperialist monster, where no expression of the spirit can have any life. They have abandoned the revolution to go there. They have preferred to be fugitives and deserters from their homeland rather than remain here even if only as spectators.

You have the opportunity to be more than spectators, you can be actors in the revolution, writing about it, expressing yourselves about it. And the generations to come, what will they ask of you? You might produce magnificent artistic works from a technical point of view, but if you were to tell someone from the future generation, 100 years from now, that a writer, an intellectual, lived in the era of the revolution and did not write about the revolution, and was not a part of the revolution, it would be difficult for a person in the future to understand this. In the years to come there will be so many people who will want to paint about the revolution, to write about the revolution, to express themselves on the revolution, compiling data and information in order to know what it was like, what happened, how we used to live.

I recently had the experience of meeting an old woman, 106 years old, who had just learned to read and write, and I proposed to her that she write a book. She had been a slave, and I wanted to know what the world looked like to her as a slave, what her first impressions were of her life, of her masters, of her fellow slaves. I believe that this old woman could write something more interesting than any of us could about that era. It is possible that in a single year someone can learn to read and write, and then write a book, at 106 years of age. That's what happens in a revolution! Who can write about what a slave endured better than she can?

And who can write about the present better than you? How many people who have not lived through the present will begin to write in the future, at a distance, selecting material from other writings?

On the other hand, let us not hasten to judge our work, since we will have more than enough judges. What we have to fear is not some imaginary, authoritarian judge, a cultural executioner. Other judges far more severe should be feared: the judges of posterity, of the generations to come. When all is said and done, they will be the ones to have the last word!

6. MANIFESTO FOR THE LIBERATION OF THE AMERICAS: "THE SECOND DECLARATION OF HAVANA"

HAVANA, FEBRUARY 4, 1962

In August 1960, at Washington's instigation, 19 of the 21 Organization of American States (OAS) members meeting in San José, Costa Rica, voted to censure Cuba for not rejecting aid from the Soviet Union and China. In response, a mass rally in Havana on September 2, 1960, adopted the "Declaration of Havana." After Cuba was finally expelled from the OAS at a meeting in Punta del Este, Uruguay, in January 1962, and after Washington imposed a blockade on the island in February, another mass assembly took place in Havana, where Fidel Castro read this "Second Declaration of Havana," asserting the right of the peoples of the Americas to sovereignty and independence.

From the people of Cuba to the peoples of the Americas and the world:

On May 18, 1895, on the eve of his death from a Spanish bullet through the heart, José Martí, the Apostle of our independence, wrote in an unfinished letter to his friend Manuel Mercado:

> Now I am able to write... I am in danger each day now of giving my life for my country and for my duty... of preventing the United States, as Cuba obtains her independence, from extending its control over the Antilles and consequently falling with that much more force on the

countries of our America. Whatever I have done so far, and whatever I will do, has been for that purpose...

The nations most vitally concerned in preventing the imperialist annexation of Cuba, which would make Cuba the starting point of that course—which must be blocked and which we are blocking with our blood—of the annexation of our American nations to the violent and brutal north that despises them, are being hindered by lesser and public commitments from the open and avowed espousal of this sacrifice, which is being made for our and their benefit.

I have lived inside the monster and know its entrails; and my sling is David's.

In 1895, Martí had already pointed out the danger hovering over the Americas and called imperialism by its name: imperialism. He pointed out to the people of Latin America that more than anyone, they had a stake in seeing to it that Cuba did not succumb to the greed of the Yankees, scornful of the peoples of Latin America. And with his own blood, shed for Cuba and Latin America, he wrote the words that posthumously, in homage to his memory, the people of Cuba place at the top of this declaration.

Sixty-seven years have passed. Puerto Rico was converted into a colony and is still a colony burdened with military bases. Cuba also fell into the clutches of imperialism, whose troops occupied our territory. The Platt Amendment was imposed on our first constitution, as a humiliating clause that sanctioned the odious right of foreign intervention. Our riches passed into their hands, our history was falsified, and our government and our politics were entirely molded in the interests of the overseers. The nation was subjected to 60 years of political, economic and cultural suffocation.

But Cuba rose up. Cuba was able to redeem itself from the bastard tutelage. Cuba broke the chains that tied its fortunes to those of the imperial oppressor, redeemed its riches, reclaimed its culture, and unfurled its banner of Free Territory and People of the Americas.

Now the United States will never again be able to use Cuba's strength against the Americas. Conversely, the United States, dominating the majority of the other Latin American states, is attempting to use the strength of the Americas against Cuba.

The history of Cuba is but the history of Latin America. The history of Latin America is but the history of Asia, Africa and Oceania. And the history of all these peoples is but the history of the most pitiless and cruel exploitation by imperialism throughout the world.

By the end of the last and the beginning of the present century, a handful of economically developed nations had finished partitioning the world among themselves, subjecting to their economic and political domination two-thirds of humanity, which was thus forced to work for the ruling classes of the economically advanced capitalist countries.

The historical circumstances that permitted a high level of industrial development to certain European countries and the United States placed them in a position to subject the rest of the world to their domination and exploitation.

What were the compelling motives behind the expansion of the industrial powers? Were they reasons of morality and civilization as they claim? No, the reasons were economic.

From the discovery of the Americas, which hurled the European conquerors across the seas to occupy and exploit the lands and inhabitants of other continents, the fundamental motive for their conduct was the desire for riches. The discovery of the Americas was carried out in search of shorter routes to the Orient, whose goods were highly paid for in Europe.

A new social class, the merchants and the producers of manufactured articles for commerce, arose from the womb of the feudal society of lords and serfs in the decline of the Middle Ages.

The thirst for gold was the cause that spurred the efforts of that new class. The desire for gain has been the incentive of its conduct throughout history. With the growth of manufacturing and commerce, its social influence also grew. The new productive forces that were developing in the womb of feudal society clashed more and more with feudalism's relations of servitude, its laws, its institutions, its philosophy, its morality, its art and its political ideology.

New philosophical and political ideas, new concepts of rights and of the state were proclaimed by the intellectual representatives of the bourgeois class, which—because they responded to the new necessities of social life—gradually entered into the consciousness of the exploited masses. At that time, these were revolutionary ideas opposed to the worn-out ideas of feudal society. The peasants, the artisans, the workers in manufacturing, led by the bourgeoisie, overthrew the feudal order, its philosophy, its ideas, its institutions, its laws and the privileges of the ruling class, that is, the hereditary nobility.

At that time, the bourgeoisie considered revolution necessary and just. It did not think that the feudal order could and should be eternal — as it now thinks its capitalist social order is.

It encouraged the peasants to free themselves from feudal servitude; it encouraged the artisans to rebel against the medieval guilds and demanded the right to political power. The absolute monarchs, the nobility and the high clergy stubbornly defended their class privileges, proclaiming the divine right of kings and the immutability of the social order. To be liberal, to proclaim the ideas of Voltaire, Diderot, or Jean-Jacques Rousseau, the spokespeople for bourgeois philosophy, at that time constituted, in the eyes of the ruling classes, as serious a crime as it is today in the eyes of the bourgeoisie to be a socialist and to proclaim the ideas of Marx, Engels and Lenin.

The bourgeoisie took political power and established on the ruins of feudal society its capitalist mode of production; and on the basis of this mode of production it erected its state, its laws, its ideas and its institutions. Those institutions sanctified, above everything, the essence of its class rule: private property.

The new society based on the private ownership of the means of production and free competition was thus divided into two basic classes: one, the owners of the means of production, ever more modern and efficient; and the other, those deprived of all wealth, possessing only their labor power, to be sold on the market as just another commodity simply in order to live.

With the feudal bonds broken, the productive forces developed extraordinarily fast. Great factories arose in which greater and greater numbers of workers were assembled.

The most modern and technically efficient factories continually displaced from the market the less efficient competitors. The cost of industrial equipment continually rose. It became necessary to accumulate more and more capital. A greater portion of production passed into a smaller number of hands. Thus arose the great capitalist enterprises and later, according to the degree and character of the association, the great industrial conglomerates through cartels, syndicates, trusts and corporations, controlled by the owners of the major portion of the stock, that is to say, by the most powerful heads of industry. Free trade, characteristic of capitalism in its first phase, gave way to monopolies, which entered into agreements among themselves and controlled the markets.

Where did the colossal quantity of resources come from that permitted a handful of monopolists to accumulate billions of dollars? Simply from the exploitation of human labor. Millions of people, forced to work for a wage of bare subsistence, produced with their strength the gigantic capital of the monopolies. The workers amassed the fortunes for the privileged classes, ever richer, ever more powerful. Through the banking institutions these classes were able to make use not only of their own money but that of society as a whole.

Thus came about the fusion of the banks with big industry, and finance capital was born. What could they do with the great surplus of capital that was accumulating in ever greater quantities? Invade the world with it. Always in pursuit of profit, they began to seize the natural resources of all the economically weak countries and to exploit the human labor of their inhabitants with much more wretched wages than what they were forced to pay the workers of their own developed countries. Thus began the territorial and economic division of the world. By 1914, eight or 10 imperialist countries had subjugated territories beyond their own borders, covering more than 83.7 million square kilometers, with a population of 970 million inhabitants. They had simply divided up the world.

But as the world, limited in size, was divided up to the very last corner of the earth, a clash ensued among the different monopolistic nations. Struggles arose for new divisions, originating in the disproportionate distribution of industrial and economic power that the various monopolistic nations had attained in their uneven development. Imperialist wars broke out that would cost humanity 50 million dead, tens of millions wounded, and the destruction of incalculable material and cultural wealth. Even before this had happened, Karl Marx had written, "capital comes into the world dripping from head to foot and from every pore with blood and dirt."

The capitalist system of production, once it had given all it was capable of giving, became an abysmal obstacle to the progress of humanity. But the bourgeoisie from its beginning carried within itself its antithesis. In its womb gigantic productive instruments were developed, but with time a new and vigorous social force developed: the proletariat, destined to change the old and worn-out social system of capitalism to a higher socioeconomic form in accordance with the historical possibilities of human society, converting into social property those gigantic means of production which the people — and no one else but the people — by their work had created and amassed. At such a stage of development of the productive forces, it became completely anachronistic and outmoded to have a regime based on private ownership and with it the economic subordination of millions and millions of human beings to the dictates of a small social minority.

The interests of humanity cried out for a halt to the anarchy of production, the waste, economic crises and the rapacious wars that are part of the capitalist system. The growing necessities of the human race, and the possibility of satisfying them, demanded the planned development of the economy and the rational utilization of its means of production and natural resources.

It was inevitable that imperialism and colonialism would experience a profound and insoluble crisis. The general crisis began with the outbreak of World War I, with the revolution of the workers and peasants that overthrew the czarist empire of Russia and founded, amid the most difficult conditions of capitalist encirclement and aggression, the world's first socialist state, opening a new era in the history of humanity. From that time until today, the crisis and decomposition of the imperialist system has steadily worsened.

World War II, unleashed by the imperialist powers — into which were dragged the Soviet Union and other criminally invaded peoples of Asia and Europe, who engaged in a bloody struggle of liberation — culminated in the defeat of fascism, the formation of the world camp of socialism and the struggle of the colonial and dependent peoples for their sovereignty. Between 1945 and 1957 more than 1.2 billion human beings conquered their independence in Asia and Africa. The blood shed by the people was not in vain.

The movement of the dependent and colonial peoples is a phenomenon of a universal character that agitates the world and marks the final crisis of imperialism.

Cuba and Latin America are part of the world. Our problems form part of the problems engendered by the general crisis of imperialism and the struggle of the subjugated peoples, the clash between the world that is being born and the world that is dying. The odious and brutal campaign unleashed against our nation expresses the desperate as well as futile effort that the imperialists are making to prevent the liberation of the peoples.

Cuba hurts the imperialists in a special way. What is hidden behind the Yankees' hatred of the Cuban revolution? What is it that rationally explains the conspiracy — uniting for the same aggressive purpose the richest and most powerful imperialist power in the contemporary world and the oligarchies of an entire continent, which together are supposed to represent a population of 350 million human beings — against a small country of only seven million inhabitants, economically underdeveloped, without financial or military means to threaten the security or economy of any other country?

What unites them and agitates them is fear. What explains it is fear. Not fear of the Cuban revolution but fear of the Latin American revolution. Not fear of the workers, peasants, intellectuals, students and progressive layers of the middle strata who by revolutionary means have taken power in Cuba; but fear that the workers, peasants, students, intellectuals and progressive sectors of the middle strata might take power by revolutionary means in the oppressed and hungry countries exploited by the Yankee monopolies and reactionary oligarchies of America; fear that the plundered people of the continent will seize the arms from their oppressors and, like Cuba, declare themselves free peoples of the Americas.

By crushing the Cuban revolution they hope to dispel the fear that torments them, the specter of revolution that threatens them. By liquidating the Cuban revolution, they hope to liquidate the revolutionary spirit of the people. They imagine in their delirium that Cuba is an exporter of revolutions. In their sleepless, merchants' and usurers' minds there is the idea that revolutions can be bought, sold, rented, loaned, exported and imported like some piece of merchandise. Ignorant of the objective laws that govern the development of human societies, they believe that their monopolistic, capitalistic and semi-feudal regimes are eternal. Educated in their own reactionary ideology, a mixture of superstition, ignorance, subjectivism, pragmatism and other mental aberrations, they have an image of the world and of the march of history that conforms to their interests as exploiting classes.

They imagine that revolutions are born or die in the brains of individuals or are caused by divine laws, and moreover that the gods are on their side. They have always thought that way—from the devout patrician pagans of Roman slave society who hurled the early Christians to the lions at the circus, and the inquisitors of the Middle Ages who, as guardians of feudalism and absolute monarchy, burned at the stake the first representatives of the liberal thought of the nascent bourgeoisie, up to today's bishops who anathematize proletarian revolutions in defense of the bourgeois and monopolist regime.

All reactionary classes in all historical epochs, when the antagonism between exploiters and exploited reaches its highest peak, presaging the arrival of a new social regime, have turned to the worst weapons of repression and calumny against their adversaries. The primitive Christians were taken to their martyrdom accused of burning Rome and of sacrificing children on their altars. Philosophers like Giordano Bruno, reformers like Hus, and thousands of other nonconformists with the feudal order, were accused of heresy and taken by the inquisitors to be burned at the stake.

Today persecution rages against the proletarian fighters and this crime brings out the worst calumnies in the monopolist and bourgeois press. In every historical epoch, the ruling classes have always committed murder. They do so invoking the "defense of society, order, country"—their "society" of the privileged minority against the exploited majority; their class "order" maintained by blood and fire against the dispossessed; the "country," whose fruits only they enjoy, depriving the rest of the people of them—all this to repress the revolutionaries who aspire to a new society, a just order, a country truly for all.

But the development of history, the ascending march of humanity cannot, and will not, be halted. The forces that impel the people, who are the real makers of history, are determined by the material conditions of their existence and by the aspirations for higher goals of well-being and liberty that emerge when the progress of humanity in the fields of science, technology and culture make it possible. These forces are superior to the will and the terror unleashed by the ruling oligarchies.

The subjective conditions of each country, that is to say, the factors of consciousness, organization, leadership, can accelerate or retard the revolution, according to its greater or lesser degree of development. But sooner or later, in every historical epoch, when the objective conditions mature, consciousness is acquired, the organization is formed, the leadership emerges and the revolution takes place.

Whether this takes place peacefully or through a painful birth does not depend on the revolutionaries; it depends on the reactionary forces of the old society, who resist the birth of the new society engendered by the contradictions carried in the womb of the old society. Revolution historically is like the doctor who assists at the birth of a new life. It does not needlessly use the tools of force, but will use them without hesitation whenever necessary to help the birth—a birth that brings to the enslaved and exploited masses the hope of a new and better life.

In many countries of Latin America, revolution is today inevitable. That fact is not determined by anyone's will. It is determined by the horrifying conditions of exploitation in which Latin Americans live, the development of the revolutionary consciousness of the masses, the world crisis of imperialism and the universal movement of struggle of the subjugated peoples.

The anxiety felt today is an unmistakable symptom of rebellion. The very depths of a continent are profoundly moved, a continent that has witnessed four centuries of slave, semi-slave and feudal exploitation beginning with its aboriginal inhabitants and slaves brought from Africa, up to the nuclei of nationalities that emerged later: white, black, mulatto, mestizo and Indian, who today are made brothers and sisters by scorn, humiliation and the Yankee yoke, and are brothers and sisters in their hope for a better tomorrow.

The peoples of Latin America liberated themselves from Spanish colonialism at the beginning of the last century, but they did not free themselves from exploitation. The feudal landowners assumed the authority of the Spanish rulers, the Indians continued in painful servitude, Latin Americans in one form or another continued to be slaves, and the tiniest hopes of the people gave way under the power of the oligarchies and the yoke of foreign capital. This has been the truth of Latin America—in one hue or another, in one variation or another. Today Latin America lies beneath an imperialism more ferocious, much more powerful and cruel than the Spanish colonial empire.

And in the face of the objective reality and the historically inexorable Latin American revolution, what is the attitude of Yankee imperialism? To prepare to wage a colonial war against the peoples of Latin America; to create an apparatus of force, the political pretexts and the pseudo-legal instruments subscribed to by the reactionary oligarchies to repress with blood and fire the struggle of the Latin American peoples.

The intervention of the US government in the internal politics of the countries of Latin America has become increasingly open and unbridled.

The Inter-American Defense Council, for example, has been and is the nest where the most reactionary and pro-Yankee officers of the Latin American armies are trained, for use later as shock troops in the service of the monopolies.

The US military missions in Latin America constitute a permanent apparatus of espionage in each nation directly tied to the Central Intelligence Agency (CIA), inculcating in officers the most reactionary sentiments and trying to convert the armies into instruments of US political and economic interests.

In the Panama Canal zone, the US high command has organized special courses to train Latin American officers in fighting against revolutionary guerrillas, with the aim of repressing the armed actions of the peasant masses against the feudal exploitation to which they are subjected.

In the United States itself the CIA has organized special schools to train Latin American agents in the most subtle forms of assassination; and in the Yankee military services the physical liquidation of anti-imperialist leaders is an accepted policy.

The Yankee embassies in the different Latin American countries are notorious for organizing, instructing and equipping fascist bands to spread terror and to attack labor, student and intellectual organizations. These bands—into which they recruit the sons of the oligarchies, lumpens and people of the lowest moral character—have already perpetrated a series of aggressive acts against the mass movements.

Nothing reveals more clearly and unequivocally the intentions of imperialism than its recent conduct in the events in Santo Domingo. Without any kind of justification, without even making use of diplomatic relations with that republic, after stationing its warships near the Dominican capital, the United States declared with its usual arrogance that if Balaguer's government sought military aid, it would land troops in Santo Domingo against the insurgent Dominican people. The fact that Balaguer's power was absolutely spurious, that each sovereign country of Latin America should have the right to resolve its internal problems without foreign intervention, that there exist international norms and world opinion, even that there exists an OAS, did not count at all in the considerations of the United States.

What did count were its designs for holding back the Dominican revolution, the reinstitution of its odious policy of landing marines, with no more basis or prerequisite for establishing this new, pirate-like concept of law than a tyrannical, illegitimate, crisis-ridden ruler's request. The significance of this should not escape the peoples of Latin America. In Latin America there are more than enough of the kind of rulers who are ready to use Yankee troops against their own people when they find themselves in a crisis.

US imperialism's declared policy of sending troops to fight the revolutionary movement of any country in Latin America, that is to say, to kill workers, students, peasants, Latin American men and women, has no other objective than the continued maintenance of its monopolistic interests and the privileges of the traitorous oligarchies that support it.

It can now be seen clearly that the military pacts signed by the US government with Latin American governments—often secret pacts and always behind the back of the people—invoking hypothetical foreign dangers that no one saw anywhere, have the sole and exclusive objective of preventing the struggle of the people. They were pacts against the people, against the sole danger—the local danger of the liberation movement—that would imperil the Yankee interests. It was not without reason that the people asked themselves: Why so many military agreements? Why the shipment of arms that although outmoded for modern war are still efficient for smashing strikes, repressing popular demonstrations, staining the land with blood? Why the military missions, the Rio de Janeiro Pact and the thousand and one international conferences?

Since the end of World War II, the countries of Latin America have become more and more impoverished; their exports have less and less value; their imports cost more; the per capita income falls; the frightful rate of infant mortality does not decrease; the number of illiterates is higher; the people lack jobs, land, adequate housing, schools, hospitals, means of communication and means of life. On the other hand, US investments exceed $10 billion. Latin America, moreover, is the provider of cheap raw materials, and the buyer of expensive finished articles. Like the first Spanish conquerors, who bartered mirrors and trinkets for gold and silver—that is how the United States trades with Latin America. To guard that torrent of riches, to gain ever more control of Latin America's resources and exploit its suffering peoples—that is what is hidden behind the military pacts, the military missions and Washington's diplomatic lobbying. This policy of gradual strangulation of the sovereignty of the Latin American nations and of a free hand to intervene in their internal affairs culminated in the recent meeting of foreign ministers at Punta del Este [in Uruguay]. Yankee imperialism gathered the ministers together to wrest from them—through political pressure and unprecedented economic blackmail in collusion with a group of the most discredited rulers of this continent—the renunciation of the national sovereignty of our peoples and the consecration of the Yankees' odious right of intervention in the internal affairs of Latin America; the submission of the peoples entirely to the will of the United States of North America, against which all our great leaders, from [Simón] Bolívar to [Augusto] Sandino, fought. Neither the US government, nor the representatives of the exploiting oligarchies, nor the big reactionary press in the pay of the monopolies and feudal lords tried to disguise their aims. They openly demanded agreements that constituted the formal suppression of the right of self-determination of our peoples; abolishing it with the stroke of a pen at the most infamous conspiracy in this continent's memory.

Behind closed doors, in reluctant meetings, where the Yankee minister of colonies devoted entire days to beating down the resistance and scruples of some ministers, bringing into play the Yankee treasury's millions in a blatant buying and selling of votes, a handful of representatives of the oligarchies of countries that together barely add up to a third of the continent's population, imposed agreements that served up to the Yankee master on a silver platter the head of a principle that has cost the blood of all our countries since the wars of independence.

The pyrrhic character of imperialism's such sad and fraudulent accomplishments, its moral failure, the broken unanimity and the universal scandal do not diminish the grave danger that agreements imposed at such a price have brought to the peoples of Latin America. At that evil conclave, Cuba's thundering voice was raised without weakness or fear, to indict the monstrous attempt before all the peoples of the Americas and the world, and to defend with a virility and dignity that will go down in the annals of history not only Cuba's rights but the abandoned rights of all our sister nations of the American continent. Cuba's voice could find no echo in that housebroken majority, but neither could it find a refutation; impotent silence was the only response to its demolishing arguments, the clarity and courage of its words. But Cuba did not speak for the ministers, Cuba spoke for the people and for history, where its words will be echoed and will find a response.

At Punta del Este a great ideological battle unfolded between the Cuban revolution and Yankee imperialism. Who did each side represent, for whom did each one speak? Cuba represented the people; the United States represented the monopolies. Cuba spoke for the exploited masses of Latin America; the United States for the exploiting, oligarchic and imperialist interests. Cuba for sovereignty; the United States for intervention. Cuba for the nationalization of foreign enterprises; the United States for new investments by foreign capital. Cuba for culture; the United States for ignorance. Cuba for agrarian reform; the United States for great landed estates. Cuba for the industrialization of the Americas; the United States for underdevelopment. Cuba for creative work; the United States for sabotage and counterrevolutionary terror practiced by its agents—the destruction of sugarcane fields and factories, bombing by their pirate planes of a peaceful people's work. Cuba for the murdered literacy workers; the United States for the assassins. Cuba for bread; the United States for hunger. Cuba for equality; the United States for privilege and discrimination. Cuba for the truth; the United States for lies. Cuba for liberation; the United States for oppression. Cuba for the bright future of humanity; the United States for the past without hope. Cuba for the heroes who fell at the Bay of Pigs to save the country from foreign domination; the United States for the mercenaries and traitors who serve the foreigner against their own country. Cuba for peace among peoples; the United States for aggression and war. Cuba for socialism; the United States for capitalism.

The agreements obtained by the United States, through methods so shameful that the entire world criticizes them, do not diminish but increase the morality and justice of Cuba's stand, which exposes the way the oligarchies sell out and betray national interests and shows the people the road to liberation. It reveals the corruption of the exploiting classes for whom their representatives spoke at Punta del Este. The OAS was revealed for what it really is—a Yankee ministry of colonies, a military alliance, an apparatus of repression against the liberation movement of the Latin American peoples.

Cuba has lived three years of revolution under the incessant harassment of Yankee intervention in our internal affairs. Pirate aircraft coming from the United States, dropping incendiary substances, have burned millions of *arrobas* of sugarcane. Acts of international sabotage perpetrated by Yankee agents, like the blowing up of the ship *La Coubre,* have cost dozens of Cuban lives. Thousands of US weapons have been dropped in parachutes by the US military services over our territory to promote subversion. Hundreds of tons of explosive materials and bombs have been secretly landed on our coast from US launches to promote sabotage and terrorism. A Cuban worker was tortured on the naval base of Guantánamo and deprived of his life with no due process and no explanation. Our sugar quota was abruptly cut and an embargo proclaimed on parts and raw materials for factories and US construction machinery, in order to ruin our economy. Cuban ports and installations have been subjected to surprise attacks by armed ships and bombers from bases prepared by the United States. Mercenary troops, organized and trained in Central America by the same government, have in a warlike manner invaded our territory, escorted by ships of the Yankee fleet and with air support from foreign bases, causing much loss of life as well as loss of material wealth. Counterrevolutionary Cubans are being trained in the US Army and new plans of aggression against Cuba are being made. All this has been going on incessantly for three years, before the eyes of the whole continent—and the OAS was not aware of it.

The ministers meet in Punta del Este and do not even admonish the US government or the governments that are material accomplices to these aggressions. They expel Cuba, the Latin American victim, the aggrieved nation.

The United States has military pacts with nations of all continents, military blocs with whatever fascist, militarist and reactionary government exists in the world: NATO, SEATO and CENTO, to which we now have to add the OAS. The United States intervenes in Laos, in Vietnam, in Korea, in Formosa, in Berlin. It openly sends ships to Santo Domingo in order to impose its law, its will, and announces its proposal to use its NATO allies to block commerce with Cuba. And the OAS is not aware of this! The ministers meet and expel Cuba, which has no military pacts with any country. Thus the government that organizes subversion throughout the world and forges military alliances on four continents, forces the expulsion of Cuba, accusing her of nothing other than subversion and ties beyond the continent!

Cuba is the Latin American nation that has made landowners of more than 100,000 peasants; ensured employment all year round on state farms and cooperatives to all agricultural workers. It has transformed garrisons into schools; given 70,000 scholarships to university, secondary and technical students; created classrooms for the entire population of children; totally eliminated illiteracy. It has quadrupled medical services; nationalized foreign interests; suppressed the abusive system that turned housing into a means of exploiting people. It has virtually eliminated unemployment; suppressed discrimination on account of race or sex; rid itself of gambling, vice and administrative corruption; and armed the people. It has made the enjoyment of human rights a living reality by freeing men and women from exploitation, lack of culture and social inequality. It has liberated itself from all foreign tutelage, acquired full sovereignty, and established the foundations for the development of its economy so as to no longer be a country producing a single crop and exporting only raw materials.

And yet it is Cuba that is expelled from the OAS by governments that have not achieved for their people any one of these objectives. How will they be able to justify their conduct before the peoples of the Americas and the world? How will they be able to deny that according to their conception the policy of land, of bread, of work, of health, of liberty, of equality and of culture, of accelerated development of the economy, of national dignity, of full self-determination and sovereignty, is incompatible with the hemisphere?

The people think very differently. The people think that the only thing incompatible with the destiny of Latin America is misery, feudal exploitation, illiteracy, starvation wages, unemployment; the policy of repression against the masses of workers, peasants and students; discrimination against women, blacks, Indians, mestizos; oppression by the oligarchies; the plundering of wealth by the Yankee monopolists; the moral stagnation of intellectuals and artists; the ruin of the small producers by foreign competition; economic underdevelopment; peoples without roads, without hospitals, without housing, without schools, without industries; the submission to imperialism; the renunciation of national sovereignty and the betrayal of the country.

How can the imperialists explain their conduct and their condemnation of Cuba? What words and what arguments are they going to use to speak to those whom they have exploited and ignored for so long?

Those who study the problems of Latin America are likely to ask: Which country has concentrated on—for the purpose of remedying—the situation of the idle, the poor, the Indians, the blacks, and the vulnerable infants, this immense number of infants—30 million in 1950 (that will be 50 million in eight more years). Yes, which country?

Thirty-two million Indians form the backbone—like the Andes—of the entire American continent. It is clear that for those who considered the Indian more as a thing than a person, this mass of humanity does not count, did not count, and, they thought, never would count. Of course, since they were considered a brute labor force, they had to be used like oxen or a tractor.

How could anyone believe in any benefit from imperialism, in any "Alliance for Progress"—under whatever oath—when under its saintly protection the natives of the south of the continent, like those in Patagonia, still experience its massacres and its persecutions, still live under strips of canvas as their ancestors did at the time the discoverers came almost 500 years ago? Those great races that populated northern Argentina, Paraguay and Bolivia, such as the Guaraní, who were savagely decimated, are hunted like animals and buried in the depths of the jungle. That reservoir of indigenous stock—

which could have served as a basis for a great Latin American civilization—
is seeing its extinction continually hastened. Across the Paraguayan swamps
and desolate Bolivian highlands, deeper into itself, Latin America has driven
these primitive, melancholy races, brutalized by alcohol and narcotics to
which they became addicted, in order at least to survive in the subhuman
conditions (not only of nutrition) in which they live.

A chain of hands stretches out almost in vain, and has done so for
centuries. Over the Andean peaks and slopes, along great rivers and in the
shadowy forests, this chain of hands stretches to unite their miseries with
those of others who are slowly perishing—Brazilian tribes and those of
the north of the continent and the coasts, reaching to the most incredibly
backward and wild confines of the Amazon jungle or mountain ranges of
Perija, to Venezuela's 100,000 Indians, then to the isolated Vapicharnas,
who await their end, now almost definitively lost to the human race, in the
hot regions of the Guianas. Yes, all these 32 million Indians, who extend
from the US border to the edges of the Southern Hemisphere, and the 45
million mestizos, who for the most part differ little from the Indians; all
these natives, this formidable reservoir of labor, whose rights have been
trampled on—yes, what can imperialism offer them? How can these people,
ignored so long, be made to believe that any benefit will come from such
bloodstained hands?

Entire tribes that live unclothed; others that are supposed to be can-
nibalistic; others whose members die like flies on their first contact with the
conquering civilization; others who are banished, that is, thrown off their
lands, pushed to the point of relocating in the jungles, mountains or most
distant reaches of the plains, where not even the smallest particle of culture,
light, bread or anything else penetrates.

In what "alliance"—other than one for their own more rapid extermination—are these native races to believe, these races who have been flogged
for centuries, shot so their lands could be taken, beaten to death in their
thousands for not working faster in their exploited labor for imperialism?

And the blacks? What "alliance" can the system of lynching and brutal
exclusion of blacks in the United States offer to the 15 million blacks and
14 million mulattos of Latin America, who know with horror and rage that
their brothers and sisters to the north cannot ride in the same vehicles as

their white compatriots, or attend the same schools, or even die in the same hospitals?

How can these disinherited racial groups believe in this imperialism, in its benefits or in any "alliance" with it, other than an alliance for lynching and exploiting them as slaves? Those masses who have not been permitted to enjoy even modestly any cultural, social or professional benefits, who— even when they are in the majority or number millions—are mistreated by the imperialists in Ku Klux Klan garb, are confined to the most unsanitary neighborhoods, in the least comfortable tenements built expressly for them, are shoved into the most menial occupations, the hardest labor and the least lucrative professions. They cannot presume to reach the universities, advanced academies or private schools.

What "Alliance for Progress" can serve as encouragement to those 107 million men and women of our America, the backbone of labor in the cities and fields, whose dark skin—black, mestizo, mulatto, Indian—inspires scorn in the new colonialists? How are they—who with bitter impotence have seen how in Panama there is one wage scale for Yankees and another for Panamanians, who are regarded as an inferior race—going to put any trust in the supposed "alliance"?

What can the workers hope for, with their starvation wages, the hardest jobs, the most miserable conditions, lack of nutrition, illness and all the evils that foster misery?

What words can be said, what benefits can the imperialists offer to the copper, tin, iron and coal miners who cough up their lungs for the profits of merciless foreign masters, or to the fathers and sons of the lumberjacks and rubber plantation workers, to the harvesters of the fruit plantations, to the workers in the coffee and sugar mills, to the peons on the pampas and plains, who with their health and lives amass the fortunes of the exploiters?

What can those vast masses expect, those who produce the wealth, who create the value, who aid in bringing forth a new world everywhere? What can they expect from imperialism, that greedy mouth, that greedy hand, with no other vista than misery, the most absolute destitution, and, in the end, cold, unrecorded death? What can this class expect, a class that has changed the course of history, that in other places has revolutionized the world, which is the vanguard of all the humble and exploited? What can it expect from imperialism, its most irreconcilable enemy?

What can imperialism offer the teachers, professors, professionals, intellectuals, poets and artists? What kind of benefits, what chance for a better and more equitable life, what purpose, what inducement, what desire to excel, to gain mastery beyond the first simple steps? What can it offer those who devotedly care for the generations of children and young people on whom imperialism will later gorge itself? What can it offer these people who live on degrading wages in most countries, who almost everywhere suffer restrictions on their right of political and social expression, whose economic future does not exceed the bare limits of their shaky resources and compensation, who are buried in a gray life without prospects, one that ends on a pension not even meeting half the cost of living? What "benefits" or "alliances" can imperialism offer them, save those that are to its total advantage?

If imperialism provides sources of aid to the professions, the arts and publications, it is always well understood that their products must reflect its interests, aims and "nothingness."

But what of the novels that attempt to reflect the reality of the world of imperialism's rapacious deeds? The poems aspiring to translate protests against imperialism's enslavement, its interference in life, in thought, in the very bodies of nations and peoples? The militant arts that try to express the forms and content of imperialism's aggression; that try to capture the constant pressure on every progressive living and breathing thing and on all that is revolutionary? The arts that teach and which—full of light and conscience, of clarity and beauty—try to guide human beings and the peoples to better destinies, to the highest summits of life and justice? All these meet imperialism's severest censure. They run into obstacles, condemnation and McCarthyite persecution. The presses are closed to them, their names are barred from its columns of print, and a campaign of the most atrocious silence is imposed against them—which is another contradiction of imperialism. For it is then that the writer, poet, painter, sculptor, the scientist—any creative person—begins truly to live in the tongue of the people, in the heart of millions of men and women throughout the world. Imperialism puts everything backwards, deforms it, diverts it into its own channels for profit, to multiply its dollars, buying words or paintings or stutterings, turning into silence the expression of revolutionaries, of progressives, of those who struggle for the people and their needs.

We cannot forget, in this sad picture, the underprivileged children, the neglected, the futureless children of the Americas.

America, a continent with a high birth rate, also has a high death rate. A few years ago the mortality of children under a year old in 11 countries was over 125 per 1,000, and in 17 others it was over 90 children. In 102 nations of the world, on the other hand, the rate is under 51. In sadly neglected Latin America, then, 74 out of 1,000 die in the first year after birth.

In some areas of Latin America that rate reaches 300 per 1,000; thousands and thousands of children up to seven years old die of incredible diseases in the Americas: diarrhea, pneumonia, malnutrition, hunger. Thousands and thousands are sick without hospital treatment or medicines; thousands and thousands walking about, victims of endemic mental deficiency, malaria, trachoma and other diseases caused by contamination and lack of water and other necessities. Diseases of this nature are common among those Latin American countries where thousands and thousands of children are in agony, children of outcasts, children of the poor and of the petit bourgeoisie with a hard life and precarious means. The statistics, which would be redundant here, are bloodcurdling. Any official publication of the international organizations collects them by the hundreds.

Regarding education, one becomes indignant merely thinking of what Latin America lacks on the cultural level. While the United States has a level of eight or nine years of schooling for those in its population 15 years and older, Latin America, plundered and pauperized by the United States, has a level of less than one year of approved schooling in the same age group.

It makes one even more indignant to know that of the children between five and 14 years, only 20 percent are enrolled in school in some countries, and even in the best countries the level is just 60 percent. That is to say, more than half the children of Latin America do not go to school. But the pain continues to grow when we learn that enrollment in the first three grades comprises more than 80 percent of those enrolled; and that in the sixth grade the enrollment fluctuates from a bare six to 22 pupils for each 100 who began in the first grade. Even in those countries that believe they have taken care of their children, the dropout rate between the first and sixth grade averages 73 percent. In Cuba, before the revolution, it was 74 percent. In Colombia, a "representative democracy," it is 78 percent. And if one looks closely at the countryside, only 1 percent of the children reach the fifth grade in the best of cases.

When one investigates this disastrous student absenteeism, there is one cause that explains it: the economy of misery. Lack of schools, lack of teachers, lack of family resources, child labor—in the last analysis, imperialism and its product of oppression and backwardness.

To summarize this nightmare that America has lived, from one end to the other: On this continent of almost 200 million human beings, two-thirds are Indians, mestizos and blacks—the "discriminated." On this continent of semi-colonies about four persons per minute die of hunger, of curable illnesses or premature old age, 5,500 per day, two million per year, 10 million every five years. These deaths could easily be avoided, but nevertheless they take place. Two-thirds of the Latin American population are short-lived and live under constant threat of death. A holocaust, which in 15 years has caused twice the number of deaths of World War I and which is ongoing. Meanwhile, from Latin America a continuous torrent of money flows to the United States: some $4,000 a minute, $5 million a day, $2 billion a year, $10 billion every five years. For each $1,000 that leaves us, one corpse remains. A thousand dollars per corpse—that is the price of imperialism! A thousand dollars per death, four times a minute!

But why did they meet at Punta del Este, despite this Latin American reality? Perhaps to take a small step toward alleviating these evils? No! The people know that at Punta del Este the ministers who expelled Cuba met to renounce national sovereignty. They know that the US government went there not only to establish the basis for aggression against Cuba, but the basis for intervention against the people's liberation movement in any Latin American nation; that the United States is preparing a bloody drama for Latin America. They know that just as the exploiting oligarchies now renounce the principle of sovereignty, they will not hesitate to solicit the intervention of Yankee troops against their own people. And they know that for this purpose the US delegation proposed a watchdog committee against subversion in the Inter-American Defense Council with executive powers, and the adoption of collective measures. "Subversion" for the

Yankee imperialists is the struggle of hungry people for bread, the struggle of peasants for land, the struggle of the peoples against imperialist exploitation.

A watchdog committee with executive powers in the Inter-American Defense Council means a continental repressive force against the peoples at the command of the Pentagon. Collective measures means the landing of Yankee marines in any country of the Americas.

To the accusation that Cuba wants to export its revolution, we reply: Revolutions are not exported, they are made by the people.

What Cuba can give to the peoples, and has already given, is its example.

And what does the Cuban revolution teach? That revolution is possible, that the people can make it, that in the contemporary world there are no forces capable of halting the liberation movement of the peoples.

Our triumph would never have been feasible if the revolution itself had not been inexorably destined to arise out of existing conditions in our socioeconomic reality, a reality that exists to an even greater degree in a good number of Latin American countries.

It inevitably occurs that in the nations where the control of the Yankee monopolies is strongest, the exploitation of the oligarchy cruelest, and the situation of the laboring and peasant masses most unbearable, the political power appears most solid. The state of siege becomes habitual, every manifestation of discontent by the masses is repressed by force. The democratic path is closed completely. The brutal character of dictatorship, the form of rule adopted by the ruling classes, reveals itself more clearly than ever. It is then that the revolutionary explosion of the peoples becomes inevitable.

Although it is true that in these underdeveloped countries of the Americas the working class generally is relatively small, there is a social class which, because of the subhuman conditions in which it lives, constitutes a potential force, which, led by the workers and the revolutionary intellectuals, has a decisive importance in the struggle for national liberation: the peasants.

Our countries combine the circumstances of an underdeveloped industry with those of an agrarian regime of a feudal character. That is why, with all the hardships of the living conditions of the urban workers, the rural population lives in even more horrible conditions of oppression and exploitation. But it is also, with exceptions, the absolute majority sector, at times exceeding 70 percent of the population in Latin America.

Not including the landlords, who often reside in the cities, the rest of that great mass gains its livelihood working as peons on the haciendas for the most miserable wages, or working the land under conditions of exploitation that in no way put the Middle Ages to shame. These circumstances determine that in Latin America the rural poor constitute a tremendous potential revolutionary force.

The armies, the forces on which the power of the exploiting classes rest, are built and equipped for conventional war. However, they become absolutely impotent when they have to confront the irregular struggle of the peasants on their own terrain. They lose 10 men for each revolutionary fighter who falls, and demoralization spreads rapidly among them from having to face an invisible and invincible enemy who does not offer them the opportunity to show off their academy tactics and their swaggering, which they use so much in military displays to curb the workers and students in the cities.

The initial struggle by small combat units is constantly fed by new forces, the mass movement begins, and the old order little by little starts to break into a thousand pieces. That is the moment when the working class and the urban masses decide the battle.

What is it that from the beginning of the struggle of those first nuclei, makes them invincible, regardless of the numbers, power and resources of their enemies? The aid of the people, and they will be able to count on the help of the people on an ever-increasing scale.

But the peasantry is a class which, because of the uncultured state in which it is kept and the isolation in which it lives, needs the revolutionary and political leadership of the working class and the revolutionary intellectuals, for without them it would not by itself be able to plunge into the struggle and achieve victory.

In the actual historical conditions of Latin America, the national bourgeoisie cannot lead the anti-feudal and anti-imperialist struggle. Experience shows that in our nations, that class, even when its interests conflict with those of Yankee imperialism, has been incapable of confronting it, for the national bourgeoisie is paralyzed by fear of social revolution and frightened by the cry of the exploited masses. Facing the dilemma of imperialism or revolution, only the most progressive layers will join with the people.

The current world correlation of forces and the universal movement for the liberation of the colonized and dependent peoples demonstrates to the working class and the revolutionary intellectuals of Latin America their true role, which is to place themselves resolutely in the vanguard of the struggle against imperialism and feudalism.

Imperialism, utilizing the great movie monopolies, its news services, its periodicals, books and reactionary newspapers, resorts to the most subtle lies to sow divisions and inculcate among the most ignorant people fear and superstition against revolutionary ideas, ideas that can and should frighten only the powerful exploiters, with their worldly interests and privileges.

Divisionism, a product of all kinds of prejudices, false ideas and lies; sectarianism, dogmatism, a lack of breadth in analyzing the role of each social layer, its parties, organizations and leaders—these obstruct the necessary united action of the democratic and progressive forces of our peoples. They are deficiencies of growth, infantile diseases of the revolutionary movement that must be left behind. In the anti-feudal and anti-imperialist struggle it is possible to bring the majority of the people resolutely behind goals of liberation that unite the spirit of the working class, the peasants, the intellectual workers, the petit bourgeoisie and the most progressive layers of the national bourgeoisie. These sectors comprise the immense majority of the population and bring together great social forces capable of sweeping away the imperialist and reactionary feudal rule. In that broad movement they can and must struggle together for the good of our nations, for the good of our peoples, and for the good of the Americas, from the old Marxist militant, right up to the sincere Catholic who has nothing to do with the Yankee monopolists and the feudal lords of the land.

This movement can pull along with it the most progressive elements of the armed forces, which have also been humiliated by the Yankee military missions, the betrayal of national interests by the feudal oligarchies and the sacrifice of national sovereignty to Washington's dictates.

Where the roads for the peoples of Latin America are closed, where the repression of workers and peasants is fierce, where the rule of the Yankee monopolists is strongest, the first and most important task is to understand that it is neither honorable nor correct to beguile people with the fallacious and convenient illusion of uprooting—by legal means that do not and will not exist — ruling classes that are entrenched in all the state institutions, monopolizing education, owning all the means of information, possessing infinite financial resources — power that the monopolies and oligarchies will defend with blood and fire and with the might of their police and armies.

The duty of every revolutionary is to make the revolution. It is understood that the revolution will triumph in the Americas and throughout the world, but it is not for revolutionaries to sit in the doorways of their houses waiting for the corpse of imperialism to pass by. The role of Job does not suit a revolutionary. Each year that the liberation of Latin America is speeded up will mean the lives of millions of children saved, millions of intellects saved for culture, an infinite amount of pain spared the people. Even if the Yankee imperialists prepare a bloody drama for Latin America, they will not succeed in crushing the peoples' struggles; they will only arouse universal hatred against themselves. And such a drama will also mark the death of their greedy and carnivorous system.

No nation in Latin America is weak — because each forms part of a family of 200 million brothers and sisters, who suffer the same miseries, who harbor the same sentiments, who have the same enemy, who dream about the same better future and who count on the solidarity of all honest men and women throughout the world.

Great as the epic struggle for Latin American independence was, heroic as that struggle was, today's generation of Latin Americans is called on to engage in an epic that is even greater and more decisive for humanity. That struggle was for liberation from the Spanish colonial power, from a decadent Spain invaded by the armies of Napoleon. Today the battle cry is for liberation from the most powerful world imperialist center, from the strongest force of world imperialism, and to render humanity a greater service than that rendered by our predecessors.

But this struggle, to a greater extent than the earlier one, will be waged by the masses, will be carried out by the people; the people are going to play a much more important role now than they did then. The leaders are less important and will be less important in this struggle than in the earlier one.

This epic before us is going to be written by the hungry Indian masses, the peasants without land, the exploited workers. It is going to be written by the progressive masses, the honest and brilliant intellectuals, who so greatly abound in our suffering Latin American lands. A struggle of masses and of ideas. An epic that will be carried forward by our peoples, mistreated and scorned by imperialism; our peoples, unreckoned with until today, who are now beginning to shake off their slumber. Imperialism considered us a weak and submissive flock; and now it begins to be terrified of that flock; a gigantic flock of 200 million Latin Americans in whom Yankee monopoly capitalism now sees its gravediggers.

This toiling humanity, these inhumanly exploited, these paupers, controlled by the system of whip and overseer, have not been reckoned with or have been little reckoned with. From the dawn of independence their fate has been the same: Indians, gauchos, mestizos, zambos, quadroons, whites without property or income, all this human mass that formed the ranks of the "nation," which never reaped any benefits, which fell by the millions, which was cut into bits, which won independence from the mother country for the bourgeoisie, which was shut out from its share of the rewards, which continued to occupy the lowest rung on the ladder of social benefits, continued to die of hunger, curable diseases and neglect, because for them there were never enough life-giving goods — ordinary bread, a hospital bed, medicine that cures, a hand that aids.

But now from one end of the continent to the other they are signaling with clarity that the hour has come — the hour of their redemption. Now this anonymous mass, this America of color, somber, taciturn America, which all over the continent sings with the same sadness and disillusionment, now this mass is beginning to enter definitively into its own history, it is beginning to write its history with its own blood, it is beginning to suffer and die for that history.

Because now in the fields and mountains of the Americas, on its plains and in its jungles, in the wilderness and in the traffic of its cities, on the banks of its great oceans and rivers, this world is beginning to tremble. Anxious hands are stretched forth, ready to die for what is theirs, to win those rights that were laughed at by one and all for 500 years. Yes, now history will have to take the poor of the Americas into account, the exploited and spurned of the Americas, who have decided to begin writing their history for themselves and for all time. Already they can be seen on the roads, on foot, day after day, in an endless march of hundreds of kilometers to the governmental "eminences," there to obtain their rights.

Already they can be seen armed with stones, sticks, machetes, in one direction and another, each day occupying lands, sinking hooks into the land which belongs to them and defending it with their lives. They can be seen carrying signs, slogans, flags; letting them fly in the mountain or prairie winds. And the wave of anger, of demands for justice, of claims for rights trampled underfoot, which is beginning to sweep the lands of Latin America, will not stop. That wave will swell with every passing day. For that wave is composed of the greatest number, the majorities in every respect, those whose labor amasses the wealth and turns the wheels of history. Now they are awakening from the long, brutalizing sleep to which they had been subjected.

For this great mass of humanity has said "Enough!" and has begun to march. And their march of giants will not be halted until they conquer true independence—for which they have died in vain more than once. Today, however, those who die will die like the Cubans at the Bay of Pigs—they will die for their own, true, never-to-be-surrendered independence.

Patria o muerte! [Homeland or death!]
Venceremos! [We will win!]
[Signed] The people of Cuba

The National General Assembly of the people of Cuba resolves that this declaration be known as the Second Declaration of Havana, and be translated into the major languages and distributed throughout the world. It also resolves to urge all friends of the Cuban revolution in Latin America to distribute it widely among the masses of workers, peasants, students and intellectuals of this continent.

Havana, Cuba
Free Territory of the Americas
February 4, 1962

7. THE OCTOBER MISSILE CRISIS

After a US spy plane photographed Soviet missiles in Cuba on October 22, 1962, President Kennedy announced a total naval blockade of Cuba. The crisis peaked by October 26 when a massive US air strike against Cuba seemed imminent. Sidelining Cuba, a secret agreement was reached between the US and Soviet governments, whereby Washington agreed not to attack or invade the island if the Soviet missiles were removed.

THE FIVE POINTS OF DIGNITY
HAVANA, OCTOBER 28, 1962

As the Missile Crisis came to a head in late October, bringing the world to the brink of a nuclear catastrophe, Fidel Castro appeared on Cuban television on October 28, outlining what he called the "Five Points of Dignity."

FIRST. The economic blockade and all of the other measures that the United States is taking all over the world to bring trade and economic pressure to bear against Cuba must cease.

SECOND. All subversive activities, airlifts and landings of arms and explosives by air and by sea, the organization of mercenary invasions, the sending of spies into our country illegally and acts of sabotage — whether carried out from US territory or from that of accessory countries — must cease.

THIRD. The pirate attacks that are carried out from bases in the United States and Puerto Rico must cease.

FOURTH. All violations of Cuba's airspace and territorial waters by US planes and warships must cease.

FIFTH. US troops must be withdrawn from the Guantánamo Naval Base, and that part of Cuban territory occupied by the United States must be returned.

ON THE MISSILE CRISIS
NOVEMBER 1, 1962

As the crisis passed, on November 1, Fidel Castro reviewed the significance of recent events.

We don't constitute an obstacle to a peaceful solution, a truly peaceful solution. We are neither a warlike nor an aggressive nation. Ours is a peaceful nation, but being peaceful doesn't mean allowing ourselves to be trampled upon. If anyone should try it, we will fight as much as need be to defend ourselves. The facts bear this out.

We will never constitute an obstacle to a truly peaceful solution. The prerequisites for a truly peaceful solution are the five-point guarantees set forth by the Cuban government.

We want the United States to start giving proof, not promises, of its good faith. Deeds, not words! It would be convincing if the United States were to return the territory it occupies at the Guantánamo Naval Base. That would be much more convincing than any words or promises.

And if the United States doesn't agree to the guarantees that Cuba wants?

Then there won't be any truly peaceful solution, and we will have to keep on living with this tension that we have endured so far. We want peaceful solutions, but they must also be honorable. We are entitled to peace, a truly peaceful solution, and, sooner or later, we will get it, because we have won that right with our people's spirit, resistance and honor...

They don't let us work in peace. More than weapons, we want to use work tools. We want to create, not kill and destroy. Our people aren't allowed to create and are constantly forced to mobilize, to place themselves on a war footing, to defend themselves, to be ready for anything. They are forced to do this; it isn't that we want that policy. It's a policy that the aggressors impose on our country. What our country wants is to work, to develop its resources, to develop its people, and to carry out its peaceful work.

We won't accept just any old formula. We will accept any formula for peace that is truly honorable. I think that with such a formula, we wouldn't be the only ones to benefit. Everyone would — the Americas, the rest of the world, the United States. That is, even those responsible for this situation would benefit from a solution of honorable peace for our country...

In the course of this crisis, while this crisis was developing, some differences arose between the Soviet and Cuban governments, but I want to tell all Cubans one thing: This isn't the place to discuss those problems, because discussing them here could help our enemies, who could benefit from such differences. We must discuss such things with the Soviets at the government and party levels; we have to sit down with them and discuss whatever is needed, using reason and principles; because, above all, we are Marxist-Leninists; we are friends of the Soviet Union. There will be no breach between the Soviet Union and Cuba.

I would like to say something else, too: We have confidence in the Soviet Union's policy of principles, and we have confidence in the leadership of the Soviet Union — that is, in the government and in the party of the Soviet Union.

If my compatriots ask me for my opinion now, what can I tell them, what advice should I give them? In the midst of a confusing situation, where things haven't been understood or not understood clearly, what should we do? I would say we must have confidence and realize that these international problems are extremely complex and delicate and that our people, who have shown great maturity, extraordinary maturity, should demonstrate that maturity now...

And, above all, there are some things that need to be said now, when some people may be annoyed because of misunderstandings or differences. It is good to remember, above all, what the Soviet Union has done for us in every one of the difficult moments we have had, what it has done to offset the economic attacks of the United States, the suppression of our sugar quota and the ending of oil shipments to our country. Every time the United States has attacked us — every time — the Soviet Union has extended its hand to us in friendship. We are grateful, and we should say so here, loud and clear...

The principal weapons used by our armed forces were sent to us by the Soviet Union, which hasn't demanded payment for them.

A few months ago, the Soviet Union decided to cancel all of our country's debt for weapons.

Some of these matters, of a military nature, must be treated with great care. However, I can tell you one thing: Cuba didn't own the strategic weapons that were used for its defense. This isn't the case with the tanks and a whole series of other weapons that do belong to us, but we didn't own the strategic weapons.

The agreements covering their shipment to our country to strengthen our defenses in the face of threats of attack stated that those strategic weapons, which are very complex and require highly specialized personnel, would remain under the direction of Soviet personnel and would continue to belong to the Soviet Union. Therefore, when the Soviet government decided to withdraw those weapons, which belonged to them, we respected that decision. I'm explaining this so you will understand about their withdrawal...

Don't think that the withdrawal of the strategic weapons will leave us unarmed. It doesn't mean that we will be unarmed.

We have impressive — very powerful — means of defense, extraordinary resources with which to defend ourselves. The strategic weapons are leaving, but all the other weapons will stay in our country. They are an extremely powerful means of defense, with which we can handle any situation that may arise. Don't misunderstand this.

Little by little, the confusion will disappear.

There is one thing that I would like to emphasize today, an appreciation that I would like to express, which refers to the people, to the way the people have behaved during the past few days. The people's attitude, in terms of determination, courage and discipline, has been more impressive than even the greatest optimists could ever have imagined...

Such a nation is invincible!

Such a nation, whose people confront such difficult situations so serenely and admirably, is a nation that has the right to get what it desires, which is peace, respect, honor and prestige.

We have long-range moral missiles that cannot and will never be dismantled. They are our most powerful strategic weapons, for both defense and attack.

That is why, here and now, I want to express my admiration for the Cuban people. Based on this experience, all revolutionaries feel doubly obliged to struggle and work tirelessly for our people. In closing, I would like to say, from the bottom of my heart, that today I am prouder than ever before of being a son of this nation.

8. FORMATION OF THE CUBAN COMMUNIST PARTY AND CHE'S FAREWELL LETTER

CHAPLIN THEATER, HAVANA
OCTOBER 3, 1965

At the closing ceremony of the Cuban Communist Party's founding meeting, where the members of the Central Committee were presented, Fidel Castro discussed the migration conflict with the United States and the Sino-Soviet split. He also used the occasion to read the letter Che Guevara wrote before he left Cuba with a brigade of Cubans on a mission to support the liberation movements in Africa.

Invited guests;
Compañeros of the Central Committee;
Compañeros of the Provincial, Regional and Local Committees;
Compañero Secretaries of the Party Cells:

I feel obliged to begin with a theme not directly related to the reason for our gathering here, but which, because it is a question of current political interest, must not be overlooked by us.

It stems from what we stated on September 28, in regard to something that has been happening for three years, and that was used by the enemy in a treacherous way to wage a campaign against the revolution, the case of the individuals who, when the flights between Miami and Cuba were suspended [in 1962] were left with one foot here and the other foot there…

I'm going to read an AP cable:

> President Johnson announced today that he would obtain a diplomatic understanding with Cuba so that Cubans who wish to leave their country can seek asylum in the United States.

This statement about a diplomatic understanding means an agreement on this [immigration] problem through diplomatic channels.

> [President Johnson] said: "I have requested the State Department to seek through the Swiss embassy in Cuba, which is in charge of US affairs, the agreement of the Cuban government in a request to the president of the International Red Cross Committee."
>
> He also said he had "instructed the State, Justice, Health, Education and Welfare Departments to make the necessary arrangements so that those in Cuba who are seeking freedom may formally enter the United States."

And another cable, longer than the others, adds that Johnson stated:

> "When many of the citizens of a regime voluntarily choose to abandon the land in which they were born for a home where there is hope for them, their decision reveals that the regime has failed. The future has little hope for any government when the present does not permit any hope for its people... [and] the refugees would be welcomed [in the United States] in the expectation that some day they might return to their country to find it cleansed of terror and free of fear."

From the beginning of the revolution there has been only one policy with regard to this [matter of immigration]. From the beginning of the revolution up until the October [Missile] Crisis, all those who wanted to go and all those who had received permission from the United States continued to leave this country.

When they stopped flights to Cuba, because of the October Crisis, the revolutionary government made no change in its policy, because nearly 300 people a month continued to leave via other routes, such as through Spain and Mexico—some 300 people a month, more than 3,000 people a year. There has not been the slightest change in our policy regarding those who wish to leave the country. What we have done is to expose the ill-intentioned hypocrisy of Yankee imperialism, the only entity responsible for having paralyzed the normal channels for leaving the country, aimed at promoting a certain type of clandestine and risky exit for propaganda purposes.

Maybe Mr. Johnson doesn't know that in the United States, when the struggle against British colonialism took place, thousands and thousands of Americans left the country after independence and went to Canada.

In all revolutions, whether the French revolution, the Russian revolution, or the Cuban revolution, the privileged classes always leave or emigrate. This is a historical fact.

Moreover, if the fact of people leaving the country in which they were born to go to another country is a reflection on a particular social regime, consider the case of Puerto Rico. More than one million people born in that country have been forced to emigrate to the United States, after Yankee imperialism seized the island and held it under a regime of colonial exploitation. Mr. Johnson forgets Puerto Rico and the million Puerto Ricans living in New York in the worst conditions, in the poorest districts, doing the most humiliating jobs.

Of course, to raise the matter of the Red Cross is a little trick Mr. Johnson uses to dramatize the affair. Really, who ever heard of needing the Red Cross to grant a visa or to authorize a few planes to land in Miami? Is there any need for the Red Cross? What does the Red Cross have to do with it? This is not like an earthquake, a catastrophe or a war. It is only a simple formality to authorize the landing of planes and the arrival of ships in the United States. The Red Cross is not necessary for that.

On the other hand, the Red Cross could well intervene by asking the US government to suspend the criminal measure banning the export of medicines to Cuba. This, indeed, would justify the intervention of the International Red Cross.

In any event, the Red Cross might do a much better job in South Vietnam, where Yankee soldiers are murdering and torturing thousands of citizens. Or in North Vietnam, where the criminal Yankee bombs are dropped indiscriminately over cities, villages, schools or hospitals.

The Red Cross could do something in the Dominican Republic, where the invading soldiers perpetrate all kinds of brutalities against the people and where they have seized schools.

It could intervene in the United States itself to prevent the massacre of black citizens, as happened in Los Angeles, California, recently. But in this matter [of Cuban émigrés], Mr. Johnson, the presence of the Red Cross is not required. It is enough for us to discuss it with the representatives of the Swiss embassy, who are also the representatives of US interests in Cuba, and we might be able to reach a perfectly satisfactory agreement as to arrangements. There is no need for anyone to intervene. We acknowledge the sincerity and dependability of the Swiss officials. But, if the US government doesn't trust or believe in the ability of the officials of the Swiss embassy, that is the US government's problem.

And now for a serious discussion on the subject of freedom: I'd like to know if Mr. Johnson could answer a couple of questions.

From the beginning of the revolution we have permitted all those who wish to leave the country to do so, and we have never refused permission to all those who want to visit their relatives and return; there are Cubans who have relatives in the United States and want to join them, and there are also Cubans who have relatives in the United States and who don't want to leave the country. Since Mr. Johnson, right there under the Statue of Liberty has taken the trouble to concoct a statement full of all this hogwash about liberty, I have to ask him whether he will allow Cubans [living in the United States] to visit their relatives in Cuba and then return to the United States. And I ask him whether those Cubans who don't wish to live in the United States can visit their relatives there and afterwards return to Cuba. And finally, I ask him whether the United States is willing to allow US citizens to come and visit Cuba.

To the government that talks about how badly a nation must be doing when its citizens want to leave, we could say in reply: A country must be even worse off when, in spite of being a nation that boasts of being free and in spite of having achieved the level of economic development that it has achieved, out of fear and terror it is afraid to permit its citizens to visit this country, a country so slandered and maligned as Cuba.

Therefore, here is a second challenge to the government of the United States: We challenge them to permit those Cubans in the United States who still have families here in Cuba, who do not wish to leave, to visit Cuba. We challenge them to permit residents of Cuba, who do not wish to emigrate, to be allowed to go to the United States to visit their relatives and return. And finally, we challenge them to permit students and any other US citizen to come to Cuba freely, in the same way that we allow any citizen of this country to leave or to return. We challenge them to permit representatives of the black or civil rights organizations in the United States to visit Cuba, so that they can see how, with the disappearance of the exploitation of human beings, racial discrimination has been eliminated in our country once and for all.

Let's see if Mr. Johnson, before the world and before the people of the United States, can reply to this challenge, in a way that is not gibberish...

And as they talk so much and boast so much about freedom, let's stop talking about phony freedom, about abstract freedoms. The fact is that a free world is not being created over there, but rather here in Cuba—so free that we don't want anyone to have to live in this society against their will. Our socialist society, our communist society, must be, above all, a truly free association of citizens. Although it is true that certain citizens who have been brought up in accord with the ideas of the past prefer to leave for the United States, it is also true that this country has become the sanctuary for the revolutionaries of this hemisphere.

It is also true that we consider worthy of the hospitality of this land not only those who were born in this land but all those who speak our language, who have a similar culture, as well as those who, though they do not speak our language, have a similar historical and ethnic origin and a similar history of exploitation. All those persecuted by bloody and imperialist oligarchies have the right to come here—and many have made use of this right. Many people born in sister nations in this hemisphere have come to live here permanently or temporarily. Many technicians and many professionals from different corners of the Americas have lived and worked here for many years.

This is not only a land for Cubans. It is a land for revolutionaries, and the revolutionaries of this hemisphere, including US revolutionaries, have the right to consider themselves our brothers. Some leaders, like Robert Williams, who was brutally persecuted there, found asylum in this land. And like Williams, all those who are persecuted by the reactionaries and exploiters over there can find asylum here. It doesn't matter that he speaks English and was born in the United States. This is the homeland for the revolutionaries of this hemisphere, just as the United States is the inevitable refuge for all the thugs, all the embezzlers, all the exploiters and all the reactionaries of this hemisphere. There is no thief, no exploiter, no reactionary, no criminal, who does not find an open door to the United States.

This is how we answer Mr. Johnson's statement, made beneath his discredited Statue of Liberty, that mass of stone and hypocrisy. No one knows what it stands for, unless it is what Yankee imperialism means today to the rest of the world.

Let's go on now to our own questions. Let's go on to the question concerning our party. I believe that all the news coming out of here, with regard to our social, economic and political achievements, constitutes very bad news for the Yankee imperialists.

Naturally, everything that permits us to strengthen and advance the revolution, everything that permits us to progress as far as we can, worries them a great deal. Now, as far as returning is concerned — yes, some day a great many of those who left will long to return, repentant. But when Mr. Johnson speaks of their returning as liberators, we can tell him that this is a "Mid-Autumn Night's Dream."

The whole country received the news of the formation of our Central Committee with joy and enthusiasm. The names and the histories of the compañeros who form this committee are very well known. If all of them are not known to everyone, all of them are known to a significant and important number of the people. We have tried to choose those who, in our judgment, represent to the fullest extent the history of the revolution. Those who, in the fight for the revolution as well as in the fight to consolidate, defend and develop the revolution, have worked and fought hard and tirelessly.

There is no heroic period in the history of our revolution that is not represented here. There is no sacrifice, there is no combat, no feat — either military or civilian, heroic or creative — that is not represented. There is no revolutionary or social sector that is not represented. I am not speaking of organizations. When I speak of a sector, I speak of the workers, I speak of the youth, I speak of the farmers, I speak of our mass organizations.

There are individuals who have held socialist ideas for many years, as is the case of compañero Fabio Grobart, who was a founder of the first communist party; the case of compañera Elena Gil, who did such extraordinary work with the schools where more than 40,000 farm girls from the mountains have studied, where they have trained thousands of teachers, where more than 50,000 young people and children have studied, work that we consider to be really exemplary; the case of compañero Arteaga, who, in addition to his history of struggle, has worked in the field of agriculture for seven years and has carried out successful plans, in some cases extraordinarily successful, such as the agricultural plan for the Escambray; the case of Lt. Tarrau, a compañero whom many may not know, but who is the compañero that the Ministry of Interior placed in charge of the rehabilitation plans on the Isle of Pines, where, in an exemplary and unselfish way, he has done a brilliant job, about which we will have to speak and write a great deal.

I have mentioned the cases of compañeros, some very well known, others less well known. The list of compañeros of the Revolutionary Armed Forces (FAR) would be endless due to their history both before and after the triumph as outstanding revolutionaries, as tireless workers, as examples of self-improvement in their studies, cultural development, cultural and political level—compañeros of extraordinary modesty, in whose hands the defense of the nation has principally rested during these seven dangerous and threat-filled years.

It is not necessary to speak about the best known. That does not mean that they are the only heroes of the nation. No, far from it! Fortunately our country has innumerable heroes and, above all, a mass of new compañeros now being developed, who will some day—without a doubt—demonstrate their sense of responsibility and honor.

If we ask ourselves whether we have left anyone out, of course we have to answer in the affirmative.

It would be impossible to form a Central Committee of 100 revolutionary compañeros without leaving out many compañeros. What is important is not those who have been left out. They will come later. What is important are those who are there, and what they represent. We know that the party and the people have received the formation of this committee with satisfaction.

This committee, which met yesterday, reached several agreements: First, it ratified the measure adopted by the former national leadership. It ratified the Political Bureau, the Secretariat and the work commissions, as well as the compañero elected as organization secretary. The committee also reached two important agreements that had been submitted by the former national leadership [of the party].

One related to our official organ. Instead of publishing two newspapers of a political nature, we are going to concentrate all human resources, all resources in equipment and paper on establishing a single morning paper of a political nature, in addition to the newspaper *El Mundo*, which is not exactly a political organ. We will concentrate all our resources and we will establish a new newspaper. It will be called *Granma*, the symbol of our revolutionary concepts and goals.

An even more important agreement refers to the name of our party. Our first name was ORI, which stood for Integrated Revolutionary Organizations. During the first stage in the uniting of all the revolutionary forces this had its positive and negative aspects. Later we became the United Party of the Socialist Revolution (PURS), which constituted an extraordinary step forward, an extraordinary step ahead in the creation of our political apparatus. This effort took three years during which time innumerable valuable individuals emerged from the inexhaustible source that the people and the workers constitute to form what we are today—not only in number, but essentially in quality. The name United Party of the Socialist Revolution says a lot, but not everything.

The name United Party suggests something that is in need of uniting, it still reminds us a little bit of the origin of each part. We consider that we have now reached that level in which all shades and all types of origin distinguishing one revolutionary from another must disappear forever. Since we have already arrived at that fortunate stage of history in which our revolutionary process has only one type of revolutionary, and since it is necessary for the name of our party to show not what we were yesterday, but what we will be tomorrow, what name should our party have now? Yes, the Cuban Communist Party!

That is the name that in view of the development of our party, of the revolutionary consciousness of its members and the objectives of our revolution, was adopted by the first Central Committee meeting yesterday.

As we explained to the compañeros yesterday, it is totally correct. The word "communist" has been maligned and distorted for centuries. Communists have existed throughout history; people with communist ideas, people who conceived of a way of life different from that into which they were born. For example, those who thought in a communist way in other times were considered utopian communists, people who 500 years ago aspired to establish a type of society that was not possible then, because of the minimal development of the productive forces of humankind at that time. To go back to the type of communism from which primitive human beings began, to live in a type of primitive communism, would not be possible except through the development of the productive forces, so that the social utilization of those forces would create the material goods and services in quantities more than sufficient to satisfy the needs of humankind.

All exploiters, all the privileged persons, have always hated the word "communist" as if it were a crime. They cursed the word "communist." For that reason, when Marx and Engels wrote the *Communist Manifesto*, outlining a new revolutionary theory, a scientific interpretation of human society and human history, they wrote, "a specter is haunting Europe, the specter of communism." The privileged classes viewed these ideas as a specter and were really afraid.

Moreover, the privileged classes in every period of history have always viewed new ideas with extraordinary fear. In its day Roman society was afraid of Christian ideas when they first arose, because these ideas were the ideas of the poor and the slaves. And due to its hatred of those new ideas, that society sent a great number of human beings to their deaths. Similarly, in the Middle Ages, as well as during feudalism, new ideas were banned and those who believed in them were slandered and treated appallingly.

Within feudal society, the emerging bourgeoisie espoused new ideas, of a political, philosophical or religious nature, for which they were cruelly condemned and persecuted.

The reactionary classes have always used every method to condemn and slander new ideas. Thus, all the paper and all the resources at their disposal are not sufficient to slander communist ideas; to slander the desire for a society in which human beings no longer exploit one another, but become real brothers and sisters; the dream of a society in which all human beings are truly equal in fact and in law — not simply in a constitutional clause as in some bourgeois constitutions which say that all men are born free and equal. Can all individuals be considered to be born free and equal in a society of exploiters and exploited, a society of rich and poor — where one child is born in a slum, in a humble cradle, and another child is born in a cradle of gold? How can it be said that these people have the same opportunities in life?

The ancient dream of humankind — a dream that is possible today — of a society without exploiters or exploited, has aroused the hatred and rancor of all exploiters.

As if they were going to offend us or as if it were an insult, the imperialists speak of the communist government of Cuba, just like they used the word "*mambí*" to denounce our liberators. But the word "communist" is not an insult but rather an honor for us.

It is the word that symbolizes the aspiration of a great part of humanity, and hundreds and hundreds of millions of human beings are concretely working toward that goal today. Within 100 years, there will be no greater glory, nothing more natural and rational, than to be called a communist.

We are on the road toward a communist society. And if the imperialists don't like it, they can lump it.

From now on, gentlemen of UPI and AP, understand that when you call us "communists," you are giving us the greatest compliment you can give.

Absent from our Central Committee is someone who possesses in the highest degree all the necessary merits and virtues to be included, but who, nevertheless, is not among those announced as members of our Central Committee.

The enemy has conjured up a thousand conjectures. The enemy has tried to sow confusion, to spread discord and doubt, and we have waited patiently because it was necessary to wait.

This differentiates the revolutionary from the counterrevolutionary, the revolutionary from the imperialist. Revolutionaries know how to wait; we know how to be patient; we never despair. The reactionaries, the counter-revolutionaries, the imperialists, all live in perpetual despair, in perpetual anguish, perpetually lying in the most ridiculous and infantile way.

When you read the things said by some of those officials, some of those US senators, you ask yourself: But how is it possible that these gentlemen are not in a stable instead of belonging to what they call Congress? Some of them come out with absolute nonsense. Furthermore, they have a tremendous habit of lying; they cannot live without lying. They live in fear.

If the revolutionary government says one thing, which is what it has consistently been saying, they see ferocious, terrible things, a plan behind everything! How ridiculous! What fear they live in! And you have to wonder: Do they believe this? Do they believe everything they say? Do they need to believe everything they say? Can't they live without believing everything they say? Do they say everything they don't believe?

It is difficult to tell. This could be a matter for doctors and psychologists. What do they have in their brains? What fear is it that makes them see everything as a maneuver, as a belligerent, frightening, terrible plan? They don't know that there is no better tactic, no better strategy than to fight with clean hands, to fight with the truth. These are the only weapons that inspire confidence, that inspire faith, that inspire security, dignity and morale. And these are the weapons we revolutionaries have been using to defeat and crush our enemies.

Lies! Who has ever heard a lie from the lips of a revolutionary? Lies are weapons that help no revolutionary, and no serious revolutionary ever needs to resort to a lie. Their weapons are reason, morality, truth, the ability to defend an idea, a proposal, a position.

In short, the moral spectacle of our adversaries is truly lamentable. The soothsayers, the pundits, the specialists on the Cuba question have been working incessantly to unravel the mystery: Has Ernesto Guevara been purged? Is Ernesto Guevara sick? Does Ernesto Guevara have differences? And things of this sort.

Naturally, the people have confidence, the people have faith. But the enemy uses these things, especially abroad, to slander us. Here, they say, is a frightening, terrible communist regime: people disappear without a trace, without a sign, without an explanation. When the people began to notice his absence, we told them that we would inform them at the appropriate time, and that there were reasons for waiting.

We live and work surrounded by the forces of imperialism. The world does not live under normal conditions. As long as the criminal bombs of the US imperialists fall on the people of Vietnam, we cannot say we live under normal conditions. When more than 100,000 US soldiers land there to try to crush the liberation movement; when the soldiers of imperialism land in a republic that has legal rights equal to those of any other republic in the world, to trample its sovereignty, as in the case of the Dominican Republic, the world doesn't live under normal conditions. When the imperialists are surrounding our country, training mercenaries and organizing terrorist attacks in the most shameless manner, as in the case of [the attack by counter-revolutionary Cuban exiles on the Spanish merchant ship] *Sierra Aránzazu*, when the imperialists threaten to intervene in any country in Latin America or in the world, we do not live under normal conditions.

When we fought in the underground against the Batista dictatorship, revolutionaries who did not live under normal conditions had to abide by the rules of the struggle. In the same way—even though a revolutionary government exists in our country—so far as the realities of the world are concerned, we do not live under normal conditions, and we have to abide by the rules of that situation.

To explain this I am going to read a letter, handwritten and later typed, from compañero Ernesto Guevara, which is self-explanatory. I was wondering whether I needed to describe our friendship and comradeship, how it began and under what conditions it began and developed, but that's not necessary. I'm going to confine myself to reading the letter.

It reads as follows: "Havana..." It has no date, because the letter was intended to be read at what we considered the most appropriate moment, but to be strictly accurate it was delivered April 1 of this year—exactly six months and two days ago. It reads:

Havana
Year of Agriculture

Fidel:

At this moment I remember many things: when I met you in the house of [Cuban revolutionary] María Antonia, when you proposed I come along, all the tensions involved in the preparations [for the *Granma* expedition]. One day, they came and asked me who should be notified in case of death, and the real possibility of that fact struck us all. Later, we knew it was true that in a revolution one wins or dies (if it is a real one). Many compañeros fell along the way to victory.

Today everything has a less dramatic tone, because we are more mature. But the event repeats itself. I feel that I have fulfilled the part of my duty that tied me to the Cuban revolution in its territory, and I say goodbye to you, to the compañeros, to your people, who now are mine.

I formally resign my positions in the leadership of the party, my post as minister, my rank of commander, and my Cuban citizenship. Nothing legal binds me to Cuba. The only ties are of another nature — those that cannot be broken as can appointments to posts.

Recalling my past life, I believe I have worked with sufficient integrity and dedication to consolidate the revolutionary triumph. My only serious failing was not having had more confidence in you from the first moments in the Sierra Maestra, and not having understood quickly enough your qualities as a leader and a revolutionary.

I have lived magnificent days, and at your side I felt the pride of belonging to our people in the brilliant yet sad days of the Caribbean [missile] crisis. Seldom has a statesman been more brilliant than you in those days. I am also proud of having followed you without hesitation, of having identified with your way of thinking and of seeing and appraising dangers and principles.

Other nations of the world call for my modest efforts. I can do that which is denied you because of your responsibility at the head of Cuba, and the time has come for us to part.

I want it known that I do so with a mixture of joy and sorrow. I leave here the purest of my hopes as a builder and the dearest of my loved ones. And I leave a people who received me as a son. That wounds a part of my spirit. I carry to new battlefronts the faith that you taught me, the revolutionary spirit of my people, the feeling of fulfilling the most sacred of duties: to fight against imperialism wherever one may be. This comforts and more than heals the deepest wounds.

I state once more that I free Cuba from any responsibility, except that which stems from its example. If my final hour finds me under other skies, my last thought will be of this people and especially of you. I am thankful for your teaching, your example, and I will try to be faithful up to the final consequences of my actions.

I have always been identified with the foreign policy of our revolution, and I continue to be. Wherever I am, I will feel the responsibility of being a Cuban revolutionary, and I shall behave as such. I am not sorry that I leave nothing material to my wife and children. I am happy it is that way.

I ask nothing for them, as the state will provide them with enough to live on and to have an education.

I have many things to say to you and to our people, but I feel they are unnecessary. Words cannot express what I would want them to, and I don't think it is worthwhile to keep scribbling pages.

Hasta la victoria siempre! [Ever onward to victory!]

Patria o muerte! [Homeland or death!]

I embrace you with all my revolutionary fervor.

Che

Those who speak of revolutionaries, those who consider revolutionaries as cold, insensitive and unfeeling people, will have in this letter the example of all the feeling, all the sensitivity, all the purity that can be held within a revolutionary soul.

And all of us could answer:

Compañero Guevara: It is not responsibility that concerns us! We are responsible to the revolution. We are responsible for helping the revolutionary movement to the best of our ability! And we assume the responsibility, the consequences and the risks. For almost seven years it has always been like that, and we know that as long as imperialism exists, and as long as there are exploited and colonized peoples, we will continue running these risks and we will calmly continue assuming that responsibility.

It was our duty to comply with and respect the feelings of that compañero, to respect that freedom and that right. That is true freedom — not the freedom of those who seek to impose chains, but the freedom of those who leave to take up a rifle against the chains of slavery!

That is another freedom our revolution proclaims, Mr. Johnson! And if those who wish to leave Cuba to go to live with the imperialists, those whom the imperialists sometimes recruit to serve in Vietnam and the Congo, can do it, let everyone know that every citizen of this country, whenever they make a request to fight — not at the side of the imperialists but at the side of revolutionaries — this revolution will not deny them permission to go!

This is a free country, Mr. Johnson, truly free for everyone!

And that was not the only letter [from Che]. Besides this letter, and the occasion on which it was to be read, we have other letters greeting various compañeros, as well as letters addressed to his children, to his parents and to other compañeros. We will deliver these letters to those compañeros and those relatives, and we are going to ask them to donate them to the revolution, because we believe they are documents worthy of being part of history.

We believe this explains everything. This was what fell to us to explain. As for the rest, let our enemies worry about it. We have enough tasks, enough things to do in our country and with regard to the world, enough duties to fulfill.

And we will fulfill them.

We will develop our own paths, our ideas, our methods, our system. We'll make use of all the experiences that can be of value to us, and we'll develop our own experiences.

A new era is emerging in the history of our country, a different form of society, a different form of government. The government of a party, the party of the workers — the best workers — established with the participation of the masses, so that we may justly and reasonably state that this party is the vanguard of the workers, and that it is the representative of the workers in our revolutionary workers' democracy.

It will be a thousand times more democratic than bourgeois democracy, because we will establish administrative and political institutions that will call for the constant participation of the masses in the problems of society. This participation will be accomplished through capable organizations, through the party, on all levels.

And we will continue developing these new forms as only a revolution can do, and we will continue developing the consciousness and the habits necessary for these new forms. And we will not stop. Our people will not stop until they have achieved their final objectives.

This step means a lot. It constitutes one of the most outstanding events in the history of our country. It marks the historic moment in which the force to unite became mightier than the forces that separate and divide. It marks the historic moment in which a revolutionary people firmly united, in which the sense of duty prevailed over everything else, in which the collective spirit triumphed over all individualism, in which the interest of the homeland overwhelmingly and definitely prevailed over individual and group interests...

We know very well where the enemy is, who our sole and real enemy is. We know it quite well, very well. We have had to fight that enemy under difficult conditions. To face that enemy, we have needed the solidarity and help of many. To defeat the aggressive policy of that enemy, to continue confronting it, we need resources and arms. Here in Cuba, thousands of miles from any other socialist country, unable to depend on anything other than our own forces and our own arms during decisive moments, we are aware of the risks we have to take and will continue taking, we have to be armed to the teeth and prepared for whatever comes.

We might disagree on some point with any other party. Due to the heterogeneity of this contemporary world, with different countries confronting dissimilar situations and most unequal levels of material, technical and cultural development, Marxism cannot be like a church, like a religious doctrine, with its Pope and ecumenical council. It is a revolutionary and dialectical doctrine, not a religious doctrine. It is a guide for revolutionary action, not a dogma. It is anti-Marxist to try to encapsulate Marxism in a sort of catechism.

This diversity will inevitably lead to different interpretations... Marxism is not private property that can be recorded in a register of deeds. It is a doctrine of revolutionaries, written by revolutionaries, developed by other revolutionaries, for revolutionaries.

We will demonstrate our confidence in ourselves and our confidence in our ability to continue to develop our revolutionary path. We might disagree on some point or various points with another party. Differences, when they are honest, are transitory. What we will never do is insult on the one hand and beg on the other. We will know how to keep any different point of view within decent boundaries. We will know how to be friends with those who know how to be friends, and we will know how to respect those who know how to respect us. These norms will always determine our conduct. We will never ask anyone's permission to do anything. We will never ask anyone's permission to go anywhere. We will never ask anyone's permission to be friendly with any party or any people.

We know these problems are transitory. Problems pass, but people remain. Individuals pass away, but peoples remain. Leaders pass away, but revolutions persist. We see something else besides temporary relationships in the relations between parties and between revolutionary countries. We see lasting and ultimate relationships.

Nothing tending to create differences will ever come from our side. We will be guided by this basic principle, because we know it is a correct position and a just principle. And nothing will separate us from the dedication of all our energies to the struggle against the enemy of humanity: imperialism.

We could never say that those who have helped us defeat the imperialists are accomplices of the imperialists.

We not only aspire to a communist society, but to a communist world in which all nations have equal rights. We aspire to a communist world in which no nation has a veto. And we hope that the communist world of tomorrow will never present the same picture as the bourgeois world torn by internal disputes. Our hope is for a free society, free nations in which all countries—large and small—have equal rights.

We will defend our point of view and our position in a rational manner through our actions and our deeds, as we have up to now. Nothing will divert us from that path.

It is not easy to maintain that line, that inflexible independence, in the face of the complexities of current problems and the present world. But we will! This revolution has not been imported from anywhere. It is a genuine product of this country. No one told us how we had to make it, and we made it! No one shall have to tell us how to continue it.

We have learned to write history, and we will continue writing it! Let no one doubt this!

We live in a complex and dangerous world. We will face the risks with dignity and firmness! Our fate will be the fate of other peoples, and our fate will be the fate of the world!

I call on all compañeros present, on all the representatives of our party, on all the secretaries of the party cells who are participating in this general assembly. I call on everyone here who represents the will of the party, of the party which in turn represents the workers, to ratify the resolutions of the national leadership!

We ask for the full and unanimous ratification of the Central Committee of our party. I ask for your full support for the line followed by the revolutionary leadership up to the present, and full support for the policy proclaimed here today.

Long live the Cuban Communist Party!
Long live its Central Committee!
Long live our socialist and communist revolution!
Patria o muerte! [Homeland or death!]
Venceremos! [We will win!]

9. ON THE LATIN AMERICAN REVOLUTION

HAVANA, AUGUST 10, 1967

Fidel Castro presented this forceful defense of armed struggle as the "fundamental road" for the Latin America revolution at the closing session of the conference of the Latin American Solidarity Organizations (OLAS).

Fellow delegates;

Invited guests;

Compañeros:

It is not easy to deliver the closing address to this first Latin American solidarity conference. In the first place, what should our attitude be? To speak as a member of one of the organizations represented here? Or to speak somewhat more freely, simply as a guest speaker.

And I wish to say that we are expressing here the views of our party and our people, which is the same opinion and the same point of view as defended by our delegation in OLAS...

The drawing together of the revolutionaries of the United States with those of Latin America is the most natural thing in the world, and the most spontaneous. Our people admire [US black rights activist] Stokely [Carmichael] for the statements he has made in the OLAS conference, because we know that it takes courage to do this. We know what it means to make such statements when you are going to return to a society that applies the most cruel and brutal methods of repression, and constantly commits the worst crimes against the black sector of the population. We know the hatred that his statements will arouse among the oppressors.

For this reason we believe that revolutionary movements all over the world must give Stokely their utmost support as protection against the repression of the imperialists, in such a way that everyone will know that any crime committed against this leader will have serious repercussions throughout the world. Our solidarity can help to protect Stokely's life.

This is why revolutionaries are getting together and internationalism is being practiced. We believe that the attitude of this US revolutionary leader is a great example of militant internationalism, characteristic of revolutionaries. We undoubtedly sympathize much more with this type of revolutionary than with the super-theorizers, who are revolutionary in word and bourgeois in deed.

This internationalism is not just proclaimed; it is practiced! The blacks in the United States are offering resistance; they are offering armed resistance. They didn't go around making theses, or talking about the need for objective conditions first in order to seize a weapon and defend their rights. We don't have to appeal to any philosophy — and, even less, to a revolutionary philosophy — to justify inaction.

We believe that if there is any country where the struggle is difficult, that country is the United States. And here we have US revolutionaries providing us with examples and giving us lessons.

We always have to bring along some cables, some papers, some news clippings, especially to a meeting of this nature. We sincerely believe that we would not be fulfilling our duty if we did not express here that the OLAS conference has been a victory for revolutionary ideas, though not a victory without struggle.

In OLAS, a latent ideological struggle has been reflected. Should we conceal it? No. What is gained by concealing it? Did OLAS intend to crush or to harm anyone? No. That is not a revolutionary method. It is not in line with the consciousness of true revolutionaries.

We believe that revolutionary ideas must prevail. If revolutionary ideas were defeated, the revolution in Latin America would be lost or would be delayed indefinitely. Ideas can hasten a process, or they can delay it considerably. We believe that the triumph of revolutionary ideas among the masses — not all the masses, but a sufficiently large part — is absolutely necessary. This does not mean that action must wait for the triumph of ideas. This is one of the essential points. There are those who believe that it is necessary for ideas to triumph among the masses before initiating action, and there are others who understand that action is one of the most effective instruments for bringing about the triumph of ideas.

Whoever stops to wait for ideas to triumph among the majority of the masses before initiating revolutionary action will never be a revolutionary. What is the difference between such a revolutionary and a *latifundista*, a wealthy bourgeois? Nothing!

Human society will, of course, continue to develop, in spite of human beings and their errors. But that is not a revolutionary attitude.

If that had been our way of thinking we would never have initiated a revolutionary process. It was enough for the ideas to take root in the minds of a sufficient number of people for revolutionary action to be initiated. Through this action, the masses began to acquire these ideas and this consciousness.

It is obvious that in many parts of Latin America there are already a number of people who are convinced of such ideas, and who have started revolutionary action. What distinguishes the true revolutionary from the false is precisely this: one acts to move the masses and the other waits for the masses to attain a certain consciousness before starting to act.

There are some principles that one should not accept without argument, but which are essential truths accepted by the majority, although with reservations on the part of a few. There is much futile discussion about ways and means of struggle: whether it should be peaceful or non-peaceful, armed or unarmed. The essence of this discussion — which we describe as futile because it resembles the argument between two deaf and dumb people — is that it distinguishes those who want to promote the revolution from those who do not. Let no one be fooled.

Different formulations have been used: whether the road [of armed struggle] is the only road or not the only road; if it is the exclusive road. The conference has been very clear in this respect. It does not say "only" road, although it might have said that. It says "fundamental" road, to which other forms of struggle must be subordinated. In the long run, it is the only road. However, to use the word "only"—even though the sense of the word is understood and even if it were true—might lead to errors about the imminence of the struggle.

That is why we understand that the declaration, by calling it the fundamental road—the road that must be taken in the long run—is the correct formulation.

Our way of thinking, and that of our party and our people, is that no one should harbor any illusions about seizing power by peaceful means in any country on this continent. Anyone trying to convince the masses of this will be completely deceiving them.

This does not mean that one has to go out and grab a rifle and start fighting tomorrow, just anywhere. That is not the question. It is a question of ideological conflict between those who want to make revolution and those who do not. It is the conflict between those who want to make revolution and those who want to curb it. Essentially, anyone can decide whether or not it is possible, whether or not conditions are ripe, whether or not to take up arms.

No one could be so sectarian or dogmatic as to say that one has to go out and grab a rifle tomorrow, anywhere. We ourselves do not doubt that there are some countries in which this is not an immediate task, but we are convinced that it will be their task in the long run.

Some people have put forward even more radical theses than Cuba has. They say we Cubans believe that in a particular country there are no conditions for armed struggle, but they claim we are wrong. The funny thing is that this is sometimes argued by representatives who are not exactly in favor of armed struggle. We are not angered by this. We prefer them to make mistakes trying to make revolution without the right conditions than to have them make the mistake of never making revolution. Of course, I hope no one will make a mistake! But no one who really wants to fight will ever be in conflict with us, and those who never want to fight will always be in conflict with us.

We understand the essence of the matter very well: The conflict is between those who want to advance the revolution and those who are deadly enemies of the ideas of the revolution. A whole range of factors have contributed to these positions.

It is not enough simply to have a correct position. Even among those who really want to make revolution, many mistakes are made, and there are still many weaknesses. But we will never have profound differences with anyone—no matter what their mistakes—who honestly takes a revolutionary position.

We believe that revolutionary thought must take a new course; that we must leave behind old vices and sectarian positions of all kinds, including the positions of those who believe they have a monopoly on the revolution or on revolutionary theory. Poor theory! How it has suffered in these processes. Poor theory! How it has been abused, and is still being abused! All these years have taught us to meditate more and analyze better. We no longer accept any truths as "self-evident." "Self-evident" truths are a part of bourgeois philosophy. A whole series of old clichés should be abolished. Marxist, revolutionary political literature itself should be renewed, because if you simply repeat clichés, phraseology and verbiage that have been repeated for 35 years you don't win anyone over, *you don't win anyone over*.

There are times when so-called Marxist political documents give the impression that all you need to do is go to the archives and ask for a form: form 14, form 13, form 12, they are all alike, with the same empty phrases. This is a language incapable of expressing real situations. Often the documents are divorced from real life. Many people are told that this is Marxism, but in what way is this different from a catechism, a litany or a rosary?

And everyone posing as a Marxist almost feels obliged to go around looking for this or that manifesto. You can read 25 manifestos of 25 different organizations, and they are all alike, copied from the same template. No one is convinced by any of them.

Nothing could be further from the thinking and style of the founder of Marxism than such empty talk that puts a straight jacket on ideas. Marx was, undoubtedly, one of the greatest, most brilliant writers of all time. But, worse than the phrases are the ideas they convey. Meaningless phrases are bad, of course, but so are the supposed meanings of certain phrases. There are some ideas that are 40 years old, such as the famous thesis about the role of the national bourgeoisie. How hard it has been to finally shake off the idea that this thesis applies on this continent. How much paper, how many phrases, how much empty talk has been wasted waiting for a liberal, progressive, anti-imperialist bourgeoisie.

Is there anyone who today believes that any bourgeoisie on this continent is playing a revolutionary role?

All these ideas have been gaining strength and have been maintained for such a long time.

I am not saying that the revolutionary movement and the communist movement in general have ceased to play a role — even an important role — in the history of the revolutionary process and of revolutionary ideas in Latin America. But the communist movement developed a certain method and style and, in some aspects, took on the characteristics of a religion. We sincerely believe that those characteristics should be left behind.

Of course, to some of these "illustrious revolutionary thinkers" we are merely petit-bourgeois adventurists lacking in revolutionary maturity. We are lucky that the revolution came before maturity! Because in the end, the mature ones are so mature they are rotten.

Nevertheless, we consider ours to be a Marxist-Leninist party, and a communist party. This is not a matter of words, it is a matter of fact.

We do not consider ourselves teachers, or that we have established a model, as some people say. But we have the right to consider our party a Marxist-Leninist party, a communist party.

We are deeply satisfied, and it is with great joy, not sadness, that we see the ranks of the revolutionary movement increasing and the revolutionary organizations multiplying. Marxist-Leninist ideas are making headway and we felt deeply satisfied when the final resolution of this conference proclaimed that the revolutionary movement in Latin America is being guided by Marxist-Leninist ideas.

This means that convent-like narrow-mindedness must be overcome. We, in our [Cuban] Communist Party, will fight to overcome that narrow-mindedness. As a Marxist-Leninist party, we belong to OLAS. As a Marxist-Leninist party we belong not to a small group within the revolutionary movement but to an organization that comprises all true revolutionaries. We will not be prejudiced against any revolutionary.

There is a much wider movement on this continent than the movement constituted simply by the communist parties of Latin America. We are a part of that wider movement, and we will judge the conduct of organizations not by what they say they are but by what they prove they are, by what they do.

We feel very satisfied that our party has wholeheartedly become part of this wider movement, the movement that has just held this first conference.

Much could be said about the importance and the vanguard role of the guerrilla, but it is not possible to do so in a meeting like this. Guerrilla experiences in this continent have taught us many things, including that it is a terrible mistake to think that the guerrilla movement can be directed from the cities.

That is the reason for the thesis that political and military commands must be united.

It is our conviction that it is not only stupid but criminal to want to direct the guerrillas from the city. We have had the opportunity to appreciate the consequences of this error many times. It is necessary that these ideas be overcome, and that is why we consider the resolution of this conference to be of great importance.

The guerrilla is bound to be the nucleus of the revolutionary movement. This does not mean that the guerrilla movement can develop without any previous work, or exist without political direction. No! We do not deny the role of the leading political organizations. The guerrilla is organized by a political movement, by a political organization. What we believe to be incompatible with correct ideas of guerrilla struggle is the concept of directing the guerrilla from the cities. And in the conditions of our continent, it will be very difficult to suppress the role of the guerrilla.

There are some who ask themselves if it would be possible in any country of Latin America to achieve power without armed struggle. Of course, hypothetically, when a great part of the continent has been liberated it would not be surprising if a revolution succeeded without opposition— but this would be an exception. However, this does not mean that the revolution is going to succeed in any country without a struggle. The blood of the revolutionaries of a specific country may not be shed, but their victory will only be possible thanks to the efforts, sacrifices and blood of the revolutionaries of the whole continent.

It would be false, therefore, to say that they had a revolution in that country without a struggle. That will always be a lie. I believe that it is not right for any revolutionary to wait with arms crossed until all the other peoples struggle and create the conditions for victory for them without a struggle. That will never be a revolutionary attitude.

To those who believe that a peaceful transition is possible in some countries of this continent, we say that we cannot understand what kind of peaceful transition they refer to, unless it is a peaceful transition in agreement with imperialism. The bourgeoisie, the oligarchies and imperialism control all the means for peaceful struggle. Sometimes you hear a revolutionary say: They crushed us, they organized 200 radio programs, so many newspapers, so many magazines, so many TV shows, so many of this and so many of the other. And one wants to ask: What did you expect? That they would put TV, radio, magazines, newspapers, printing shops, everything at your disposal? Are you unaware that those are precisely the instruments the ruling class uses to crush revolutions?

They complain that the bourgeoisie and the oligarchies crush them with their media campaigns, as if it is a surprise. The first thing that a revolutionary has to understand is that the ruling classes have organized the state in such a way as to maintain themselves in power by all possible means. And they use not only arms, but all possible instruments to influence, deceive and confuse.

Those who believe that they are going to win elections against the imperialists are just plain naive; and those who believe that the day will come when they will take power through elections, are super-naive. It is necessary to have experienced a revolutionary process and to understand the repressive apparatus by which the ruling classes maintain the status quo, and just how much one has to struggle — how difficult it is.

This does not imply the negation of all other forms of struggle. When someone writes a manifesto in a newspaper, attends a demonstration, holds a rally, propagates an idea, they may be using the famous so-called legal means. We must do away with that differentiation between legal or illegal means, and call them revolutionary or non-revolutionary means.

The revolutionary, in pursuit of revolutionary aims, uses various methods. The essential question is whether the masses will be led to believe that the revolutionary movement, that socialism, can take power without a struggle. That is a lie! Those who assert, anywhere in Latin America, that they will take power peacefully will be deceiving the masses.

We are talking about conditions in Latin America. We don't want to involve ourselves in any other problems, which are already significant enough, of other revolutionary organizations in places such as Europe. We are addressing Latin America. If only they would also confine their mistakes to themselves... but no! They try to encourage the errors of those who are already mistaken on this continent! And to such an extent that part of the so-called revolutionary press has made attacks against Cuba for our revolutionary stand in Latin America. That's a fine thing! They don't know how to be revolutionaries over there, yet they want to teach us how to be revolutionaries over here!

But we are not anxious to start arguments. We already have enough to think about. However, we will not overlook direct or indirect, overt or covert attacks from some neo-social democrats in Europe.

These are clear ideas. We are absolutely convinced that in the long run there is only one solution, as expressed in the resolution: the role of the guerrilla in Latin America.

Does this mean that if a garrison rises in rebellion, because there are some revolutionaries in it, we should not support the rebellion because it is not a guerrilla struggle? No! But it is stupid to think, as one organization did, that the revolution would be made with the rebellion of garrisons only. It is stupid to have a rebellion in a garrison, and afterwards let it be crushed by overwhelming forces as has happened on some occasions.

New situations may arise — we do not deny that. For example, in Santo Domingo a case came up when a military uprising began to acquire a revolutionary character. But of course, this doesn't mean that the revolutionary movement must wait and see what happens. No one was able to foresee the form or character that the revolutionary movement acquired, especially after the imperialist intervention.

In other words, by stressing the role of the guerrilla as an immediate task in all those countries where real conditions exist, we do not discard other forms of revolutionary armed struggle.

The revolutionary movement must be in a position to take advantage of and support any form of struggle that may arise and that can develop or strengthen their position. But I believe that no one who considers themselves a revolutionary should wait for a garrison to rebel in order to make a revolution. I believe that no revolutionary can dream of making a revolution with the rebellion of garrisons.

The uprising of military units may constitute an unforeseen factor that may arise, but no really serious revolutionary movement would begin with that as a starting point.

Guerrilla warfare is the main form of struggle, but that does not exclude all other expressions of armed struggle that may arise.

It is necessary to clarify these ideas because we have had very bitter experiences; not the blows or reverses of a military engagement, but frustrations — in the long run sad and disastrous for the revolutionary movement — of a political nature that were the consequence of wrong concepts. The most painful case was that of Venezuela.

In Venezuela the revolutionary movement was growing and it has had to pay dearly for the absurd mistake of wanting to lead the guerrilla movement from the city, of wanting to use the guerrilla movement as an instrument for political maneuvers and low politics. They have suffered the consequences of incorrect attitudes, and on many occasions, immoral attitudes.

The case of Venezuela is a very worthwhile case to consider, because if we do not learn the lessons of Venezuela, we will never learn anything.

Or course, the guerrilla movement in Venezuela is far from being crushed, in spite of treason. And we, gentlemen, have every right to use the word "treason." Some here will not like it; a few will even feel offended. I hope that some day they will be convinced that they have no reason to be offended unless they carry the seeds of treason in their hearts.

The case of Venezuela is eloquent in many aspects, because in Venezuela a group — which was in the leadership of a party with all these wrong concepts — almost achieved what neither imperialism nor the repressive forces of the regime could.

The party, or rather not the party but the rightist leadership of the Venezuelan [Communist] Party, has adopted a position that is practically that of an enemy of revolution, an instrument of imperialism and the oligarchy. And I do not say this just for the sake of it. I am not a slanderer.

We have some unfinished business with that group of traitors. We do not encourage polemics and we do not incite conflicts. For a long time we have silently endured a barrage of documents and attacks from that rightist leadership, whilst they abandoned the guerrilla fighters and took the road of conciliation and submission.

We were the victims of deceit. First they spoke to us about something strange—for many of these problems began with a series of strange things—they began to talk of democratic peace. And we would say: "What the devil does democratic peace mean? What does that mean? It is strange, very strange." But they would say: "No, that is a revolutionary slogan to widen the front, to join forces, to present a broad front." "A broad front?" "Well, a broad theoretical front, who will oppose that? Trust us!"

Then, after a few months, they began to speak of tactical retreats. Tactical retreats? How odd! If they had told us the truth we might have disagreed, we might have had doubts. But they never did. A "tactical retreat"—that is what they told the militants and the people. The tactical retreat was followed by an attempt to end the struggle, an attempt to suppress the guerrilla movement. Everyone knows that in a guerrilla movement there is no tactical retreat, because a guerrilla that retreats is like an airplane that cuts the engine in mid-flight—and falls to the ground. Such a tactical retreat must have been conjured up by those genius inventors of high-flown revolutionary theories. Anyone with any idea of what a guerrilla is, who hears talk of retreat by guerrillas, says: "This person is talking a lot of nonsense. A guerrilla unit can be totally withdrawn, but it cannot retreat."

Bit by bit they began to unmask themselves, until one day they removed the mask completely and said: "Let's have an election." Thus, they became electoralists.

But even before they declared themselves in favor of elections, they committed one of the most vile deeds that a revolutionary party can commit: They began to act as informers, as public accusers against the guerrillas. They took advantage of the case of Iribarren Borges and openly and publicly denounced the guerrilla movement, practically delivering it into the jaws of the beasts of the regime. The government had the weapons and the soldiers with which to pursue the guerrillas, who would not retreat. The so-called party, or the rightist leadership of the party, had taken control of the guerrilla command and had armed the repressive forces that persecuted the guerrilla forces, both morally and politically.

We must ask ourselves honestly, how could we, a revolutionary party, cover up for a convent-like party that was trying to morally arm the repressive forces against the persecuted guerrilla forces.

Then came the rhetoric. They began to accuse us, saying that we were guilty of creating divisions! They were not discussing a group of charlatans. They were talking about a group of guerrillas that had been in the mountains for years: combatants who had gone into the mountains and who were completely abandoned and forgotten. But how can a revolutionary say: "Yes, once more you are correct; you who have been deceiving us — speaking to us about one thing and then doing something else?"

Naturally we condemned them publicly, after a series of statements had already been issued by the right-wing leadership against our party, accusing us in a treacherous manner and using the Iribarren incident to spread calumnies and to attack revolutionaries.

That provoked an irate and indignant protest from the right-wing leadership, which made us the butt of a series of tirades. They did not answer a single one of our arguments; they were unable to answer even one, and they wrote a maudlin reply to the effect that we were ignoble, that we had attacked an underground party — a combative, heroic anti-imperialist organization.

Why has it been necessary to bring this up here? Because that document [from the Venezuelan Communist Party] became the argument of a whole gang of detractors and slanderers of the Cuban revolution. That incident triggered a real international conspiracy against the Cuban revolution...

In the first place, there has been a deliberate attempt to distort our views. Furthermore, these gentlemen of the rightist leadership of the Venezuelan Communist Party had a goal, and they pursued it in a very immoral manner. Once, when [President] Leoni's administration was trying to establish diplomatic relations with the Soviet Union, we were asked for our opinion. These gentlemen were also asked, and they responded negatively to the idea.

Why do these gentlemen resort to dragging up a problem that was not being discussed with them? Clearly it forms part of the conspiracy in which they and their fellows are participating, together with imperialism, to create a serious conflict between the Cuban revolution and the socialist countries. It is unquestionable that this argument is one of the lowest, most despicable, most treacherous and provocative. It pretends to counterpose our position to our trade with capitalist countries. Until recently this argument was not openly published. The capitalist press published it, and the letter was published by the counterrevolutionary organizations, but this low argument was also employed, *sotto voce*, in small groups by the conspirators against and critics of the Cuban revolution.

In the first place, they are lying when they state that Cuba is opposed to trade. In every international body, economic conference and organization that Cuba has taken part in as a state, we have repeatedly denounced the imperialist policy of blockade and the acts of the US government against our country as a violation of free trade and of the right of all countries to trade with each other. Cuba has inflexibly maintained that position at all times. That has been a policy pursued by our country and the history of our commercial relations bears that out. Our position does not refer to commerce and it has never referred to commerce. This position of ours is known to the Soviet people, because we have stated our viewpoint to them.

The problem of a socialist state giving financial and technical help to the Latin American oligarchies is another issue. Let these things not be confused. Some socialist states even offered dollar loans to Mr. Lleras Restrepo [of Colombia] because he was having difficulties with the International Monetary Fund (IMF).

And we asked ourselves: How can this be? This is absurd! Dollar loans to an oligarchic government that is repressing, persecuting and assassinating guerrillas. War is conducted with money—among other things—because the oligarchies have nothing with which to wage war except money, with which they pay their mercenary forces.

Such things seem absurd to us—as does everything that involves financial and technical aid to any of those countries that are repressing the revolutionary movement or are accomplices in the imperialist blockade against Cuba, which we condemn. It is unfortunate that we have to go into this problem in detail, but naturally it is the number one argument employed by this gang.

It is logical. Cuba is a small country against which the United States practices a cruel blockade. At Gran Tierra we explained to some of those present how the imperialists do everything within their power to prevent our obtaining even such insignificant things as a handful of seeds, for rice or cotton or vegetables or grain, or any kind at all.

No one can imagine the lengths to which the imperialists will go to extend their economic blockade against our country. And all those governments have violated and are continuing to violate the most elementary principles of free trade. Those governments help imperialism in its attempts to starve the people of Cuba. And if that is the case, if internationalism exists and solidarity is a word worthy of respect, then the least we can expect of any state in the socialist camp is that it will lend no financial or technical assistance of any sort to those governments.

It is truly repugnant that this vile argument is used to test the revolutionary steadfastness of this country, or to provoke conflicts with it. And, truly, this nation is steadfast and its policy is based on principles. It acts in a responsible way, yes! We are careful to prevent polemics and conflicts wherever possible, yes! But never believe that under any circumstance, no matter how difficult, no matter how great the problem, will they be able to drive our dignity and revolutionary consciousness to the wall! Because if that was the kind of leadership our party has, we would have surrendered long ago in the face of the great and mortal dangers engendered by imperialism.

It is equally repugnant that they try to find a contradiction between this position and Cuba's commercial policy with the capitalist world. The imperialists have tried to break us with the blockade. The question is not what countries we trade with, but how many countries throughout the world we do not trade with simply because, one by one, and under the constant and growing pressure of the imperialists, they break trade relations with us.

We have never broken off those relations. Imperialism has taken care of that, in the same way that it has seen to it that they break off diplomatic relations with Cuba, one by one. These are weapons that imperialism has used against the Cuban revolution, in diplomatic and commercial relations.

And it is worthwhile to speak about commercial relations because some of the mafia—and I cannot use any other term for those who attack our revolution in such a slanderous and base fashion, without any serious and powerful argument—have spoken of the fact that we have not broken off diplomatic relations with the state of Israel. Nor did our country break off relations with Albania when a great number of countries from the socialist camp did. We did not break off relations with the Federal Republic of Germany [West Germany], but they did not want to accept our establishing relations with the German Democratic Republic [East Germany]. And even though we knew that the consequences would be the rupture of diplomatic and commercial relations, this country had not the slightest hesitation of being among the first to establish diplomatic relations with the German Democratic Republic. This country has never hesitated to put our political principles above economic interest, for if this were not so we would have found a million reasons to reconcile ourselves with imperialism a long time ago, and even more so today when that has become quite fashionable.

The slightest insinuation of our following a sordid policy of self-interest in our international relations is to forget the price this country has paid for its unyielding stand in solidarity with a great number of countries—Algeria among them, notwithstanding the fact that this gave another country [France], which was one of the biggest buyers of Cuban sugar, an excuse to stop buying our sugar.

Our people always saw, and we thought that everyone understood quite clearly, that each time imperialist pressure against anyone selling to us or buying from us failed, it was a victory for our revolution in the face of the blockade. We always saw it, in a certain sense, as self-defense, and we have spoken publicly about it. We have spoken in Revolution Plaza quite recently about Europe and why, in spite of its economic and industrial development, Europe has to resist the competition of Yankee monopolies, and how, owing to a question of self-interest, it was impossible for them to bow to imperialist pressure. Because Cuba was a growing market, Cuba paid, and paid promptly, and the imperialists failed utterly in their attempts to have the whole capitalist world break off commercial relations with Cuba.

What has this to do with our arguments? What has it to do with our statements? If the imperialists had succeeded, the road of the revolution would have been much more difficult.

Do we trade with the socialist camp? Yes, it is a trade that is practically all barter, using the so-called clearing currency, which has a value only in the country with which the agreement is signed. And if the country needs medicines of a certain kind, or other things essential for the life of our people, and the trade organizations in any socialist country say "we do not have it," we must look for those items in other markets and pay in the currency of that country. It is here that imperialism tries to crush us. If we have to buy medicines in capitalist countries — because we cannot get them in a socialist country to save the lives of sick people, including children, to reduce the child mortality rate (and we have reduced it), or the mortality rate in general and attain the excellent position Cuba holds today in public health and in many other fields — apparently we are criminals. Apparently we are people without principles or morals. Apparently we are the opposite of what we proclaim.

And they have tried the same tactic concerning the breaking off of relations with the state of Israel. No one could have the slightest doubt about the position of Cuba on that painful problem. We have a firm, principled and uncompromising position [on the Middle East]. It is just that we do not like petty subterfuges.

What is Israel? It is an instrument of Yankee imperialism, and the United States is the instigator, the protector, of that state. That is why I ask those of the mafia, who intend to slander Cuba with their arguments, why don't they break relations with the United States? It just happens that if we are not obedient yes-men, we are immoral, a people without principles and full of ideological contradictions. All this is but part of a repugnant conspiracy to create a conflict between the Cuban revolution and the states of the socialist camp.

We are not instigators of conflict; we do not seek to unnecessarily or gratuitously create conflicts of that nature. Actually, I believe that the interdependence of the revolutionary movements, parties and states will grow, as we face a powerful enemy.

We want this very much, being a small country with no possibility of economic autonomy, in need of arms to defend ourselves from Yankee imperialists. It is unimaginable that we would act in an irresponsible manner and create problems that could be avoided. But between Cuba's attitude and the idea that this country can be intimidated with provocations of that sort, there is a profound abyss.

At the bottom of all this there is a conspiracy of the reactionary mafia within the revolutionary movement and Yankee imperialism — a conspiracy to create a conflict between our revolution and the states of the socialist camp. What they attempt, what they demand, what they urge, is that the socialist camp also joins in the imperialist blockade against Cuba. They do not hide it...

We do not deliberately seek conflict, problems or difficult situations. That will never be the attitude of the revolution. They will never see an irresponsible, absurd attitude adopted by the revolution. No! But neither will they see the revolution hesitating, giving up or yielding one iota of its principles! For *"Patria o muerte"* has many meanings. It means being revolutionary until death. It means being a proud people until death! And the fact that we speak about *"Patria o muerte"* does not mean that we are fatalists. It is an expression of determination. When we say "death," we mean not that only we would be dead, but that many of our enemies would be dead too. Kill our people? All the soldiers of Yankee imperialism could not do it!

These facts, these attitudes are calling us all to order; they are calling us all to reason and to clarify things. These attitudes are not the result of development, but rather of the deterioration of revolutionary ideas and revolutionary consciousness.

The resolutions of OLAS do not mean that everything is done. They do not mean that the struggle is won. The Tricontinental conference also passed resolutions, and there were those who signed the resolutions and forgot all about them afterwards.

There must be a struggle. We have to struggle. Saying that Cuba wants to set itself up as a judge or leader is more than ridiculous. No! And I am going to tell you what we really think: There is no reason why there should be leading peoples or leading individuals! It is leading ideas that are needed! Revolutionary ideas will be the true and only guide for our peoples. We fight for our ideas! We defend ideas! But to defend ideas does not mean the pretension to lead anyone. The world does not need countries that lead, parties that lead or individuals that lead. The world, and above all our Latin American world, needs ideas that lead.

The ideas will open the road. We know the process. At the beginning, when a few people began to think about the idea of an armed struggle in our country and we began to struggle, very few believed in this possibility — very few. For a long time we were very few. And afterwards, little by little, these ideas began to gain prestige, began to catch on, and the time came when everyone believed and the revolution won.

It was very difficult to win acceptance for the idea that the struggle of the people against modern professional armies was possible in order to make a revolution! And when that was finally demonstrated, after the triumph of the revolution, what happened? Everyone believed in this truth in such a way that the counterrevolutionaries also believed that it could also be true for them.

Then followed the organization of opposition guerrilla groups and counterrevolutionary gangs. Even the most gentle, the most peaceful of the counterrevolutionaries, the most charlatan of counterrevolutionary park-benchers, joined a gang and took to the hills. Then it became necessary to show them they were mistaken — that that kind of action was a revolutionary action to be used against the oligarchies. A counterrevolution of oligarchs — a guerrilla warfare of oligarchs and of reactionaries against a social revolution — is impossible.

It was extremely difficult until we were finally able to prove this. We have had to point out more than once that it is impossible for oligarchs to defend themselves against the people's struggle; that it is impossible for the people to be defeated by counterrevolutionary guerrilla gangs. The CIA knows this. Do you know who are probably the most convinced of the effectiveness of armed revolutionary guerrilla warfare and the incapacity of the oligarchies to oppose the armed guerrilla struggle of the people? Do you know who? The CIA, Johnson, McNamara, Dean Rusk, Yankee imperialism. That's who are the most convinced.

One could ask: How is it possible for these counterrevolutionaries to let themselves be deceived and dragged into the armed struggle against the revolution if it is impossible for them to win? We are forced to admit that it is because these counterrevolutionaries are more consistent than many who call themselves super-revolutionaries.

They are most consistent. Naturally, afterwards they say that they were fooled, that they were deceived, that they believed that the army, that the militia… All that. For us it is a scratched record.

Logically, the ideas in our country have had to develop dialectically, through struggle and through conflict. And it will be the same in every country, and no country will escape from this conflict of ideas. These conflicting ideas survive even in Cuba. The fact that we have a revolutionary people does not mean that there are no antagonisms or contradictions. Here we find the contradiction with the counterrevolution and imperialism, and there are also conflicts with those who share the ideas of the reactionary gentlemen of the Venezuelan party.

In this country we also have our micro-faction. We can't call it a faction, because it has no volume, no size and no potential. Where does that micro-faction come from? From the old resentful sectarians. Because our revolution has its history. I said that at the beginning very few believed, but afterwards many believed. Our revolution has its own history. Our revolution passed through the phase of sectarianism, and the sectarians created serious problems for us with their ferocious opportunism and their inexorable policy of persecution against many people. They brought corruption into the revolution. Naturally, the revolution patiently made criticisms; it was generous toward that sectarianism. Moreover, we had to be careful to prevent sectarianism from creating neo-sectarianism in the ranks of the revolution, and we succeeded. But some sectarian elements held on; they swallowed their resentment but each time they had a chance they expressed it. There are those who never believed in the revolution unless it was in an opportunistic way—trying to profit by the efforts of the revolutionary people; trying to climb the ladder in a shameful way. They never believed in revolution and they haven't learned in eight years, or in 10 years, and they will never learn.

Let it be clearly understood: I am not referring to old communists, because the worst expression of sectarianism and the worst activities of those sectarians have been their attempts to identify the old communists with their pseudo-revolutionary attitudes. We have to say that the revolution counts, and always counted, on the support of the real communists in this country. Naturally, at the time of sectarianism, many cowards who had deserted the ranks of the old party turned up again. Opportunism and sectarianism brings all this in its wake and, isolated from the masses, tries to strengthen itself by means of favoritism. Then follow the incomes, and higher incomes, and higher incomes and privileges.

Logically, when the revolution put a brake on sectarianism, it also prevented the emergence of sectarianism of another kind. That has always been our method, to try to find the best solution without excesses of any type, preferring to sin by omission than by excess.

So here we also have our micro-faction, composed of old sectarian groups — which are not the same as the old communists. And I repeat, the greatest harm is that they have tried, although in vain, to instill their unhealthy and resentful ideas into the old and tried revolutionaries. They were the ones who, for example, at the time of the October [Missile] Crisis, thought that we should let Yankee imperialism inspect us, search us from head to foot, and let the planes fly low over us, in fact, everything. They have been systematically opposed to all the concepts of the revolution; to the most pure and sincere revolutionary attitudes of our people; to our concepts of socialism, of communism, of everything.

This micro-faction has the same attitudes as the larger group. It constitutes a new form of counterrevolutionary activity, in that it has the same goals as Alpha 66, Faria, Pompeyo and company, the same as McNamara, Johnson and all those people.

Now the CIA has a new plan. Why does it want to prepare so many personal attacks and so many other things? Its plan now is that Castro has to be eliminated in order to destroy the revolution, because imperialism is losing ground. In the beginning, it wanted to do away with everything revolutionary — now, the more it loses ground, the more frightened it gets. Now its plan is to moderate the line of the revolution, to change its course, so that Cuba will take a more moderate position. In this, Alpha 66, Johnson, Faria, the micro-factionalists and similar political groups coincide. They are all harboring illusions.

I'm not really interested in buying a life insurance policy. I don't give a damn! Let them believe what they want. I don't want to be indebted to our enemies for their ceasing to consider me a true enemy. I don't want to be indebted to them for their not doing whatever they want. They have their rights and they are within their rights. I have no intention of buying any insurance policy.

But, to all of you, I think it is unnecessary to say that the line of this revolution is not the Castro line; it is the line of a people, it is the line of a leading group that has a real revolutionary history, and it is the natural line of this revolution!

The counterrevolutionaries encourage one another. Their international organization has been greatly encouraged by the idea that insurmountable antagonisms may develop between the Cuban revolution and the socialist camp. In reality, the only thing that we can say is that it is an honor to our revolution that our enemies give it so much thought. It must likewise be an honor for all Latin American revolutionaries that imperialism has paid so much attention to the problem of OLAS. They issued threats, they postponed the OAS conference and said they were going to "clean the place up," and that OLAS could not take place. But the OLAS conference has been held — representing a genuine revolutionary movement whose ideas are solid because they are based on reality. OLAS is the interpreter of tomorrow's history, interpreter of the future, because OLAS [the Spanish word for "waves"] is a wave of the future, a symbol of the revolutionary wave sweeping a continent of 250 million people. This continent is pregnant with revolution. Sooner or later, it will be born. Its birth may be more or less complicated, but it is inevitable.

We do not have the slightest doubt: There will be victories, there will be reverses, there will be advances and there will be retreats; but the arrival of a new era is inevitable. The victory of the peoples in the face of injustice, exploitation, oligarchy and imperialism, whatever mistakes are made and whatever mistaken ideas may be obstacles on the road, is inevitable.

We have spoken to you with complete and absolute frankness. We know that the true revolutionaries will always be in solidarity with Cuba; we know that no true revolutionary or communist on this continent, or among our people, will ever let themselves be induced to take positions that would lead them into an alliance with imperialism; that would make them go hand in hand with the imperialist masters against the Cuban revolution and against the Latin American revolution.

We do not condemn anyone *a priori*. We do not close the doors to anyone and nor do we attack anyone en masse. We express our ideas, we defend and debate our ideas. And we have absolute confidence in the revolutionaries, in the true revolutionaries, in the true communists.

They will not fail the revolution, the same as our revolution will never fail the revolutionary movement of Latin America.

We do not know what awaits us, what vicissitudes, what dangers and what struggles lie ahead. But we are prepared, and every day we try to prepare ourselves better, and every day we will be better and better prepared.

One thing we can say: We are calm, we feel safe, and this little island will always be a revolutionary wall of granite against which all conspiracies, all intrigues and all aggressions will be smashed. And high upon this wall there will fly forever a banner with the words: *Patria o muerte! Venceremos!*

10. THE DEATH OF CHE GUEVARA

REVOLUTION PLAZA, HAVANA
OCTOBER 18, 1967

Che Guevara was wounded and captured in an ambush by the Bolivian army on October 8, 1967. The following day he was executed in cold blood, on Washington's instructions. When this news was confirmed, a memorial rally was held in Havana's Revolution Plaza on October 18, attended by almost one million people, where Fidel Castro made the following remarks:

I first met Che one day in July or August 1955. And in one night—as he recalls in his account—he became one of the future *Granma* expeditionaries, although at that time the expedition possessed neither boat, nor arms, nor troops. That was how, together with Raúl, Che became one of the first two on the *Granma* list.

Twelve years have passed since then; they have been 12 years filled with struggle and historic significance. During this time death has cut down many brave and invaluable lives. But at the same time, throughout those years of our revolution, extraordinary individuals have arisen, forged from among the people of the revolution, and between them, bonds of affection and friendship have emerged that surpass all possible description.

Tonight we are meeting to try to express, in some degree, our feelings toward one who was among the closest, among the most admired, among the most beloved, and, without a doubt, the most extraordinary of our revolutionary comrades. We are here to express our feelings for him and for the heroes who have fought with him and fallen with him, his internationalist army that has been writing a glorious and indelible page of history.

Che was one of those people who was liked immediately, for his simplicity, his character, his naturalness, his comradely attitude, his personality, his originality, even when one had not yet learned of his other characteristics and unique virtues.

In those first days he was our troop doctor, and so the bonds of friendship and warm feelings for him were ever increasing. He was filled with a profound spirit of hatred and contempt for imperialism, not only because his political education was already considerably developed, but also because, shortly before, he had had the opportunity of witnessing the criminal imperialist intervention in Guatemala through the mercenaries who aborted the revolution in that country.

A person like Che did not require elaborate arguments. It was sufficient for him to know Cuba was in a similar situation and that there were people determined to struggle against that situation, arms in hand. It was sufficient for him to know that those people were inspired by genuinely revolutionary and patriotic ideals. That was more than enough.

One day, at the end of November 1956, he set out on the expedition toward Cuba with us. I recall that the trip was very hard for him, since, because of the circumstances under which it was necessary to organize the departure, he could not even provide himself with the medicine he needed. Throughout the trip, he suffered from a severe attack of asthma, with nothing to alleviate it, but also without ever complaining.

We arrived, set out on our first march, suffered our first setback, and at the end of some weeks, as you all know, a group of those *Granma* expeditionaries who had survived was able to reunite. Che continued to be the doctor of our group.

We came through the first battle victorious, and Che was already a soldier of our troop; at the same time he was still our doctor. We came through the second victorious battle and Che was not only a soldier, but the most outstanding soldier in that battle, carrying out for the first time one of those singular feats that characterized him in all military action. Our forces continued to develop and we soon faced another battle of extraordinary importance.

The situation was difficult. The information we had was erroneous in many respects. We were going to attack in full daylight—at dawn—a strongly defended, well-armed position at the edge of the sea. Enemy troops were at our rear, not very far, and in that confused situation it was necessary to ask people to make a supreme effort.

Compañero Juan Almeida had taken on one of the most difficult missions, but one of the flanks remained completely without forces—one of the flanks was left without an attacking force, placing the operation in danger. At that moment, Che, who was still functioning as our doctor, asked for three or four combatants, among them one with a machine gun, and in a matter of seconds set off rapidly to assume the mission of attack from that direction. On that occasion he was not only an outstanding combatant but also an outstanding doctor, attending the wounded comrades and, at the same time, attending the wounded enemy soldiers.

After all the weapons had been captured and it became necessary to abandon that position, undertaking a long return march under the harassment of various enemy forces, someone had to stay behind with the wounded, and it was Che who did so. Aided by a small group of our soldiers, he took care of them, saved their lives, and later rejoined the column with them.

From that time onward, he stood out as a capable and valiant leader, one of those who, when a difficult mission is pending, do not wait to be asked to carry it out.

Thus it was at the battle of El Uvero. But he acted in a similar way on a previously unmentioned occasion during the first days when, following a betrayal, our little troop was attacked by surprise by a number of planes and we were forced to retreat under the bombardment. We had already walked a distance when we remembered some rifles of some peasant soldiers who had been with us in the first actions and had then asked permission to visit their families, at a time when there was still not much discipline in our embryonic army. At that moment, we thought the rifles might have to be given up for lost. But I recall it took no more than simply raising the problem for Che, despite the bombing, to volunteer, and having done so, quickly go to recover those rifles.

This was one of his principal characteristics: his willingness to instantly volunteer for the most dangerous mission. And naturally this aroused admiration—and twice the usual admiration, for a fellow combatant fighting alongside us who had not been born here, a person of profound ideas, a person in whose mind stirred the dream of struggle in other parts of the continent and who nonetheless was so altruistic, so selfless, so willing to always do the most difficult things, to constantly risk his life.

That was how he won the rank of commander and leader of the second column, organized in the Sierra Maestra. Thus his standing began to increase. He began to develop as a magnificent combatant who was to reach the highest ranks in the course of the war.

Che was an incomparable soldier. Che was an incomparable leader. Che was, from a military point of view, an extraordinarily capable person, extraordinarily courageous, extraordinarily combative. If, as a guerrilla, he had his Achilles' heel, it was this excessively combative quality, his absolute contempt for danger.

The enemy believes it can draw certain conclusions from his death. Che was a master of warfare! He was an artist of guerrilla struggle! And he showed that an infinite number of times. But he showed it especially in two extraordinary deeds. One of these was the invasion, in which he led a column, a column pursued by thousands of enemy soldiers over flat and absolutely unknown terrain, carrying out—together with Camilo [Cienfuegos]—an extraordinary military accomplishment. He also showed it in his lightning campaign in Las Villas province, especially in the audacious attack on the city of Santa Clara, entering—with a column of barely 300 combatants—a city defended by tanks, artillery, and several thousand infantry soldiers. Those two heroic deeds stamped him as an extraordinarily capable leader, as a master, as an artist of revolutionary war.

However, now after his heroic and glorious death, some people attempt to deny the truth or value of his concepts, his guerrilla theories. The artist may die—especially when he is an artist in a field as dangerous as revolutionary struggle—but what will surely never die is the art to which he dedicated his life, the art to which he dedicated his intelligence.

What is so strange about the fact that this artist died in combat? It is stranger that he did not die in combat on one of the innumerable occasions he risked his life during our revolutionary struggle. Many times it was necessary to take steps to keep him from losing his life in actions of minor significance.

And so it was in combat—in one of the many battles he fought—that he lost his life. We do not have sufficient evidence to enable us to deduce what circumstances preceded that combat, or how far he may have acted in an excessively combative way. But, we repeat, if as a guerrilla he had an Achilles' heel, it was his excessive combativity, his absolute contempt for danger.

And this is where we can hardly agree with him, since we consider that his life, his experience, his capacity as a seasoned leader, his authority, and everything his life signified, were more valuable, incomparably more valuable than he himself, perhaps, believed.

His conduct may have been profoundly influenced by the idea that individuals have a relative value in history, the idea that causes are not defeated when one person falls, that the powerful march of history cannot and will not be halted when leaders fall.

That is true, there is no doubt about it. It shows his faith in the people, his faith in ideas, his faith in examples. However—as I said a few days ago—with all our heart we would have liked to see him as a forger of victories, to see victories forged under his command, under his leadership, since people of his experience, his caliber, his really unique capacity, are not common.

We fully appreciate the value of his example. We are absolutely convinced that many people will strive to live up to his example, that people like him will emerge.

It is not easy to find a person with all the virtues that were combined in Che. It is not easy for a person to spontaneously develop a character like his. I would say that he is one of those people who are difficult to match and virtually impossible to surpass. But I would also say that the example of people like him contributes to the appearance of others of the same caliber.

In Che, we admire not only the fighter, the person capable of performing great feats. What he did, what he was doing, the very fact of his confronting, with a handful of combatants, the army of the oligarchy, trained by US advisors sent in by US imperialism, backed by the oligarchies of all neighboring countries—that in itself constitutes an extraordinary feat.

If we search the pages of history, it is likely that we will find no other case in which a leader with such a limited number of combatants has set about a task of such importance; a case in which a leader with such a limited number of combatants has set out to fight against such large forces. Such proof of confidence in himself, such proof of confidence in the people, such proof of faith in people's capacity to fight, can be looked for in the pages of history — but the likes of it will never be found.

And he fell.

The enemy believes it has defeated his ideas, his guerrilla concepts, his point of view on revolutionary armed struggle. What they accomplished, by a stroke of luck, was to eliminate him physically. What they accomplished was to gain an accidental advantage that an enemy may gain in war. We do not know to what degree that stroke of luck, that stroke of fortune, was helped along, in a battle like many others, by that characteristic of which we spoke before: his excessive combativity, his absolute disdain for danger.

This also happened in our War of Independence. In a battle at Dos Ríos they killed [José Martí], the Apostle of our independence; in a battle at Punta Brava, they killed Antonio Maceo, a veteran of hundreds of battles [in the Cuban War of Independence]. Countless leaders, countless patriots of our wars of independence were killed in similar battles. Nevertheless, that did not spell defeat for the Cuban cause.

The death of Che — as we said a few days ago — is a hard blow, a tremendous blow for the revolutionary movement because it deprives it, without a doubt, of its most experienced and able leader.

But those who boast of victory are mistaken. They are mistaken when they think that his death is the end of his ideas, the end of his tactics, the end of his guerrilla concepts, the end of his theory. For the man who fell, as a mortal being, as a person who faced bullets time and again, as a soldier, as a leader, was a thousand times more able than those who killed him by a stroke of luck.

How should revolutionaries face this serious setback? How should they face this loss? If Che had to express an opinion on this point, what would it be? He gave his opinion, he expressed this opinion quite clearly when he wrote in his message to the [Tricontinental] Latin American Solidarity Conference that if death surprised him anywhere, it would be welcome as long as his battle cry had reached a receptive ear and another hand reached out to take up his rifle.

His battle cry will reach not just one receptive ear, but millions of receptive ears! And not one hand, but millions of hands, inspired by his example, will reach out to take up arms! New leaders will emerge. People with receptive ears and outstretched hands will need leaders who emerge from their ranks, just as leaders have emerged in all revolutions.

Those hands will not have available a leader of Che's extraordinary experience and enormous ability. Those leaders will be formed in the process of struggle. Those leaders will emerge from among the millions of receptive ears, from the millions of hands that will sooner or later reach out to take up arms.

It is not that we feel that his death will necessarily have immediate repercussions in the practical sphere of revolutionary struggle, that his death will necessarily have immediate repercussions in the practical sphere of development of this struggle. The fact is that when Che took up arms again he was not thinking of an immediate victory; he was not thinking of a speedy victory against the forces of the oligarchies and imperialism. As an experienced fighter, he was prepared for a prolonged struggle of five, 10, 15 or 20 years, if necessary. He was ready to fight five, 10, 15 or 20 years, or all his life if need be! And within that perspective, his death — or rather his example — will have tremendous repercussions. The force of that example will be invincible.

Those who attach significance to the lucky blow that struck Che down try in vain to deny his experience and his capacity as a leader. Che was an extraordinarily able military leader. But when we remember Che, when we think of Che, we do not think fundamentally of his military virtues. No! Warfare is a means and not an end. Warfare is a tool of revolutionaries. The important thing is the revolution. The important thing is the revolutionary cause, revolutionary ideas, revolutionary objectives, revolutionary sentiments, revolutionary virtues!

And it is in that field, in the field of ideas, of sentiments, of revolutionary virtues, of intelligence, that — apart from his military virtues — we feel the tremendous loss his death means to the revolutionary movement.

Che's extraordinary character was made up of virtues that are rarely found together. He stood out as an unsurpassed man of action, but Che was not only that — he was also a person of visionary intelligence and broad culture, a profound thinker. That is, the man of ideas and the man of action were combined within him.

But it is not only that Che possessed the double characteristic of the man of ideas — of profound ideas — and the man of action, but that Che as a revolutionary united in himself the virtues that can be defined as the fullest expression of the virtues of a revolutionary: a person of total integrity, a person with a supreme sense of honor and absolute sincerity, a person of stoic and Spartan living habits, a person in whose conduct not one stain can be found. He constituted, through his virtues, what can be called a truly model revolutionary.

When someone dies it is usual to make speeches, to emphasize their virtues. But rarely can one say of a person with greater justice, with greater accuracy, what we say of Che on this occasion: that he was a pure example of revolutionary virtues!

But he possessed another quality, not a quality of the intellect or of the will, not a quality derived from experience, from struggle, but a quality of the heart. He was an extraordinary human being, extraordinarily sensitive!

That is why we say, when we think of his life, when we think of his conduct, that he constituted the singular case of a most extraordinary human being, able to unite in his personality not only the characteristics of the man of action, but also the man of thought, the person of immaculate revolutionary virtues and of extraordinary human sensibility, joined with an iron character, a will of steel, indomitable tenacity.

Because of this, he has left to the future generations not only his experience, his knowledge as an outstanding soldier, but also, at the same time, the fruits of his intelligence. He wrote with the virtuosity of a master of our language. His narratives of the war are incomparable. The depth of his thinking is impressive. He never wrote about anything with less than extraordinary seriousness, with less than extraordinary profundity—and we have no doubt that some of his writings will pass on to posterity as classic documents of revolutionary thought.

As fruits of that vigorous and profound intelligence, he left us countless memories, countless narratives that without his work, without his efforts, might have been lost forever.

An indefatigable worker, during the years that he served our country he did not know a single day of rest. The responsibilities assigned to him were many: president of the National Bank, director of the Central Planning Board, minister of industry, commander of military regions, the head of political or economic or fraternal delegations.

His versatile intelligence was able to undertake with maximum assurance tasks of any kind. He brilliantly represented our country in numerous international conferences, just as he brilliantly led soldiers in combat, just as he was a model worker in charge of any of the institutions he was assigned to. And for him there were no days of rest; for him there were no hours of rest!

If we looked through the windows of his offices, he had the lights on all hours of the night, studying, or rather, working and studying. For he was a student of all problems; he was a tireless reader. His thirst for learning was practically insatiable, and the hours he stole from sleep he devoted to study.

He devoted his scheduled days off to voluntary work. He was the inspiration and provided the greatest incentive for the work that is today carried out by hundreds of thousands of people throughout the country. He stimulated that activity in which our people are making greater and greater efforts.

As a revolutionary, as a communist revolutionary, a true communist, he had a boundless faith in moral values. He had a boundless faith in the consciousness of human beings. And we should say that he saw, with absolute clarity, the moral impulse as the fundamental lever in the construction of communism in human society.

He thought, developed and wrote many things. And on a day like today it should be stated that Che's writings, Che's political and revolutionary thought, will be of permanent value to the Cuban revolutionary process and to the Latin American revolutionary process. And we do not doubt that his ideas—as a man of action, as a man of thought, as a person of untarnished moral virtues, as a person of unexcelled human sensitivity, as a person of spotless conduct—have and will continue to have universal value.

The imperialists boast of their triumph at having killed this guerrilla fighter in action. The imperialists boast of a triumphant stroke of luck that led to the elimination of such a formidable man of action. But perhaps the imperialists do not know or pretend not to know that the man of action was only one of the many facets of the personality of that combatant. And if we speak of sorrow, we are saddened not only at having lost a man of action. We are saddened at having lost a man of virtue. We are saddened at having lost a man of unsurpassed human sensitivity. We are saddened at having lost such a mind. We are saddened to think that he was only 39 years old at the time of his death. We are saddened at missing the additional fruits we would have received from that intelligence and that ever richer experience.

We have an idea of the dimension of the loss for the revolutionary movement. And, here is the weak side of the imperialist enemy: They think that by eliminating a man physically they have eliminated his thinking—that by eliminating him physically they have eliminated his ideas, eliminated his virtues, eliminated his example.

They are so shameless in this belief that they have no hesitation in making it public, as if it were the most natural thing in the world, the by now almost universally accepted circumstances in which they murdered him after he had been seriously wounded in action. They do not even seem aware of the repugnance of the procedure, of the shamelessness of the acknowledgement. They have publicized it as if thugs, oligarchs and mercenaries had the right to shoot a seriously wounded revolutionary combatant.

Even worse, they explain why they did it. They assert that Che's trial would have been quite an earth shaker, that it would have been impossible to place this revolutionary in the dock.

And not only that. They have not hesitated to spirit away his remains. Whether it is true or false, they certainly announced they had cremated his body, thus beginning to show their fear, beginning to show that they are not so sure that by physically eliminating the combatant, they can eliminate his ideas, eliminate his example.

Che died defending no other interest, no other cause than the cause of the exploited and the oppressed of this continent. Che died defending no other cause than the cause of the poor and the humble of this earth. And the exemplary manner and the selflessness with which he defended that cause cannot be disputed even by his most bitter enemies.

In history, people who act as he did, people who do and give everything for the cause of the poor, grow in stature with each passing day and find a deeper place in the heart of the peoples with each passing day. The imperialist enemies are beginning to see this, and it will not be long before it will be proved that his death will, in the long run, be like a seed that will give rise to many people determined to imitate him, many people determined to follow his example.

We are absolutely convinced that the revolutionary cause on this continent will recover from the blow, that the revolutionary movement on this continent will not be crushed by this blow.

From the revolutionary point of view, from the point of view of our people, how should we view Che's example? Do we feel we have lost him? It is true that we will not read new writings of his. It is true that we will never again hear his voice. But Che has left a heritage to the world, a great heritage, and we who knew him so well can become in large measure his beneficiaries.

He left us his revolutionary thinking, his revolutionary virtues. He left us his character, his will, his tenacity, his spirit of work. In a word, he left us his example! And Che's example will be a model for our people. Che's example will be the ideal model for our people!

If we wish to express what we expect our revolutionary combatants, our militants, our people to be, we must say, without hesitation: Let them be like Che! If we wish to express what we want the people of future generations to be, we must say: Let them be like Che! If we wish to say how we want our children to be educated, we must say without hesitation: We want them to be educated in Che's spirit! If we want the model of a person, the model of a human being who does not belong to our time but to the future, I say from the depths of my heart that such a model, without a single stain on his conduct, without a single stain on his action, without a single stain on his behavior, is Che! If we wish to express what we want our children to be, we must say from our very hearts as ardent revolutionaries: We want them to be like Che!

Che has become a model of what future human beings should be, not only for our people but also for people everywhere in Latin America. Che carried to its highest expression revolutionary stoicism, the revolutionary spirit of sacrifice, revolutionary combativeness, the revolutionary's spirit of work. Che brought the ideas of Marxism-Leninism to their freshest, purest, most revolutionary expression. No other person of our time has carried the spirit of proletarian internationalism to its highest possible level as Che did.

When one speaks of a proletarian internationalist, and when an example of a proletarian internationalist is sought, that example, high above any other, will be the example of Che. National flags, prejudices, chauvinism and egotism had disappeared from his mind and heart. He was ready to shed his generous blood spontaneously and immediately, on behalf of any people, for the cause of any people!

Thus, his blood fell on our soil when he was wounded in several battles, and his blood was shed in Bolivia, for the liberation of the exploited and the oppressed, of the humble and the poor. That blood was shed for the sake of all the exploited and all the oppressed. That blood was shed for all the peoples of the Americas and for the people of Vietnam — because while fighting there in Bolivia, fighting against the oligarchies and imperialism, he knew that he was offering Vietnam the highest possible expression of his solidarity!

It is for this reason, compañeros of the revolution, that we must face the future with firmness and determination, with optimism. And in Che's example, we will always look for inspiration — inspiration in struggle, inspiration in tenacity, inspiration in intransigence toward the enemy, inspiration in internationalist feeling!

Therefore, after tonight's moving ceremony, after this incredible demonstration of vast popular recognition — incredible for its magnitude, discipline and spirit of devotion, which demonstrates that our people are a sensitive, grateful people who know how to honor the memory of the brave who die in combat, that our people recognize those who serve them; and which demonstrates the people's solidarity with the revolutionary struggle and how this people will raise high and maintain ever higher revolutionary banners and revolutionary principles — today, in these moments of remembrance, let us lift our spirits and, with optimism in the future, with absolute optimism in the final victory of the peoples, say to Che and to the heroes who fought and died with him:

Hasta la victoria siempre! [Ever onward to victory!]
Patria o muerte! [Homeland or death!]
Venceremos! [We will win!]

11. ONE HUNDRED YEARS OF STRUGGLE FOR CUBAN INDEPENDENCE

LA DEMAJAGUA MONUMENT, MANZANILLO
OCTOBER 10, 1968

Cuba's first declaration of independence was made by the wealthy landowner Carlos Manuel Céspedes on October 10, 1868, at La Demajagua sugar mill in Oriente province, sparking the Ten Years' War against Spain. On October 10, 1968, Fidel Castro reminded Cubans of the historical continuity of their revolutionary struggle for nationhood.

Relatives of the heroes of our struggle for independence;
Guests;
Compañeros who are present here tonight representing every corner of our nation:

The importance of today's commemoration surpasses that of any other occasion. It would seem that nature is again putting us to the test, but this is indeed part of the commemoration itself. Apparently, immediately after the proclamation of Cuba's independence, when the *mambises* were on their way to the town of Yara, at about this same time of day, a heavy rainstorm suddenly developed — symbolically, as the first indication of the hardships they would face. Certainly, our first *mambises* at the time had only a few shotguns when they were about to engage in their first combat. Their ammunition got wet from the rain, and so they couldn't use their firearms that night, that night when the first blood was shed by Cubans in this 100-year struggle, when for the first time they began a life of incredible privation that lasted for 10 long years.

Today we are commemorating the 100th anniversary of that day. This first centennial of the beginning of the revolutionary struggle in our homeland is, for us, the most significant commemoration that has been celebrated in the history of our country.

What does October 10, 1868, signify for our people? What does this glorious date mean for the revolutionaries of our nation? It simply marks the beginning of 100 years of struggle, the beginning of the revolution in Cuba, because in Cuba there has been one revolution: that which was begun by Carlos Manuel de Céspedes on October 10, 1868, the revolution that our people are now carrying forward.

There is, of course, no doubt that Céspedes symbolized the Cuban spirit of that time. He symbolized the dignity and rebelliousness of a people — still heterogeneous in nature — which began to take shape as a nation over the course of history.

It was without doubt Céspedes who, among the conspirators of 1868, was the firmest in his determination to rise up in arms. A number of interpretations have been made of his position, when in reality he had only one motive in all his actions. In every meeting of the conspirators, Céspedes always took the firmest stand. At the meeting held on August 3, 1868, in the region between Las Tunas and Camagüey, Céspedes argued for an immediate uprising. In later meetings with the revolutionaries of the province of Oriente, at the beginning of October, he insisted on the need to go into action at once. Until finally, on October 5, 1868, in a meeting at a certain sugar mill, the Rosario mill, the most resolute revolutionaries met and set October 14 as the date for the uprising.

It is historically documented that at this place Céspedes learned about a telegram sent by the governor general of Cuba on October 8 instructing the provincial authorities to arrest him.

But Carlos Manuel de Céspedes gave the authorities no time to act. He didn't allow them to take the initiative. Then and there, he issued the necessary orders, and on October 10, at this very spot, he proclaimed Cuba's independence.

It is true that the history of many a revolutionary movement—the vast majority, in fact—ends in prison or on the gallows. Certainly, Céspedes had a clear idea that the uprising could not be postponed for long. The delay involved in the long process of creating an organization and establishing an armed force with a significant number of weapons before beginning the struggle was too great a risk, since the conditions in our country at that time were very difficult. So Céspedes made the decision to act.

On this subject, Martí commented, "Céspedes provided the impetus; Agramonte, the virtue"—although Agramonte also provided impetus, and Céspedes also had virtue. Martí further explained Céspedes's conflicts with other revolutionaries concerning the postponement of the uprising, saying that the postponement would "perhaps have given the repressive colonial authorities the chance to crush the uprising."

History has proved that Céspedes was correct, that such a resolute stand proved to be the very spark that ignited a heroic war that lasted 10 years, a war begun with no resources whatsoever, by a people that was virtually unarmed and from then on had to adopt the classic strategy for obtaining weapons: seizing them from the enemy.

In the history of this 100-year struggle, this was not the only occasion when our people, lacking weapons and totally unprepared for war, saw the need for taking up the struggle and wresting weapons from the enemy. The history of our people in these 100 years of struggle confirms this axiomatic truth: If we had postponed the struggle until the ideal conditions existed, until all the necessary arms and supplies were assured, then the struggle would never have begun at all. If a people has decided to take up arms, the weapons needed will be found in the enemy's garrison, in the oppressors' garrisons.

This truth has been demonstrated in all our struggles, in all our wars.

When, at the beginning of the struggle in 1895, Maceo landed in the Baracoa region, he had only a handful of combatants, very poorly armed. And on a dark and stormy night, when Martí, along with Máximo Gómez, disembarked at a place on the southern coast of Oriente province—a rough, inhospitable part of the coast—he, too, was accompanied by only a few combatants. He had no army; the army was here, among the people. And the weapons were here, in the hands of the ruling forces.

A few days later, while advancing toward the interior of the province, they joined up with José Maceo, at the head of a large army, fighting near Guantánamo. Later they joined up with [Antonio] Maceo, who after landing had wandered all alone in the mountains and woods of the Baracoa region — absolutely alone! Nonetheless, just a few weeks later, when Antonio Maceo received Máximo Gómez and Martí, he had an army of 3,000 combatants from Oriente province, a well-organized army that was ready for combat.

These events provided us with an extraordinary example. They taught us a great deal during our difficult times, when we had no resources and no weapons; but these circumstances did not prove an obstacle to our struggle because there was a people in whom we had faith.

This is not only an example for Cuban revolutionaries but a tremendous example for revolutionaries all over the world.

Our revolution, with its own methods and essential characteristics, has deep roots in the history of our homeland. That is why I have said — and all revolutionaries should clearly understand this — our revolution is a single revolution, a revolution that began on October 10, 1868.

This commemoration today is like an encounter between the people and their history. It is a search by the present generation for its own roots. Nothing could teach us better how to understand what a revolution is, nothing could better teach us to understand what the term "revolution" means, than an analysis of the history of our country, a study of the history of our people, of our people's revolutionary roots.

Perhaps there are some people who have regarded the nation and the homeland as simply a matter of natural evolution. Perhaps many think that the Cuban nation and national consciousness have always existed. And perhaps many people have seldom taken the time to think about how the Cuban nation was born, how our awareness as a people and our revolution-ary consciousness came into being.

One hundred years ago, this consciousness did not exist. One hundred years ago, Cuban nationality did not exist. One hundred years ago, a nation, in the sense of a people with a common interest and a common destiny, did not actually exist. A century ago, our people were simply a motley mass, made up in the first place of citizens of the Spanish colonial power; there was also a mass of citizens born in this country, many direct descendants of Spaniards, others more distant, some of whom favored colonial rule, while others resisted that rule; and a large mass of slaves, criminally brought to our country to be pitilessly exploited after the exploiters had already virtually annihilated the indigenous population.

Of course, the owners of the country's wealth were primarily Spaniards, who owned the businesses and the land. There were also the descendants of the Spaniards, called creoles, who owned the sugar mills and large plantations. And, of course, in a country in which there was tremendous ignorance, access to books and education was limited to a very small and exclusive group of creoles, who came from these wealthy families.

In the first decades of the last century, when the rest of Latin America had already won its independence from Spain, Spanish power still retained a very firm grip over our country, which they called the last and the most precious jewel in the Spanish crown.

The emancipation of Latin America had very little real impact on our nation. We know that the liberators of Latin America had the idea of sending an army to Cuba to liberate our people. But the truth is that there was no nation; there were no people to liberate, because there were no people who were aware of the need for liberation. At the beginning of the last century — in fact, during the entire first half of that century — the most educated sectors of the population, the people capable of forming political ideas, supported ideas that were not exactly in favor of Cuba's independence.

At that time, the main issue under discussion was slavery. The land-owners, the wealthy, the oligarchy that ruled the country, whether they were Spaniards or Cubans, greatly feared the abolition of slavery. In other words, their interests as proprietors, their interests as a class — and thinking exclusively in terms of these interests — led them to favor the annexation of Cuba to the United States.

Thus, one of the first political currents, the annexationist trend, emerged in Cuba. This political trend was based, fundamentally, on the economic interests of a class that wanted to maintain the shameful institution of slavery through annexation to the United States, where a large number of states continued to support slavery. Since the North and the South were already at odds over the question of slavery, the politicians of the southern, slave-holding states also encouraged the idea of the annexation of Cuba — with the aim of creating another state to support them and guarantee their congressional majority.

This is the background to the mid-century expedition headed by Narciso López. When we studied about Narciso López in school, we learned that he was a patriot, that Narciso López was a liberator. In fact, we were taught so many incredible distortions that—even after the republic of Cuba had supposedly been established—we were made to believe that Narciso López came to liberate Cuba. The truth is that Narciso López was encouraged by the politicians from the slave-holding South of the United States, who wanted to secure another state which would support the most inhuman and backward of institutions: the institution of slavery.

On one occasion, Martí described it as an unfortunate expedition, organized precisely by those interests. Thus in that period, the annexationist currents held sway over our country. We must bear this in mind, because this trend, for one reason or another, in one guise or another, has periodically appeared throughout the history of Cuba.

There came a time when the annexationist forces began to lose ground and another current emerged in opposition to some aspects of Spanish rule in our country. This reformist current did not demand the independence of Cuba, but instead proposed certain reforms within the Spanish colony. At that time, there was still no independence movement, no movement for real independence. The repeated deceptions and tricks of the Spanish colonial regime did, however, arouse the spirit and consciousness of a small group of Cubans, creoles who belonged to the wealthy educated and landed sectors, who were well informed about what was happening in the world. It was this group, which, for the first time, conceived of the idea of winning their rights through revolutionary methods, through armed struggle, in an open challenge to colonial rule.

Let no one think that this group of Cubans necessarily had the support of the majority of the population, that they obtained widespread support because—as I have already explained—at that time, the idea of Cuban nationhood did not exist.

There was one factor that deeply divided that sector of wealthy creoles. Naturally, the Spaniards opposed reforms, and independence even more so. But many rich creoles also opposed the idea of independence, because of the issue of slavery. Thus, the question of slavery was the fundamental issue that divided the most radical sectors, which were largely creole—for there were still no Cubans in the true sense of the word. And naturally, these creoles were primarily concerned with their own economic interests, which meant they were chiefly concerned with maintaining the institution of slavery. Therefore, they supported the annexationist movement at first, then reformism—anything but the idea of independence or the idea of winning their rights through armed struggle.

And this is a very important question, because we see how this history, this contradiction, repeats itself regularly throughout 100 years of struggle.

Finally, the first small group of patriots—a group of wealthy and illustrious gentlemen born in this country—decided to strike for their rights through armed struggle. They faced a complex situation and deep contradictions, which necessarily involved a long and hard struggle.

What really earned them the title of revolutionaries was, above all, their consciousness that there was only one way to win those rights; their decision to adopt this way; their breaking with the tradition, with reactionary ideas; and their decision to abolish slavery.

Perhaps today that decision seems simple, but the decision to end slavery was a most revolutionary measure—the most radical, revolutionary measure imaginable in a society based on slavery.

What makes Céspedes a great man is not only his firm and resolute decision to take up arms, but his actions that followed that decision. His first act after the proclamation of independence was the emancipation of his own slaves. He proclaimed his commitment to end slavery in our country, although initially he hoped for the widest possible support from Cuban landowners.

In Camagüey, the revolutionaries proclaimed the abolition of slavery from the very beginning, and the Guáimaro constitution of April 10, 1869, definitively established the right of all Cubans to freedom, completely abolishing the hateful, centuries-old institution of slavery.

As often happens in such circumstances, many of those rich Cubans were hesitant about supporting the revolution and drew back from the struggle, and in fact began to collaborate with the colonial power. In other words, as the revolution became more radical, this group of Cubans became more isolated—the same group of creoles who had already begun to depend on the support of the only people capable of carrying out the revolution, the poor people and the recently emancipated slaves.

During those first days of the revolutionary struggle in Cuba, the laws of every revolutionary process inevitably came into play, and revolutionary ideas began to undergo a process of radicalization and strengthening which continues today.

During those days, of course, there was no discussion about the ownership of the means of production. The discussion was about the ownership of some human beings by others. And when the revolution—a radical revolution from the moment it ended a centuries-old privilege, from the moment it abolished that so-called right enshrined over centuries—abolished that ownership, it carried out a profoundly radical act in the history of our country; and from that moment on, for the first time, the concept and the consciousness of nationhood began to develop, and also for the first time, the adjective "Cuban" was used to describe all those who had taken up arms and were struggling against the Spanish colonial power.

We all know how the war was waged. We all know that very few nations in the world had the opportunity or were able to endure such great, incredibly difficult sacrifices as those endured by the Cuban people during that 10-year struggle. To ignore those sacrifices is a crime against justice, a crime against culture; it is a crime for any revolutionary.

While our sister nations of Latin America which had freed themselves from Spanish domination some decades before were living under servitude, under the tyranny of the social interests which in those nations replaced the Spanish tyranny, our country, absolutely alone and single-handedly—and not the whole country, but a small portion of our country—fought for 10 years against a still powerful European nation which had, and mobilized, an army of hundreds of well-armed men to combat the Cuban revolutionaries.

It is a recognized fact that Cuba received virtually no help from abroad. We all know the story of the schisms abroad, which obstructed and finally blocked the aid from the exiles to the Cubans-in-arms.

Nevertheless, our people—making incredible sacrifices, and heroically carrying the weight of that war, overcoming great difficulties—succeeded in mastering the art of war and in organizing a small army, which armed itself with the enemy's weapons.

From the ranks of the poor, from the ranks of the fighters who came from the people, from the ranks of the peasants and the emancipated slaves—for the first time, officers and leaders of the revolutionary movement rose from the ranks of the people. The most worthy patriots, the most outstanding fighters, began to come to the fore, among them the Maceo brothers, examples of these exceptional men.

After 10 years this heroic struggle was defeated—not by Spanish arms, but by one of the worst enemies the Cuban revolutionary movement has always had—by dissension among the Cubans themselves, who sank into quarrels, regionalism, caudillismo. In other words this enemy—which was permanently present in the revolutionary process—destroyed that struggle.

It is a recognized fact, for example, that Máximo Gómez, after invading Las Villas province and achieving great military victories, was practically expelled from that province because of regionalism and sectionalism. This is not the time to analyze the role of each person in that struggle; instead, it is our intention to analyze the process and describe how disagreements, regionalism, sectionalism and caudillismo ruined that heroic 10-year effort.

But we should also keep in mind that we cannot expect those Cubans— those first Cubans who laid the foundations of our country—to have the level of political consciousness that we have today, even though they had a profound patriotic consciousness. We cannot analyze the events of that period within the framework of today's concepts. Things that are quite clear today, unquestionable truths, neither were nor could have been clear at that time. Communication was difficult; the Cubans had to fight under great hardship; they were constantly persecuted and, of course, we could not expect those problems to have been avoided—problems that arose again in the struggle of 1895, problems that arose again during the second half of this century, throughout our revolutionary process.

After the Cuban forces had been undermined by the disagreements, and the enemy stepped up its offensive, those weaker revolutionary elements began to vacillate. And it was at the time of the Zanjón Pact that ended that heroic war that Antonio Maceo emerged as the truest representative of the people, coming from the most humble ranks of the people, with all his strengths and his exceptional greatness.

That decade gave rise to exceptional leaders, with incredible merits, such as Céspedes, Agramonte, Máximo Gómez, Calixto García and count-less others—the list is endless. By no means are we trying to judge the merits—which were all extraordinary—of each one of them; we simply want to explain how the process developed, and how, when that 10-year-long struggle ended, how Antonio Maceo came to represent a radical, revolutionary consciousness and spirit, in the face of the Zanjón Pact. The Zanjón treaty was more than a treaty, it was a surrender of Cuban arms. In the historic Baraguá Protest, Maceo affirmed his intention of continuing the struggle, expressing the most resolute and unyielding spirit of our people by declaring that he did not accept the Zanjón Pact. And, in fact, the war continued.

Even after the agreements had been reached, Maceo scored a series of crushing victories against the Spanish forces. But at that time, Maceo was reduced to the role of commander of part of the forces of Oriente province; as a black man at a time when there was so much racism and prejudice, Maceo did not have the support of all the revolutionaries because, unfortunately, reactionary and unjust prejudices were held by many of the combatants and their leaders. That is why, although Maceo saved the flag that time, saved the cause, and raised the revolutionary spirit of the people of nascent Cuba to its highest level, in spite of his tremendous ability and heroism, he could not continue to wage the war, and he was forced to wait for the conditions that would allow him to resume the struggle.

The defeat of the revolutionary forces in 1878 also had its political aftermath. Taking advantage of the sense of defeat and disappointment, those people who, decades before, had represented the annexationist and reformist currents, began to promote a new political current, that of autonomy, which was counterposed to the radical theses of independence and the only road to achieve that independence: armed struggle.

So, after the Ten Years' War a new pacifist tendency, this conciliationist current emerged in Cuban politics. In the same way, the annexationist tendency was revived to a certain degree, a tendency which still existed at the beginning of the Ten Years' War, when many Cubans naively viewed the United States as the model of a free country, a democratic country, and recalled that nation's struggle for independence, the [US] Declaration of Independence, Lincoln's policy and so on. There were still Cubans who at the beginning of the war in 1868 held vestiges of that annexationist tendency, which they gradually abandoned in the course of the armed struggle.

A new stage began, lasting almost 20 years from 1878 to 1895. This period was of great importance in the development of our country's political awareness. The revolutionary banners were not abandoned; the radical theses were not forgotten. On the basis of that tradition created by the people of

Cuba, on the basis of that consciousness born of the heroism and struggle of those 10 years, a new, even more radical and advanced revolutionary thought began to emerge.

That war brought to the fore many leaders from among the ranks of the people, but that war also inspired the person who was, without doubt, the most brilliant and most universal of all Cuban political figures: José Martí.

Martí was very young when the Ten Years' War broke out. He suffered imprisonment and exile; his health was not good, but he had an extraordinarily brilliant mind. In his student years, he was a champion of the cause of independence, and when barely 20 years old, he wrote some of the finest documents in the political history of our country.

After the Cuban forces were defeated in 1878, Martí became the main theoretician and champion of revolutionary ideas. He took up the banners of Céspedes, Agramonte and the heroes who fell in that 10-year struggle, and developed Cuban revolutionary ideas of that period to their highest level. Martí understood the factors that led to the failure of the Ten Years' War. He analyzed the causes profoundly and dedicated his energies to preparing for a new war. He planned this war for almost 20 years without ever becoming discouraged, developing his revolutionary theory, uniting forces, rallying the veterans of the Ten Years' War. Ideologically, he fought the autonomists and the annexationists that opposed the revolutionary current in the Cuban political arena.

Martí advocated his ideas constantly and at the same time organized the Cuban émigrés [in the United States]; in fact, Martí organized the first revolutionary party—that is, the first party that united all the revolutionaries. With outstanding tenacity, moral courage and heroism, with no resources other than his intelligence, his convictions and his correct position, he dedicated himself to that task.

We can state that our country had the privilege of having at its disposal one of the richest political treasures, one of the most valuable sources of political education and knowledge, in the thought, writings, books, speeches and all the other extraordinary works of José Martí.

We Cuban revolutionaries, more than anyone else, need to study these ideas as thoroughly as possible, to study that inexhaustible source of political, revolutionary and human wisdom.

We haven't the slightest doubt that Martí was the greatest political and revolutionary thinker from this continent. It is not necessary to make historical comparisons, but Martí worked in exile under extraordinarily difficult circumstances, fighting without resources against the colonial power after a military defeat, against those sectors that had at their disposal the press and the economic resources with which to combat revolutionary ideas. Martí labored to free a small country controlled by hundreds of thousands of soldiers armed to the teeth, a country not only burdened with that domination but also threatened by a still greater power — the danger of its absorption by a powerful neighbor whose imperialist claws were visibly growing. With his pen, with his words, Martí tried to inspire the Cubans and develop their consciousness in order to overcome the discord and correct the errors in leadership and methods that had brought about defeat in the Ten Years' War, while at the same time uniting the émigrés around the same revolutionary ideas, uniting the older generation that began the struggle and the younger generation, uniting those outstanding and distinguished military heroes. He combated, in the field of ideas, the Spanish colonialists; the campaigns of the autonomists, whose pettifogging, electoral and deceitful methods would never lead our country anywhere; and the new annexationist currents that included not only the wealthy sectors that were committed to maintaining the institution of slavery, but also the developing economic and political forces of the emerging imperialist power. Considering all this, we can state with assurance that the Apostle of our independence faced greater difficulties and problems than have ever been faced by any other revolutionary and political leader in the history of this continent.

Thus, a new star appeared in the firmament of our country, that complete patriot, that complete human being, that complete model, who — together with Maceo and Máximo Gómez, the battle heroes — recommenced the war for Cuban independence...

So the war of 1895 began, a war equally filled with extraordinary heroism, with incredible sacrifices, with military feats. But as we all know, it was a war that did not attain the objectives pursued by our ancestors; it did not end with a complete victory — although none of our struggles really ended in defeat, because each one was a step forward, a leap toward the future. The fact is that at the end of that struggle, Spanish colonial power, Spanish domination, was replaced by the domination of the United States over our country — political and military domination achieved through intervention.

Cubans had fought for 30 years; tens of thousands of Cubans had died on the battlefields; hundreds of thousands perished in that struggle, while the Yankees lost only a few hundred soldiers in Santiago de Cuba. They seized Puerto Rico, they seized Cuba, they seized the Philippine archipelago, 6,000 miles from the United States, and they seized other possessions. This was something that Martí and Maceo had feared the most. Political consciousness and revolutionary thought had already developed to such an extent that the key leaders of the War of Independence in 1895 had very clear, absolutely clear, ideas about the objectives, and fervently rejected the idea of annexation — and not just annexation, but even the intervention of the United States in that war.

Tonight, one of Martí's best known passages was read here, the letter written on the eve of his death, which is almost his testament, in which he relates his essential ideas to his friend, what he had struggled for, what had inspired his actions and his life, what deep inside gave him the most joy — to live on the battlefield, to have the chance to give his life, and to fulfill his duty "of preventing the United States, as Cuba obtains her independence, from extending its control over the Antilles and consequently falling with that much more force on the countries of our America."

This is one of the most revealing and profound documents, typifying the revolutionary and radical thought of Martí, who was already exposing imperialism for what it was, who had foreseen its role in this hemisphere, and who had described it with an analysis that could very well be considered Marxist, because of its thorough and dialectical nature and because of his ability to see that the US policy toward the rest of the world was based on the unsolvable contradictions of that society. As early as 1895 Martí was describing the future so clearly, writing with his powerful eloquence and sharply attacking the annexationist tendencies as the worst political trends in Cuba. Our generation is amazed by not only Martí, but by Maceo, as well, because of his clear vision, his ability to thoroughly analyze the phenomenon of imperialism.

It is a well-known fact that on one occasion, when a young man spoke to Maceo about the possibility of the Cuban star joining the constellation in the US flag, Maceo answered that although he thought it would be impossible, perhaps that would be the only issue on which he would side with Spain.

Like Martí, a few days before his death, Maceo wrote with extraordinary clarity of his unyielding opposition to US intervention in the struggle in Cuba, stating, "It is preferable to rise or fall without help than to contract a debt of gratitude to such a powerful neighbor." Prophetic words, inspired words, words which our two most important leaders in the war of 1895 expressed a few days before their deaths.

We all know what happened. When Spanish power was virtually exhausted, motivated by purely imperialist aims, the US government joined the war, after 30 years of Cuban struggle. With the aid of the *mambí* fighters, the US forces landed, seized the city of Santiago de Cuba and sank Admiral Cervera's fleet, which consisted of museum pieces and was sent out to a certain sinking out of pure, traditional Quixotism, since the fleet was an easy target for the US battleships. Calixto García was not even allowed to enter Santiago de Cuba. The United States completely ignored the revolutionary government-in-arms, completely ignored the leaders of the revolution. It negotiated with Spain without Cuba's participation, and they decided on the military intervention of their armies in our country.

They proceeded to do this and, in fact, took over our country both militarily and politically.

The people were not really informed of this. Why? Because who would be interested to inform them of this monstrous fact? Who? The old autonomists? The old reformists? The old annexationists? The old slave owners? Who? Those who had been allies of the colony during the wars? Who? Those who didn't want Cuban independence, preferring annexation to the United States? They had no interest in explaining these historical truths, these bitter truths to our people.

What did they tell us in school? What did those lying books tell us about these events? They told us that the imperialist power was not an imperialist power, but that the US government, out of its generosity and its desire to give us liberty, intervened in the war, and that because of this we were free. We were not free because of the thousands of Cubans who died during 30 years of combat, we were not free because of the heroic deeds of Carlos Manuel de Céspedes, the "Father of our Country," who began the struggle and who even preferred to see his son executed rather than make a single concession; we were not free because of the heroic efforts of so many Cubans; we were not free because of Martí's teachings; we were not free because of the heroic feats of Máximo Gómez, Calixto García and all the other illustrious leaders; we were not free because of the blood shed by Antonio Maceo with his more than 20 wounds and his heroic death at Punta Brava. We were free simply because Theodore Roosevelt landed with a few Rangers at Santiago de Cuba to fight against an exhausted and practically defeated army, and because US battleships sank one of Cervera's old junks in Santiago Bay.

These were the monstrous lies, the incredible falsehoods, that were taught in our schools.

Perhaps few things can help so much to make us revolutionaries as recalling the extent of that infamy; the extent to which the truth was distorted; the extent to which cynicism was used to destroy the consciousness of the people about their path, their destiny; the extent to which the people were kept criminally ignorant of their own merits, virtues and capacities—a people that made sacrifices equaled by few peoples in the world—in order to destroy their self-confidence and faith in the future.

Those who collaborated with Spain during those 30 years, those who fought in the colony, those who shed the blood of the *mambises*, now became the allies of the Yankee interventionists, of the Yankee imperialists, and tried to do what they had not been able to do for 30 years. They even tried to distort the history of our country, altering it to fit their own interests: annexationist interests, imperialist interests, anti-Cuban and counterrevolutionary interests.

Who collaborated with the imperialist intervention? The Spanish merchants and the autonomists. It must be pointed out that in the first government of the republic there were several ministers who came from the ranks of the autonomists, who had condemned the revolution. They became allies of the large landholders, of the annexationists, of the worst elements. And under the protection of the military intervention, under the protection of the Platt Amendment, they began without the slightest scruples to cleverly adulterate the republic and pave the way for taking over our country.

This history must be known, our people must know their own history; today's feats, today's achievements, today's triumphs must not make us forget—unjustly and criminally—our historical roots. Our present consciousness, our present ideas, our present political and revolutionary development—assets that we have today but which those who began the struggle could not have had—must not make us underestimate for one moment or forget for a single instant that what we have today rightfully belongs not so much to this generation, but—and it must be said with all sincerity—to those who rose up on this very site 100 years ago, freed the slaves, proclaimed independence and started out on the road of heroism, initiating the struggle that served as an encouragement and example for later generations.

That example inspired the generation of 1895; that example inspired revolutionary combatants throughout 60 years of the false republic; and that example of heroism and that tradition inspired the combatants who fought the most recent battles in our country.

This is not just said for this occasion, because we are commemorating this anniversary; on the contrary, it has always been said—it was said at the Moncada trial. When the judges asked for the name of the intellectual author of the attack on the Moncada barracks, we replied without hesitation: "Martí was the intellectual author of the attack on the Moncada barracks!"

It is possible that ignorance, or forgetfulness, or the euphoria of present achievements might lead the present generation to underestimate how much our people owe those fighters.

They were the ones who paved the way; they were the ones who created the conditions; and they were the ones who had to swallow the most bitter dregs: the bitter draft that was the Zanjón Pact, the end of the struggle in 1878; the even more bitter draft that was Yankee intervention, the bitter draft of the transformation of this country into a colonial establishment and a strategic pontoon—as Martí had feared; the bitter draft of seeing opportunists and corrupt politicians, the enemies of the revolution, allied with the imperialists, ruling the country.

They had to live through the exceedingly bitter experience of seeing this country governed by a Yankee ambassador; and seeing an insolent functionary aboard a battleship anchored in Havana Bay issuing instructions to everyone—to ministers, to the head of the army, to the president, to the House of Representatives, to the Senate.

These are well-known facts, historically confirmed facts. In other words, they are not so well known as confirmed, because for a long time the masses were not aware of the facts; for a long time they were kept in ignorance. It is necessary to go to the archives, to exhume the documents, so that our people, our present generation, can have a clear idea of how the imperialists governed; how, through memorandums and papers, and with great insolence, they governed this country—a country they pretended to call a "free," "independent" and "sovereign" nation. Our people should know what kind of liberators these were and the crude and repugnant methods they used in their relations with this country. Our present generation must be informed about all of this because if it is not informed its revolutionary consciousness will not be sufficiently developed. If this country's origins and history are not known the political culture of our masses will not be sufficiently well developed. We could not even understand Marxism, we could not even call ourselves Marxists, if we didn't begin with an understanding of our own revolutionary process and of the process of the development of consciousness and political and revolutionary thought in our country over the period of 100 years. If we don't understand that, we can know nothing of politics.

Unfortunately, we lived in ignorance of many historical facts for a long time. If it was convenient for those who allied themselves here with the imperialists to conceal the history of Cuba, to distort Cuban history, to play down the heroism, the extraordinary merits, the thought and example of our heroes, it is we, the revolutionaries, who are called upon to bring that history to light, in knowing that history, in knowing our roots, in divulging those truths.

They had as many reasons to hide that history and ignore it as we have to demand that all stages of that history, from October 10, 1868, until today, be made known. That history is filled with very harsh, very painful, very bitter, very humiliating episodes, from the Platt Amendment until 1959.

Our people must also be informed of how the imperialists took over our economy. Our people have suffered from the consequences of this. They don't know how it happened, but they know it happened, they know that it did happen.

The men and women of this country—above all, those who live in this province, in which the struggle was initiated and which continued to be the scene of constant struggle for the nation's liberty—know that almost overnight, everything passed from Spanish hands to the hands of the North Americans. They know that the railroads, the electricity companies, the best lands, the sugar mills, the mines, everything passed into their hands. They know that this happened; and they know that between 1915 and 1920 workers had to be brought in from other islands of the Antilles because of the labor shortage, and only some years later, during the 1920s, 1930s, 1940s and 1950s — each decade worse than the one before — there was more unemployment, more and more destitute families, more and more ignorance.

In this country, where today the number of workers — liberated workers — is insufficient to develop the infinite wealth of our soil, to develop the unlimited abilities of our people, workers remained idle for entire months and had to beg for work, and not just during the "dead season," but at the height of the harvest season as well.

These lands were drenched with the blood of tens of thousands of our forebears, tens of thousands of our *mambises*. The Cuban people under the truncated republic were deprived not only of the right to receive the fruits of their sacrifices, but even of the right to work. Our fighters for independence shed their blood for the future happiness of this country, but their brothers, their descendants and their children did not even have the right to earn a living by the sweat of their brow.

What kind of a republic was that in which not even a person's right to work was guaranteed? What kind of republic was it, in which not only culture, so essential to human beings, but even justice and the possibility of good health, instead of disease and epidemics, were not guaranteed? What kind of a republic was it, that could not offer the least opportunity to the children of the people — the people, who had not only given their lives in the hundreds of thousands, but who had done so at a time when the number of true Cubans did not even reach a million; the people, who had immolated themselves in a singular holocaust? What kind of a republic was that in which a person was not even guaranteed the right to work, the right to earn their daily bread on that land so often drenched with the blood of patriots?

And they tried to pass that off to us as a republic; they tried to pass it off as a just state. In few other regions of the country have the people suffered directly from these experiences as have the people of Oriente — from the tens of thousands of peasants who, in order to live, had to seek refuge in the mountains, almost all the way up to Turquino Peak, to the cane field workers or their parents who lived through those terrible years. What kind of future awaited this country!

The fact of the matter was that the Yankees took over our economy. In 1898, US holdings in Cuba amounted to 50 million pesos; in 1906 they amounted to some 160 million; and in 1927, to 1.45 billion.

I don't believe there is another country in which economic penetration has taken place so incredibly quickly, allowing the imperialists to take over our best lands, all our mines, our natural resources. They controlled the public services, the greater part of the sugar industry, the most efficient industries, the electricity industry, the telephone service, the railroads, the most important businesses and the banks.

In taking over the banks, they began to practically buy the country with the Cubans' own money, because those who had money, whether it was a little or a lot, deposited it in the banks. And the owners of the banks controlled that money.

And so, by 1927, in a period of less than 30 years, the imperialists' holdings in Cuba had climbed to 1.45 billion pesos. They had taken over everything, with the compliance of the annexationists, neo-annexationists and autonomists—those who had fought against Cuba's independence. With the help of the US intervention governments, they received incredible concessions.

In 1901 a certain Mr. Preston bought 75,000 hectares of land in the Nipe Bay area for $400,000—that is, less than $6 a hectare. The valuable hardwood forests that covered that land and that went into the furnaces of the sugar mills were alone worth many times more, incomparably more than that sum. With bulging pockets, they came to a country impoverished by 30 years of struggle, to buy up the nation's best land at less than $6 a hectare.

In that same year, a certain Mr. McCann bought 32,000 hectares in the southern part of Pinar del Río province. And—if my memory doesn't fail me—Mr. James bought 27,000 hectares of land that same year at Puerto Padre.

In other words, in just one year—their pockets bulging with money—they acquired well over 100,000 hectares of the nation's best land from a people still prostrated by the impoverishment of 30 years of struggle. And so it was that they were able to take over this country—without bloodshed, and at bargain prices.

Our people must know this history.

I cannot imagine why, faced with tasks as urgent and important as the need for research on the history of this country, for delving into the roots of this country, only a few people have devoted themselves to this. Too many prefer to devote their talents to other matters—looking for easy success through "effect" writing—when they have such an incredible source, such an extraordinary wealth of material at their disposal in which to discover the important roots of this country. We are more interested in this than what some—following the latest fad—are trying to introduce into our culture, while the serious task, the imperative task, the urgent task, the just task of delving into the roots of this country awaits.

As revolutionaries, when we say it is our duty to defend this land, to defend this country, to defend this revolution, we must realize that we are not defending the efforts of just 10 years; we must realize that we are not just defending the revolution of this generation. We must realize that we are defending the efforts of 100 years. We must realize that we are defending not just that for which thousands of our comrades fell, but that for which hundreds of thousands of Cubans fell during these 100 years!

With the victory of 1959, fundamental questions for our people's lives presented themselves once again—this time on a much higher plane. If in 1868 one of the matters under discussion was whether or not to abolish slavery, to abolish the ownership of one human being by another, in our era, in our century, with the advent of our revolution, the fundamental question, the essential question, that which can define the revolutionary nature of this era and of this revolution, is no longer the question of the ownership of human beings, but that of the ownership of other human beings' means of earning a living.

Whereas formerly the debate centered on whether a person could have 10, 100 or 1,000 slaves, now it is on whether a Yankee enterprise, an imperialist monopoly, has the right to own 10,000, 100,000 or 200,000 hectares of land; now it is about what right the slaveholders of yesterday have to own the best lands of our country. Whereas formerly the debate was about what right a person had to claim another human being as their property, now it is about what right a monopoly or anyone—the owner of a bank that holds the money of all depositors, a monopoly or an oligarch—has to own a sugar mill where 1,000 workers labor; whether it is fair that a monopoly or an oligarch owns an electricity plant, a mine or an industry worth tens of thousands, hundreds of thousands, or millions, or tens of millions of dollars; whether it is justifiable for the members of an exploiting minority to own chains of warehouses solely in order to line their own pockets by raising the prices of all products imported into this country.

If, during the past century, it was argued whether or not a person had the right to own other human beings, in this century — in short — it is argued whether individuals have the right to own the means by which human beings live. In reality, what existed was no more than a fictitious freedom. There could be no real abolition of slavery as long as human beings formally liberated from being owned by others still had to earn their living working on the land and in the industries that were and continued to be the property of other individuals. Those who had formerly enslaved human beings directly now enslaved and exploited them equally ruthlessly through a monopoly on the wealth of the country and the means of production.

That is why, if a revolution in 1868 had to begin by setting the slaves free to be called a revolution, a revolution in 1959, to have the right to be called a revolution, is obliged to liberate the wealth monopolized and exploited by a minority for its exclusive benefit, to liberate society from the monopoly on wealth by virtue of which a minority exploited other human beings.

What difference was there between the slave's quarters of 1868 and the wage laborer's quarters of 1958? What difference was there, except that — with human beings allegedly free — the owners of the plantations and sugar mills in 1958 did not care whether or not that worker died of hunger? If he died, 10 workers were waiting to take his job. Since workers were no longer a piece of property that could be bought or sold on the market, the owner did not care whether or not a worker, his wife or his children died. This is the reality that the people of Oriente know only too well.

And so the direct ownership of human beings was suppressed, but the ownership of human beings by private property and a monopoly on wealth and the means of production endured. To eradicate the exploitation of one human being by another was to suppress the right to the private ownership of that wealth, to suppress the right to monopolize those means of livelihood which belong and must belong to society as a whole.

If slavery was a brutal and repugnant institution, a direct means of exploiting human beings, capitalism was an equally brutal and repugnant institution that also needed to be abolished. And, if the abolition of slavery is completely understood by present generations, the day will come when the coming generations will be astonished to learn that a foreign monopoly—managed by an insolent official—once owned over 100,000 hectares of land, of which it was the lord and master, the owner of lives and property, just as we are shocked today when we learn that there once was a time when one person was the owner of dozens, hundreds or even thousands of slaves.

Whereas the idea of a human being in chains was reasonable for the generations of that time, that idea will seem monstrous to coming generations—even more so than to our own generation. People often become accustomed to seeing monstrous things without realizing their monstrosity, and become accustomed to seeing certain social phenomena as naturally as they see the moon come out at night or the sun rise in the morning, or rain or sickness, so that in the end, they consider monstrous institutions as normal as natural disasters or illness.

Naturally, the privileged who monopolized the wealth of this country were hardly likely to teach the people these ideas, these concepts, to open their eyes or provide them with teachers and schools. It would not be the privileged and the exploiting minority who would vindicate the history of our country, who would honor with dignity those who made possible a future of progress for our homeland. Those who were interested not in revolution but in preventing revolutions, those who were interested not in justice but in prosperity and enriching themselves through injustice, would never be interested in revealing to the people their beautiful history, their just revolution, their heroic struggle for dignity and justice.

That is why it has fallen to this generation to have meaningful experiences and to learn of the expeditions—preceded by bombardments and pirate-like attacks, organized abroad by the "grandees" of imperialism and here by those who in a matter of 30 years took over the wealth of this country—to crush the revolution and to reestablish a monopoly on our wealth by privileged minorities, by exploiters of human beings.

It has also fallen to this generation to recognize the annexationists of today, the eternal weaklings, the "volunteers" of today—that is, not in the sense the word has now, or in the sense the word "guerrilla" has today, but in the sense of yesterday—"volunteers" of yesterday, *guerrilleros* of yesterday, which is the name they gave at that time to those who fought against revolutionary combatants, to those who murdered students, to those who made machete attacks on wounded patriots when they were recovering in the poor, ill-equipped and undefended field hospitals.

We recognize them in those who now attempt to destroy the wealth of the country, in those who serve the imperialists, in those cowards unfit for work and sacrifice who desert this country. When the hour of hard work arrived, when the time to build the homeland arrived, when the time came to liberate our natural and human resources and fulfill the destiny of our people, they abandoned their country and went to their masters abroad, placing themselves at the service of the infamous cause of imperialism, the enemy not only of our people but of all the peoples of the world.

So it has fallen to this generation to understand the ideological struggle against the electoralists and in defense of the legitimate revolutionary ideas; it has fallen to this generation to understand the great ideological battles that followed the triumph of the revolution; to go through the experiences of the revolutionary process; to confront Yankee imperialism, its blockade, its hostility and its defamation campaigns against the revolution; and to face the tremendous problem of underdevelopment.

We must point out that the struggle repeats itself on a different scale but also under different conditions. In 1868, in 1895 and during the nearly 60 years of the pseudo-republic the revolutionaries were a minority; the levers of power were in the hands of the reactionaries; the colonialists and the autonomists held power and made laws against the revolutionaries. This held true throughout the struggle of 1895 and continued until 1959.

Today our people face similar tendencies: the same old reactionary ideas brought back to life, the new interpreters of autonomism and annexationism, the pro-imperialists and the imperialists, but under very different conditions.

In 1868 the Cubans organized their own government in the backcountry. It was beset with dissension and discord. Similar things have taken place in the course of these 100 years. The heroic proletarian combatants of the years of the pseudo-republic—Baliño, Mella, Guiteras, Jesús Menéndez—had to confront police thugs and the exploiters backed by their foremen and Rural Guards. They were cut down by murderous bullets while in exile or here in their own country—in Mexico or in El Morrillo or Manzanillo—or, like so many other revolutionaries, such as this town's native son, Paquito Rosales, they were simply made to disappear.

Throughout 90 of these 100 years, the revolution had been unable to cover the whole country; the revolution had been unable to take power; the revolution had been unable to constitute itself as a government; the revolution had been unable to release the tremendous force of the people; the revolution had been unable to set the country in motion. It is not a case of the revolutionaries of yesterday being less capable than those of today — no, not at all. It is rather that the revolutionaries of today had the privilege of gathering the fruits of the hard and bitter struggles waged by the revolutionaries of yesterday. We, the revolutionaries of today, found the way already paved, a nation already formed; a people with an already well-developed awareness of its common interests; a more homogeneous people, a truly Cuban people; a people with a history, a history written by these leaders; a people with a tradition of struggle, of rebellion and heroism. It was the present generation that had the privilege of reaching the stage in which the people — after 90 years — constituted themselves in power, established themselves in power. It was no longer the power of the colonialists and their allies; it was no longer the power of the intervening Yankee imperialists and their allies, the autonomists and neo-annexationists — the enemies of the revolution.

That is why at that time the power of the people, the genuine power of the people and for the people, was constituted. Not the power confronting the people, against the people — the kind of power that had been known for more than four centuries, since the time of the colony, since the Spaniards, right in this zone, burned the Indian Hatuey alive, right through until Batista's henchmen, on the eve of their defeat, murdered revolutionaries, burning them to death. For the first time, this popular power confronted the monopolies, the vested interests; the privileges, the powerful social magnates. It was the power confronting privilege and against privilege, confronting exploitation, confronting colonialism and confronting imperialism. For the first time, this power was with the homeland and for the homeland; for the first time, it was the power of the people and for the people. It was not the weapons of the mercenaries, the weapons of the imperialists, but the weapons that the people took away from the oppressor, took away from the gendarmes and the guardians of the interests of imperialism, that became the weapons of the people. The people became an army. For the first time in history, this generation had the opportunity to initiate its work on the basis of this new power, on this revolutionary power that had extended to the entire country.

Naturally, the class enemies, the exploiters, the oligarchs, the imperialists — whose holdings were worth 1.45 billion — could not possibly support this power; they were against it. The corrupt politicians; the sinecure holders; the parasites of every kind; the speculators; the exploiters of gambling and vice; the propagators of prostitution; the thieves; those who openly stole the funds earmarked for hospitals, schools and roads; the owners of hundreds of thousands of hectares of the best lands; the owners of the finest factories; the exploiters of our farmers and workers, could not support that power — they have to oppose that power.

Since then, the people in power have been waging their struggle — a no less difficult, no less arduous struggle — confronting the Yankee imperialists and against Yankee imperialism, against the most powerful imperialist country, the world's gendarme of reaction. A power accustomed to destroying governments that show the slightest leaning toward the road to liberation, accustomed to overthrowing them by means of a coup d'état or a mercenary invasion, accustomed to destroying political movements by means of economic reprisals — its methods, its resources and its power have crashed against the fortress of the revolution.

The revolution is the result of 100 years of struggle, the result of the development of the political movement and revolutionary consciousness, armed with the most up-to-date political thinking, armed with the most up-to-date, scientific concept of society, history and economics — which is Marxism-Leninism — the weapon that completed the wealth, the arsenal of revolutionary experience and the history of our country.

Our people are armed not only with that experience and that consciousness; they are also a people that has been able to overcome the factions that divided it, the group divisions, caudillismo and regionalism, to become a single, undivided revolutionary people. When we speak of the people, we speak of revolutionaries; when we speak of a people ready to fight and to die, we are not thinking of the *gusanos* [literally: worms], of the few faint-hearted individuals who are still around. We are thinking of those who have the legitimate right to be called Cubans and the Cuban people — the same legitimate right our combatants and our *mambises* had — a people integrated, united and led by a revolutionary party, a party that constitutes a militant vanguard.

What did Martí do, in order to make the revolution? He organized the party of the revolution, organized the party of the revolutionaries. There was only one revolutionary party. Those who were not in the party of the revolutionaries were in the party of the Spanish colonialists, in the party of the annexationists or in the party of the autonomists.

In the same way today, the people with their party, which is their vanguard, armed with the most up-to-date concepts, armed with the experience of 100 years of struggle, having developed their revolutionary political and patriotic consciousness to the highest level, have succeeded in overcoming age-old vices and have built this unity and this power of the revolution.

The Ten Years' War—as Martí said—was lost not because the enemy seized the sword from our hands, but because we let the sword fall. After 10 years of struggle, confronting imperialism, neither have the imperialists been able to seize our sword, and our people, united, will never let it fall!

The revolution enjoys the privilege of having with it—and having at its disposal—the united revolutionary people, whose consciousness is constantly developing and whose unity is indestructible. A revolutionary people armed with the most revolutionary concepts, with the most profound patriotism—an internationalist consciousness in no way excludes patriotism. Revolutionary patriotism is perfectly reconcilable with revolutionary internationalism. A people armed with such resources and under such favorable circumstances will be an invincible people.

This anniversary comes at a time when the development of a revolutionary consciousness and the people's spirit of work are at their highest. Proof of this are the feats such as the one achieved on October 8, when in celebration of the centennial and also in honor of the Heroic Guerrilla [Che Guevara]—who met a hero's death on a day that almost coincided with October 10—the people decided to make an effort worthy of this celebration and proceeded to plant 13,815 hectares of land with sugarcane in a single day.

Let this be a simple example of what a people can do when its intelligence, energy and human potential are put into motion.

I must say that the figure I just gave you surpasses the highest, the most optimistic figure that could ever have been imagined. It takes a truly hard-working people to do these things. It takes a truly conscientious and inspired people to do these things.

This act of homage, this anniversary, takes place at the time when the development of the revolution is at its highest in every field. This in no way means that in these 100 years we have reached the summit of the struggle, the end of the struggle. No one can tell how many years of struggle we have ahead of us. But one thing must be said: We have never been in a better situation that the one we are in today; we have never been more organized or better armed, not only with weapons, with "hardware," but also with thoughts and ideas. Never, never before, have we been better armed with both ideas and "hardware," or better organized. And we shall continue to arm ourselves in both ways. We shall continue to organize ourselves and make ourselves ever stronger.

We have imperialism right there, virtually across the street, and its attitude is insolent and threatening. The most reactionary forces are coming to the fore, and the most reactionary, aggressive groups are becoming dominant factors in that country's policy.

We commemorate this anniversary, this centennial, these 100 years, not in an atmosphere of beatific peace, but rather in an atmosphere of struggle, threats and danger. But never before have we been so aware, never before have things become so clear to all of us.

This generation will not limit itself to having reached the end of a stage or certain specified objectives; to having been able to reach a goal or complete the historic task today: that of having a free homeland, a truly free homeland, a victorious revolution, a power of the people and for the people. This revolution must defend this power, because our enemies will not resign themselves to this state of affairs easily, because the imperialists, making use of all their resources, will not let us live in peace. The enemy's hatred grows to the extent that the revolution grows stronger, to the extent to which their efforts have been futile.

How far can they go? They go to incredible extremes in every field. In fact, at times they even look totally ridiculous.

Only recently, we read a news dispatch which mentioned a Spanish priest in Miami who organized prayer meetings against the revolution—a Spanish priest who, according to the dispatch, prayed for the destruction of the revolution and even held a mass and prayed that the revolutionary leaders would die in an accident or in an assassination attempt as a way to crush the revolution.

How wrong these people are, if they believe that the revolution can be crushed, in whatever way! We don't even have to say it. Now less than ever before! But we must say that the philosophy of the reactionaries, this philosophy of the imperialists, certainly attracts our attention.

They themselves admitted that whenever they organized a counterrevolutionary meeting, less than 200 people showed up; but when they organized a prayer meeting, thousands of *gusanos* came running. This only proves that all the counterrevolution has been left with are the ridiculous, fanatical *gusanos* who get together to attend mass. That is some kind of religious spirit: a priest who prays for people to die or to be murdered!

We must say that if that priest told us there was a surefire prayer for destroying the imperialists, we would absolutely refuse to make use of such a prayer; and if that priest said there was a prayer to repel the imperialists if they invaded this country, we would say to him: "To hell with your prayers. We'll take care of annihilating the invaders, the imperialists, right here, with a storm of bullets and shells!"

The Vietnamese say no prayers against the imperialists. The heroic people of Korea said no prayers against the imperialists. Neither did our militiamen say prayers against the mercenaries who came armed with skulls and crossbones, crucifixes and what-have-you; the mercenaries who came here in the name of God — with a priest and everything — to murder peasant women, to murder boys and girls, to destroy the wealth of this country.

Now we see the degree of degeneration the reactionaries have reached, to what degree they have prostituted their doctrines, to what extremes they can go, and the kind of feelings they harbor. But, after all, that is typical of the imperialists' *gusano* allies.

Naturally, the priest, his prayers and his motley congregation of fanatics are far from being matters of concern to the revolution. We are concerned with imperialism and its technical and military resources. And it is imperialism and its threats that we must always be ready for, always improving our preparation.

The study of the history of our country will not only develop our consciousness, our thinking, but it will also help us to find an inexhaustible source of heroism, an inexhaustible source of spirit of sacrifice, a spirit of struggle and combat.

What those combatants [in Cuba's independence wars] — virtually unarmed — were able to accomplish will always be a source of inspiration for the revolutionaries of today; it will be a source of confidence in our people, in their strength, in their capacity for struggle, in their future; it will make our country confident that nothing and no one in this world will ever defeat us, that nothing and no one in this world will ever be able to crush us and that this revolution will never be defeated by anyone!

This is because our people — who fought for their future for 100 years — can fight through another 100 years for that same future.

Our people — who have had the courage to sacrifice themselves more than once — will have the courage to sacrifice themselves as often as necessary.

The banners that flew over Yara, La Demajagua, Baire, Baraguá and Guáimaro; the banners that presided over the solemn event where slavery was eradicated; and the banners that have led the way throughout the revolutionary history of our country will never be lowered. Our people will defend those banners and what they represent to the last drop of their blood.

Our people know what they were yesterday, what they are today and what they will be tomorrow. We cannot say that 100 years ago we had a Cuban nationality, that there was a Cuban people; 100 years ago we were the last on this continent... One day, when Martí was still alive, the insolent imperialist press, with incredible scorn, described the people of Cuba as effeminate, arguing, among other things, that the Cuban people had stood for Spanish domination for years on end. This showed the imperialists' absolute ignorance of the historical and social factors that made up the people, and their ignorance of the conditions existing in Cuba at that time. Martí refuted the argument vigorously in a brilliant article entitled "Vindication of Cuba."

Very well. Back in 1868 they could hurl such insults against the homeland, ignoring her heroic deeds and her solitary struggle against great odds. They could even say that we were the least important country of the continent. That was the truth, but this nation could not be blamed for it. It would be impossible to blame a nation that did not exist and a people that did not exist as a people. But the nation that has existed ever since it sprang to life from the blood of those who took up arms here on October 10, 1868; the people forged in that tradition; the people that began their ascent in history, that began to develop their political thinking and consciousness; the people that had the good fortune of having those extraordinary leaders as thinkers and combatants — that people will not be called the last anymore, by anyone. We are no longer the people that abolished slavery 100 years ago; we are no longer the last to abolish slavery — the ownership of human beings — today, we are the first people of this continent to abolish the exploitation of one human being by another! It is true that we were the last to begin, but it is also true that we have gone further than anyone else. We have eradicated the capitalist system of exploitation; we have made the people the true owners of their future and their wealth. We were the last to break the chains of the colony, but we have been the first to throw off the chains of imperialism. We were the last to break free from a slave-type mode of production, but the first to throw off the capitalist mode of production — and, by so doing, free ourselves of its rotten political and ideological structure. We have exposed the lies with which they attempted to deceive us for so many years. We are vindicating the truth of history. We have recovered our wealth, our mines, our factories, our woods, our mountains, our rivers and our lands.

The land so often soaked with the blood of patriots is now soaked with the honest sweat of people who, with the sweat of their brow, working that land won with the blood of their sons and daughters, will now earn, honestly, the bread that was formerly snatched out of our hands and out of our mouths. Today we are the human community with the highest degree of consciousness and the highest political level on this continent. We are the first socialist state! Yesterday we were the last. Today we are the first in the advance toward the communist society of the future! The true society of human beings, of humankind.

We no longer struggle just to eradicate the vices and institutions that have a detrimental effect on the relationship between human beings and the modes of production; we are also trying to develop human consciousness to its highest level. Our struggle is no longer just against the institutions that enslaved human beings, but also against the selfish feelings that still enslave some people; against individualism, that isolates some people from the strength of the community. In short, it is no longer a case of simply liberating human beings from the tyranny of things, but of liberating human beings from the age-old ideas that still enslave them.

That is why we can state that ever since October 10, 1868, the road of our people has been a road of uninterrupted progress, of great strides forward, rapid advances and new stages of progress.

We have ample reasons for viewing this history with pride. We have ample motives for regarding this history with profound satisfaction. Our history is now 100 years old—not the history of the colony, which is older; but the history of the Cuban nation, the history of the Cuban homeland, the history of the Cuban people, of their political ideas, of their revolutionary consciousness!

The stretch of road we have covered in these 100 years is long, and our determination to continue marching forward without hesitating is also unending; we are steadfast in our determination to go on building this beautiful history, with more confidence than ever, with more work than ever, with more tasks ahead than ever, confronting Yankee imperialism, defending the revolution in whatever field may be necessary; confronting underdevelopment, in order to make use of all the potential of our resources, in order to release all the energies of our people, all the potential of their intelligence.

Our tasks will be the following: to defend the revolution in the face of imperialism, to strengthen our political consciousness on the journey toward the future, to strengthen our revolutionary thought by studying our history, to probe into the roots of this revolutionary thought and to carry forward the battle against underdevelopment.

Someone mentioned the [campaign for] 10 million tons of sugarcane, and this is a battle that has practically been won by this nation—thanks to the momentum of our work in the fields, thanks to the tremendous drive of our working people. And the campaign for 10 million tons is part of this major battle, the battle against underdevelopment, against poverty. These are our tasks for the future.

Many times, from the speakers' platform, the hypocritical, lying, thieving, stealing politicians would invoke the names of the patriots of our independence. Many times they desecrated, by merely bringing to their lips, the name of Martí, the name of Maceo, the name of Céspedes, the name of

Agramonte, the names of all our outstanding citizens. They hypocritically mentioned these names. In their hearts they forgot everything, abandoned everything.

In this country there should be a plaque, a marker, at each point where the Cubans fought, at each spot where they waged battles. They did not concern themselves with leaving a marker even at the exact place where the battle of Peralejo, or Las Guasimas, or Palo Seco was fought, or of recording the battles of the invasion. They left them to lie in oblivion, covered with brush and dust, without a single marker.

The swindlers often attempted to use the names of our heroes to serve their politicking ends.

That is why today, we, the revolutionaries of this generation, our revolutionary people, can feel the intimate and profound satisfaction of paying homage to Céspedes, to the combatants of our independence — the only homage, the most honest, the most sincere, the most profound homage — the tribute of a people that has gathered the fruits of their sacrifices and that, after 100 years, pays them this tribute of a united people, of a people's power, of a politically aware people, of a victorious revolution that is determined to continue marching ever onward, firmly and invincibly marching forward.

Long live free Cuba!
Long live October 10!
Long live the victorious revolution!
Long live 100 years of struggle!
Patria o muerte! [Homeland or death!]
Venceremos! [We will win!]

12. REVOLUTION AND COUNTERREVOLUTION IN ALLENDE'S CHILE

NATIONAL STADIUM, SANTIAGO DE CHILE
DECEMBER 2, 1971

After spending almost one month in Chile, at the end of the first year of President Salvador Allende's Popular Unity government, Fidel Castro addressed a mass meeting in the National Stadium in Santiago, warning about the dangers of fascism and the lessons of the Cuban revolution.

Beloved President;

Revolutionary Chileans;

Chileans:

President Allende's words have made such an impact on us that we have to calm ourselves a bit. The president has said some very moving and courageous things, analyzing a number of current events. But in my case, although I have been a part of some of them, I am a visitor, and I must not concern myself with such events. We must and can speak of other things that are common to the interests of all our peoples. We must and can concern ourselves with other questions that are common to all revolutionary processes.

There's one question that's very common among Chileans, one we have run into almost everywhere and which reveals the great patriotic spirit and something of the patriotic pride of you Chileans. For you fill your lungs, breathe deeply and ask, "What do you think of our country?" —although you already know the answer, you already know what impression it has made. Or you ask, "How have you been treated in this country?" — although you already know how we feel toward those who truly love this land.

Of course, one can say many things about one's impressions, about the majesty of the mountains, the blue of the sky, the beauty of the moon, your natural resources and your impressive landscape. But we aren't geologists or naturalists. And, unfortunately, the only thing in the way of poetry that comes to mind is the refrain that attributes a little poetry and a little madness to everyone. I imagine you Chileans are also familiar with this refrain.

But there are other things that interest us far more. We are interested, above all, in the human landscape, in the people, in you Chileans.

We have dedicated our lives to the human question, the social question, the revolutionary question. What most stirs our interest is the struggle of the peoples and of humankind, the historical march of humanity, advancing from the human being who lived in primitive hordes to the human being of today. What interests us the most is the living spectacle of a process in its critical moments.

The march of humankind has been slow. Sometimes it has halted. Occasionally it has even gone backward. But it has also speeded up at times. And these are moments of crisis, these are revolutionary moments.

We haven't come to Chile as tourists. We have visited Chile as revolutionaries, as friends, as supporters of this process and of this country. Here you must permit us a small difference of opinion with the president, though not a constitutional difference or one of protocol. He said that we hadn't come to learn or to teach. And where I beg to differ with him is that although we are absolutely in agreement that we didn't come to teach — and I don't know what kind of fear exists in those who go around with their little libels saying that they have nothing to learn and who, in the very saying, are reflecting some kind of complex, some unconscious fear. Nevertheless, we would like to say in all frankness that we did come to learn.

But, let no one think that the libelers and seditious proponents of reactionary political theories were right when they said how great it was that we had come to learn about elections, parliament, certain kinds of freedom of the press and so on. That's all very interesting, but we've already learned more than enough about those things. We've learned a great deal during the past 50 years about those bourgeois, capitalist freedoms; and we know only too well about their institutions. Now, we don't say they aren't good. Greek democracy was good, too, in its time. In its time the Roman republic, with its millions of slaves, its gladiator circuses and its Christians devoured by lions, also signified an extraordinary advance of human society. The medieval period was also considered an advance over primitive slavery, despite feudal servitude. The historic and famous French revolution also signified an advance over medieval society and the absolute monarchs who enjoyed prestige in their time—who were themselves once considered a step forward in the march of human progress. And there were even some so-called "enlightened despots."

It was the advent of a new form of production, and the creation of new relationships of production and ownership and of the appropriation of products that gave rise to all those superstructures, once considered advances in the march of humanity.

But anyone claiming that any particular society or social system and the superstructure that it represents is eternal is mistaken, because history has proved otherwise. One social form succeeds another and is, in turn, succeeded by yet another, and so on, each new social form being superior to the old.

Even the bourgeoisie, in its era—before there was any such thing as a proletariat—was revolutionary, a revolutionary class, and led the people in the struggle for a new social form, led the peasants who were serfs of the feudal lords, and led the artisans. There was no such thing as a proletariat at the time. And human society continued its march.

To claim that the form which emerged two centuries ago is eternal, to claim that it is the highest expression of human advancement, to claim that humanity's progress culminated with it, is simply ridiculous, from any historical or scientific point of view.

Moreover, all decadent social systems and societies have defended themselves when threatened with extinction. They have defended themselves with tremendous violence throughout history.

No social system resigns itself to disappearing from the face of the earth of its own free will. No social system resigns itself to revolution. As we said before, all those systems were once good. It is only today that they are condemned by history as decadent, as anachronistic. And anachronisms hang on just as long as they can. Anachronisms exist as long as the people lack the force to do away with them. Anachronisms exist only as long as they can't be replaced. But just because something can't be done away with at a given moment of a process doesn't mean that it is here to stay.

In our country, which has known various forms of the exploitative state, those instruments that served the exploiters to repress the exploited, their institutions, have been changed. It is scarcely a secret that changes have taken place in Cuba.

In the Technological University, responding to a question, we said in effect that we were not representatives of democracy. We were not representatives of democracy! Much less when you know perfectly well who have been called representatives of democracy in this hemisphere!

And we said that in our country our people need no one to represent them because the people represent themselves.

Very profound changes have taken place in our country. Very profound! It is difficult to understand from a distance. It is very difficult to understand, especially through the prism of the lies and calumnies in which reactionaries have specialized throughout history. There is a difference between the revolutionary and the reactionary. The difference is that the revolutionary lives by inner convictions, by deep motivations, and to lie is a violation of character, the lie is a violation of a human being's innermost feelings. The lie is the weapon of those in the wrong. The lie is the weapon of those with no argument. The lie is the weapon of those who disparage others and, above all, of those who disparage the people.

Truth, reason, ideas, thought, awareness and culture constitute the revolutionary's arsenal and the weapon of the contemporary revolutionary is the correct interpretation of the scientific laws that govern the march of human society.

We do not lie, nor will we ever lie! And we are not afraid to confront any adversary in the realm of ideas. The truth will always emerge victorious in the long run. The task of the revolutionary above all is to arm the spirit, to arm the spirit! For it is true that no physical weapon is worth anything if the spirit is not well armed beforehand.

We don't expect you to understand the problems of our country from such a distance. We don't expect that. It isn't even a basic question. All we mean when we say we came here to learn is that we didn't come to learn about decadence or anachronisms in human history. Nor are we fundamentally interested in the day or the hour, how or when a people decides to sweep away the anachronisms. No one anywhere will sweep them away unless they are able. No one can sweep them away before their time. But may they always be swept away as soon as possible.

We have come to learn about a living process. We have come to learn how the laws of human society operate. We have come to see something extraordinary. A unique process is taking place in Chile. Something more than unique: Rare! Rare! It is the process of a change. It is a revolutionary process in which revolutionaries are trying to carry out changes peacefully. A unique process, practically the first in human history—we won't even say in the history of contemporary societies. It is unique in the history of humankind, trying to carry out a revolutionary process by legal and constitutional methods, using the very laws established by the society or by the reactionary system, the very mechanism, the very forms that the exploiters created to maintain their class domination.

So it is really something unique, something rare.

And what has our attitude been? We, the revolutionaries, did nothing unique, nothing unusual. The Cuban revolutionaries at least have the merit of having had the first socialist revolution in Latin America. But we don't have the merit of having made it in an unusual and unique form. But what has our attitude been? Solidarity with the process in Chile. Solidarity with the people who have chosen this road. Our understanding, our moral support, our curiosity, our interest.

Because, as we have said on other occasions, revolutionaries did not invent violence. It was class society throughout history that created, developed and imposed its system, always through repression and violence. In every epoch, the instigators of violence have been the reactionaries. Violence has been imposed on the people in every epoch by the reactionaries.

We observe, and the world observes with enormous interest, how this Chilean process is developing today, even with the present correlation of world forces.

For us, then, this constitutes an extraordinary event.

We have been asked on several occasions—in an academic way—if we consider that a revolutionary process is taking place here. And we have said without the slightest hesitation: Yes! But when a revolutionary process is begun, or when the moment arrives in a country when what can be called

a revolutionary crisis occurs, then the struggle and the battles become tremendously acute. The laws of history are brought to bear.

Anyone who has lived in this country three weeks, anyone who has seen
and analyzed the factors, the first measures taken by the Popular Unity
government—measures that hit hard at powerful imperialist interests,
measures that culminated in the recuperation of the basic wealth of the
nation, measures characterized by the advancement of social sectors and
by the application of the law of agrarian reform (which was not passed by
the Popular Unity government, but which had been passed previously and
only timidly applied)—these measures, it can be said, have proved the great
historical fact that a process of change generates a dynamic of struggle. The
measures already carried out, which constitute the beginning of a process,
have released social dynamics, the class struggle; they have released the fury
and resistance—as is true in all social processes of change—of the exploiters,
the reactionaries.

All right. The question that immediately strikes a visitor observing this
process is whether or not the historical law of resistance and violence by the
exploiters will be fulfilled. We have said that there is no case in history in
which the reactionaries, the exploiters, the privileged members of a social
system, resigned themselves to change, resigned themselves to peaceful
change.

Therefore, this is, in our opinion, a matter of vital importance, an aspect
that has aroused our interest and which has taught us a great deal in the past
few days. Yes, gentlemen—especially those who didn't want me to come
here to learn—I have learned a great deal. I have learned how the social laws
operate, how the revolutionary process operates, how each sector reacts and
how the various forces struggle. We have gone through these experiences.
And we've felt it in our own flesh—not because our flesh was bruised by
a rock or a bullet. I haven't even seen a rock—not even at a distance. As a
visitor, as a friend, as a person in solidarity with you, I have felt another
type of aggression, with which I am more than familiar: an aggression in the
form of insults and campaigns.

We do not ignore the fact that our visit might very well aggravate a number of problems. In fact, it might even be a stimulus to those who wanted
to create difficulties for the Popular Unity government. At a time when, according to what is being said, there are hundreds and hundreds of journal-

ists here from all over the world covering our visit; at a time when people all over the world—in Europe, Asia, Africa and Latin America—are talking about this visit, about this meeting between Chileans and Cubans, between two processes which had such different beginnings; at a time when the image of Chile is in everyone's mind, it is obvious that this visit might cause some irritation, some feeling of discomfort, some exasperation which, in turn, might lead to the worsening of certain attitudes.

As a visitor, representing the people of Cuba, I have received extraordinary affection. We have had the opportunity to appreciate, to see how these phenomena are manifested.

Unquestionably, the person visiting this country was not Benito Mussolini. The person visiting this country was not Adolf Hitler. The person visiting was not a fascist, or a tool of the Yankee monopolies. The person visiting this country was not a friend of the powerful and the privileged. The person visiting this country was a friend of the humble people, a friend of the workers, a friend of the farmers, a friend of the students, a friend of the people!

This is why, after having been invited by the president, when we spoke with Chilean compañeros and they asked us what we would like to see on our visit here, we said we wanted to see the mines, the saltpeter, the copper, the iron, the coal, the workplaces, the agricultural centers, the universities, the mass organizations, the parties of the left, everything and everyone; we wanted to talk with the revolutionaries and even with those who, though they could not be considered revolutionaries, were decent people. We could not think of a better way to spend our visit.

And this is the way our visit was organized.

Why did we want it this way? Because we know where we can find our friends, among which social class. We know that wherever the workers, the farmers, the people of humble origin are, there we find our friends.

And that is why we got the kind of reception we received everywhere—in every town, university and agricultural region—the extraordinary reception we got in every workplace without exception. In every one of them! In fact, even in those places where the reactionaries had done their best to confuse the thinking of the workers. Even there!

The spirit of the workers, of the humble people, of those who create wealth with their sweat, was the same spirit the law of history dictates.

This is why we took the opportunity to confirm this; how this phenomenon arises despite the deluge of calumny and lies about Cuba emanating from the news agencies controlled by the Yankee monopolies. Despite all their efforts, what did they achieve?

Naturally, we didn't expect to be given a friendly reception from those interests opposed to the workers, the farmers and the humble people of this country. You'd have to be out of your mind to think that. We knew that our presence here wouldn't be welcomed by the powerful, the landowners, the reactionaries.

In a nutshell, Chileans, we didn't expect to be given a warm welcome by the fascists.

And, I repeat, we have learned something else. We have witnessed the verification of another law of history — we have seen fascism in action. We have been able to confirm a fact of modern day life: that the desperation of the reactionaries, the desperation of the exploiters today leads toward the most brutal, most savage forms of violence and reaction.

You all know the history of fascism in many countries, in those countries that are the cradle of that movement. You are all familiar with the history of how the privileged, the exploiters, destroy the institutions they once created — the very institutions they established to maintain their class domination, the laws, the constitution, the parliament — when they are no longer of any use to them. When I say they invent a constitution, I mean a bourgeois constitution, because the socialist revolutions create their own constitutions and forms of democracy.

What do the exploiters do when their own institutions no longer guarantee their domination? How do they react when the mechanisms they depend on historically to maintain their domination fail them? They simply go ahead and destroy those institutions. Nothing is more anti-constitutional, more illegal, more anti-parliamentarian, more repressive and more criminal than fascism.

Fascism, in its violence, wipes out everything. It attacks, closes and crushes the universities. It attacks the intellectuals, represses them and persecutes them. It attacks the political parties and trade unions. It attacks all mass organizations and cultural organizations.

Therefore, there is nothing more violent, more reactionary, more illegal than fascism. And we have been able to confirm, in this unique process, the manifestations of that law of history in which the reactionaries and the exploiters, in their desperation—and mainly supported from the outside—generate that political phenomenon, that reactionary current: fascism.

We say this in all sincerity; we have had the opportunity to see fascism in action. We sincerely believe that nothing else could teach us as much as this visit has.

Of course, it is said that nothing can teach the people as much as a revolutionary process itself. Every revolutionary process teaches the people things that would otherwise take dozens of years to learn.

This raises a question: Who will learn more and sooner? Who will develop more of an awareness faster? The exploiters or the exploited? Who will be quicker to learn the lessons of this process? The people or the enemies of the people?

Are you absolutely sure—you, the protagonists in this drama being written by your country—are you completely sure that you have learned more than your exploiters have?

Then, allow me to say that I disagree—not with the president, but with the masses.

Tomorrow there'll be a headline in some paper somewhere in the world, reading, "Castro disagrees with the masses." We disagree on one aspect of the appreciation of the situation.

In this sort of dialogue on scientific and historical matters, we can say that we are not completely sure that in this unique process the people, the humble people—who constitute the majority of the population—have learned more rapidly than the reactionaries, than the old exploiters.

And there's something else: The rulers of the social system that revolutions transform have had many years of experience to their credit, many, many years of experience! They went on accumulating experience, culture, technology and tricks of every kind to use against revolutionary processes. They confront the people, who lack all that experience, know-how and technology, armed with this experience and technology accumulated over the years.

If you don't mind our speaking frankly, and as we have said, we are incapable of lying: We may be wrong, we may get the wrong impression about certain things, but we will never say anything we don't believe. We sincerely believe that the enemy, the reactionaries, have learned much quicker than the masses.

Is it because the people lack something? Is it because the people of Chile lack patriotic virtues, character, courage, intelligence and firmness? No! We have been deeply impressed by the qualities of the Chilean people. And yet, when we spoke with the farmers here, after having chatted with them for half an hour, we asked them how far they'd gone in school, and they answered, "We don't even know how to read or write."

We were deeply impressed by the fiery Chilean character. Everywhere we went, at receptions, during our tours, we witnessed this courage, this determination; we saw how the people swarmed over our cars. Moreover, very often we saw how the women, holding children in their arms, stood firmly across the road, with an impressive determination and courage.

We have seen in the Chilean people qualities that our people lacked in the early days of the revolution: a higher level of culture, a higher level of political culture. Listen to this carefully! A higher level of political culture, a much higher level of political culture! This is because the situation in our country was different from here, where, for example, there was an electoral victory for the Marxist parties, and other organizations that supported those parties.

In regard to political culture, you have started from a higher level than ours. Moreover, you start from a patriotic tradition dating back 150 years, a national tradition which dates back 150 years. You start from a much higher level of patriotic awareness, a higher awareness of the problems in your country.

Imperialist ideology had made deep inroads in our country. Our country had been invaded by the imperialist culture, by the way of life and the customs of that society so close to us, US society.

Therefore, in that sense, we were much weaker than you. You can see that there is a whole series of factors that reveal your people started from a much higher level than we did. From the economic standpoint, Chile has more resources than Cuba. Chile has an incomparably higher level of economic development than Cuba based on natural resources which it now owns. In other words, Chile now owns its own copper, where 30,000 workers produce close to one billion dollars in foreign exchange. It produces oil, almost two million tons. It has hydroelectric power resources, iron, coal, a food industry much more highly developed than Cuba's, and a textile industry. In other words, you start from a technological and industrial level much higher than the one that existed in Cuba.

Therefore, all the human conditions, all the social conditions necessary for progress exist in this country.

However, you are faced with something we didn't have to face. In our country, the oligarchs, the landowners, the reactionaries, didn't have the experience that their colleagues here have. Over there, the landowners and the oligarchs weren't in the least concerned about social changes. They said, "The Americans" — they called everyone from the United States "Americans" — "will take care of that problem. There can't be a revolution here!" And they lay back to wait.

This is not the case in Chile, though!

The reactionaries and the oligarchs here are much better prepared than they were in Cuba. They are much better organized and better armed to resist changes, from the ideological standpoint. They have all the weapons they need to wage a battle on every front in the face of the advancing process. A battle on the economic front, on the political front, and on the front of the masses — I repeat — on the front of the masses!

Now then, that is the essential difference, but there are others. There are others! I won't discuss them because they concern totally different issues.

However, when our revolution won, when it began — we say that January 1 marked the triumph of the revolution, but, historically, we consider it as the beginning of the process — we also met with some resistance. Don't ever think that the reactionaries and oligarchs in Cuba never put up any resistance. There was plenty of it! They resorted to everything they had, to every weapon at hand, with the direct aid of the imperialists. They challenged us on every front — mark my words — on every front. They fought us on the ideological front. They tried to fight us on the front of the masses and they fought us on the front of armed struggle.

It might be said of us that we started a process of armed struggle in Cuba, but we did not invent armed resistance. That's something that comes at a high price. The armed resistance of reaction cost our country more blood and more victims than the revolutionary war. Just listen to this: More people were killed as a result of reactionary violence than during the revolutionary war. The struggle cost us hundreds upon hundreds of lives, hundreds upon hundreds of millions of dollars. This is because of the sabotage, the bands of armed mercenaries practically all over our territory, the infiltration of spies, the dropping of weapons by parachute; all these things cost us many years of struggle. The mercenary invasion of the Bay of Pigs, the threats at the time of the October [Missile] Crisis—a crisis brought on by the imperialists—have forced us to keep fighting all these years.

All right, now we have beaten them everywhere. We beat them first on the ideological front; second, on the front of the masses; and third, on the front of armed struggle!

In our opinion, the problem of violence in these processes—including the Cuban process—once the revolution is in power, does not depend on the revolutionaries. It would be absurd, incomprehensible and illogical for revolutionaries to engage in violence when they have an opportunity to advance, to create, to work, to march toward the future. Therefore, it isn't the revolutionaries who promote violence in these circumstances. And, in case you didn't know this, you'll find out through experience.

That's the experience we went through when the Cuban revolutionary movement won.

Don't ever think that we had it easy! Believe me, it wasn't. And you can believe something else, too. There were more political parties in Cuba than there are here! We had everything there. Therefore, you shouldn't be discouraged. There were all sorts of differences, but, on the other hand, there was always a drive to unite, an awareness of the need to unite, to increase our forces. That's one thing that was never lacking.

You all know that in our country the parties were not merged by decree. No one should think that the parties had to merge. No! In Cuba, the revolutionary forces gradually merged together. It was a gradual process that took years.

Today, there's one revolutionary force in Cuba—the revolutionary force of the people of Cuba.

I have no idea how many people are here now. You might know more or less how many. But I can tell you that it takes 10 minutes to get as many people together in Cuba. And we can get together 10 times as many in a couple of hours! And yet the population of our capital is two-thirds the population of Santiago de Chile.

Our country has reached a high level of unity, a high level of revolutionary awareness. A very sound, really solid form of patriotism has been created, which makes our country a bulwark of the revolution and one trench among the nations of America that the imperialists will never be able to destroy.

We were simply amazed when we heard the president [Allende] say that a very important newspaper in Washington—or New York—has published statements by a high-ranking government official who said "the days of the popular government in Chile are numbered."

I would like to point out—regardless of the rudeness and intrusion, the unheard-of prophecy, the offense and insolence—that it's been many a year since some crazy US official had the idea of saying that the days of the Cuban revolution were numbered.

It would be logical, in view of a statement like that, not only to get angry, to protest the insult to one's dignity, to protest against the offense, but also to ask what makes them believe such a thing and why they feel so confident about it. What kind of calculations did they make? What computers did they put into operation to figure this out? This doesn't mean that Yankee computers don't make mistakes. In the case of the Bay of Pigs, the Pentagon's computers, the CIA's computers, the US government's computers, everybody's computers were wrong—a million times wrong.

Nevertheless, one must ask what are the grounds for such optimism, for such an assurance, and where does the encouragement come from. And you are the only ones who can supply the answer.

Or maybe you'd be interested in hearing the opinion of a visitor who is not a tourist? Do I have your permission to express it?

All those in favor, raise their hands.

Well, in view of the permission granted me in this sort of plebiscite to express my opinion in such matters, I say that this confidence is based on the very weakness of the revolutionary process, on weaknesses in the ideological battle, on weaknesses in the mass struggle, on weakness in the face of the enemy! And the enemy abroad, which supports the enemy at home, tries to take advantage of the slightest breach, of the slightest weakness. In fact, we should say that it is the result of weakness in the effort to consolidate your forces, to unite them and to increase them.

You're going through a period that is very special, albeit not a new one, in the matter of class struggle. There are countless examples of this. You're going through that period in the process in which the fascists—to call them by their right name—are trying to beat you to the streets; they are trying to isolate you from the middle strata of the population. There is a specific moment in every revolutionary process when fascists and revolutionaries engage in a struggle for the support of the middle strata.

The revolutionaries are honest. They don't go around telling lies. They don't go around sowing terror and distress or cooking up terrible schemes.

The fascists stop at nothing. They'll try to find the weakest spot. They'll invent the most incredible lies. They'll try to sow terror and unrest among the middle strata by telling the most incredible lies. Their objective is to win over the middle strata. Moreover, they'll appeal to the basest sensibilities. They will try to arouse feelings of chauvinism—that narrow-minded nationalism—and all sorts of selfish feelings. They will resort to every method they can think of. They will try to arouse feelings of chauvinism, arouse the lowest passions, arouse the most groundless terror. The fascists stop at nothing.

We've seen it here, because we had the opportunity to see certain things during our long, hectic trip—long in distance and long in time (and here we are in agreement with the complainers)—we've had an opportunity to hear the lies, the sort of things they say. Where were they aimed? With respect to our visit, what was the purpose of all these lies? To be honest, there was only one way to visit this country and that was by remaining speechless, by not uttering a word. What they wanted was a deaf-mute or something like that—and someone who wouldn't even use sign language, because it's possible to say a great many things by signing. First there was the pharisaical attitude: "He's here. He was received. We hope he will remember where he is, that he will mind his own affairs." Then, later, the business with the pie, "The man eating a pinon pie," and "The man having his picture taken with the girls with the hot pants." Then the lies: "Fidel hooted at in Los Andes," and "Fidel gets cold welcome in Chuquicamata."

It's always the same story, an attempt to arouse chauvinism, to present every gesture, every attitude, every word, every answer to a question put by a student, as meddling. We have seen this day after day, how everything is used as a pretext to arouse mistrust, fear and resentment. They are quite adept at this kind of thing. And, from our standpoint as observers we see how the fascists are trying to make headway and gain ground among the middle strata, and to beat you to the streets. They are trying to demoralize the revolutionaries. There are places where we have found the revolutionaries looking hard hit, and there are places where they even appeared discouraged.

If we weren't sincere, if we didn't believe in the truth, we wouldn't dare say what we just said. It might even sound as if we were saying something that the enemy might use to its advantage, to gain ground. No! The only way in which the enemy can gain ground is by deceit, by confusion, by ignorance, by lack of awareness about the problems!

If you want my opinion, the success or the failure of this unusual process will depend on the ideological battle and the mass struggle. It will also depend on the revolutionaries' ability to grow in numbers, to unite and to win over the middle strata of the population. This is because in our countries—less developed countries—these middle strata are quite large and are susceptible to lies and deceit. However, in the ideological struggle, no one is ever won over except through the truth, sound arguments and by right. There is no question about that.

Yes, I hope you will win. We want you to win. And we believe that you will win!

There was something today that made a deep impression on us, and that was the words of the president, especially when he reaffirmed his commitment to defend the cause of the people and the will of the people. Most especially when he made a history-making statement—that he was the president by the will of the people and that he would fulfill his duty until his term was over or until his body was taken out of the palace. Those of us who know him know very well that the president is not a person of words but a person of deeds. All of us who know his character know that this is the way he is.

When you can count on such a sense of dignity; when the people know they can depend on the person who represents them today and who, in those few words, expressed his determination to resist the attacks of the enemy abroad who are complicit with the reactionaries at home; when the people know this and the enemy knows it, too, that in itself means assurance, confidence, a banner.

And as Latin Americans, we congratulate the president for his courageous, dignified statement.

We saw how the people reacted to the president's words.

[Responding to someone in the audience]

I wouldn't put it that way, "By right or by force." There are phrases that are historical, which have a value in themselves due to their historic character, and have become symbols. By right, by the force of right and by the physical power and the people's power that accompanies right!

When the chiefs, the leaders, are ready to lay down their lives for a cause, the men and the women of the people are ready to lay down their lives too!

The people are the makers of history. The people write their own history. The masses make history. No reactionary, no imperialist enemy can crush the people! And our country's recent history proves this!

How did we manage to resist and why? Because of the unity of our people, because of the strength that such unity generates.

We said that it would take two hours for us to get together 10 times as many people as there are here now. And we also say that we can have 600,000 people in arms within 24 hours!

A close, unbreakable unity between the people and the armed forces has been created in our country. This is why we say our defense is strong.

There's something that experts in the history of war and professional soldiers know: The individual plays a decisive role in battle; moral factors play a decisive role in battle; and morale of the combatant plays a decisive role in battle. Those familiar with history and great military deeds know that when the forces are united, inspired and deeply motivated, they can overcome any obstacle. They can assail and take any position and make the most incredible sacrifices.

What is it that gives our people this deep motivation in their defense against threats from outside? The fact that, when it comes to defending our homeland, that homeland is not divided into millionaires and paupers, wealthy landowners with all the privileges in the world and miserable peasants without land or work, living a life of poverty; the fact that our homeland is not divided into oppressors and oppressed, exploiters and exploited, ladies overloaded with jewelry and girls forced to lead a life of prostitution. Our homeland is not divided into privileged and dispossessed.

When our campesinos are called to form part of the armed forces, they know that they will not be defending a country of exploiters and oppressors, a country of privileged men and women, but rather a country of all the people and for all the people, a country that provides bread for all instead of abundance for some and hunger for others, instead of honors and grandeur for some and humiliation for others.

We have seen this, we have experienced all this—the deep motivation, the spirit of our people, of men and women, everybody, in combat. They know what they are fighting for. They have developed a great awareness of what dignity means. Ours is a people united behind a just cause, a people defending its own cause, defending a flag which means more now than it ever did before.

The people are so noble, and patriotic feelings are so aroused in them that even in class societies, in a society of exploiters and exploited, they have been capable of fighting and dying because they had a symbol of the homeland, an idea of what homeland meant, for which they were willing to lay down their lives. Even though they were the humble, the scorned and the exploited in that homeland, they still defended it!

Imagine their motivations, their degree of heroism, when they know that they are defending a country that is theirs in the fullest sense of the word!

No people, no armed force, has more power to fulfill the sacred duty of defending the homeland than where exploiters and exploited are a thing of the past. In other words, where the exploitation of human beings has disappeared.

It is not by accident that history taught us a lesson not too long ago. In World War II, which brought about the collapse of a number of powerful armies, what was it that the fascists did to attack Europe, to invade France, Belgium, Holland and practically all of the western world? They sowed their fifth column, promoted division and morally disarmed the people. When the fascist hordes attacked with their armor, when their motorized divisions broke through, they made their greatest gains from the demoralization of the people.

But when one day, two years later—in June 1941—four million experienced veterans of that same fascist army launched a surprise invasion of the Soviet Union, what did they find? They found stiff resistance, from the very first moment, from the very first day, from the very first hours. They found a people ready to fight and to die, a people who lost 18 million lives, who had the most extraordinary experience of war in recent times.

And don't let it be said that the Westerners learned how to fight! With fabulous superiority in their favor, and at a time when the Nazi army was practically destroyed, they landed in Normandy and reached the border with no difficulty. And then, in that famous episode of the Ardennes, a few armored divisions pushed them back scores of miles.

Now then, the fascists threw more than 300 divisions into their attack on the Soviet Union, and the people of the Soviet Union resisted and put up a fight. What a mistake the fascists made! They thought the whole thing would be like a military parade — but that treacherous attack ended in Berlin. And it was the Soviet army that crushed the fascist hordes!

Here we have a perfect lesson from history. Never before, notwithstanding the proverbial patriotism of that nation, had they put up such a heroic, determined resistance. This was because the society of the feudal lords and serfs, of the czars with their absolute power, no longer existed. The socialist state resisted even more. And what's really extraordinary is that this socialist state, made up largely of peasants, became the strong industrial power it is today, and the country which has helped small nations such as Vietnam and Cuba to resist such great dangers as imperialism.

Military men know what a people united, militant and deeply motivated means: that such a people makes victory possible, that such a people can beat all odds against them and that such a people can demonstrate all kinds of heroism.

We mentioned the French revolution. You will recall that when the bourgeoisie was a revolutionary class and led the people, the same thing happened — the country, invaded by a great many nations, not only resisted but went on to defeat the aggressors. This is because, in a revolution, the people become united when age-old injustices disappear, and forces come forward that nothing and nobody can defeat.

Somebody, a historian of that revolution, once said, "When a people embarks on revolution no force in the world can stop it." This is why we say that our country is powerful and united. We have made progress and we feel satisfied. However, if you'll allow me to express, in all sincerity, one of our conclusions and one of our impressions to you Chileans — who are so curious, who are so interested in impressions—I'll tell you an impression that comes from my very heart. When I see history unfolding, when I see these struggles, when I see how hard the reactionaries are trying to demoralize the people, when I see the means they resort to, I come to one conclusion, one that comes from the bottom of my heart: I will return to Cuba more of a revolutionary than when I came here! I will return to Cuba more of a radical than when I came here! I will return to Cuba more of an extremist than when I came here!

I am trying to express an idea. When we wish to express something we try to find the words to reflect our ideas. The lessons I have learned and the experiences I've gone through make me feel more and more identified with the process our country has gone through; they make me feel an even greater love for our revolution; they make me appreciate our successes and our progress.

I don't want to dwell on this subject.

I am deeply grateful for your kindness and patience. You know I must leave and you know that you don't need me here.

I am very grateful for those words that I take as a kind of apology for those who tried to throw a wet blanket on my visit, demanding that I leave and practically promoting a law to have me expelled.

Yesterday, we were even joking about it, and we did joke about it until yesterday. However, today, we are not in the mood for joking, having read about something I won't comment on. I'll only refer to the way one feels when one reads news of injuries, of fires, and of a lot of things that happened when we were having a reception in the Cuban embassy, attended by more than 600 prominent Chileans. And, until then, we'd be joking and saying, "What are the requirements for becoming a Chilean citizen?" There was a lawyer there and we asked him, "How long does it take? How long does one have to reside here?" and, "Where are the forms that should be filled out? I want to fill out one of those forms," and things like that.

It was all right to joke at all the insults and the rest. In fact, I was tempted to carry the joke a little further. After all, you wouldn't deny a Latin American the right to become a Chilean citizen, provided he met all the requirements, would you? Maybe in 10 or 20 years? I don't know. The whole thing was a joke.

To a certain extent, we feel that we are the children of a whole community, part of a world much larger than Cuba and Chile, and that is Latin America.

The day will come when we'll all have the same citizenship, without losing one iota of our love for our homeland, for that corner of our hemisphere where we were born; for our flags, which will be sister flags; for our anthems, which will be sister anthems; for our traditions, which will be sister traditions; and for our cultures, which will be sister cultures. The day will come when our peoples will have the power to take an honored place in the world, when the powerful will no longer be able to insult us, when the empire, proud and arrogant, will no longer be able to threaten us with tragedy and defeat or make any other kind of threat. Because it is not the same thing to threaten a small country as it is to threaten a union of sister nations that may become a large and powerful community in the world of tomorrow.

The day will come when reactionary ideology will be defeated, when all narrow-minded nationalism, the ridiculous chauvinism which the reactionaries and the imperialists utilize to maintain a situation of division and hostility among our peoples, peoples who speak the same language, who can understand one another as we understand each other now will be defeated. Reactionary ideology makes for division.

For America to be united and become "Our America," the America Martí spoke of, it will be necessary to eradicate every last vestige of those reactionaries who want the peoples to be weak so they can hold them in oppression and in subjection to foreign monopolies. After all, that is nothing but the expression of a reactionary philosophy, the philosophy of exploitation and oppression.

Allow me, not to extend my visit, but only to express a few more ideas, if I may.

What is it that we want to say? Among other things, an elementary expression of gratitude to all those with whom we have been in contact—and we've had ample contact with the people of Chile. We have met and talked at length with the workers, the students, the campesinos and the people in general in our visits to so many places here. We have talked with journalists and intellectual workers and with economists and technicians, like those in the ECLA. We have met and talked with deputies, with the leaders of the parties of Popular Unity, with the leaders of the organizations of the left; with everybody.

We have met with the workers' representatives. We have met with the women of Chile. We have met with the cardinal of Chile. We have met with more than 100 progressive priests who make up quite an impressive movement. We have talked with members of the army, the navy and the carabineers. We were met with affection and respect everywhere. And we have tried our very best to answer all the questions put to us.

Of all these meetings, those that provoked the greatest irritation and criticism were the meetings with the cardinal, the meetings with the progressive priests and the meetings with the members of the army, the navy, the air force and the carabineers.

It is necessary that we explain the essence of these meetings and the reason why they came about. Have we, perhaps, been engaged in a campaign of demagoguery or acted in contradiction to our own convictions? We say this because we noticed the special emphasis that was placed on a number of these things.

It could be said that if anyone had to bear as many insults as I did it was the cardinal. We had many things to talk about with the Christian left and with the Chilean priests, many, many things based on principles rather than on opportunism, on profound reason, on convictions rather than on profits; based on the possibility—and the need—of bringing together this Latin American community of Marxist revolutionaries and Christians, the Marxist revolutionaries and the Christian revolutionaries.

We spoke at length with the priests about the foundations for our convictions now and always. Let's not confuse these meetings with the problems that the oligarchs in our country created by trying to use the church to fight the revolution!

We have often spoken of the history of Christianity—that Christianity which gave rise to so many martyrs, to so many people who sacrificed themselves defending their faith. Those who can lay down their lives for the sake of their faith will always have our deepest respect. However, we will never feel the slightest respect for those who defend illegitimate interests—their egotism, their full stomachs—and who are incapable of sacrificing their lives for anything or anyone.

We examined the many points of coincidence that might exist between the purest precepts of Christianity and the objectives of Marxism. There are many who have tried to use religion to defend exploitation, poverty and privilege; to transform peoples' lives in this world into a hell, forgetting that Christianity was the religion of the humble, of the slaves of Rome, of the tens of thousands who were devoured by the lions in the arena and who had very definite ideas about human solidarity or human love, and condemned greed, gluttony and selfishness.

That was a religion which, 2,000 years ago, called the merchants and Pharisees by their name, which condemned the rich and said that they would not enter the kingdom of heaven. That was the religion which multiplied the loaves and the fishes — precisely what the revolutionary today intends to do with technology, with human hands, with the rational, planned development of the economy.

When you search for the similarities between the objectives of Marxism and the most beautiful precepts of Christianity, you will find many points of coincidence. You will see why a humble priest who knows what hunger means because he is in close contact with it, who knows what sickness and death and human pain mean, or why some of those priests who practice their religion among the miners or among humble peasant families become identified with them and fight shoulder to shoulder with them. You will see why there are unselfish people who devote their whole lives to the care of people afflicted with the worst diseases.

When you find all those points of coincidence you will see how such a strategic alliance between Marxist revolutionaries and Christian revolutionaries is possible.

The imperialists — and, of course, all the reactionaries — don't want such an alliance to take place.

We also spoke at length with the military. And when we say military we mean members of every branch of the armed forces. However, these talks came about spontaneously. They were not planned. They were the result of the official attention given us, of the extraordinary attentions with which the president, the ministers and other government authorities showered us. At the airports, everywhere, those in uniform and their representatives were there, too. Thus, a series of conversations took place, spontaneously, at the receptions and during our meetings with the authorities. It was obvious that those in uniform and our delegation had many things to talk about.

In the first place, our country has been forced to live through a tremendous experience. We, the Cuban revolutionaries, had to go through many unique experiences during the various stages of our struggle. First, as irregular fighters, in the beginning. Then as fighters with certain ideas and tactics of struggle. We, the Cuban revolutionaries, were forced to fight against great odds throughout our revolutionary war.

We went through many stages—adversity, success, very difficult moments and total victory. Later, we went through other experiences—our country was invaded by mercenary bands and we had to fight them for years. These bands were armed with the best weapons made in the United States, radio equipment and other war materiel.

We have lived through the experience of the Bay of Pigs and through the experience of the October [Missile] Crisis, when our country lived through days of tension and danger, when our country was threatened by dozens of nuclear missiles.

We have lived through the experience of having to organize combat units in the face of a real, a great danger. We have had to develop powerful armed forces, create schools, learn how to handle modern armaments, learn new combat techniques. We have studied the experience, the reports and the documents of the last world war.

Undoubtedly, from the technical point of view, from the professional point of view, there were many things we might have discussed. Interest in Cuba's experience, Cuba's process, and the natural curiosity about historical events that everyone possesses. In addition, there were issues of a human nature, the competence, efficiency, traditions and history of each country, the present and the future. What will be the future of our peoples in the face of the technological gaps that are growing between the developed nations and those that have been left behind? What are the prospects in weapons, the new systems of armaments?

That is, from both the professional and human points of view, as things related to the future of our peoples, there were plenty of broad themes of this kind on which our talks developed.

We had the chance to meet many very talented, upright, efficient people, many worthy individuals, thanks to those talks. We had the chance to speak on matters related to our traditions. We have learned—all of us—many things.

So was this a sin? Was this a conspiracy? Was this a crime? Was there anything that anyone could feel offended by? And why, since we talked with the priests, the cardinal and the ECLA technicians, shouldn't we talk with those in uniform in Chile? Why did they fear these talks so much? Whom have we offended with them?

Even during the revolutionary war [in Cuba] we held talks. While fighting, we held talks with the enemy, and we discussed things. While fighting, we analyzed who was right and who was wrong. If we talked with those fighting against us, why shouldn't we talk with those who treated us with every courtesy, kindness, every consideration and full respect?

This is why we would also like to express our thanks to them today for their attention — today, December 2, which, without anyone's planning it this way, is singularly appropriate for this, as it marks the 15th anniversary of the landing of the *Granma*, which brought a group of 82 combatants to a swampy coast in Cuba.

Comparing all of Batista's forces to ours, the odds were a thousand to one. In all, counting the various branches, he had around 80,000 combatants. A few days later, our situation was much worse, and only seven of us armed men regrouped. The odds: Ten thousand to one, or even greater. A little more than ten thousand. Ten thousand to one! And we weren't unnerved. We didn't lose heart!

Perhaps this will help you to understand why we aren't afraid to show what the weaknesses of the revolutionaries or of a process are at a given time.

Ten thousand to one! And we didn't lose heart. We kept on going, overcoming very difficult circumstances, and always fighting against overwhelming odds. Even at the end of the war, the odds were a little over 20 to one against us. That's what our process has gone through.

I'm telling you this, Chilean revolutionaries, in relation to this day, which it is our duty to commemorate, in order to show that there's no way on earth to defeat a revolutionary people, a people armed with a doctrine, with an idea; a people determined to defend a cause — there's no way on earth to crush it.

We have said this so that there may never be any discouragement in the revolutionary ranks! So there may never be discouragement! So morale may never be other than at its peak! The actions of the enemy don't matter! We must always say, "Forward!"

Revolutionaries are moved by profound motivations, by great ideas. They do not promote fear. No! Even though they are familiar with the fate of crushed revolutions. To cite two examples: The revolution of the Roman slaves, led by Spartacus, which was crushed by the oligarchs, and cost the lives of tens of thousands of people who were nailed to crosses along the roads leading to Rome; and the revolution of the Paris communards which was drowned in blood.

We could cite some more recent examples. Every time a revolution gets under way, fascism appears along with all its tricks and schemes, all its maneuvers, all its hypocrisy and pharisaism, all its tactics of promoting fear and making use of lies and the most criminal methods. But there's nothing to fear! Fight back with arguments! Fight back with reason! Fight back with the truth! Fight back with conviction! Fight back without fear of the consequences of defeat! Fight for an idea! Fight for a just cause! Fight back knowing that you're right! Fight back knowing that the inexorable laws of history are on your side! Fight back knowing that the future is yours! Advance with the masses! Advance with the people! Advance with ideas! Advance uniting forces! Advance gathering forces!

And all this that I'm saying to you today, all these things about which I've spoken at length—thanks to your patience and understanding—all these things I've said about tactics and unity, about the possibility that we may all participate in this great crusade on behalf of our sister America, was not an invention I made for my visit to Chile, are not just things that are said in passing. We have here this document, proclaimed 10 years ago, and known as the Second Declaration of Havana, and we believe that it would be appropriate to read a few paragraphs which sum up our revolutionary strategy since that time. Perhaps they may be of some use to you.

On leaving you, what could we possibly leave as a memento? If some of these ideas, some of these concepts can be of use to you, we will be very satisfied, at least in a spiritual sense, for having in some way reciprocated your affection.

The paragraphs I refer to and which run consecutively, read as follows:

Imperialism, utilizing the great movie monopolies, its news services, its periodicals, books and reactionary newspapers, resorts to the most subtle lies to sow divisions and inculcate among the most ignorant people fear and superstition against revolutionary ideas, ideas that can and should frighten only the powerful exploiters, with their worldly interests and privileges.

Divisionism, a product of all kinds of prejudices, false ideas and lies; sectarianism, dogmatism, a lack of breadth in analyzing the role of each social layer, its parties, organizations and leaders — these obstruct the necessary united action of the democratic and progressive forces of our peoples. They are deficiencies of growth, infantile diseases of the revolutionary movement that must be left behind. In the anti-feudal and anti-imperialist struggle it is possible to bring the majority of the people resolutely behind goals of liberation that unite the spirit of the working class, the peasants, the intellectual workers, the petit bourgeoisie and the most progressive layers of the national bourgeoisie. These sectors comprise the immense majority of the population and bring together great social forces capable of sweeping away the imperialist and reactionary feudal rule. In that broad movement they can and must struggle together for the good of our nations, for the good of our peoples, and for the good of the Americas, from the old Marxist militant, right up to the sincere Catholic who has nothing to do with the Yankee monopolists and the feudal lords of the land.

This movement can pull along with it the most progressive elements of the armed forces, which have also been humiliated by the Yankee military missions, the betrayal of national interests by the feudal oligarchies and the sacrifice of national sovereignty to Washington's dictates.

These ideas were expressed 10 years ago and do not vary one iota from the ideas we hold today.

Our revolution has stood firm by its principles. It is not dogmatic. It moves forward, advances. Its development even includes significant strides forward. But, at all times, it has stuck to a principle, has followed one line, one road. The revolution is characterized by its confidence in the people, in the masses, in ideas and in victory. It is characterized by its firmness and its uncompromising attitude. A broad-minded attitude on the one hand, and firmness in principles on the other!

We have met and spoken at length with many Chileans. The only ones we haven't spoken with—and will never speak with—are the exploiters, the reactionaries, the oligarchs and the fascists.

We have never talked with the fascists, and we never will!

As far as the rest of the Chileans are concerned, it has been a great honor for us to have met them, to get to know them, to have talked with them and to have exchanged views with them.

Beloved Compañero Salvador Allende, we will be leaving this beautiful country very soon. We will soon be saying goodbye to this hospitable, magnificent, warm-hearted people. We are taking back with us a memento of our visit—the indelible memory of our stay here, of all the affection, all the attention, all the honors that you heaped on our delegation as the representatives of the people of Cuba and the Cuban revolution.

All we want to say to you, beloved president, and to all Chileans, is that you can count on Cuba. You can count on her unselfish, unconditional solidarity, on what that flag and that homeland really mean. Not the homeland of the exploited, but the homeland of free human beings! A homeland to which the revolution gave equality and justice! A homeland where humankind regained its dignity!

To those who attempt to deny the legitimacy of the revolution, let them observe its force and then try to explain how it is possible for us to resist the powerful Yankee empire on the cultural front, on the political front and on the military front, if we don't have a conscious, united people, a people who knows what dignity and freedom mean.

There's our country, firm and staunch! There's our flag; a flag which represents the dignity of Cuba, which represents the nation in the broadest sense of the word, which represents patriotism in its most fraternal sense, as sons and daughters of Cuba and sons and daughters of America!

These two symbols that today wave together here also represent the closeness of our peoples, of our ideas, of our cause and of our motives.

Because today is December 2, allow me to end the way we do in Cuba:

Patria o muerte! [Homeland or death!]
Venceremos! [We will win!]

13. ON BEHALF OF THE MOVEMENT OF NONALIGNED COUNTRIES

UN GENERAL ASSEMBLY, NEW YORK
OCTOBER 12, 1979

On October 12, 1979, Fidel Castro addressed the United Nations General Assembly in New York on behalf of the 95 members of the Movement of Nonaligned Countries. Despite pressure from the United States, the sixth summit of the nonaligned movement had been held in Havana the previous month and had elected Fidel Castro as chair.

Most Esteemed President;
Distinguished Representatives of the world community:

I have not come to speak about Cuba. I am not here to denounce before this assembly the aggressions to which our small but honorable country has been subjected for 20 years, neither have I come to injure, with unnecessary adjectives, our powerful neighbor in his own house.

We have been charged by the sixth summit conference of the heads of state or government of the Movement of Nonaligned Countries to present to the United Nations the results of its deliberations and the positions derived from them.

We are 95 countries from all continents, representing the great majority of humanity. We are united by the determination to defend the cooperation between our countries, free national and social development, sovereignty, security, equality and self-determination.

We are united in our determination to change the present system of international relations, based as it is on injustice, inequality and oppression. In international politics we act as an independent world force.

Meeting in Havana, the movement has just reaffirmed its principles and confirmed its objectives.

The nonaligned countries stress that it is imperative to do away with the enormous inequality separating the developed countries from the developing countries. We are struggling to eradicate the poverty, hunger, disease and illiteracy from which hundreds of millions of human beings still suffer.

We aspire to a new world order, one based on justice, fairness and peace; one that will replace the unjust and unequal system prevailing today, in which, as the final summit declaration states: "Wealth is concentrated in the hands of a few powers whose wasteful economies are maintained by the exploitation of workers as well as by the transfer and plunder of the natural and other resources of the peoples of Africa, Latin America, Asia and other regions of the world."

Among the problems to be debated in the present session of the General Assembly, peace is a concern of the first order. The search for peace is also an aspiration of the Movement of Nonaligned Countries and has been the subject of its attention at the sixth summit conference. But for our countries, peace is indivisible. We want a peace that will equally benefit the large and the small, the strong and the weak, a peace that will embrace all regions of the world and reach all its citizens.

Since its very inception, the Movement of Nonaligned Countries has considered that the principles of peaceful coexistence should be the cornerstone of international relations, constituting the basis for the strengthening of peace and international security, for the relaxation of tensions, and the expansion of this process to all regions of the world and to all aspects of international relations. And they must be applied universally in relations among states.

At the same time, the sixth summit conference considered that these principles of peaceful coexistence should also include the right of peoples under alien and colonial domination to self-determination, independence, sovereignty and territorial integrity; the right of every country to put an end to foreign occupation and the acquisition of territory by force; and the right of every country to choose its own social, economic and political system.

Only in this way can peaceful coexistence be the foundation for all international relations. This cannot be denied. Analyzing the structure of the world today, we see that these rights of our peoples are not yet guaranteed. The nonaligned countries know full well who our historical enemies are, where the threats come from and how to combat them.

That is why, in Havana, we reaffirmed, "the quintessence of the policy of nonalignment, in accordance with its original principles and essential character, involves the struggle against imperialism, colonialism and neocolonialism, apartheid, racism (including Zionism) and all forms of foreign aggression, occupation, domination, interference or hegemony, as well as the struggle against great power and bloc policies."

It will therefore be understood that the final declaration also linked the struggle for peace with "political, moral and material support for the national liberation movements and joint efforts to eliminate colonial domination and racial discrimination."

The nonaligned countries have always attached great importance to the possibility of and necessity for détente among the great powers. The sixth summit conference pointed with great concern to the fact that in the period after the Colombo summit conference [of 1976], there was a certain stagnation in the process of détente, which has continued to be limited "both in scope and geographically."

On the basis of that concern, the nonaligned countries—who have made disarmament and denuclearization one of the permanent and most prominent objectives of their struggle, and who took the initiative in convening the 10th special session of the [UN] General Assembly on disarmament— examined the results of negotiations on strategic arms and the agreements known as SALT II. They feel that those negotiations constitute an important step for the two main nuclear powers and could open up prospects for more comprehensive negotiations leading to general disarmament and the relaxation of international tensions.

But as far as the nonaligned countries are concerned, those treaties are only part of the progress toward peace. Although negotiations between the great powers constitute a decisive element in the process, the nonaligned countries once again reiterated that the endeavor to consolidate détente, to extend it to all parts of the world and to avert the nuclear threat, the arms buildup, and war, is a task in which all the peoples of the world should participate and exercise their responsibility.

Mr. President, basing ourselves on the concept of the universality of peace, and on the need to link the search for peace, extended to all countries, with the struggle for national independence, full sovereignty and full equality among states, we, the heads of state or government who met at the sixth summit conference in Havana, gave our attention to the most pressing problems in Africa, Asia, Latin America and other regions.

It is important to stress that we started from an independent position that was not linked to policies that might stem from the contradictions between the great powers. If, in spite of our uncommitted and objective approach, our review of international events became a denunciation of imperialism and colonialism, this merely reflects the essential reality of today's world.

Thus, having begun the analysis of the situation in Africa and recognizing the progress made in the African peoples' struggle for their emancipation, the heads of state or government stressed that a fundamental need of the region is the elimination from the continent, and especially in southern Africa, of colonialism, racism, racial discrimination and apartheid.

It was imperative to stress the fact that the colonialist and imperialist powers are continuing their aggressive policies with the aim of perpetuating, regaining or extending their domination and exploitation of the African nations.

This is the dramatic situation in Africa. The nonaligned countries could not fail to condemn the attacks on Mozambique, on Zambia, on Angola, on Botswana, the threats against Lesotho, the constant efforts to destabilize the area and the role played by the racist regimes of Rhodesia [Zimbabwe] and South Africa. The pressing need for Zimbabwe and Namibia to be completely and quickly liberated is not just the cause of the nonaligned countries or of the most progressive forces of our era, but is already contained in resolutions and agreements of the international community through the United Nations. It implies duties that must be accomplished and infractions that must be denounced internationally.

Therefore, when in the final declaration the heads of state or government condemned by name a number of Western countries, headed by the United States, for their direct or indirect collaboration in maintaining racism, oppression and South Africa's criminal policy of apartheid, and when on the other hand they recognized the role played by the nonaligned countries, the United Nations, the Organization of African Unity [OAU], the socialist countries, the Scandinavian countries and other democratic and progressive forces in supporting the struggle of the peoples of Africa, this did not reflect the slightest manifestation of an ideological leaning. It was simply the expression of an objective reality. To condemn South Africa without mentioning those who make its criminal policies possible would have been incomprehensible.

More forcibly and urgently than ever, the sixth summit conference expressed the need to end the situation in which the Zimbabwean and Namibian peoples' right to independence is denied, and the pressing need of South Africa's black men and women to attain equality and respect as human beings. It also affirmed the need to guarantee conditions of respect and peace for all the countries of the region.

The decision to continue support for the national liberation movements, the Patriotic Front [of Zimbabwe] and for SWAPO [of Namibia], was as unanimous as it was expected. Let us state very clearly now that this is not a case of expressing a unilateral preference for solutions through armed struggle.

It is true that the conference praised the Namibian people, and SWAPO, their sole, authentic representative, for having stepped up and advanced the armed struggle, and that it called for total and effective support for that form of combat. But that was due to the fact that the South African racists have slammed the door on any real negotiations and that the efforts to achieve a negotiated solution go no further than simple maneuvers.

The attitude toward the Commonwealth's decisions at its Lusaka meetings last August to have the British government, as an authority in Southern Rhodesia, call a conference to discuss the problems of Zimbabwe, confirmed that the nonaligned countries are not opposed to solutions that may be achieved without armed struggle, so long as they lead to the creation of a genuine majority government and so long as independence is achieved in a manner satisfactory to the fighting peoples, and that this is done in accordance with the resolutions of such bodies as the OAU, the United Nations and our own Movement of Nonaligned Countries.

Mr. President, once more the sixth summit conference had to express its regret over the fact that Resolution 1514 of the UN General Assembly, concerning the granting of independence to colonial countries and peoples, has not been applied to Western Sahara. We should recall that the decisions of the nonaligned countries and the resolutions of the United Nations, and more specifically Resolution 3331 of the General Assembly, have all reaffirmed the inalienable rights of the people of Western Sahara to self-determination and independence.

In this problem Cuba feels a very special responsibility since it has been a member of the UN commission investigating the situation in Western Sahara, and our representatives were able to confirm the Saharawi people's total desire for self-determination and independence.

We repeat here that the position of the nonaligned countries is not one of antagonism toward any country. The welcome that we gave to the agreement between the Republic of Mauritania and the Polisario Front, and to Mauritania's decision to withdraw its forces from Western Sahara, is in keeping with our principles and the agreements of the United Nations. The same is true for our censure of the extension of Morocco's armed occupation of the southern part of Western Sahara, previously administered by Mauritania. Therefore, the conference expressed its hope that the committee established at the 16th OAU summit conference would make it possible to ensure that the people of Western Sahara are allowed to exercise their right to self-determination and independence as soon as possible.

Those same principles and positions determined the resolution on Mayotte and the Malagasy Islands and the need for them to be reintegrated into Comoros and Madagascar respectively.

Mr. President, there can be no doubt that the problem of the Middle East has become one of the situations of greatest concern in today's world. The sixth summit conference examined the problem's two-fold dimension.

The conference reaffirmed that Israel's determination to continue its policy of aggression, expansionism and colonial settlement in the occupied territories, with the support of the United States, constitutes a serious threat to world peace and security. The conference also examined the problem from the standpoint of the rights of the Arab countries and the question of Palestine.

For the nonaligned countries the Palestinian question is the crux of the problem of the Middle East. They form an integral whole and neither can be settled in isolation from the other.

No just peace can be established in the region unless it is based on total and unconditional withdrawal by Israel from all the occupied Arab territories, as well as the return to the Palestinian people of all their occupied territories and the restoration of their inalienable national rights, including their right of return to their homeland, to self-determination and to the establishment of an independent state in Palestine in accordance with Resolution 3236 of the UN General Assembly [November 22, 1974].

All measures taken by Israel in the occupied Palestinian and other Arab territories, including the establishment of colonies or settlements on Palestinian land or other Arab territories—whose immediate dismantlement is a prerequisite for a solution to the problem—are illegal, null and void.

As I stated in my address to the sixth summit:

> We are not fanatics. The revolutionary movement has learned to hate racial discrimination and pogroms of any kind. From the bottom of our hearts, we repudiate the merciless persecution and genocide that the Nazis once visited on the Jews, but there is nothing in recent history that parallels it more than the dispossession, persecution and genocide that imperialism and Zionism are currently practicing against the Palestinian people.
>
> Pushed off their lands, expelled from their own country, scattered throughout the world, persecuted and murdered, the heroic Palestinians are a vivid example of sacrifice and patriotism, living symbols of the most terrible crime of our era.

Can anyone be surprised that the conference, for reasons stemming not from any political prejudice but rather from an objective analysis of the facts, was obliged to point out that US policy, in aligning itself with Israel and working to attain partial solutions favorable to Zionist aims that guarantee the fruits of Israel's aggression at the expense of the Palestinian Arabs and the entire Arab nation, played a major role in preventing the establishment of a just and comprehensive peace in the region?

The facts—and only the facts—led the conference to condemn US policies and maneuvers in that region.

When the heads of state or government reached a consensus condemning the Camp David agreement and the Egypt-Israel treaty of March 1979, their formulations had been preceded by long hours of detailed study and exchange which had allowed the conference to consider those treaties not only as a complete abandonment of the cause of the Arab countries, but also as an act of complicity with the continuing occupation of Arab territories.

These words are harsh, but they are true and just. It is not the Egyptian people who have been subjected to the judgment of the Movement of Non-aligned Countries. The Egyptian people command the respect of each and every one of our countries and enjoy the solidarity of all our peoples.

The same voices that denounced the Camp David agreements and the Egypt-Israel treaty eulogized Gamal Abdel Nasser, a founder of the non-aligned movement and an upholder of the fighting traditions of the Arab nation. No one has been, is or ever will be ignorant of Egypt's historical role in Arab culture and development, or of its merits as a founding nation and a driving force in the Movement of Nonaligned Countries.

The conference also considered the problems of Southeast Asia. The growing conflicts and tensions that have been created in the region are a threat to peace that must be avoided.

Similar concern was expressed by the sixth summit conference in relation to the situation of the Indian Ocean. The declaration adopted eight years ago by the UN General Assembly that the Indian Ocean should be a zone of peace has not been fulfilled. Far from being reduced, the military presence in the region is growing. Military bases have been extended as far as South Africa and are also serving as a means of surveillance against the African liberation movements. The talks between the United States and the Soviet Union are still suspended, despite the recent agreement between the two countries to resume them.

All this led to the sixth summit's invitation to all states concerned to work effectively to fulfill the objectives of the UN declaration on the Indian Ocean as a zone of peace.

The sixth summit conference also analyzed other issues of regional and world interest, such as European security and cooperation, the problem of the Mediterranean, the tensions that still exist there and that have now been increased as a result of Israel's aggressive policy and the support given it by certain imperialist powers.

The conference studied the situation in Cyprus, still partially occupied by foreign troops, and in Korea, still divided despite the Korean people's desire for a unified homeland. This led the nonaligned countries to reaffirm and broaden resolutions of solidarity aimed at fulfilling the aspirations of both peoples.

It would be impossible to refer to all the political decisions of the sixth summit conference. If we were to do so we would be unable to touch upon what we consider to be one of the most fundamental aspects of that sixth summit: its economic perspectives — the clamor of the people of the developing countries, weary as they are of their underdevelopment and the suffering it engenders. Cuba, as the host country, will present to all members of the international community copies of the conference's final declaration and additional resolutions. But before informing you of how the nonaligned countries view the world economic situation, what demands they make and what their hopes are, perhaps you will allow me to take a few more moments to inform you of the movement's approach to current Latin American issues.

The fact that the sixth summit conference was held in Latin America gave the heads of state or government meeting the opportunity to recall that the peoples of that region began their efforts to obtain independence at the very beginning of the 19th century. They also did not forget, as the declaration states:

> Latin America is one of the regions of the world that historically has suffered the most from the aggression of the imperialism, colonialism and neocolonialism of the United States and Europe.

The participants in the conference were forced to point out that remnants of colonialism, neocolonialism and national oppression remain in that region. The conference called for the eradication of colonialism in all its forms and manifestations. It condemned the presence of foreign military bases in Latin America and the Caribbean, such as those in Cuba and Puerto Rico, and again demanded that the US government and other colonial powers restore to those countries the parts of their territory occupied by those bases against the will of their people.

The experience in other areas led the heads of state or government to reject and condemn any attempt to create in the Caribbean a so-called "security force," a neocolonial mechanism that is incompatible with the sovereignty, peace and security of these countries.

By calling for the restitution of the Malvinas [Falkland] Islands to

Argentina, by reaffirming its support for the inalienable right of the people of Belize to self-determination, independence and territorial integrity, the conference once again showed what its declaration had defined as the very quintessence of nonalignment.

It welcomed the fact that as of October 1, the treaties on the Panama Canal concluded between the Republic of Panama and the United States would enter into force. It gave its full support to those treaties, calling for them to be fully respected in both letter and spirit, and it called on all the states of the world to adhere to the protocol under the treaty concerning the permanent neutrality of the Panama Canal.

The heads of state and government reiterated their solidarity with the struggle of the Puerto Rican people and their inalienable right to self-determination, independence and territorial integrity, despite all the pressure, threats and flattery that was brought to bear by the US government, and the demand that the issue of Puerto Rico be considered a domestic matter for the United States. They called upon the US government to refrain from any political or repressive maneuvers perpetuating the colonial status of that country.

No more appropriate tribute could be paid to the Latin American traditions of freedom and to the heroic people of Puerto Rico, who in recent days have just celebrated another anniversary of the Cry of Lares, which expressed their indomitable will for freedom almost 100 years ago.

When speaking about the Latin American reality, the heads of state or government, who had already analyzed the significance of the liberation struggle in Iran [1979], could not fail to refer to the revolutionary upheaval in Grenada and the remarkable victory of the Nicaraguan people and their vanguard, the Sandinista National Liberation Front (FSLN), or to emphasize the historic significance of that event for the peoples of Latin America and of the world. The heads of state or government also highlighted something new in Latin American relations that sets an example for other regions of the world: the way in which the governments of Panama, Costa Rica and Mexico, as well as the member countries of the subregional Andean Pact—Bolivia, Colombia, Ecuador, Peru and Venezuela—acted in solidarity and unity to achieve a just solution to the Nicaraguan problem, as well as Cuba's traditional solidarity with the cause of that people.

I confess that these considerations on Latin America would alone have justified the Cuban people's efforts to give a worthy reception to the fraternal nations of the Movement of Nonaligned Countries in Havana, but for Cuba there was much more than this. There is something for which, on behalf of our people, we would like to acknowledge at this forum of the United Nations.

The Havana summit supported the Cuban people's right to choose their own political and social system, and their claim to the territory occupied by the Guantánamo [US naval] base, and the blockade with which the US government continues to isolate and destroy the Cuban revolution was condemned.

We appreciate the deep feeling and the universal resonance of the movement's recent denunciation, in Havana, of the hostile acts, pressures and threats against Cuba by the United States, declaring them to be a flagrant violation of the UN Charter and the principles of international law, and a threat to world peace.

Once again we respond to our brothers and sisters, assuring the international community that Cuba will remain true to the principles of international solidarity.

Mr. President, history has taught us that when a people frees itself from a colonial or neocolonial system and obtains its independence, this is simultaneously the last act in a long struggle and the first in a new and difficult battle. This is because the independence, sovereignty and freedom of our supposedly free peoples are constantly threatened by foreign control over their natural resources, by financial impositions on the part of official international bodies and by the precarious situation of their economies, all of which diminish their full sovereignty.

For this reason, at the onset of their analysis of the world's economic problems, the heads of state or government again emphasized:

> ...the paramount importance of consolidating political independence through economic emancipation... and that the existing international economic system runs counter to the basic interests of the developing countries, and that it is profoundly unjust and incompatible with the development of the nonaligned countries and other developing countries, and that it does not contribute to the elimination of the economic and social evils that afflict those countries.

Furthermore, they pointed to:

> ...the historic mission that the Movement of Nonaligned Countries should play in the struggle to obtain the economic and political independence of all developing countries and peoples; to exercise their full and permanent sovereignty and control over their natural and all other resources and economic activities; and to promote a fundamental restructuring of the world economy through the establishment of the new international economic order.

The statement concludes with the following words:

> The struggle to eliminate the injustice of the existing international economic system and to establish a new international economic order is an integral part of the people's struggle for political, economic, cultural and social liberation.

It is not necessary to delve into how profoundly unjust and incompatible the existing international economic system is with the development of the underdeveloped countries. The figures are so familiar it is unnecessary for us to repeat them here. There is a debate about whether there are only 400 million undernourished people in the world or whether that figure is now 450 million, as certain international documents have stated. Even 400 million hungry men and women is enough of an indictment.

But no one doubts that all the hopes raised in the developing countries appear to have been dashed and extinguished at this end of the second development decade.

The director general of the Food and Agricultural Organization [FAO] has acknowledged:

> Progress is still disappointingly slow in relation to the long-term development goals contained in the International Development Strategy, in the Declaration and the Program of Action on the Establishment of the New International Economic Order, in the resolution of the World Food Conference and in several subsequent conferences.

We are still a long way from achieving the modest 4 percent annual average increase in the developing countries' food and agricultural production, which was proposed 10 years ago to solve some of the most pressing problems of world hunger and to approach consumption levels that are still too low. As a result of this, food imports by the developing countries, which right now constitute an aggravating factor in their unfavorable balance of payments, will soon, according to FAO figures, reach unmanageable proportions. In the face of this, official commitments of foreign aid for agriculture in the developing countries are dropping.

This panorama cannot be prettied up. At times, certain official documents reflect circumstantial increases in the agricultural production of some areas of the underdeveloped world, or stress the cyclical price increases registered by some agricultural items, but these are transitory advances and short-lived advantages. The developing countries' agricultural export revenues are still unstable and insufficient to meet their import needs for food, fertilizer, and other items required to raise their own production. Per capita food production in Africa in 1977 was 11 percent less than that of 10 years earlier.

While backwardness in agriculture is perpetuated, the process of industrialization cannot advance. It cannot advance because most of the developed countries view the industrialization of the developing countries as a threat.

In 1975, the Lima World Conference on Industrialization proposed that the developing countries set themselves the goal of achieving 25 percent of the world's manufacturing output by the year 2000. But the progress made since that conference has been so insignificant that if the measures proposed by the sixth summit conference are not implemented, and if a crash program is not put into effect to modify the economic policies of most of the developed countries, that target will never be met. We currently account for less than 9 percent of the world's manufactured output.

Moreover, our dependency is further demonstrated by the fact that the countries of Asia, Africa and Latin America import 26.1 percent of the manufactured goods that enter into international trade while exporting only 6.3 percent of them.

It may be said that some industrial expansion is taking place, but it does not occur at the necessary pace, or in the key industries. This was pointed out at the Havana summit. The world redistribution of industry, the so-called industrial redeployment, should not consist of a renewal of the deep economic inequalities that emerged in the colonial era of the 19th century.

At that time we were condemned to be producers of raw materials and cheap agricultural products. Now, an effort is being made to take advantage of the abundant labor power and starvation wages and to transfer the low technology industries to our countries, the industries of lowest productivity and those that most pollute the environment. We categorically reject this.

The developed market economies today absorb more than 85 percent of the world's manufactured goods, including those whose industrial production requires the most advanced technology. They also control more than 83 percent of all industrial exports, and 26 percent of those exports go to the developing countries, whose markets they monopolize. The most serious aspect of this structure of dependence is that our imports — consumer items as well as capital goods — are all manufactured according to the demands, needs and technology of the most developed industrial countries, and the patterns of consumer societies, which are thus introduced through the cracks by way of our trade, contaminating our own societies and adding a new element to the already permanent structural crisis.

The result, as was noted in Havana, is that the gap between the developed and the developing countries not only persists, but has substantially increased. The relative share of the developing countries in world output has decreased considerably during the last two decades, with even more disastrous effects on such problems as malnutrition, illiteracy and poor sanitation.

Some would like to solve the tragic problem of humanity with drastic measures to reduce the population. They remember that in other eras wars and epidemics helped to reduce population. They wish to go even further. They want to blame underdevelopment on the population explosion.

The population explosion is not the cause but the result of underdevelopment. Development will bring solutions to the problems of poverty, and education and culture will help our countries to attain rational and adequate rates of growth.

A recent World Bank report paints an even bleaker picture. It is possible, the report states, that by the year 2000, some 600 million people on this earth may still be submerged in absolute poverty.

Mr. President and distinguished representatives: The state of agricultural and industrial backwardness from which the developing countries have not managed to emerge is undoubtedly the result of unjust and unequal international relations. As the final declaration also points out, to this is now added the prolonged world economic crisis.

I will not dwell too long on this aspect. But, let us state that we heads of state or government consider that the crisis of the international economic system is not a phenomenon of a cyclical nature, but is rather a symptom of the underlying structural maladjustments and of a lack of equilibrium that are part of its very nature. We also believe that this imbalance has been aggravated by the refusal of the developed market economies to control their external imbalances and their high rates of inflation and unemployment. That inflation has been engendered precisely in those developed countries that now refuse to implement the only measures that could eliminate it. Let us further point out, and this is something to which we will return and which has been set down in the final declaration, that this crisis is also the result of persistent inequality in international economic relations, and that eliminating the inequality, as we propose, will contribute to reducing and eliminating the crisis itself.

What are the main guidelines formulated in Havana by the representatives of the Movement of Nonaligned Countries?

We condemned the persistent diversion of human and material resources into an arms race, which is unproductive, wasteful and dangerous to humanity. We demanded that a substantial part of the resources now devoted to arms, particularly by the major powers, be used for economic and social development.

We expressed our grave concern over the negligible progress that has been made in the negotiations for the establishment of a new international economic order. We pointed out that this was due to a lack of political will on the part of most of the developed countries and we specifically censured the delaying, diversionary and divisive tactics adopted by those countries. The failure of the fifth UN Conference on Trade and Development [UNCTAD] session highlighted this very situation.

We confirmed that the unequal exchange in international economic relations, defined as an essential characteristic of the system, has, if possible, become even more unequal. While the prices of manufactured goods, capital goods, foodstuffs and services that we import from the developed countries are constantly rising, the prices of the raw materials we export are stagnating and are subject to constant fluctuation. The terms of exchange have worsened. We emphasized that protectionism, one of the factors aggravating the Great Depression of the 1930s, has been reintroduced by some developed countries.

The conference deplored the fact that in the General Agreement on Tariffs and Trade [GATT] negotiations the developed countries did not take into account the interests and concerns of the developing countries, especially the least developed among them. The conference also denounced the way in which certain developed countries are intensifying their use of domestic subsidies for certain products, to the detriment of the products of the developing nations. The conference further deplored the shortcomings in the scope and operation of the Generalized System of Preferences and, in that spirit, condemned the discriminatory restrictions contained in the US Foreign Trade Act and the inflexible positions adopted by some developed countries, which prevented an agreement on these problems at the fifth session of UNCTAD.

We expressed our concern over the constant deterioration of the international monetary situation. The instability of the exchange rate of the main reserve currencies, along with inflation, increases the imbalance in the world economic situation. It creates additional economic difficulties for the developing countries, by lowering the real value of their export earnings and reducing the value of their foreign currency reserves.

We also pointed out that the disorderly growth of international liquidity, mainly through the use of devalued US dollars and other reserve currencies, is a negative factor. We noted that while the inequality of international economic relations is increasing the developing countries' accumulated foreign debt to over $300 billion, the international financial bodies and the private banks are raising their interest rates, imposing shorter terms of loan amortization, and thus strangling the developing countries financially.

The conference denounced these as elements of coercion in negotiations, allowing the developed countries to obtain additional political and economic advantages at the expense of our countries.

The conference noted the neocolonialist determination to prevent the developing countries from exercising their full, effective and permanent sovereignty over their natural resources and it reaffirmed this right. For this reason it supported the efforts of developing countries producing raw materials to obtain just and remunerative prices for their exports and to improve, in real terms, their export earnings.

Moreover, the conference paid a great deal of attention to the strengthening of economic relations and to scientific, technical and technological exchanges among the developing countries. The concept of what could be defined as "collective self-reliance," that is, mutual support and collaboration among the developing countries so that they will depend, in the first place, on their own collective forces, is given greater emphasis in the Declaration of Havana than ever before.

Cuba, as chair of the movement and coordinating country, together with the Group of 77, intends to do everything necessary to promote the program of action on economic cooperation drawn up by the conference.

Nevertheless, we cannot conceive of that "collective self-reliance" as anything even remotely resembling self-sufficiency. Rather, we consider it to be a factor in international relations that will mobilize all the possibilities and resources of that considerable and important part of humanity represented by the developing countries, incorporating them into the general current of resources and economies of both the capitalist camp and the socialist countries.

Mr. President, the sixth summit conference rejected the attempts of certain developed countries to try to use the question of energy to divide the developing nations.

The energy problem can only be examined in its historical context, taking into account the fact that the wasteful consumption patterns of some of the developed countries and the role played by transnational oil corporations has led to the squandering of hydrocarbons, and noting the pillaging role of transnational corporations that have benefited from cheap energy supplies—which they have used irresponsibly—until only recently. The transnationals have been exploiting both the producers and the consumers and reaping unjustified windfall profits, while at the same time falsifying facts by shifting the blame for the present situation on to the oil-exporting developing countries.

Permit me to recall that in my opening remarks to the conference I pointed to the desperate situation of the non-oil-producing underdeveloped countries, especially the least developed ones, and I expressed my confidence that the nonaligned oil-producing countries would devise formulas to help alleviate the unfavorable situation of those countries, which had already been hit by world inflation and unequal trade relations and who suffer serious balance-of-payments deficits and sharp increases in their foreign debt. But this does not obviate the principal responsibility of the developed countries, their monopolies and their transnational corporations.

In adopting this approach to the energy issue, the heads of state or government stressed that this subject should be the main focus of global negotiations within the United Nations, with the participation of all countries and linking the energy question to all the development problems, to financial and monetary reforms, to world trade and raw materials, so as to make a comprehensive and global analysis of all aspects that bear on the establishment of the new international economic order.

No review of the main problems confronting the developing countries within the context of the world economy would be complete without an examination of the functioning of the transnational corporations. Once again their policies and practices were declared unacceptable. It was charged that in their search for profits they exhaust the resources, distort the economies and violate the sovereignty of developing countries. They undermine the rights of people to self-determination, they violate the principles of non-interference in the affairs of states and they frequently resort to bribery, corruption and other undesirable practices, through which they seek to subordinate and succeed in subordinating the developing countries to the industrialized countries.

In view of the inadequate progress achieved in the United Nations to draw up a code of conduct regulating the activities of transnational corporations, the conference reaffirmed the urgency of early completion of this work, in order to provide the international community with a legal instrument by which to control and regulate, at the least, the activities of the transnational corporations in accordance with the objectives and aspirations of the developing countries.

In setting forth all the overwhelming negative aspects of the economic situation of developing countries, the sixth summit conference called special attention to the mounting problems of the least developed and most disadvantaged countries, those landlocked or isolated in the hinterlands, and asked that urgent measures be adopted to alleviate their problems.

This, Mr. President and distinguished representatives, was the far from optimistic, rather somber and discouraging picture which the members of the Movement of Nonaligned Countries considered when they met in Havana. But the nonaligned countries did not allow themselves to be overcome by frustration or exasperation, however understandable that might have been. While drawing up strategic concepts for advancing and continuing in their struggles, the heads of state or government repeated their demands and defined their positions.

The first and fundamental objective in our struggle consists of reducing and finally eliminating the unequal exchange prevailing today that converts international trade into a very useful vehicle for plundering our wealth. Today the product of one hour's labor in the developed countries is exchanged for 10 hours of labor in the underdeveloped countries.

The nonaligned countries demand that serious attention be paid to the Integrated Program for Commodities which, until now, has been manipulated and juggled in the so-called North-South negotiations. Similarly, we demand that the Common Fund, which was supposed to act as an instrument of stabilization establishing a permanent linkage between the prices we receive for our products and those paid for our imports, and which has scarcely begun to have an impact, be given a real boost.

For the nonaligned countries this linkage—which permanently ties the prices of their exports to the prices of basic equipment, industrial products, raw materials and technology that they import from the developed countries—constitutes an essential pivot for all future economic negotiations.

The developing countries demand that the countries that have created inflation and stimulated it through their policies adopt the necessary measures to control it and thus put an end to the aggravation of the unequal exchange between our countries.

The developing countries demand—and will continue their struggle to achieve—access to the markets of the developed countries for the industrial products of their incipient economies. They demand a halt to the vicious protectionism that has been reintroduced in the international economy and that threatens once again to lead us into a deadly economic war. And they demand that a general system of nonreciprocal tariff preferences be applied generally and without deceptive falsehoods so that the young industries of the developing countries can develop without being crushed in the world market by the superior technological resources of the developed countries.

The nonaligned countries consider that the negotiations about to be concluded on the Law of the Sea should not be used as certain developed countries seek to use them—to ratify and endorse the existing imbalance as regards sea resources—but should serve as a vehicle for equitable redress. The conference on the Law of the Sea has once again highlighted the arrogance and imperialist determination of some countries that, placing their technological possibilities ahead of the spirit of understanding and accommodation requested by the developing nations, threaten to take unilateral action in carrying out deep-sea mining operations.

The foreign debt of the developing countries has now risen to $335 billion. It is estimated that about $40 billion a year goes to servicing this foreign debt, which represents more than 20 percent of their exports. Moreover, the average per capita income in the developed countries is now 14 times that of the underdeveloped countries. This situation is not sustainable.

The developing countries need a new system of financing that enables them to obtain the necessary financial resources to ensure continuous and independent development of their economies. These financing methods should be long-term and low-interest. The use of these financial resources should be completely at the discretion of the developing countries. This will enable them to establish a system of priorities for their own economies, in accordance with their own plans for industrial development, and it will help prevent those funds from being absorbed, as they are today, by transnational corporations that use alleged financial contributions for development to aggravate the distortions of the developing countries' economies and reap maximum profits from the exploitation of these countries' resources.

The developing countries, and on their behalf the Movement of Nonaligned Countries, demand that a substantial portion of the immense resources now being squandered by humanity on the arms race be dedicated to development. This would contribute both to reducing the danger of war and helping improve the international situation.

Expressing the position of all the developing countries, the nonaligned countries call for the establishment of a new international monetary system to put an end to the disastrous fluctuations to which the main currencies used in the international economy are subject, especially the US dollar. That financial disorder hits the developing countries, which hope that when the outlines of the new international monetary system are drawn up, they, as the majority of the countries in the international community, representing more than 1.5 billion people, may be given a voice in the decision-making process.

Mr. President and distinguished representatives:

Unequal exchange is ruining our peoples. It must end!

Inflation, which is being exported to us, is crushing our peoples. It must end!

Protectionism is impoverishing our people. It must end!

The existing imbalance in the exploitation of the resources of the sea is abusive. It must be abolished!

The financial resources received by the developing countries are insufficient. They must be increased!

Arms expenditures are irrational. They must cease and the funds thus released must be used to finance development!

The international monetary system prevailing today is bankrupt. It must be replaced!

The debts of the least-developed countries, and of those in a disadvantageous position, are impossible burdens to bear, and have no solution. They must be cancelled!

Indebtedness oppresses the rest of the developing countries economically. There must be relief!

The economic chasm between the developed countries and the countries seeking development is not narrowing but widening. It must be closed!

These are demands of the underdeveloped countries.

Mr. President and distinguished representatives: Response to these demands, some of which have been systematically presented by the developing countries in international forums through the Group of 77 and by Movement of Nonaligned Countries, would permit a change of course in the international economic situation that would provide the developing nations with the institutional conditions for organizing programs that would definitively place them on the road to development.

But even if all these measures were implemented, even if all the mistakes and evils of the present system of international relations were rectified, the developing countries would still lack one decisive element: external financing.

All the domestic efforts, all the sacrifices that the peoples of the developing countries are making and are willing to make, and all the opportunities for increasing their economic potential by improving the conditions in which their foreign trade is carried out, would not be enough.

In light of their true present financial situation, they need further resources to be able both to pay their debts and to make the enormous expenditures required on a global level for the leap into development. Here again, it is not necessary to repeat the figures.

The sixth summit conference was concerned not only because the debts of the underdeveloped countries are practically unbearable, but also because that debt is growing each year at an alarming rate. The data contained in the recent World Bank report, which came out while we were holding the conference in Havana, confirmed that the situation was growing worse every day. In 1978 alone, the foreign public debt of 96 developing countries rose by $51 billion. This rate of growth has raised the foreign debt to the astronomical figures already mentioned.

We cannot, Mr. President, resign ourselves to this gloomy prospect!

The most renowned economists, both Western and those who ascribe to Marxist concepts, admit that the system of international indebtedness of the developing world is completely irrational and that its persistence endangers the entire precarious and unstable world economic balance.

Some try to explain the surprising economic fact that the international banking centers continue to provide funds to countries that are technically bankrupt by arguing that these are generous contributions to help those countries meet their economic difficulties. But this is not so. In fact, they are operations for saving the international capitalist order itself. In October 1978, the Commission of European Communities admitted by way of clarification:

> The present balance of the world economy depends to a considerable extent on continuing the flow of private loans to non-oil-producing developing countries... on a scale unprecedented prior to 1974, and any obstacle to that flow will endanger that balance.

World financial bankruptcy would be very hard, most of all for the underdeveloped world and workers in the developed capitalist countries. It would affect even the most stable socialist economies. It is doubtful that the capitalist system would be able to survive such a catastrophe. It is likely that the resulting economic situation would engender a world conflagration. There is already talk of special military forces to occupy the oil fields and the sources of other raw materials.

While it is everyone's responsibility to be concerned about this somber prospect, first and foremost it is the duty of those who possess the greatest wealth and material abundance.

In any case, the prospect of a world without capitalism is not too frightening to us revolutionaries.

It has been proposed that instead of a spirit of confrontation we employ a sense of world economic interdependency that will enable us to call on the resources of all our economies to obtain joint benefits. But the concept of interdependency is acceptable only when you begin by admitting the intrinsic and brutal injustice of the present interdependency.

The developing countries will not accept the unjust and arbitrary international division of labor that was imposed on them by modern colonialism with the English industrial revolution, and that was intensified by imperialism as "interdependency."

If we wish to avoid confrontation, which seems to be the only road open to the developing countries—a road offering long and arduous battles of proportions no one can predict—then we must all seek and find formulas for cooperation to solve the great problems, which, while affecting our peoples, cannot be solved without also affecting the most developed countries in one way or another.

Not so many years ago we stated that the irrational squandering of material goods and the subsequent waste of economic resources by developed capitalist societies had already become intolerable. Is that not the cause of the dramatic energy crisis that we face right now? Who, if not the non-oil-producing underdeveloped countries, are bearing the main brunt of it?

This desire to put an end to the waste of resources by the consumer societies is very widely held. A recent document of the UN Industrial Development Organization states, "The present way of life, especially in the industrialized countries, may have to undergo a radical and painful change."

Naturally, the developing countries cannot and do not hope that the transformation they seek and the financing they require will be given to them as a gift, coming as a result of a mere analysis of international economic problems. In this process, which implies conflict, struggle and negotiation, the nonaligned countries must rely first of all on their own decisions and efforts.

That conviction emerges clearly from the sixth summit. In the economic section of the final declaration, the heads of state or government acknowledge the need to carry out in their countries the necessary economic and social structural changes. They consider that this is the only way to eliminate the present vulnerability of their economies and to turn simple statistical growth into genuine development.

The heads of state and government recognize that this is the only way their people will be willing to pay the price required of them to become the main protagonists in the process. As I said at the summit, "If the system is socially just, the possibilities of survival and economic and social development are incomparably greater." The history of my own country provides irrefutable proof of this.

The emerging and desperate need to solve the problem of underdevelopment brings us back, Mr. President, to the problem I mentioned a little while ago, which is the last one I would like to submit to this 34th Session of the General Assembly. I refer specifically to international financing.

One of the most serious phenomena accompanying the accelerated indebtedness of the developing countries, as we have already said, is that the majority of funds they receive from outside go to covering their trade balances and negative current accounts, renewing their debts and making interest payments.

If we take as an example the non-oil-exporting developing countries, to whose situation I referred at the Havana conference, we note that in the last six years alone they have run up deficits in their balance of payments of over $200 billion.

In view of this, the investments required by the developing countries are enormous, and they need them primarily, almost without exception, in those branches of production that yield low profits and therefore do not appeal to private foreign lenders or investors.

To increase the production of foodstuffs so as to do away with the malnutrition that affects those 450 million people I mentioned earlier, we must provide extensive new land and water resources. According to estimates of specialists, an additional 76 million hectares of land in the developing countries would have to be cultivated and over 10 million additional hectares of land irrigated in the next 10 years to meet these needs.

Irrigation systems for 45 million hectares of land would have to be repaired. Therefore, and even the most modest estimates admit—I refer to aid and not the total flow of resources—that between $8 billion and $9 billion a year will be required to achieve an agricultural growth of between 3.5 to 4 percent in the developing countries.

With regard to industrialization, the estimates are far higher. The UN Conference on Industrial Development, when defining the goals for the Lima session, stated that at the heart of international development policy there should be a target to achieve by the year 2000 annual levels of growth of between $450 billion and $500 billion a year, of which a third, that is, from $150 billion to $160 billion, will have to be financed from external sources.

But Mr. President and distinguished representatives, development includes more than agriculture and industrialization. Development primarily involves attention to human beings, who should be the protagonists and the goal of all development efforts.

To cite the example of Cuba alone, I will point out that during the last five years our country has invested an average of nearly $200 million a year in school construction. Investment in medical equipment and construction of public health facilities averages over $40 million a year. Cuba is only one of nearly 100 developing countries, and is one of the smallest in terms of land mass and population.

It can easily be deduced that the developing countries will need billions of dollars more to be invested every year to overcome the results of backwardness in education and public health services.

This is not, ladies and gentlemen, our problem alone, a problem solely for the countries victimized by underdevelopment and insufficient development. It is a problem for the international community as a whole. On more than one occasion, it has been said that we were forced into underdevelopment by colonization and imperialist neocolonization. The task of helping us to emerge from underdevelopment is therefore first and foremost a historic and moral obligation for those who benefited from the plunder of our wealth and the exploitation of our men and women for decades and for centuries. But at the same time, it is the task of humanity as a whole.

The socialist countries did not participate in the plunder of the world and they are not responsible for the phenomenon of underdevelopment. But even so, because of the nature of their social system, in which international solidarity is a foundation, they understand and assume the obligation of helping to overcome it.

Likewise, when the world expects the oil-producing developing countries to contribute to the universal flow of external financing for development, it does not present this as a historic obligation and duty, which no one can impose, but as an expression and a recognition of the duty of solidarity among underdeveloped countries.

Those developing countries that are relatively more advanced should also make their contributions. Cuba, which is not speaking here on behalf of its own interests and which is not defending national objectives, is willing to contribute, in accordance with its means, thousands or tens of thousands of technicians: doctors, teachers, agronomists, hydraulic engineers, mechanical engineers, economists, middle-level technicians, skilled workers and so on.

The time has come for all of us to join in the task of drawing entire peoples, hundreds of millions of human beings, out of the backwardness, poverty, malnutrition, disease and illiteracy that keeps them from enjoying full human dignity and pride.

We must therefore mobilize our resources for development. This is our joint obligation.

Mr. President, there are so many special multilateral funds, both public and private, whose purpose it is to contribute to some aspect of development, whether it is agricultural, industrial, or meeting deficits in the balance of payments. Therefore it is not easy for me, in presenting to this General Assembly a report on the economic problems discussed at the sixth summit conference of nonaligned countries, to formulate a concrete proposal for the establishment of a new fund.

But there can be no doubt that the problem of financing should be discussed thoroughly and fully in order to find a solution. In addition to the resources already mobilized by various banking channels, loan organizations, international bodies and private finance agencies, we must discuss and decide on the strategy for the next development decade, so that it will include an additional contribution of no less than $300 billion at 1977 real value, to be invested in the underdeveloped countries and to be made in annual installments of at least $25 billion from the very beginning. This aid should be in the form of donations and long-term, moderate and low-interest credits.

It is imperative that these additional funds be gathered, as the contribution of the developed world and of other countries with resources to the underdeveloped world, over the next 10 years.

If we want peace, these resources will be required. If there are no resources for development there will be no peace.

Some may think that we are asking too much, but I think that the figure itself is still modest. According to statistical information, the world's annual military expenditure amounts to more than $300 billion.

With $300 billion you could, in one year, build 600,000 schools with a capacity for 400 million children; 60 million comfortable homes for 300 million people; 30,000 hospitals with 18 million beds; 20,000 factories with jobs for more than 20 million workers. Or you could build irrigation systems to water 150 million hectares of land, which, with appropriate technology, could feed a billion people. Humanity wastes this much every year on its military spending. Furthermore, consider the enormous waste of youthful human resources, of technicians, scientists, fuel, raw materials and other things. This is the fabulous price of preventing a true climate of confidence and peace from existing in the world.

In the 1980s, the United States alone will spend six times this much on military activities.

We are requesting less for 10 years of development than is spent in a single year by the ministries of war, and much less than a 10th of what will be spent for military purposes in 10 years.

Some may consider our proposal irrational, but true irrationality lies in the madness of our era; the peril threatening humanity. The enormous responsibility of analyzing, organizing and distributing these resources should be entrusted entirely to the United Nations. These funds should be administered by the international community itself on an absolutely equal basis for all countries, whether they are contributors or beneficiaries, with no political conditions attached and without the size of the donations having any influence on voting power to decide when loans are to be granted and to whom.

Even though the flow of resources should be measured in financial terms, it should not consist only of money. It may well be composed of equipment, fertilizer, raw materials, fuel and complete factories valued in the terms of international trade. Aid in the form of technical personnel and their training should also be considered as a contribution.

Mr. President and distinguished representatives: With the support of the UN secretary general, assisted by the president of the General Assembly and with all the prestige and weight of this organization behind them, and supported from the very outset by the developing countries and especially the Group of 77, we are convinced we would be able to call together the various factors we have mentioned and initiate discussions in which there would be no room for the so-called North–South, East–West antagonisms. Instead, all forces would be joined together in a common undertaking, a common duty, a common hope. That is how this idea we are now submitting to the General Assembly could be crowned with success.

This is not a project that will only benefit the developing nations. It will benefit all countries. As revolutionaries we are not afraid of confrontation. We have placed our trust in history and people. But as a spokesperson and interpreter of the feelings of 95 nations, I have the duty to struggle to achieve cooperation among people, a cooperation which if achieved on a new and just basis, will benefit all the countries of the international community and will especially improve the prospects for peace.

Development in the short term may well be a task entailing apparent sacrifices and even donations that may seem irrecoverable. But the vast world now submerged in backwardness with no purchasing power and extremely limited consumer capacity will, with its development, add a flood of hundreds of millions of consumers and producers to the international economy. It is only in this way that the international economy can be rehabilitated and help the developing countries emerge from crisis.

The history of international trade has shown that development is the most dynamic factor. A major portion of the trade of today takes place among fully industrialized countries. We can assure you that as industrialization and progress spread throughout the world, so too will trade spread to the benefit of all.

For this reason, on behalf of the developing countries, we advocate our cause and we ask you to support it. This is not a gift we seek from you. If we do not come up with effective solutions we will all be equal victims of the catastrophe.

Mr. President, distinguished representatives: Human rights are very often spoken of, but we must also speak of humanity's rights.

Why should some people go barefoot so that others may ride in expensive cars?

Why should some live for only 35 years so that others may live for 70?

Why should some be miserably poor so that others can be excessively rich?

I speak on behalf of the children of the world who don't even have a piece of bread. I speak on behalf of the sick who lack medicine. I speak on behalf of those who have been denied the right to life and to human dignity.

Some countries border the coast; others do not. Some have energy resources, others do not. Some possess abundant land on which to produce food, others do not. Some are so glutted with machinery and factories that you cannot breathe the air because of the poisoned atmosphere. And others have only their own emaciated bodies with which to earn their daily bread.

In short, some countries possess abundant resources, other have nothing. What is their fate? To starve? To be eternally poor? Why then civilization? Why then the conscience of humanity? Why then the United Nations? Why then the world?

You cannot speak of peace on behalf of tens of millions of human beings all over the world who are starving to death or dying of curable diseases. You cannot speak of peace on behalf of 900 million illiterate people.

The exploitation of the poor countries by the rich must cease.

I address myself to the rich nations, asking them to contribute. And I address myself to the poor nations, asking them to distribute.

Enough of words! We need deeds!

Enough of abstractions. We want concrete action! Enough speculating about a new international economic order, which no one understands. We must now speak of a real, objective order that everyone understands!

I have not come here as a prophet of the revolution. I have not come here to ask or to wish that the world be violently convulsed. I have come to speak of peace and cooperation among the peoples. And I have come to warn that if we do not peacefully and wisely resolve the present injustices and inequalities, the future will be apocalyptic.

The rattling of weapons, threatening language and overbearing behavior on the international arena must cease.

Enough of the illusion that the problems of the world can be solved by nuclear weapons. Bombs may kill the hungry, the sick and the ignorant; but bombs cannot kill hunger, disease and ignorance. Nor can bombs kill the righteous rebellion of the peoples. And in the holocaust, the rich, who have the most to lose in this world, will also die.

Let us say farewell to arms, and let us, in a civilized manner, dedicate ourselves to the most pressing problems of our times. This is the responsibility, this is the most sacred duty of all the leaders of all the world. This, moreover, is the basic premise for the survival of humankind.

Thank you.

14. RECTIFYING THE ERRORS OF THE CUBAN REVOLUTION

KARL MARX THEATER, HAVANA
APRIL 19, 1986

In the last part of his speech on the 25th anniversary of the Bay of Pigs invasion, Fidel Castro challenged some of the attitudes and practices that he considered were vestiges of capitalism that were corrupting the Cuban revolution. This was further discussed at the special session of the Cuban Communist Party in December 1986 and later became known as the "rectification campaign."

Compañeros, the party program is now being discussed in our country by all our people. The program will be studied and approved by the delegates to the third party congress in a special meeting later this year.

The conditions under which this ambitious program is going to be carried out are not easy. In fact, the conditions under which we have to meet our economic plans—the 1986 plan, the five-year plan, and the longer-term plans—are anything but easy. Today we must also consider these things. There are circumstances, some of which have arisen after the party congress, that make our task more difficult, although not impossible.

Late last year our country was affected by a natural disaster, a hurricane that flattened 70 percent of our sugarcane, and that made the sugar harvest more difficult. Despite the great efforts made by our workers, there's no doubt that in the end our sugar plans will be affected by at least half a million tons. And if the figure does not run to a million or a million and a half, it will be thanks to the efforts of our sugar workers.

But it wasn't only the hurricane. Paradoxical and incredible as it may seem, we were also affected by the drop in the value of the dollar.

Many may wonder how a drop in the value of the dollar could affect Cuba. Right now the imperialists are trying to reduce the value of the dollar because they have a tremendous trade deficit, and in order to compete with the Japanese and the Europeans — the big capitalist countries came to an agreement on this — they took measures to devalue the dollar.

We sell our sugar and all other export products on the basis of dollars — which is the universal practice. If the price of sugar is quoted at four centavos, it means four cents of a dollar, and so a devaluation of the dollar represents a drop in the price paid for our exports.

But basically what affects us is that the price we must pay for imports from the hard currency area increases because we cannot import from the United States. We import from Japan and Europe, where we obtain less German marks, less French francs, less British pounds sterling, and less Japanese yen for each dollar. When we sell a ton of sugar to any of those countries we obtain less products in exchange for that ton.

If we could import from the United States, the situation would be advantageous for us, because the dollar is now cheaper. These are the paradoxes that a country like ours, under a blockade, must put up with, and we suffer some consequences, along with other Third World countries, every time the dollar is overvalued, such as high interest rates, or when the dollar is devalued.

But that's not all. There's another surprising thing: The drop in the price of oil is also affecting us to a considerable extent. It's very simple: We also export oil, that is, a part of our production and all the oil we save from the oil we import from the Soviet Union is exported.

I spoke about this at the Energy Forum, what saving a gallon of fuel meant in terms of hard currency, a barrel, a ton, cent by cent. In the last few years, thanks to the great efforts made to economize and while sugar prices were exceedingly low, oil exports were a key source of hard currency in our country, earning us hundreds of millions of dollars.

With the drop in prices, we have been affected by about two-thirds the value of the oil, and we've lost hundreds of millions of dollars in hard currency, just like that, hundreds of millions! This largely shattered the great effort we were making to economize, an effort we must still make.

This problem with oil happened a few weeks after our congress. It means more problems for the country and forces us to make even greater efforts.

Why talk about these issues on the 25th anniversary [of the Bay of Pigs invasion]? Because now the enemy isn't the mercenaries, we don't have mercenary invasions, but we do have another type of mercenary, or people who act like them. Among them are people viewed as good people, ready to fight for the revolution in the event of war, but who do things that go against the revolution and its interests; and there are others who don't have a profound revolutionary awareness. This obliges us to make an effort.

Precise guidelines were set out at the party congress. There was strong and penetrating criticism of persistent problems, and we pledged to struggle against them. As I said before, we are discussing the program. Without these problems I'm referring to we would have to implement the line set out at the congress, but now with the added problems we have, fulfillment becomes much more important and decisive.

We must be much more intransigent regarding all forms of misconduct and wrongdoing. We must be much more effective in our struggle against problems that persist and new ones that crop up. That's what I told the Pioneers during their 25th anniversary, and with more reason the issue must be raised with our people as a whole.

I repeat, our problems are not the same as those we had 25 years ago, but we do have people who are indolent, people who are negligent, and people who, as I told the Pioneers, don't want to get worked up about problems; irresponsible people, people who aren't demanding enough in the sphere where they have responsibility, people who are lax. We have people who seek privileges; people who seek easy money, not from work but from shady deals, speculation and illicit trade.

On such a day as this, I don't want to mention many things, but there are those who put us to shame. For example, some people have earned 100,000 pesos or more a year apparently through legitimate means. How can this be in a socialist society? I know of some people who paint and sell their paintings or do decorating work, mostly for state agencies, who have even earned over 200,000 pesos a year. This is just one example of excessive incomes which I do not believe are the fruits of labor because, let's face it, the paintings are not by Picasso or Michelangelo.

Obviously, some state officials are irresponsible, because it's the people's money that's being spent in this way. On the other hand, some people have confused freelancing with capitalism or the right to engage in capitalist trade; some people have certainly confused one with the other. Yes, we have these kinds of problems.

Just consider, the person who makes 100,000 pesos is making 20 times the annual salary of those doctors performing heart transplants — 20 times! I have met those dedicated, modest doctors, with their salaries of 5,000 or 6,000 pesos a year; while other people are making 100,000 or more through shady deals.

You all know how critical I was of the free farmers' market, where some people could sell a head of garlic at a peso and pocket the profit themselves without any benefit for the people.

It wasn't the honest hardworking peasant who receives all the benefits of the revolution such as education for their children and medical care, all the benefits without exception. They were people who, rather than making money honestly by working the land, got rich through trading, theft and selling at very high prices.

This coupled with other goings-on, such as goods that were pledged to the state because of credits, seed, and other benefits and guarantees granted which wound up on the other market, was a practical experience.

We ourselves have brought on some of these problems, and we must set them right in time, because unfortunately, there are people who confuse money earned through work with that earned through speculation and shady deals that border on theft, or are theft.

Some of our heads of enterprises have also become capitalist-like entrepreneurs. The first thing a socialist, a revolutionary, a communist cadre must ask themselves is not if their particular firm is making more money, but how the country makes more. Whenever we have so-called entrepreneurs who worry more about the enterprise than the interests of the country, we have a capitalist in every sense of the word.

The economic management and planning system was not set up so that we can play at capitalism; and some people are shamefully playing at capitalism; we know this, we see it, and this must be set right.

Then there are those who want their enterprises to be profitable by increasing prices and distributing bonuses by charging the earth for anything; that way any enterprise can be profitable, right?

Not long ago I visited Almeijeiras Hospital and I noticed they had well-maintained elevators reinforced with stainless steel. I'd gone to see a new piece of equipment that we had purchased, very sophisticated, useful and humane that is already functioning. One is really amazed at the efforts made by doctors, specialists, all the workers at that hospital.

I was told, "You know how much they wanted to charge us for installing the sheets of stainless steel? Ten thousand pesos!" Finally they settled for 5,000. I asked them how many people did the work. Two, was the answer. And how many days did it take? Fifteen. Well, in wages the outlay must have been about 300 pesos. The hospital provided the stainless steel, and this was a state enterprise charging those prices!

One must really have gall—I don't mean the workers but those who organize such ventures—to charge 30 times more for a job that took two weeks. That way any outfit can be profitable, and we have seen this sinister attitude.

The hospital was charged 40,000 pesos for work on a floor, some sort of polishing job.

We already mentioned this at the congress among the problems that had to be combated. We also know about diverting resources; we've seen examples.

Not long ago I was touring an area to look at some problems concerning the economy, and I came across a crane. A person was putting a cement roof on his house with a 16-ton Japanese Kato crane, a Japanese-made cement mixer, a truck to carry the cement and a water truck, all belonging to the state.

He had purchased a pig for his helpers, beer and other things; the three trucks came from three different places, the crane was from the brigade building the thermoelectric power plant in Santa Cruz—I saw this with my own eyes, it's not something someone told me. The other truck with the cement mixer came from the oil enterprise across the way from the José Martí children's city, and the water truck came from a quarry along the highway.

Thanks to his friends and connections, this single individual had a crane, a cement mixer, a truck to carry it, and a water truck all together. Who knows where the materials came from! He was building a house; we're glad, of course, that people build houses, but they should do it honestly.

The house was 150 square meters, although this person makes 199 pesos a month working as the head of a storeroom at a restaurant. Were he to sell it, he could get 40,000 pesos. He would find a buyer for sure, because those who steal one way or another and make large sums from sources other than their work would just as soon buy a house as the Capitol building if it were for sale.

So there is this kind of problem. Where do those thousands of pesos come from? Not from work.

The state provides resources and credit to repair or build homes, it provides many facilities and has just approved a generous law that allows people to own their existing homes or those they are about to receive, at a reasonable price, with no profit. What need is there to divert resources, what need is there to resort to shady deals, even though the need is great in this field?

When I was telling the head of the Planning Board about my experience he said, "On Sunday I saw a crane doing the same thing, but this was a 40-ton crane."

Can you imagine? What we do here on large building sites to cast concrete, we haul it up in buckets with cranes, the most sophisticated equipment we have in construction technique; and there are people here with such initiative and such connections, and there are so many people who aren't subject to controls that they use this state technology to build a roof for their house.

It would be worthwhile asking the brigade and the enterprise building the Oriente power plant how was it possible that a 16-ton crane truck purchased with hard currency was off the work site for three days? They took it Friday and it was returned on . Somebody gave the papers to justify its use to cover up for others and all sorts of things like that which we know exist because we know there are people who seek privileges at all cost and who divert resources.

This is, of course, a struggle. When we talk about the party program and the congress and the measures to take, it doesn't mean a transitory campaign which will be soon forgotten. We aren't advocating a cultural revolution here, we don't want to use extremist measures to solve problems or throw the people against those responsible for such infuriating acts.

I am convinced, however, that in an organized and disciplined manner, the masses can help win this battle. Between the masses, the members of the party, and the Union of Young Communists (UJC) this can be done. It also requires greater alertness on the part of the Committees for the Defense of the Revolution (CDRs), because they know what's going on when suddenly somebody starts building a big house and then sells it for an enormous sum.

We can't accept misconduct. We can't fall prey to confusion. Can anyone here engage in shady deals without the people, the masses, finding out? We don't want to unleash the masses, I repeat, against the guilty parties for them to stop such activity on their own, because we have the party and the UJC, we have the mass organizations. What we must do is engage in a systematic, serious and tenacious struggle, applying pressure from the top down, and from the bottom up, with great force!

Our party must be very alert! There are 500,000 members in the party, including full members and candidates—if only we'd had an organization of 500,000 members when we started the struggle against the dictatorship—plus another 500,000 Young Communists, what an incredible force; the mass organizations, millions of men and women organized into unions, the CDRs, the Federation of Cuban Women (FMC), the Pioneers, it's a tremendous, incredible force! If well used, we can put an end to all these things without extremism.

We don't have to resort to extremism or campaigns lasting a few months, no! This must be a sustained struggle. As I told the Pioneers, we must continue the struggle against the vestiges of the old system, against the vestiges of capitalism, the capitalist ideology, parasitical attitudes, privileges, and the tendency to try to get something out of proportion to what one contributes to society. We have mentioned the socialist formula: from each according to their ability, to each according to their work! This is a clear formula which is obviously not egalitarian.

I'd like to know by virtue of what miracle or what diabolical mechanism someone can make 10 times the salary of a distinguished doctor who saves lives? Things that are not functioning well and consciences that are not in good shape. We must say it: consciences that are not in good shape! And functionaries that aren't doing their jobs properly, since they don't keep a record of the money and resources they administer.

There are those who think socialism can be built without political work. Well, there are even some people who think it can be built without physical work. Yes, these people exist!

We are involved in a project with all the hospitals in the capital because of problems that existed. We met with all the hospital directors, party and Young Communist leaders, head nurses and union leaders; this is being done with the help of the party. The party in Havana province has worked hard on this score, and the results are evident in the new enthusiasm and spirit at the hospitals.

It won't happen overnight, and the party in Havana has monthly meetings with the secretaries of hospital party committees. That's political work, and with political work we can solve many problems. We thought about some economic measures that were fair, such as taking into account abnormal working conditions for auxiliary personnel.

We are also considering ways of having staff do several things and better pay for auxiliary personnel as was done with doctors and nurses. All this, of course, is within the socialist formula, seeking more rational and better use of labor; the country will never develop if we try to solve disorganization, inefficiency or low productivity by putting more people to work. This is basically political work.

In regard to hospitals and schools we should not talk about profitability because they cannot be economic enterprises with bonuses. If there is too much talk of bonuses, we will be corrupting workers and saying that the only way to get things done is through bonuses.

Although we recognize that there is room for bonuses under socialism, they must be the result of good work, and real work, not because of fabricated profits, inflated prices, and charging 40,000 pesos for a floor and 10,000 pesos for what actually costs 500. That way any outfit can be profitable, and it's easy to conceal disorganization and inefficiency by raising prices.

Some important construction brigades like that in Cienfuegos at the nuclear power plant have to achieve maximum productivity. We sent a compañero out there because we began to hear talk that 16,000 workers were needed in that construction project. So we sent them a message, saying no, they would have to make do with the 12,000 agreed to earlier. Another form of concealing disorganization and inefficiency is the lack of control over what each worker accomplishes, asking constantly for more workers instead of controlling and rigorously assessing their work.

Believe me, that is a good brigade [in Cienfuegos], with very good leaders. There the workers have been given benefits—special uniforms, special work boots and special food. When I heard about the request for 16,000, I said, "No, they'll have to make do with 12,000—with 12,000!" Yes, and furthermore, construction workers are putting in more than eight hours a day. It is wrong to conceal inefficiency and disorganization with more and more workers so that later there are 20,000 and then 25,000 at peak times.

I'm mentioning some of the kinds of problems, and I'm talking about a good brigade and magnificent workers, to whom I have made certain commitments—and who have made commitments to me—through the efforts we have made to improve their standard of living in general.

There is often a tendency, instead of going to tell the worker, "make a greater effort, meet your obligations"—in other words, to do political and organizational work—to go about fabricating things, asking for more people. This is easier to do, but much more costly for the country. Our resources might run out, and then we would not be able to give them special uniforms and special shoes if that was to occur.

These are the kinds of things I meditate on. Not long ago I read in the newspaper about the problems in a textile mill in Santiago de Cuba, problems that I spoke about during the congress, a large textile mill with a capacity of 80 million square meters.

Recently there was a meeting at that mill, where different groups were brought together from the party and from the state. What I read in the paper rather surprised me because they were saying that such and such problems had to be solved in order to bring the mill to full capacity because there wasn't enough stability in the work force, that they had to guarantee more recreation, and who knows what else, cultural things, construct more housing, guarantee the possibility of higher education. I don't know how much they were supposed to guarantee. Finally, a compañero said that it would be very difficult to achieve this goal by 1990, but that they would try.

Imagine if this textile mill were in Brazil, what would happen? In a country with so much unemployment, so much hunger, so many social problems, would so many promises be necessary to get the mill to produce to its full capacity?

Is this how socialism is built? Do we believe that socialism can be built in this way? With no appeal to the workers' sense of obligation? Without an appeal to young people's sense of duty, reminding them that ours is an underdeveloped country that needs to develop, and that this cannot be on the basis of offering pie in the sky promises—just so that the factory can function? We have to know how to remind these young people and the workers of their duty, by simply saying, "Produce!"

We must know how to tell the workers "Stabilize yourselves. Reach the limits of production. Work, because production must come first, and then the rewards!" We must tell them that the revolution has made great efforts to guarantee work to all young people, but that we are an underdeveloped country, confronted by imperialism and blockaded by imperialism. It cannot only be on the basis of promises, everyone must be asked to fulfill their duty, everyone!

I believe that on a day like today, we must talk about these things. In order to have the many things that today are within our reach, we have struggled, we have shed blood and made many sacrifices. But it seems that many people don't know this, or pretend not to know, and they don't seem to know what world they're living in.

We haven't come together just to exalt our past glories, to pay tribute to the dead; to pay them tribute, we would need more than one or two hours, more than a minute, or a second, or one day every 25 years or every year. To the dead, to those who sacrificed themselves for the revolution, generation after generation, one must pay tribute every day, every hour, every minute, and every second!

What can we say to the mothers who have lost their sons? What can we say to the women who have lost their husbands? What can we say to the children who have lost their fathers or their grandfathers in the revolutionary struggle? I see children here of six, eight and 10 years old, relatives of the dead. Are we going to tell them that if a person doesn't have a house next door to the factory where they work they won't work in the factory?

If houses can't be built—even though it might be quite right to build houses next door to the factory—we still need cloth, and we have, for example, the spinning mill in Havana that can produce up to 15,000 tons of thread for our textile factories. But, hold on! There is not enough stability in the work force; we must build houses, we will wait until we have all the houses ready. But houses alone won't solve the labor problem because later on the workers living there might take jobs elsewhere.

I believe that we must also solve the problems with morale, honor and principles, that it is necessary to appeal—and it would be demagogic not to appeal—to our compatriots' and our workers' sense of duty.

It is clear that it was poor planning to build the textile mill without also building a number of housing units close to the factory. We should be aware of these problems. But the revolution doesn't have the resources to solve everything at once.

I believe that these are weaknesses and these weaknesses are our enemy now. All those who look for privileges and cushy jobs, who divert resources, who seek to pocket money that they haven't earned by the sweat of their brow, engaging in rackets and schemes, they are doing the mercenaries' work. All this can be found in the vineyards of the Lord.

They are not the majority—to the contrary—but we have a duty to combat them, because these minorities can only do those things when the majority is passive, lazy, and does not exercise a critical spirit. And I know the critical spirit of our people, I know the qualities of our people.

This struggle will be long, much longer than just a five-year period. We will have to fight against this tendency for our entire lives, because there are always two factions, as Martí said: those who build up and those who tear down. There is a large faction that builds up. But there are those of the other faction, where the irresponsible and lazy can be found. And these don't have to be counterrevolutionaries; there are those who don't realize that this is one way to act like a mercenary!

We must appeal to the honor and dignity of our fellow citizens, which has been so evident throughout our history.

I believe this to be an appropriate theme for a day like today. Everything we have said, everything we have recalled, reflects the world in which we live. Everything I said about Mr. Reagan's Hitlerian methods is showing us that all our efforts at national defense are not in vain.

We know that even though our schools have many needs—there are old schools, some in bad condition, especially primary schools—that there is a shortage of housing, that we lack sports and cultural centers, that we lack many things; for all those things that we desire, we must invest hundreds of millions every year in fortification, in defense; we have to dedicate scores of millions of labor-hours to train the people in defense.

All of this takes energy and effort away from productive work that must be redirected into military training. We have to devote hundreds of thousands of tons of cement, steel, all kinds of materials and the efforts of a countless number of workers every year just to defend ourselves. This is another price imperialism forces us to pay!

Today, on this anniversary and in light of these meditations, we see how right we are in preparing the people for this struggle. Because we were strong, we liberated ourselves from a terrible war 25 years ago. This is another lesson of the Bay of Pigs: We must be strong to liberate ourselves, perhaps, from another terrible war!

To the extent that we are strong, efficient and hardworking, and that we meet all our obligations, we will help to avoid imperialist aggression! The imperialists are opportunists, and they know to attack where there is weakness; but where there is strength they hold back. A population is not just made strong by its patriotism, by the arms that it has, but also by its general behavior.

The imperialists would love to see all these problems and vices to which I have referred multiply, because they know that this would weaken us and our resistance.

So then, patriotism obliges us not just to train ourselves, to join a combat unit and to arm ourselves but also to fulfill all our obligations every day of our lives.

The revolution has moved forward, has made great advances, has achieved great successes, but those who think that the new generations don't have equal or greater tasks ahead of them than those of the generation of the Bay of Pigs, or their predecessors, are mistaken. They are truly mistaken!

The struggle will be long and hard; these last 25 years have taught us this. Imperialism's crimes continue to demonstrate it to us, as we face an imperialism that is ever more aggressive, arrogant and overbearing.

This is a goal for the whole world, for all the revolutionary forces, for all the socialist countries, for all the democratic and progressive forces of the world. It is a tremendous challenge, a tremendous struggle. No one should believe that a single generation did it all. One generation did a single part, and if you will, a small part. The new generations have to do a great deal, and those that follow will also have much to do. This is the reality.

These are the realities of which I wish to make our compatriots aware, on a day like today, upon which we meditate and on which we can say to our heroes, to our martyrs, to those who had to make more sacrifices than others, that we will never permit the fruits of their labor to become sullied or the fruits of their sacrifice to be misappropriated or squandered; that we will fight with the same courage, with the same steadfastness as at the Bay of Pigs; that we will fight with tenacity and without rest against everything that continues to weaken the revolution.

And in the face of foreign enemies and the danger that lies in wait for us beyond our shores, we can also tell our heroes and martyrs, those who gave everything for the revolution and those who by their sacrifice brought pain to their loved ones: The revolution will not only be able to defend itself from weaknesses, its own weaknesses, but also from its foreign enemies; this country will never return to capitalism, and this country will never again be the property of imperialism.

Finally, we will tell them, as was expressed in Antonio Maceo's immortal words: "Whoever tries to conquer Cuba will gain nothing but the dust of her blood-soaked soil — if they do not perish in the struggle first!"

Patria o muerte! [Homeland or death!]
Venceremos! [We will win!]

15. CUBAN INTERNATIONALISM AND THE COLLAPSE OF THE SOCIALIST BLOC

HAVANA, DECEMBER 7, 1989

At a memorial ceremony held at El Cacahual on December 7, 1989, for Cubans who had died on military and civilian missions in Africa and elsewhere, Fidel Castro discussed the imminent collapse of the Soviet Union and its significance.

Compañero President José Eduardo Dos Santos of Angola and other guests;
Relatives of our fallen compañeros;
Members of the armed services;
Compatriots:

This date, December 7, the date on which Antonio Maceo, the most illustrious of all our soldiers, and his young aide-de-camp were killed, has always been very meaningful for all Cubans. Their remains lie here, in this sacred site of their homeland.

By choosing this day for laying to rest the remains of our heroic internationalist fighters who have died in different parts of the world — mainly in Africa, the land of birth of Maceo's ancestors and many of our forebears — we make it a day for honoring all those Cubans who gave their lives while defending their country and all humankind. Thus, patriotism and internationalism — two of humanity's most treasured values — will be joined forever in Cuba's history.

Perhaps, some day, a monument will be erected not far from this site to honor them.

The remains of all the internationalists who died while carrying out their missions are being laid to rest in their hometowns all over Cuba right now.

The imperialists thought we would conceal the number of our combatants killed in Angola during that complex, 14-year-long mission—as if it were a dishonor or a discredit to the revolution. For a long time they dreamed that the blood shed had been to no avail, as if those who died for a just cause had died in vain. Even if victory were the way to measure the value of people's sacrifices in their legitimate struggles, they also returned victorious.

The Spartans used to tell their fighters to return with their shields or on them. Our troops are returning with their shields.

Still, it is not my intention, on this solemn occasion, to boast of our achievements or to humiliate anyone—not even those who were our adversaries. Our country sought neither glory nor military prestige. We always applied the principle of achieving our goals with the lowest possible number of casualties. To do this, we had to be strong, unemotional and always willing to do our utmost.

All of our soldiers knew that the whole country supported them and that all of us were concerned about their health and safety.

When political and diplomatic efforts became feasible for attaining the final goals, we did not hesitate to use political and diplomatic channels, and, while we always employed the necessary firmness, at no time during the negotiation process were we arrogant, overbearing or boastful. We were flexible whenever flexibility was advisable and fair.

The final stage of the war in Angola was the most difficult. It demanded our country's total determination, tenacity and fighting spirit in support of our Angolan brothers and sisters.

In fulfilling this duty of solidarity, not only to Angola but also to our own troops fighting under difficult conditions there, the revolution did not hesitate to risk everything. When the imperialist threats against our own country became very serious, we did not hesitate in sending a large part of our most modern and sophisticated military equipment to the southern front of the People's Republic of Angola. Over 50,000 Cuban troops were in that sister nation—a truly impressive figure, in view of the distance and our country's size and resources. It was a veritable feat by our Revolutionary

Armed Forces and our people. Such chapters of altruism and international solidarity are very rare.

Therefore, we greatly appreciate the fact that José Eduardo Dos Santos is attending this ceremony. It was an entirely spontaneous gesture. "I want to be with you on this occasion," he said. Also spontaneously, as soon as they learned of this ceremony, only a few days ago, the leaders of Ethiopia, SWAPO and other countries and revolutionary organizations stated that they wanted to send representatives to be here with us today when we laid to rest all our internationalists who died in Africa and in other lands.

There are historic events that nothing and no one can obliterate. There are revolutionary examples that the best men and women of future generations, both within and outside our country, will always remember. This is one of them, yet we should not be the ones to judge it; history will do that.

We will never forget that the soldiers of the Angolan Armed Forces were our comrades in arms. Tens of thousands of the best sons and daughters of that nation lost their lives in the struggle. Our unity and close cooperation made victory possible.

We also had the honor of fighting alongside the courageous sons and daughters of Namibia, the patriots of Guinea Bissau and the unmatched Ethiopian soldiers. Years earlier, in the difficult period immediately following Algeria's independence, our internationalist fighters were at her side — as, later, they helped defend Syria, another sister Arab nation that was a victim of foreign aggression and requested our cooperation.

Every legitimate African cause received our people's support. Che Guevara and a large group of Cuban revolutionaries fought against white mercenaries in the eastern part of what is now Zaire, and doctors and teachers are now working in the Saharawi Republic, helping its people, who are fighting for their freedom.

All these countries were then or are now independent, and those that have not yet won their independence will do so, sooner or later.

In just a few years, our fighters wrote an extraordinary chapter of solidarity of which our people can be proud. Combatants from other countries also fought at our side in our own struggles for independence. Máximo Gómez, who was born in the Dominican Republic, was the most outstanding of all and due to his extraordinary merits, became the chief of our liberation army. In the years prior to our revolution, 1,000 Cubans organized by the first communist party fought in Spain to defend the republic. They wrote memorable chapters of heroism that were recorded for history by Pablo de la Torriente Brau, until death put an early end to the life of that brilliant revolutionary journalist.

That was how our gallant internationalist spirit was forged. It reached its zenith with the socialist revolution.

Wherever Cuban internationalists have gone, they have set examples of respect for the dignity and sovereignty of those countries. The trust that those peoples have placed in them is the result of their irreproachable behavior. Their exemplary selflessness and altruism is remembered everywhere.

A prominent African statesperson once said in a meeting of leaders of the region: "Cuban fighters are ready to give their lives for the liberation of our countries. The only things they will take back with them, in exchange for that assistance to our freedom and our peoples' progress, are the bodies of those who died fighting for freedom." That continent, which experienced centuries of exploitation and plunder, has recognized the full extent of the unselfish nature of our internationalist contribution.

Now, our battle-seasoned troops are returning victoriously. The joyful, happy, proud faces of mothers, wives, brothers, sisters, sons and daughters—of all our people—welcome them with affection and love. Peace has been achieved with honor, and their sacrifice and effort have been amply rewarded. Our sleep is no longer disturbed by constant concern over the fate of our troops fighting thousands of kilometers away from their homeland.

The enemy thought that the return of our troops would cause social problems, since it would be impossible to provide jobs for them all. Most of those combatants—aside from those who have made the military their career—had jobs here in Cuba and will go back to their old jobs or be given better ones. None of them has been forgotten. Many of them already knew where they would be working even before returning home.

Of all the young people in military service who, shortly after graduating from high school, volunteered for the honor of going to Angola on an internationalist mission, none has had to wait before going back to school or joining the ranks of our working people.

Our country is working hard, implementing ambitious socioeconomic development programs. The irrational laws of capitalism do not guide our actions, and every man and woman in our country has a place in education, production or the services.

No close relatives of those who died while fulfilling their mission or who suffered serious injuries have been forgotten. They have received, are receiving and will continue to receive all the care and consideration due them for the sacrifices made by their loved ones and for their own devoted, selfless, generous, even heroic behavior.

The hundreds of thousands of Cuban who carried out military or civilian internationalist missions have earned the respect of present and future generations. They have honorably upheld our people's glorious fighting and internationalist traditions.

On their return, they have found their country engaged in a tremendous struggle for development while continuing to confront the criminal imperialist blockade with exemplary dignity. This is in addition to the current crisis in the socialist camp, from which we can only expect negative economic consequences for our country.

People in most of those countries aren't talking about the anti-imperialist struggle or the principles of internationalism. Those words aren't even mentioned in their press. Such concepts have been virtually removed from their political vocabulary. Meanwhile, capitalist values are gaining unheard-of strength in those societies.

Capitalism means unequal terms of trade with the peoples of the Third World, the exacerbation of individual selfishness and national chauvinism, the reign of irrationality and chaos in investment and production, the ruthless sacrifice of the peoples on behalf of blind economic laws, the survival of the fittest, the exploitation of human beings by other human beings, a situation of every person for themselves. In the social sphere, capitalism implies many more things: prostitution; drugs; gambling; begging; unemployment; abysmal inequalities among citizens; the depletion of natural resources, the poisoning of the air, seas, rivers and forests; and especially the plundering of the underdeveloped nations by the industrialized capitalist countries. In the past, it meant colonialism; now, it means neocolonialism for billions of human beings, using the most sophisticated — and cheapest, most effective and most ruthless — economic and political methods.

Capitalism, its market economy, its values, its concepts and its methods can never pull socialism out of its present difficulties or rectify whatever mistakes have been made. Most of those difficulties are the result not just of errors but also of the tight blockade and isolation imposed on the socialist countries by imperialism and the major capitalist powers, which have monopolized most of the world's wealth and the most advanced technologies by plundering their colonies, exploiting the working class and promoting a large-scale brain drain from the underdeveloped countries.

Devastating wars were unleashed against the first socialist state, taking a toll of millions of lives and destroying most of the means of production. Like a phoenix, the first socialist state had to rise more than once from its ashes. It has performed great services to humankind by defeating fascism and decisively supporting the liberation movements in countries still under colonial rule. Now, all this is being forgotten.

It is disgusting to see how many people, even in the Soviet Union itself, are engaged in denying and destroying the history-making feats and extraordinary merits of that heroic people.

That is not the way to rectify and overcome the undeniable errors made by a revolution that emerged from czarist authoritarianism in an enormous, backward, poor country. We shouldn't blame Lenin now for having chosen czarist Russia as the place for the greatest revolution in history.

Thus we didn't hesitate to stop the circulation of certain Soviet publications that are full of poison against the Soviet Union itself and against socialism. You can see that imperialism, reactionary forces and the counterrevolution are behind them. Some of those publications have already started calling for an end to the fair and equitable trade relations that were established between the Soviet Union and Cuba during the Cuban revolutionary process. In a word, they want the Soviet Union to begin practicing unequal trade with Cuba by selling its products to us at ever higher prices and buying our agricultural produce and raw materials at ever lower prices, just as the United States does with other Third World countries. In short, they want the Soviet Union to join the US blockade against Cuba.

Imperialism's undermining actions and the systematic destruction of the values of socialism, combined with the mistakes that have been made, have accelerated the destabilization of the Eastern European socialist countries. The United States designed and implemented a long-term policy of treating each country differently and undermining socialism from within.

Imperialism and capitalist powers cannot hide their glee over the way things are turning out. They are convinced—not without reason—that at this point, the socialist bloc has virtually ceased to exist. Groups of US citizens, including US presidential advisors, are planning capitalist development programs in some of those Eastern European countries right now. A recent news dispatch reported that they were fascinated by that "exciting experience." One of them, a US government official, favored the application in Poland of a program similar to the New Deal, with which Roosevelt tried to alleviate capitalism's severe crisis. This would be to help the 600,000 Polish workers who will lose their jobs in 1990, and half of the country's 17.8 million workers, who will have to be retrained and change jobs as a result of the implementation of a market economy.

Imperialism and the NATO capitalist powers are persuaded—not without reason—that at this point, the Warsaw Pact no longer exists and is nothing but a fiction, and that those societies which have been corroded and undermined from within will not be able to resist.

It has been stated that socialism must be improved. No one can deny this principle, which is inherent and permanently applicable to every human endeavor. But can socialism be improved by forsaking Marxism-Leninism's most basic principles? Why must the so-called reforms be along capitalist lines? If those ideas are truly revolutionary, as some claim, why do they receive the imperialist leaders' unanimous, enthusiastic support?

In an amazing statement, the president of the United States described himself as the number-one advocate of the doctrines currently being applied in many countries in the socialist camp.

History has never recorded an instance of a truly revolutionary idea as having received the enthusiastic support of the leader of the most powerful, aggressive and greedy empire known to humankind.

During compañero Gorbachev's visit to Cuba in April this year—a visit during which we had a frank, in-depth exchange of views—I publicly expressed my opinion to the National Assembly that if any socialist country wants to build capitalism, its right to do so should be respected, just as we demand complete respect for any capitalist country's right to build socialism.

I believe that revolution cannot be imported or exported; a socialist state cannot be founded through artificial insemination or by means of an embryo transplant. A revolution requires certain conditions within society, and the people in each individual nation are the only ones who can create it. These ideas don't run counter to the solidarity that all revolutionaries can and should extend to one another. Moreover, a revolution is a process that may advance or regress, a process that may even be derailed. But, above all, communists must be courageous and revolutionary. Communists are duty-bound to struggle under all circumstances, no matter how adverse they may be. The Paris communards struggled and died in the defense of their ideas. The banners of the revolution and of socialism are not surrendered without a fight. Only cowards and the demoralized surrender — never communists and other revolutionaries.

Now, imperialism is urging the European socialist countries to become recipients of its surplus capital, to develop capitalism and to join in plundering the Third World countries.

It is a well-known fact that a large part of the developed capitalist world's wealth comes from the unequal terms of trade it maintains with the Third World countries. For centuries, those nations were plundered as colonies. Millions of their sons and daughters were enslaved; their gold, silver and other mineral resources were exhausted; they were pitilessly exploited; and underdevelopment was imposed on them. Underdevelopment was the most direct and clearest consequence of colonialism. Now, those nations are being squeezed dry by means of interest payments on an endless, unpayable debt, while ridiculously low prices are paid for their commodities and they are forced to pay ever higher prices for the industrial goods they import. Financial and human resources are constantly being drawn away from those nations through the flight of capital and the brain drain. Their trade is blocked by dumping, high tariffs, import quotas, synthetic substitutes produced through advanced technological processes, and subsidies for the developed capitalist countries' products when they aren't competitive.

Now, imperialism is inviting the European socialist countries to join it in this colossal plunder — an invitation which seems not to displease the theoreticians of capitalist reforms. Thus, in many of those countries, no one speaks about the tragedy of the Third World, and their discontented multitudes are guided toward capitalism and anticommunism — and, in one country, toward pan-Germanism. Such developments may even lead to fascist trends. The prize promised by imperialism is a share of the plunder wrested from our peoples, the only way of building capitalist consumer societies.

Right now, the United States and the other capitalist powers are much more interested in investing in Eastern Europe than in any other part of the world. What resources can the Third World—in which billions of people live in sub-human conditions—expect from such developments?

They speak to us of peace, but what kind of peace? Of peace between the major powers, while imperialism reserves the right to intervene in and attack the Third World countries. There are many examples of this.

The imperialist government of the United States demands that no one help the Salvadoran revolutionaries and tries to blackmail the Soviet Union into ending its economic and military assistance to Nicaragua and Cuba because we express solidarity with the Salvadoran revolutionaries, even though we abide strictly by our commitments concerning the weapons supplied by the Soviet Union, in accordance with the agreements signed between our sovereign nations. Meanwhile, that same imperialist government which is demanding an end to solidarity with the Salvadoran revolutionaries is helping the genocidal Salvadoran government and sending special combat units to El Salvador, supporting the counterrevolution in Nicaragua; organizing coups d'état and the assassination of leaders in Panama; sending military aid to UNITA in Angola—in spite of the successful peace agreements in southwestern Africa—and continuing to supply the rebel forces in Afghanistan with large amounts of weapons, ignoring the Geneva Accords and the fact that the Soviet troops have withdrawn.

Only a few days ago, US Air Force planes insolently intervened in the internal conflict in the Philippines. Regardless of whether or not the rebel forces had good cause for their action—which it is not our place to judge— the US intervention in that country is a very serious matter and is an accurate reflection of the current world situation, showing that the United States has taken upon itself the role of gendarme, not only in Latin America—a region it has always considered as its backyard—but also in any other Third World country.

The consecration of the principle of universal intervention by a major power spells an end to independence and sovereignty in the world. What kind of peace and security can our peoples have other than that which we ourselves achieve through our own heroism?

The elimination of nuclear weapons is an excellent idea. If it were more than simply a utopian idea and could be achieved some day, it would be of unquestionable benefit and would increase world security—but only for a part of humanity. It would not bring peace, security or hope to the Third World countries.

Imperialism doesn't need nuclear weapons to attack our peoples. Its powerful fleets, which are stationed all over the world; its military bases everywhere; and its ever more sophisticated and lethal conventional weapons are enough to ensure its role as the world's master and gendarme.

Moreover, 40,000 children who could be saved die every day in our world because of underdevelopment and poverty. As I've said before— and this is worth repeating—it's as if a bomb similar to the ones dropped on Hiroshima and Nagasaki were dropped every three days on the poor children in the world.

If these developments continue on their present course and the United States isn't forced to renounce these concepts, what new way of thinking can we speak of? Following this course, the bipolar world which emerged in the postwar period will inexorably become a unipolar world under US hegemony.

In Cuba, we are engaged in a process of rectification. No revolution or truly socialist rectification is possible without a strong, disciplined, respected party. Such a process cannot be advanced by slandering socialism, destroying its values, casting slurs on the party, demoralizing its vanguard, abandoning the party's guiding role, eliminating social discipline and sowing chaos and anarchy everywhere. This may foster a counterrevolution, but not revolutionary changes.

The US imperialists think that Cuba won't be able to hold out and that the new situation in the socialist community will inexorably help them to bring our revolution to its knees.

Cuba is not a country in which socialism arrived in the wake of the victorious divisions of the Red Army. In Cuba, our people created our socialist society in the course of a legitimate, heroic struggle. The 30 years in which we have stood firm against the most powerful empire on earth that sought to destroy our revolution bear witness to our political and moral strength.

Those of us in our country's leadership aren't a bunch of bumbling parvenus, new to our positions of responsibility. We come from the ranks of the old anti-imperialist fighters who followed [Julio Antonio] Mella and [Antonio] Guiteras; who attacked the Moncada barracks and came on the

Granma; who fought in the Sierra Maestra, in the underground struggle and at the Bay of Pigs; who were unshaken by the October [Missile] Crisis; who have stood firm against imperialist aggression for 30 years; who have performed great labor feats and have carried out glorious internationalist missions. Men and women from three generations of Cubans are members and hold posts of responsibility in our battle-seasoned party, our marvelous vanguard young people's organization, our powerful mass organizations, our glorious Revolutionary Armed Forces and our Ministry of the Interior.

In Cuba, the revolution, socialism and national independence are indissolubly linked.

We owe everything we are today to the revolution and socialism. If Cuba were ever to return to capitalism, our independence and sovereignty would be lost forever; we would be an extension of Miami, a mere appendage of US imperialism; and the repugnant prediction that a US president made in the 19th century — when that country was considering the annexation of Cuba — that our island would fall into its hands like a ripe fruit, would prove true. Our people are and will always be willing to give their lives to prevent this. Here, at Maceo's tomb, we recall his immortal phrase: "Whoever tries to conquer Cuba will gain nothing but the dust of her blood-soaked soil — if they do not perish in the struggle first!"

We Cuban communists and the millions of our people's revolutionary soldiers will carry out the role assigned to us in history, not only as the first socialist state in the Western Hemisphere but also as staunch front-line defenders of the noble cause of all the destitute, exploited people in the world.

We have never aspired to having custody of the banners and principles that the revolutionary movement has defended throughout its heroic and inspiring history. However, if fate were to decree that one day we would be among the last defenders of socialism in a world in which US imperialism had realized Hitler's dreams of world domination, we would defend this bulwark to the last drop of our blood.

These men and women whom we are honorably laying to rest today in the land of their birth gave their lives for the most treasured values of our history and our revolution.

They died fighting against colonialism and neocolonialism.

They died fighting against racism and apartheid.

They died fighting against the plunder and exploitation to which the Third World peoples are subjected.

They died fighting for the independence and sovereignty of those peoples.

They died fighting for the right of all peoples in the world to well-being and development.

They died fighting so there would be no hunger or begging; so that all sick people would have doctors, all children would have schools, and all human beings would have jobs, shelter and food.

They died so there would be no oppressors or oppressed, no exploiters or exploited.

They died fighting for the dignity and freedom of all men and women.

They died fighting for true peace and security for all nations.

They died defending the ideals of Céspedes and Máximo Gómez.

They died defending the ideals of Martí and Maceo.

They died defending the ideals of Marx, Engels and Lenin.

They died defending the ideals of the October revolution and the example it set throughout the world.

They died for socialism.

They died for internationalism.

They died for the proud, revolutionary homeland that is today's Cuba.

We will follow their example!

Eternal glory to them!

Socialism or death!

Patria o muerte! [Homeland or death!]

Venceremos! [We will win!]

16. RETURN OF CHE GUEVARA'S REMAINS TO CUBA

SANTA CLARA, OCTOBER 17, 1997

In July 1997 the remains of Che Guevara and his compañeros killed in combat in Bolivia were discovered and returned to Cuba. Fidel Castro gave this speech at the memorial built to honor Che and the other guerrilla fighters in Santa Clara, Cuba.

Families of the compañeros who fell in combat;

Guests;

Villaclareños;

Compatriots:

With profound emotion we experience one of those moments that will never again be repeated.

We are not here to say farewell to Che and his heroic compañeros. We are here to welcome them.

I see Che and his combatants as reinforcements, as a movement of invincible combatants, which on this occasion not only includes Cubans, but also Latin Americans who came to fight with us and write new pages of history and glory.

I also see Che as a moral giant who grows with each passing day, whose image, strength, and influence have multiplied throughout the earth.

How can he fit beneath a memorial stone?

How can he fit into this square?

How can he fit into our beloved, but small, island?

Only in the world that he dreamed of, which he lived and fought for, is there enough space for him.

The greater the injustice, the greater the exploitation, the greater the inequality, the greater the unemployment, the greater the poverty, hunger and misery that prevail in human society, the greater his figure will be.

The values he defended will appear more elevated in the face of growing imperialist power, hegemony, domination and interventionism that deny the most sacred rights of humanity, particularly the rights of the weak, underdeveloped and poor peoples in what were for centuries colonies of the West and sources of slave labor.

His profound humanism will always stand in stark contrast to growing abuse, egotism, alienation, discrimination against indigenous peoples, ethnic minorities, women and immigrants. It will stand against child labor and the sexual commodification of hundreds of thousands of children. It will stand against ignorance, disease, unemployment and insecurity.

His example as an upright, revolutionary and principled person will be ever more outstanding, as long as corrupt politicians, demagogues and hypocrites exist everywhere.

Admiration for his personal bravery and revolutionary integrity will grow as long as the numbers of cowards, opportunists and traitors on earth increase. While others flinch from their duty, the greater will be the respect for his iron will. The more people lacking integrity, the greater his sense of honor and dignity; the more skeptics there are, the greater his faith in humanity; the more pessimists there are, the greater his optimism; the more fear there is, the greater his daring; the more idlers there are who waste the products of the labor of others in luxury and leisure, the greater his austerity and his spirit of work and study.

Che was a true communist and is today an example and a paradigm of the revolutionary and the communist.

Che was a teacher who forged men and women like himself. Consistent with his actions, he never failed to do what he preached, or demand of himself what he demanded of others.

Whenever a volunteer was required for a difficult mission, he was the first in line, both in war and in peace. His great dreams depended on his willingness to give his life generously. Nothing was impossible for him, and he was capable of making the impossible possible.

The invasion from the Sierra Maestra through vast and unprotected plains and the capture of the city of Santa Clara with just a few combatants are among those feats that show his amazing capabilities.

His ideas on revolution in his own country and in the rest of Latin America, in spite of enormous difficulties, were possible. Had he made them a reality, perhaps today the world might be different. Vietnam proved it could fight against the interventionist forces of imperialism and defeat them. The Sandinistas triumphed against one of the most powerful puppet governments of the United States. The Salvadoran revolutionaries were just about to win victory. In Southern Africa, apartheid was defeated in spite of the state possessing nuclear weapons. China, thanks to the heroic struggle of its workers and peasant farmers, is today one of the most promising countries in the world. Hong Kong was returned after 150 years of an occupation established through the Opium Wars.

Not all historical eras or circumstances require the same methods and the same tactics. But nothing can stop the march of history; its objective laws are immutable. Che based himself on these social laws and had an absolute faith in humanity. Very often revolutionaries and those seeking profound social change do not have the privilege of seeing their dreams realized as quickly as they had hoped or desired, but sooner or later they are victorious.

A combatant may die, but not their ideas. What was a man from the US government doing up there where Che was wounded and taken prisoner? How could they believe that by killing Che he would cease to exist as a combatant? Now, he is not in La Higuera; instead he is everywhere, wherever there is a just cause to defend. Those who wanted to kill him, to make him disappear, were not able to understand that he would leave an indelible footprint in history and that his luminous prophet's gaze would transform him into a symbol for all the earth's poor in their millions upon millions. Young people, children, the elderly, men and women who have learned about him, honest people throughout the world, regardless of their social background, admire him.

Che is taking up and winning more battles than ever. Thank you, Che, for your history, your life and your example!

Thank you for coming to fortify us in this difficult battle we are engaged in today to save the ideas you fought so hard for, to save the revolution, our country and the achievements of socialism, where some of the great dreams you cherished have come true!

To carry forward this heroic achievement, to defeat the imperialists' plans against Cuba, to resist the blockade, to achieve victory, we count on you.

As you can see, this land is your land, these people are your people, and this revolution is your revolution. We continue to fly the socialist banner with honor and pride.

Welcome, heroic compañeros of the reinforcement! The trenches of ideas and justice that you defend together with our people will never be conquered by the enemy! And together we will continue to fight for a better world!

Hasta la victoria siempre! [Ever onward to victory!]

17. INAUGURATION OF PRESIDENT CHÁVEZ IN VENEZUELA: "THE BATTLE OF IDEAS"

UNIVERSITY OF VENEZUELA, CARACAS
FEBRUARY 3, 1999

On visiting Venezuela for the inauguration of President Hugo Chávez, Fidel Castro reminisced about his visit 40 years earlier in the weeks immediately after the overthrow of the Batista dictatorship in Cuba in January 1959. In this speech, that has become known as "the battle of ideas," he considered the ideological offensive against socialist ideas that arose in the wake of the collapse of the European socialist bloc.

I was going to say that today, February 3, 1999, it is exactly 40 years and 10 days since I first visited this university and we met in this same place. Of course, you understand that I am moved—without the melodrama you find in certain soap operas—as it would have been unimaginable then that one day, so many years later, I would return to this place…

Several weeks ago, on January 1, 1999, on the occasion of the 40th anniversary of the triumph of the [Cuban] revolution, I stood on the same balcony in Santiago de Cuba where I had spoken on January 1, 1959. I was reflecting with the audience gathered there that the people of today are not the same people who were there at the time, because of the 11 million Cubans we are today, 7.19 million have been born since. I said that they were two different peoples and yet one and the same eternal Cuban people.

I also reminded them that the immense majority of those who were 50 years old then are no longer alive, and that those who were children at that time are over 40 today.

So many changes, so many differences, and how special it was for us to think that the people had started a profound revolution when they were practically illiterate, when 30 percent of adults could not read or write and perhaps an additional 50 percent had not reached fifth grade. We estimated that out of a population of almost seven million, possibly a little over 150,000 people had gone beyond fifth grade, while today university graduates alone number 600,000, and there are almost 300,000 teachers and professors.

I told my fellow compatriots—in paying tribute to the people who had achieved that first great triumph 40 years before—that in spite of an enormous educational backwardness, they had been able to undertake and defend an extraordinary revolutionary feat. Furthermore, their political culture was probably lower than their educational level.

Those were times of brutal anticommunism, the final years of McCarthyism, when by every possible means our powerful and imperial neighbor had tried to sow in the minds of our noble people all kinds of lies and prejudices. I would often meet an ordinary citizen and ask them a number of questions: whether they believed we should undertake land reform; whether it would be fair for families to own the homes for which at times they paid almost half their salaries. Also, if they believed that the people should own all the banks in order to use those resources to finance the development of the country. Whether those big factories—most of them foreign-owned—should belong to, and produce for, the people... things like that. I would ask 10, 15 similar questions and they would agree absolutely: "Yes, that would be great."

In essence, if all those big stores and all those profitable businesses that now only enrich their privileged owners belonged to the people, and were used to enrich the people, would you agree? "Yes, yes," they would answer immediately. So, then I asked them: "Would you agree with socialism?" Answer: "Socialism? No, no, no, not with socialism." Let alone communism... There was so much prejudice that this was an even more frightening word.

Revolutionary legislation was what contributed the most to creating a socialist consciousness in our people. At that time it was that same people— illiterate or semi-illiterate at the beginning—who had to start by teaching many of its children to read and write. That same people who, out of love for liberty and a yearning for justice, had overthrown the dictatorship and carried out, and heroically defended, the most profound social revolution in this hemisphere.

In 1961, only two years after the triumph of the revolution, with the support of young students working as teachers, about one million people learned how to read and write. They went to the countryside, to the mountains, to the most remote places, and there they taught people who were up to 80 years old how to read and write. Later on, there were follow-up courses and the necessary steps were taken in a continuing effort to attain what we have today. A revolution can only be born from culture and ideas.

No one becomes revolutionary by force. Those who sow ideas never have any need to suppress the people. Weapons in the hands of that same people are now used to fight those abroad who try to take away their achievements.

Forgive me for touching on this issue because I did not come here to preach socialism or communism and I don't want to be misunderstood. Nor did I come here to propose radical legislation or anything of the sort. I was simply reflecting on our experience that showed us the importance of ideas, the importance of believing in humanity, the importance of trusting in the people. This is extremely important when humankind is facing such complicated and difficult times.

Naturally, on January 1 this year in Santiago de Cuba it was fitting to acknowledge, in a very special way, the fact that the revolution, which had managed to survive 40 years without folding its banners, without surrendering, was mainly the work of the people gathered there, young people and mature men and women. They had received their education under the revolution and were capable of that feat, thus writing pages of noble and well-earned glory for our nation and for our brothers and sisters in the Americas.

We could say that thanks to the efforts of three generations of Cubans, vis-à-vis the mightiest power, the biggest empire in humanity's history, this sort of miracle came about: that a small country could undergo such an ordeal and achieve victory.

Our even greater recognition went to those compatriots who in the past decade had been willing to withstand the double blockade resulting from the collapse of the socialist camp and the demise of the Soviet Union, which left our neighbor as the sole superpower in a unipolar world, unrivalled in the political, economic, military, technological and cultural fields. I don't mean the value of their culture, but rather the tremendous power they exercise to impose their culture on the rest of the world.

But they have been unable to defeat a united people, a people armed with just ideas, a people endowed with a great political consciousness, because that is most important for us. We have resisted everything and are ready to continue resisting for as long as necessary, thanks to the seeds planted throughout those decades, thanks to the ideas and the consciousness developed during that time.

This has been our best weapon and it shall remain so, even in nuclear times. Even in times of "smart" weapons, which apparently sometimes make mistakes and strike 100 or 200 kilometers away from their targets, but which have a certain degree of precision. Human intelligence will always be greater than any of these sophisticated weapons.

It is a matter of concepts. The defense doctrine of our nation is based on the conclusion that in the end — the end of our invaders — it would be hand-to-hand combat with the invaders.

We have had to wage, and will have to continue waging, a more difficult battle against that extremely powerful empire — a ceaseless ideological battle. They stepped up this battle after the collapse of the socialist camp when, fully confident in our ideas, we decided to continue forward — moreover, to continue forward alone. And when I say alone I am thinking of state entities, without ever forgetting the immense and invincible solidarity of the peoples that we have always had, which makes us feel under an even greater obligation to struggle.

We have accomplished honorable internationalist missions. Over 500,000 Cubans have taken part in difficult missions abroad. The children of the Cuban people who could not read or write developed such a high consciousness that they have shed their sweat, and even their blood, for other peoples — for any people in other parts of the world.

When the special period began we said: "Now, our first internationalist duty is to defend this bulwark." By this we meant what [José] Martí had described in the last words he wrote the day before his death, when he said that the main objective of his struggle had to go undeclared in order to be accomplished. Martí, who was not only a true believer in [Simón] Bolívar's ideas but also a wholehearted follower, set himself an objective. Martí, in his own words, saw it as his duty to prevent "the United States from spreading through the Antilles, as Cuba gains its independence, and from overpowering with that additional strength our lands of America. All I have done so far, and all I will do, is for this purpose."

It was Martí's political will and life's aspiration to prevent the fall of that first trench which the northern neighbors had so many times tried to occupy. That trench is still there, and will continue to be there, with a people willing to fight to the death to prevent the fall of that trench of the Americas. The people there are capable of defending that last trench, and whoever defends the last trench and prevents anyone from taking it begins, at that very moment, to attain victory.

Compañeros—if you allow me to call you that, because that is what we are at this moment—I believe that we are defending a trench here, too. And trenches of ideas—forgive me for quoting Martí again—are worth more than trenches of stone.

We must discuss ideas here, and so I go back to what I was saying. Many things have happened over these 40 years but the most transcendental is that the world has changed. This world of today does not resemble the world of those days.

The revolutionary fever we had come down with from the mountains only a few days before accompanied us when speaking [here 40 years ago] of revolutionary processes in Latin America and focusing on the liberation of the Dominican people from Trujillo's clutches. I believe that issue took most of the time at that meeting—with a tremendous enthusiasm shared by all.

Today, that would not be an issue. Today, there is not one particular people to liberate. Today, there is not one particular people to save. Today, a whole world, all of humankind needs to be liberated and saved. And it is not our task; it is *your* task...

Yes, we all hope to live for a long time, all of us! In the ideas that we believe in and in the conviction that those following in our footsteps will carry them forward. However, your task—it must be said—will be more difficult than ours...

I was saying that we are living in a very different world; this is the first thing we need to understand. Furthermore, the world is globalized, truly globalized. It is a world dominated by the ideology, the ethics and the principles of neoliberal globalization.

In our view, globalization is nobody's whim; it is not even anybody's invention. Globalization is a law of history. It is a consequence of the development of the productive forces — excuse me, please, for using this phrase which might still scare some people due to its authorship — it is a consequence of scientific and technological development, so much so that even the author of this phrase, Karl Marx, who had great confidence in human abilities, was probably unable to imagine it.

Certain other things remind me of some of the basic ideas of that thinker among great thinkers. It comes to mind that even what he conceived as an ideal human society could never come true — and this is increasingly clear — if it was not a globalized world. Not for a second did he think that in the tiny island of Cuba — just to give you an example — a socialist society, or the building of socialism, would be attempted, least of all so close to such a powerful capitalist neighbor.

Yes, we have tried. Furthermore, we made it and we have defended it. And we have also known 40 years of blockade, threats, aggression and suffering.

Today, since we are the only ones, all the propaganda, all the mass media in the world are used by the United States in the ideological and political warfare against our revolutionary process, in the same way that it uses its immense power in all fields, including its economic power, and its international political influence in the economic warfare against Cuba...

We have withstood that warfare, and like in all battles — whether military, political or ideological — there are casualties. There are those who may be confused, some are weakened by a combination of economic difficulties, material hardships, the parading of luxury in consumer societies and the nicely sweetened but rotten ideas about the fabulous advantages of their economic system, based on the mean notion that humans are animals moved only by a carrot or when beaten with a whip. We might say that their whole ideology is based on this.

There are casualties, but also, like in all battles, other people gain experience, fighters become veterans, they develop their character and help preserve and increase the morale and strength needed to continue fighting.

We are winning the battle of ideas. The battlefield is not limited to our small island, although our small island has to fight. Today, the world is the battlefield—everywhere, on every continent, in every institution, in every forum. This is the good side of the globalized struggle. We must defend the small island while fighting throughout the gigantic world they dominate or try to dominate. In many fields they have almost total domination, but not in all fields, or in the same way, or in absolutely every country.

They have discovered very intelligent weapons but we, the revolutionaries, have discovered an even more powerful weapon: Humans think and feel. We have learned this around the world, in the countless internationalist missions we have discharged in one place or another. Suffice it to mention a single figure: 26,000 Cuban doctors have taken part in these missions...

I was saying that life has taught us many things, and this is what nurtures our faith in the people, our faith in humanity. We didn't read this in some book, we have lived it; we have had the privilege of living it.

There is no need here for an extensive explanation of what neoliberalism is all about. How can I summarize it? Well, I would say this: Neoliberal globalization wants to turn all countries, especially all our countries, into private property.

What will be left for us of their enormous resources? They have accumulated an immense wealth by not only looting and exploiting the world but also by working the miracle alchemists longed for in the Middle Ages: turning paper into gold. At the same time, they have turned gold into paper and with it they buy everything, everything but souls, or rather, everything but the overwhelming majority of souls. They buy natural resources, factories, whole communication systems, services and so on. They are even buying land all around the world, assuming that if it is cheaper than in their own countries it is a good investment for the future.

I wonder, what are they going to leave us after turning us virtually into second-class citizens—pariahs would be a more precise term—in our own countries? They want to turn the world into a gigantic free-trade zone. It might be more clearly understood this way, because what is a free-trade zone? It is a place with special characteristics where taxes are not paid;

where raw materials, spare parts and components are brought in and assembled, or various goods produced, especially in labor-intensive sectors. At times, they pay not more than 5 percent of the salary they must pay in their own countries and these meager salaries are the only thing they leave us with.

Sadder still, I have seen how they have made many of our countries compete with one another by favoring those who offer more advantages and tax exemptions to investors. They have made many Third World countries compete with one another for investments and free-trade zones.

There are countries suffering such poverty and unemployment that they have had to establish dozens of free-trade zones as an option within the established world order. Otherwise they won't even have the free-trade zone factories and jobs with certain salaries, even if these amount to only 7 percent, 6 percent, 5 percent or less of the salaries the owners of those factories would have to pay in the countries they come from...

That is the future we are offered by neoliberal globalization. But you should not think that this is offered to the workers only. It is also being offered to the national businesses and to the small- and medium-size owners. They will have to compete with the transnational companies' technology, with their sophisticated equipment, and their worldwide distribution networks; then they will have to look for markets without the substantial trade credits their powerful competitors can use to sell their products...

These past eight years since 1991—in other words, since the collapse of the Soviet Union—have been hard years for us in every sense, especially in terms of ideas and concepts. Now we see that the high and mighty, those who thought they had created a system or an empire that would last a thousand years, are beginning to realize that the foundations of that system, of that empire, are falling apart.

What is the legacy of this global capitalism or this neoliberal capitalist globalization? Not only the capitalism that we know from its very origins, that capitalism from which this one was born, which was progressive yesterday but reactionary and unsustainable today. This is a process many of you, historians, and those who are not, like the students of economics, must know. Capitalism has a history of 250 to 300 years, whose primary theoretician, Adam Smith, published his book in 1776, the same year as the Declaration of Independence of the United States. He was a great talent, undoubtedly, a great intellect. I don't regard him as a sinner, a culprit or a bandit. He studied the economic system that emerged in Europe while it was in full bloom. He examined and outlined the theoretical bases of capitalism—the capitalism of his day. Adam Smith could have never imagined capitalism as it is today.

In those days of small workshops and factories, Smith felt that personal interest was the primary stimulus to economic activity, and that private and competitive quest constituted the basic source of public welfare. It was not necessary to appeal to an individual's humanity but one's love of oneself.

Private property and control were totally compatible with the world of small-scale industry that Adam Smith knew. He did not even live to see the enormous factories and the impressive masses of workers at the end of the 19th century. He could much less imagine the gigantic corporations and modern transnational companies with millions of shares, managed by professional executives who have nothing to do with the ownership of these entities and whose main function is to occasionally report to the shareholders. (Those executives decide, however, which dividends are paid, and how much and where to invest.) These forms of property, management and enjoyment of the wealth produced have nothing to do with the world [Smith] lived in.

Nevertheless, the system continued to develop and gained considerable momentum during the English industrial revolution. The working class emerged and so did Karl Marx, who in my view, with all due respect to those who have a different view, was the greatest economic and political thinker of all time. No one learned more about the laws and principles of the capitalist system than Marx. Right now, more than a few members of the capitalist elite, concerned about the current crisis, are reading Marx, seeking a possible diagnosis and remedy for today's evils. Socialism, as the antithesis of capitalism, arose with Marx…

Allow me to point out some facts to answer the question I asked: What is the legacy of capitalism and neoliberal globalization? After 300 years of capitalism, the world now has 800 million hungry people. Now, at this very moment, there are one billion illiterates, four billion poor, 250 million children who work regularly and 130 million people who have no access to education. There are 100 million homeless and 11 million children under five years of age dying every year of malnutrition, poverty and preventable or curable diseases.

There is a growing gap between the poor and the rich, within countries and between countries; a callous and almost irreversible destruction of nature; an accelerated squandering and depletion of important nonrenewable resources; pollution of the air and underground waters, rivers and oceans; and climate change with unpredictable but already perceptible consequences. During the past century, more than one billion hectares of virgin forests have been devastated and a similar area has become either desert or wasteland.

Thirty years ago hardly anyone discussed these issues; now it is crucial for our species. I don't want to give any more figures. All this is very easy to demonstrate and its disastrous results are self-evident. In face of all this, perhaps many are wondering what can be done. Well, the Europeans have invented their own recipe: They are uniting. They have already approved and are in the process of implementing a single currency. The good wishes of the United States, according to their spokespersons, have not been lacking — good wishes which are as great as they are hypocritical, because everyone knows that what they really want is for the euro to fail...

And what will we do? This is a question that we must all ask ourselves within this context, at a time when they are trying to swallow our countries. You can rest assured that this is what they would like to do. We should not expect another miracle like when the prophet was delivered from the gut of a whale, because if that whale swallows us, we'll be thoroughly digested very rapidly.

Yes, this is our hemisphere and I am here speaking from no other place than Venezuela, Bolívar's glorious homeland, where he dreamed, where he conceived the idea of the unity of our nations and worked for its attainment at a time when it took three months to travel from Caracas to Lima on horseback, when there were no cellular phones, no planes, no highways, no computers, or anything of the sort. And yet, he foresaw the danger that those few, recently independent colonies far up north could pose. He was prophetic when he said, "The United States seems destined by Providence to plague the Americas with misery in the name of liberty." He launched the idea of our peoples' unity and struggled for it until his death. If it was a dream then, today it is a vital necessity.

How can solutions be worked out? They are difficult, very difficult. As I said, the Europeans have set a goal and are immersed in a tough competition with our neighbor to the north; this strong and growing competition is obvious. The United States does not want anyone to interfere with its interests in what it considers to be its hemisphere. It wants everything absolutely for itself. On the other hand, China in the Far East is a huge nation and Japan is a powerful, industrial country.

I believe that globalization is an irreversible process and that the problem is not globalization per se, but rather the type of globalization. This is why it seems to me that for this difficult and tough undertaking, for which the peoples do not have much time, the Latin Americans are the ones who should hurry the most and struggle for unity, through agreements and regional integration, not only within Latin America but also between Latin America and the Caribbean. There we have our English-speaking sister nations of the Caribbean, the CARICOM members, who after barely a few years of independence have acted with impressive dignity...

What is it that suits the neoliberals? What is it they are after? They want to see the day when there will be no tariffs, when their investments will not be affected by the tax authorities in any country. They obtain years of tax exemption as a concession from underdeveloped countries thirsty for investments, where they get the lion's share and the right to do as they please in our countries with no restrictions whatsoever. They also impose the free circulation of capital and goods throughout the world. Of course, the exception is the commodity that is Third World people—the modern slaves, the cheap labor power so abundant on our planet—who flood the free-trade zones in their own lands or sweep streets, harvest vegetables and do the hardest and worst-paid jobs when legally or illegally admitted into the former metropolis.

This is the type of global capitalism they want to impose. Our countries, full of free-trade zones, would have no other income but the meager salaries of those fortunate enough to get jobs, while a bunch of billionaires accumulates untold wealth...

What second millennium are we going to celebrate, and what kind of a new century will we live in? The world will reach the 21st century with people wrapped in newspapers living under bridges in New York, while others amass enormous fortunes. There are many tycoons in that country but the number of those living under bridges, in the doorways of buildings or in slums is incomparably higher. In the United States, millions live in critical poverty, something in which the fanatical advocates of the economic order imposed upon humanity cannot take pride...

I am discussing this so that you know what Cuba is today, why Cuba is like it is and what the prevailing ethics are in Cuba, a country so miserably slandered in matters of human rights. A country where in 40 years of revolution there has never been a disappeared person, where there has never been a tortured person, where there are no death squads and no political assassinations — nothing like that has ever happened. A country where there are no elderly people abandoned, no children living in the streets or without schools or teachers, no people left to their own devices.

We know very well what has happened in some of the places where our neighbors to the north have been, such as those who organized the 1954 ousting of the [Árbenz] government in one of the most important countries in the Central American region. They brought in their advisors with their handbooks on torture, repression and death. For many years there were no prisoners, this category did not exist, only the dead and disappeared. One hundred thousand disappeared in just one country! And 50,000 killed. We could also mention what happened in many other countries with torture, murders, disappeared, repeated US military interventions under any pretext or no pretext whatsoever.

They don't remember that, they don't speak about that; they have lost their memory. In the light of the terrible experiences of the peoples of our America, we challenge them. We will demonstrate with actual facts, with reality, who has a humane approach to life, who has true humanitarian sentiments and who is capable of doing something for humankind that is not lies, slogans, misinformation, hypocrisy, deception and everything they have been doing in our region throughout this century.

I know you don't need me to explain all this to you but since I raised the subject I feel it is my duty. One frequently meets misinformed persons who believe at least some of the tons of lies and slanders that have been cast against our country in an attempt to batter us, to weaken us, to isolate us, to divide us. They have not been able to divide us and they won't be able to divide us!

I have said all this to you in the greatest intimacy. I could not come now and speak to you as I did in 1959 about organizing an expedition to solve a problem in a neighboring country. We know very well that today no country can solve its problems by itself. That is the reality in this globalized world. We can say here: Either we are all saved or we all sink.

Martí said: "Humanity is my homeland." This is one of the most extraordinary things he said. That is how we have to think: Humanity is our homeland!...

It is the Latin American countries' duty to unite without losing a single minute; the Africans are trying to do it. In Southeast Asia they have ASEAN and they are looking for other forms of economic integration. Europe is doing it at a rapid pace. In other words, there will be subregional and regional alliances in various parts of the world.

Bolívar dreamed of an extensive regional federation from Mexico to Argentina. As you well know, the gentlemen from the north sabotaged the Amphictyonic Congress. They opposed Bolívar's idea of sending an expedition commanded by [General] Sucre to liberate the island of Cuba and remove all risks of threat or counterattack by the fearful and tenacious Spanish metropolis; so we were not forgotten in Venezuelan history. Now that we are free from the domination of a much stronger power, our most sacred duty is to defend our freedom in the very interests and security of our brothers and sisters in this hemisphere.

Obviously, we must work out various forms of cooperation and integration, step by step, but swiftly if we want to survive as a regional entity with the same culture, the same language and so many things in common. Europe does not have a common language — I don't know how an Italian understands an Austrian or a Finn, how a German speaks with a Belgian or a Portuguese — but they have been able to create the European Union and they are quickly advancing toward greater economic integration. Why can't we consider this type of formula? Why don't we encourage all the unitary and integrationist trends in every country sharing our language, our culture, our beliefs and the mixed blood running through the immense majority of us? And where there is no mixed blood in our veins there should be mixed blood in our souls.

Who were those who fought in the Ayacucho battle? People from the lowlands and from Caracas; Venezuelans from the west and the east, Colombians, Peruvians and Ecuadorans who were side by side; that is how they were able to do what they did. There was also the unforgettable co-operation of the Argentines and the Chileans. Our greatest sin is that we lost this after almost 200 years.

Eleven years from now we will celebrate the 200th anniversary of the proclamation of Venezuelan independence, and later that of other countries. Almost 200 years! What have we done in those 200 years, divided, frag-mented, Balkanized, submissive as we have been? It is easier to control the seven dwarfs than to control a boxer, even if he is a lightweight. They have wanted to keep us as divided, neighboring dwarfs so they can control us...

I began by telling you that [Venezuela] is a country I love dearly. This is when I began to tell you about my love for history, for world history, for the history of revolutions and wars, for the history of Cuba, the history of Latin America, and especially for that of Venezuela. That is why I identify so much with Bolívar's life and ideas.

Fate would have it that Venezuela was the country to fight the most for the independence of this hemisphere. It began here, and you had a legend-ary precursor like [Francisco] Miranda, who even led a French army in campaign, waging famous battles, which during the French revolution prevented an invasion of French territory. He also fought in the United States for that country's independence. I have a wide range of books about Miranda's great life, although I have not been able to read them all. The Venezuelans, therefore, had Miranda, the forefather of Latin America's independence, and later Bolívar, the Liberator, who was always for me the greatest among the greatest people in history.

[Responding to the audience:] Please, put me in the 40,000th place. One of Martí's phrases is deeply engraved in my mind: "All the glory in the world can fit into a kernel of corn." Many great people in history were concerned about glory and that is no reason to criticize them. Perhaps it was the concept of their times, a sense of history, the future, the importance of events in their lives that they took for glory. This is natural and understandable. Bolívar liked to speak about glory; he spoke very strongly about glory. He cannot be criticized; a great aura of glory will be attached to his name forever.

Martí's concept, which I share entirely, associates glory with personal vanity and self-exaltation. The role of the individual in important historical events has been very much debated. What I like especially about Martí's phrase is the idea of the insignificance of an individual as compared to the enormous significance and transcendence of humanity and the immeasurable reach of the universe, the reality that we are really like a small speck of dust floating in space. That reality, however, does not diminish human greatness. On the contrary, it is enhanced when, as in Bolívar's case, he carried in his mind a whole universe of just ideas and noble sentiments. That is why I admire Bolívar so much. That is why I consider his work so immense. He doesn't belong to the stock of those who conquered territories and nations, or founded empires that brought fame to others; he created nations, freed territories and tore down empires. He was also a brilliant soldier, a distinguished thinker and prophet.

Today, we are trying to do what he wanted to do and what still remains to be done. We are trying to unite our peoples so that tomorrow human beings will be able to know and live in a united, fraternal, just and free world. That is what he wanted to do with the white, black, native and mixed peoples of our America.

I perceive at this moment an exceptional situation in the history of Venezuela. I have witnessed two unique moments here: First, that moment in January 1959 [in my first visit], and 40 years later, I have seen the extraordinary volatility of the people on February 2, 1999. I have seen a people reborn. A people such as I saw in Plaza del Silencio where I was a bit more silent than I have been here... Those were unquestionably revolutionary masses.

It was once again very impressive to see the people in such extraordinary high spirits, although under different circumstances. Back then hope had been abandoned. I don't want to explain why; I leave that to the historians. This time hope lies ahead. I see in these hopes a true rebirth of Venezuela, or at least an exceptionally great opportunity for Venezuela. I see it coming not only in the interest of Venezuelans; I also see it in the interest of Latin

Americans. I see it as something in the interest of other peoples in the world as it advances—because there is no other choice—toward a universal globalization.

There is no way of escaping it, and there is no alternative. So I am not trying to flatter you with my words. Rather, I am reminding you of your duty, the duty of the nation, of the people, of all those who were born after that visit [in 1959], of the youngest, of the more mature, who really have a great responsibility ahead. Opportunities have often been lost, but you could not be forgiven if you lose this one.

The person speaking to you here has had the privilege and the opportunity of accumulating some political experience, of having lived through a revolutionary process in a country where, as I have already said, people did not even want to hear about socialism. And when I say people, I mean the vast majority. That same majority supported the revolution, supported the leaders, and supported the Rebel Army—but there were ghosts that they were afraid of. Like Pavlov did with his famous dogs, the United States created conditioned reflexes in many of us, including who knows how many millions of other Latin Americans.

We have had to fight hard against scarcity and poverty. We have had to learn to do a lot with very little. We had good and bad times, the former especially when we were able to establish trade agreements with the socialist bloc and the Soviet Union and demand fairer prices for our export products. We resorted to diplomacy and the eloquence that revolutionaries in a country that had to overcome so many obstacles must have.

Actually, the Soviets felt great sympathy for Cuba and great admiration for our revolution. It was very surprising for them to see that after so many years a tiny country, right next to the United States, would rebel against that mighty superpower. They had never contemplated such a possibility and they would have never advised it to anyone. Luckily we never asked anyone for advice, although we had already read almost a whole library of the works of Marx, Engels, Lenin and other theoreticians. We were convinced Marxists and socialists.

With that fever and that blind passion that characterizes young people, and sometimes old people too, I absorbed the basic principles from those books and they helped me understand the society in which I lived. Until then it was for me an intricate puzzle for which I could not find any convincing explanation. I must say that the famous *Communist Manifesto*, which Marx and Engels took so long to write—you can tell that its main authors worked conscientiously—impressed me tremendously. For the first time in my life I realized a few truths.

Before that, I was a sort of utopian communist, drawing my own conclusions while taking the first political economy course they taught us in law school from an enormous book with some 900 mimeographed pages. It was a conception of political economy inspired by the ideas of capitalism but which mentioned and analyzed very briefly the different schools of thought. Later, in the second course, I paid much more attention to the subject and after meditating on it all, I became a utopian communist. I call it that because my doctrine had no scientific or historical basis whatsoever but was based on the good intentions of a student recently graduated from a Jesuit school. I am very grateful because [the Spanish Jesuits] taught me some things that have helped me in life—although far removed from any of the ideas I have today—above all, to have strength, a certain sense of honor and definite ethical principles.

I left that school an athlete, an explorer and a mountain climber. I entered the University of Havana ignorant about politics, without a revolutionary mentor, who would have been so useful to me at that stage of my life.

That is how I came to have my own ideas, which I maintain with increased loyalty and fervor. Maybe it is because I now have a little more experience and knowledge, and maybe also because I have had the opportunity of meditating about new problems that did not exist during Marx's time…

So I am wearing the same jacket I wore when I came to this university 40 years ago, the same one I wore when I attacked the Moncada barracks [in July 1953], and when we disembarked from the *Granma* [in December 1956]. I would venture to say, despite the many pages of adventure that anyone can find in my revolutionary life, that I always tried to be wise and sensible, although perhaps I have been more wise than sensible.

In our conception and development of the Cuban revolution, we acted as Martí said when, on the eve of his death in combat, he addressed the great anti-imperialist goal of his struggle: "I have had to work quietly and somewhat indirectly, because to achieve certain objectives, they must be kept under cover; to proclaim them for what they are would raise such difficulties that the objectives would not be attained."

I was discreet, but not as much as I should have been, because I would explain Marx's ideas about class society to everyone I met. So, they began to take me for a communist in the popular movement whose slogan in the fight against corruption was "Dignity against money." I had joined that movement as soon as I arrived at the university. Toward the end of my university studies, I was no longer a utopian communist but rather an atypical communist who was acting independently. I based myself on a realistic analysis of our country's situation.

Those were the times of McCarthyism and Cuba's Marxist party, the Popular Socialist Party, was almost completely isolated. However, within the movement I had joined, which had now become the Cuban People's [Orthodox] Party, in my opinion, there was a large mass that had a class instinct but lacked a class consciousness: peasants, workers, professionals, middle-class people—good, honest, potentially revolutionary people. Its founder and leader [Eduardo Chibás], a person of great charisma, had dramatically taken his own life a few months before the 1952 coup d'état. The younger ranks of that party later became an important part of our movement.

I was a member of that political organization which, as usually happens, was already falling into the hands of rich people, and I knew what was going to happen after the inevitable electoral triumph. But I had come up with some ideas on my own—just imagine the things a utopian can dream!— about what had to be done in Cuba and how to do it, despite the United States. Those masses had to be led along a revolutionary path. Maybe that was the merit of the tactic we pursued. Of course, we were reading the books of Marx, Engels and Lenin.

When we attacked the Moncada barracks we left one of Lenin's books behind, and the first thing the propaganda machine of Batista's regime said during the trial was that it was a conspiracy of corrupt members of the recently overthrown government, bankrolled with their money, and communist, too. No one knows how both categories could be reconciled!

In the trial, I assumed my own defense. It was not that I considered myself a good lawyer but I thought that I was the person who could best defend myself at that time. I put on a gown and took my place with the other lawyers. It was a political and not a penal trial. I did not intend to be acquitted but to disseminate ideas. I began to cross-examine all those killers who had murdered dozens upon dozens of our compañeros and who were there as witnesses; I turned the trial against them. So the next day they took me out of there, they put me away and declared me unwell.

That was the last thing they did although they really wanted to do away with me once and for all; but I knew very well why they checked themselves. I knew the psychology of all of those people. It was due to the mood and the situation with the people, the rejection and great indignation caused by all the murders they had committed. I also had a bit of luck; but the fact is that at the beginning, while they were questioning me, this book by Lenin shows up. Someone takes it out and says, "You people had a book by Lenin."

We were explaining who we were: followers of Martí, and that was the truth; and that we had nothing to do with that corrupt government that they had ousted from power. However, we didn't say a word about Marxism-Leninism, and we did not have to. We said what we had to say, but since the subject of the book came up at the trial, I felt really angry and said, "Yes, that book by Lenin is ours, we read Lenin's books and other socialist books, and whoever doesn't read them is ignorant." That is what I told the judges and the rest of the people there. It was insufferable; we were not going to say, "Listen, that little book was planted there by someone..."

Our program had been presented when I defended myself at the trial. Therefore, if they did not know what we thought it was because they did not want to know. Perhaps they tried to ignore that speech, which became known as *History Will Absolve Me*. As I explained, I was ejected, they declared me unwell, they tried all the others and sent me to a hospital to try me in a small ward [of the hospital]. They did not exactly hospitalize me, but put me in an isolated prison cell. In the hospital, they turned a small ward into a courtroom with the judges and a few other people crammed into it, most of them from the military. They tried me there, and I had the pleasure of saying there everything that I thought, everything, quite defiantly.

I wonder why they were not able to deduce our political thought, for it was all out there in the open. You might say it contained the foundation of a socialist program, although we were convinced the time was not yet ripe, that the right time and stages would come. At the time we spoke about land reform among many other things of a social and economic nature. We said that all the profits obtained by all those gentlemen with so much money — in other words, the surplus value but without using such terminology — should be used for the development of the country, and I hinted that it was the government's responsibility to look after the development of the country and that surplus money.

I even spoke about the golden calf; I referred to the Bible again and singled out "those who worshipped the golden calf," in a clear reference to those who expected everything from capitalism. That was enough for them to figure out what we thought.

Later, I realized that it is likely that many of those who might be affected by a true revolution did not believe what we said, because in the 57 years of Yankee neocolonialism many a progressive or revolutionary program had been proclaimed. The ruling classes never believed our program to be possible or permissible by the United States. They did not pay much attention to it; they heeded it and even found it amusing. At the end of the day, all those other programs had been abandoned and people became corrupt. So they probably thought, "Yes, the illusions of these romantic young people are very pretty, very nice, but why worry about that?"

They did not particularly like Batista; so they admired our frontal attack against his abusive and corrupt regime, and they possibly underestimated our declaration, which was the basis of what we later did and of what we think today. The difference is that many years of experience have further enriched our knowledge and perceptions of all those problems. So, as I have said, that is the way I have thought since then.

We have undergone the tough experience of a long revolutionary period, especially during the last 10 years, confronting extremely powerful forces under very difficult circumstances. Well, I will tell you the truth: We achieved what seemed impossible. I would venture to say that near miracles were performed. Of course, the laws were passed exactly as they had been promised, always with the angry and arrogant opposition of the United States. It had had great influence in our country, so it made itself felt and the process became increasingly radicalized with each blow and each aggression we suffered.

Thus began the long struggle we have waged up to now. The forces in our country became polarized. Fortunately, the vast majority was in favor of the revolution and a minority, around 10 percent or less, was against it. So there has always been a great consensus and a great support for that process up to now. We made a great effort to overcome the prejudices that existed, to convey ideas, to build a consciousness, and it was not an easy task.

I remember the first time I spoke about racial discrimination. I had to go on television about three times. I was surprised at how deep-rooted those prejudices brought to us by our northern neighbors were, prejudices that meant that certain clubs were for white people only and others were not admitted. Almost all the beaches, especially in Havana, were exclusively for whites. There were even segregated parks and promenades, where according to the color of your skin you had to walk in one direction or another. What we did was to open all the beaches for everyone and from the very first days of the revolution we prohibited discrimination in all places of recreation, parks and promenades. Such humiliating injustice was incompatible with the revolution.

One day when I spoke about these issues, there was such a reaction, so many rumors and so many lies! They said we were going to force white men to marry black women and white women to marry black men. Well, just like that other preposterous fabrication that we were going to deprive families of the parental custody of their children. I had to go on television again to discuss the subject of discrimination in order to respond to all those rumors and machinations. That phenomenon of racism, which was nothing but an imposed racist culture, a humiliating, cruel prejudice, was very hard to eradicate.

In other words, during those years, we devoted a great deal of our time to two things: defending ourselves from invasions, threats of foreign aggression, the dirty war, assassination attempts, sabotage, etc., and building consciousness. There was a time when there were armed mercenary bands in every province of our country, promoted and supplied by the United States. But we confronted them immediately, so that they did not have the slightest chance to prosper. Our own experience in irregular [guerrilla] warfare was very recent and we were one of the few revolutionary countries that totally defeated these counterrevolutionary bands despite the logistical support they received from abroad. Nevertheless, we had to devote a lot of our time to this.

One source of concern I have is that many expectations have been raised here in Venezuela by the extraordinary election results, and this is only logical. What do I mean? I mean the natural, logical tendency of the people to dream, to wish that a great number of accumulated problems might be solved in a matter of months. As an honest friend, in my opinion, I think there are problems here that will not be solved in months, or even years...

What do I fear? It is this: You people have lived through periods of abundance — okay, long ago. In 1972 the price of oil was $1.90 a barrel. For example, at the triumph of the revolution, Cuba could buy the four million tons of fuel it consumed with a few hundred thousand tons of sugar, at the normal world sugar price existing then. When the price of fuel suddenly rose we were saved by the already mentioned price [agreement with the Soviet Union]. But when the crisis came — after the Soviet Union was lost and our basic market with it, as well as all our agreed prices — we had to cut by half the 13 million tons of oil that we were consuming at that time. A large part of what we were exporting we had to invest in fuel, and we learned to save...

These are times of abundance for neither Venezuela nor the world. I am fulfilling an honest duty, the duty of a friend, of a brother, by suggesting to you, who are a powerful, intellectual vanguard, to meditate profoundly about these topics. We want to express to you our concern that these logical, natural and human hopes, stemming from a sort of political miracle that has taken place in Venezuela might, in the short term, turn into disappointment and a weakening of such an extraordinary process.

I ask myself, what economic feats or miracles can be expected immediately with the prices of Venezuelan export commodities so low and oil at $9 a barrel? With the lowest price in the last 25 years, a dollar has a lot less purchasing power now, with a larger population, an enormous accumulation of social problems, an international economic crisis and a neoliberally globalized world?

I cannot and should not say a word about what we would do in such circumstances. I cannot. I am here as a guest, not as an advisor, an opinion giver or anything like that. I am simply meditating. Allow me to say that there are some important countries, whose situation is worse than yours, which I hope can overcome their difficulties. Your situation is difficult, but not catastrophic. That would be our view if we were in your place. I will say more with the same frankness. You cannot do what we did in 1959. You will have to be more patient than we were, and I am referring here to the sector that wants radical economic and social changes in the country.

If the Cuban revolution had triumphed in a moment such as this, it would not have been able to sustain itself. By this, I mean that same Cuban revolution which has done everything it has done. It emerged—and not because it was so calculated, but by a rare historical coincidence—14 years after World War II, in a bipolar world. We did not know a single Soviet citizen, and we never received a single bullet from the Soviets to carry out our struggle and our revolution. Nor did we let ourselves be guided by any type of political advice after the triumph, nor did anyone ever attempt it, because we were very reluctant to accept that advice. We Latin Americans in particular, do not like to be told what to do.

At that moment, of course, there was another powerful pole and so we anchored ourselves to that pole, which had come out of a great social revolution. It helped us to face the monster that cut off our oil and other vital supplies and reduced its imports of Cuban sugar, bringing them down to zero as soon as we enforced a land reform law. Therefore, from one minute to the next, we were deprived of a market that had taken more than a century to establish.

The Soviets, on the other hand, sold us oil. At the world price, yes; to be paid in sugar, yes; at the world price of sugar, yes, but we exported our sugar to the Soviet Union and we received oil, raw materials, food and many other things. It gave us time to build a consciousness; it gave us time to sow ideas; it gave us time to create a new political culture. It gave us time! Enough time to build the strength that enabled us later to resist the most incredibly hard times.

All the internationalism that we have practiced, which has already been mentioned, also made us stronger...

Now we can say the same thing a lieutenant said who took me prisoner in a forest near Santiago de Cuba in the early hours of dawn, several days after the attack against the Moncada barracks. We had made a mistake—there is always a mistake. We were tired of sleeping on the ground, on roots and stones, so we fell asleep in a makeshift hut covered with palm fronds. Then we woke up with rifles pointed against our chests. It was a lieutenant, a black man, with a group of obviously bloodthirsty soldiers who did not know who we were. We had not been identified. At first, they did not recognize us. They asked our names. I gave a false name. Prudence, huh? Shrewdness? Perhaps it was intuition or maybe instinct. I can assure you that I was not afraid because there are moments in life when you consider yourself as good as dead, and then it is rather your honor, your pride, your dignity that reacts.

If I had given them my name, that would have been it — tah, tah, tah! They would have done away with that small group immediately. A few minutes later they found some weapons nearby. Some compañeros who were not physically able to continue the struggle had left these behind. Some of them were wounded and we had all agreed they should return to the city to turn themselves in to the judicial authorities. Only three of us stayed, only three armed compañeros! And we were captured.

But that lieutenant... what an incredible thing! I have never publicly told this story in detail. This lieutenant was trying to calm down the soldiers but he could hardly restrain them. When they found the other compañeros' weapons while searching the surroundings, they were wild. They had us tied up with their loaded rifles pointing at us. But the lieutenant moved around calming them down and repeating in a low voice: "You cannot kill ideas, you cannot kill ideas." What made this man say that?

He was a middle-aged man. He had taken some university courses and he had that notion in his head, and he felt the urge to express it in a low voice, as if talking to himself: "You cannot kill ideas." Well, when I saw this man and I saw his attitude, in a critical moment when he was hardly able to keep those angry soldiers from shooting us, I got up and spoke to him alone: "Lieutenant, I am so and so, first in command of the action. Seeing your chivalrous attitude, I cannot deceive you. I want you to know whom you have taken prisoner." And the man said, "Don't tell anyone! Don't tell anyone!" I applaud that man because he saved my life three times within a few hours.

A few minutes later they were taking us with them and the soldiers were still very agitated. They heard some shots not far away, got ready for combat, saying to us, "Drop down to the ground." I remained standing and I said, "I will not drop to the ground!" I thought it was some kind of trick to eliminate us, so I said, "No." I also told the lieutenant, who kept insisting that we protect ourselves, "I am not dropping to the ground; if they want to shoot, let them shoot." Then he says—listen to what he says: "You boys are very brave." What an incredible reaction!

I don't mean that he saved my life at that moment, but he made that gesture. After we reached a road, he put us in a truck and there was a major there who was very brutal. He had murdered many of our compañeros and wanted the prisoners handed over to him. The lieutenant refused, saying we were his prisoners and he would not hand us over. He had me sitting in the front seat of the truck. The major wanted him to take us to the Moncada [barracks] but he did not hand us over to the major. So he saved our lives for the second time. He did not take us to the Moncada barracks. He took us to the precinct, in the center of the city, saving my life for the third time. You see, he was an officer of the army we were fighting against. After the revolution, we promoted him to captain and he became aide to the first president of the country.

As that lieutenant said, ideas cannot be killed. Our ideas did not die; no one could kill them. And the ideas we sowed and developed during those 30 odd years until 1991, when the special period began, were what gave us the strength to resist. Without those years we had had to educate, sow ideas, build awareness, instill feelings of solidarity and a generous internationalist spirit, our people would not have had the strength to resist.

I am speaking of things that are somewhat related to matters of political strategy. Very complicated things because they can be interpreted in different ways. I have said that not even a revolution like ours, which triumphed with the support of over 90 percent of the population—with unanimous, enthusiastic support, great national unity, and a tremendous political force—would have been able to resist. We would not have been able to preserve the revolution under the current circumstances of the globalized world.

I do not advise anyone to stop fighting, one way or another. There are many ways, among them the action of the masses, whose role and growing strength are always decisive.

Right now, we ourselves are involved in a great combat of ideas, disseminating our ideas everywhere; that is our job. It would not occur to us today to tell anyone to make a revolution like ours. Under the circumstances that we think we understand quite well, we would never suggest: Do what we did. Maybe if we were in those times we would say: Do what we did. But the world was different then and the experience was different. Now we are more knowledgeable, more aware of the problems, and of course, respect and concern for others should always come first.

At the time of the revolutionary movements in Central America, when the situation had become very difficult because the unipolar world already existed, and not even the Nicaraguan revolution could stay in power, when peace negotiations were initiated, visitors came quite often because of the longstanding friendship with Cuba, and we were asked our views. We would tell them: "Don't ask for our views about that. If we were in your place, we would know what to do, or we might be able to imagine what we should do. But one cannot tell others what to do if you are not the people who will have to take action on matters as vital as fighting to the death or negotiating. Only the revolutionaries of each country themselves can take that decision. We will support whatever decision you make."

It was a unique experience, which I am relating in public for the first time. Everyone has their own opinions, but no one has the right to convey to others their own philosophy on matters of life and death. That is why I say that giving opinions is a very delicate matter.

This does not, however, hold true for global issues that affect the entire planet, and questions of tactics and strategies of struggle related to those issues. As citizens of the world and as part of the human race, we have the right to clearly express our thoughts to those who want to hear, whether or not they are revolutionaries.

We learned a long time ago how to approach relations with the progressive and revolutionary forces. Here, I limit myself to conveying ideas, reflections and concepts in keeping with our common condition as Latin American patriots, because I repeat, I see a new hour has arrived in Venezuela, an immovable and inseparable pillar of the history of our America. One has the right to trust one's own experience or viewpoint, not because one is infallible or because one has not made mistakes, but because of having had the opportunity to take a 40-year-long course in the academy of the revolution.

That is why I have told you that you do not have a catastrophic situation, but you do have a difficult economic situation that entails risks for the opportunity that is looming. There have been very impressive coincidences.

This situation in Venezuela has taken place at a critical moment in the integration of Latin America; a special moment when those further to the south, in their endeavor for unity, need help from those in northern South America. In other words, they need your help. This has come at a moment when the Caribbean countries need you. It has come at a moment when you can be the link, the bridge, the hinge, whatever you want to call it: a steel bridge between the Caribbean, Central America and South America.

Nobody like you is in such a position to struggle for unity and integration, something so important and so much of a priority at this difficult moment. It concerns the survival not only of Venezuela but of all the countries sharing our culture, our language and our race.

Today more than ever we must be followers of Bolívar. Now more than ever we must raise the banner that states "Humanity is our homeland," aware that we can only be saved if humankind is saved. We can only be free—and we are very far from being free—if and when humanity is free, if and when we achieve a truly just world, which is possible and probable, although from much observation, meditation and reading, I have reached the conclusion that humanity has very little time left to achieve this.

This is not only my opinion but the opinion of many other people...

[In Cuba] we have some resources. Tourism, developed mainly with our own resources, has gained momentum in these years and we have made several decisions that have proved effective. I am not going to explain how we have managed to achieve what I have already explained. But I should say that we did it by avoiding shock policies, the famous shock therapy that has been so insensitively applied elsewhere.

We consulted with the people about the austerity measures we applied. We discussed this with the trade unions, the workers and the peasants. We discussed what to do with the price of a given item, what prices to increase and why, what prices not to increase and why. That was also discussed with students in hundreds of thousands of assemblies. Then the measures were submitted to the National Assembly and later they were taken back to the grassroots again. Every decision was discussed so that nothing was implemented unless there was a consensus and consensus is something that cannot be achieved by force.

The wise men in the north believe or pretend to believe that the Cuban revolution is sustained by force. They have not been clever enough to realize that in our country, a country educated in important revolutionary and humane concepts, that would be absolutely impossible. This is only achieved through consensus and nothing else; no one in the world can do this without the people's massive support and cooperation. But consensus has its own rules. We learned to create it, to maintain it and to defend it. A united people ready to fight and win can be tremendously strong...

So what you need is unity, political culture and the conscious and militant support of the people. We built that through a long process. You, Venezuelans, will not be able to create it in a few days, or in a few months.

If instead of being an old friend, someone to whom you have given the great honor of receiving with affection and trust, if instead of being an old and modest friend—I say it candidly, since I am totally convinced of it—if it were one of the Venezuelan forefathers who was here. I dare say more, if it were that great and talented man who dreamed of Latin American unity who was here, talking to you right now, he would say: "Save this process! Save this opportunity!"

I think you can be happy, and you will be happy, with many of the things you can do. Many are already within reach and depend on subjective factors and on very little resources. Yes, you can find resources, and you can find them in many things to meet priorities, fundamental, essential requirements. But you cannot dream that the Venezuelan society will now have the resources it once had, under very different circumstances. The world is in crisis, prices for raw materials are very low, and the enemy will try to make use of that.

Rest assured that our neighbors to the north are not at all happy with the process that is taking place here in Venezuela, and they do not want it to succeed.

I am not here to sow discord, quite the opposite. I would recommend wisdom and caution, all the necessary caution, but no more than necessary. But you have to be skilled politicians. You will even need to be skilled diplomats. You should avoid frightening many people. Based on my own experience of many years, not on my own intelligence, I suggest that you subtract as few people as possible.

A transformation, a change, a revolution in the sense that word has today — when you look farther than the piece of land where you were born, when you think of the world, when you think of humankind — requires the participation of the people. Better to add than subtract. Look how that lieutenant who commanded the platoon that took me prisoner was added to our cause, not subtracted from it. I took that man the way he was, and I have met some others like him throughout my life. I would probably say I have met many like him.

It is true that the social environment, the social situation, is the main factor in forging the human consciousness. After all, I was the son of a landowner who had quite extensive land in a country the size of Cuba, though perhaps it would not be considered so extensive in Venezuela. My father had about 1,000 hectares of land of his own and 10,000 hectares of leased land that he exploited. He was born in Spain and as a poor, young peasant was enlisted to fight against the Cubans...

He was a conscript. He was brought here as they brought hundreds of thousands of other people. When the war ended, he was repatriated to Spain and he came back to Cuba a little later to work as a farmhand.

Later, he became a landowner. I was born and I lived on a large estate; it did not do me any harm. I had my first friends there, the poor children of the place, the children of waged workers and modest peasants, all victims of the capitalist system. Later I went to schools that were more for the elite, but I came out unscathed, luckily. I really mean luckily. I had the fortune of being the son, and not the grandson, of a landowner. If I had been the grandson of a landowner I would have probably been born and brought up in the city among rich children, in a very high-class neighborhood, and I would have never developed my utopian or Marxist, communist ideas or anything similar.

No one is born a revolutionary or a poet or a warrior. It is the circumstances that make an individual or give them the opportunity of being one thing or the other.

If Columbus had been born a century before, no one would have heard of him. Spain was still under Arab occupation. If he had not been wrong and there had really been a route directly to China by sea without a continent in between, he would have lasted 15 minutes on the coast of China. Remember that the Spaniards conquered Cuba with just 12 horses and in those days the

Mongols already had cavalries with hundreds of thousands of soldiers. See how things come to be!

I will not comment on Bolívar, because he was born where he should have been born, the right day and in the way he should—that's it! I leave aside the scenario of what would have happened if he had been born 100 years before or 100 years later, because that was impossible...

Now I will really finish. Some businesspeople are waiting for me. Will I change my discourse for them? Well, I will tell them the same thing: honesty above all else. I believe that in this country there is a place for every honest person, for every feeling person, for every person who can hear the message of the homeland and of the times. I would say, the message of humanity is the one to be conveyed to your fellow countrymen and women.

18. RESPONSE TO THE US DECLARATION OF THE "WAR AGAINST TERRORISM"

HAVANA, SEPTEMBER 22, 2001

While expressing his condemnation of the September 11 terrorist attacks on Washington and New York and his sympathy for the victims, Fidel Castro attacked the belligerent response of the US president.

No one can deny that terrorism constitutes today a dangerous and ethically indefensible phenomenon that should be eradicated, in the face of its deep origins and the economic and political factors that brought it and those responsible for it into being.

The human and psychological damage brought on the people of the United States, the unexpected and shocking deaths of thousands of innocent people—whose images have shaken the world—have caused understandable and unanimous anger. But who has profited? The extreme right, the most backward and right-wing forces, those in favor of crushing a growing world rebellion and sweeping away everything progressive that still remains on the planet. Whoever organized or is responsible for such acts committed an enormous error, a huge injustice and a great crime. But this tragedy should not be used to recklessly begin a war that in reality could unleash endless carnage on people who are also innocent—in the name of justice and under the singular and bizarre title of "Infinite Justice" [later renamed "Operation Enduring Freedom"].

In the last few days we have witnessed the hasty establishment of the premise, the conception, the true purpose, the spirit and the conditions for such a war. No one could say that this was not something thought out well in advance, just waiting for its chance to materialize. After the so-called end of the Cold War, those who continued a military build-up and the development of the most sophisticated means to exterminate human beings were aware that their large military investments would privilege them to impose absolute and complete dominance over other peoples of the world. The ideologues of the imperialist system knew very well what they were doing and why they were doing it.

Now, after the shock and sincere pain felt by all peoples on earth at this atrocious and insane terrorist attack that targeted the US people, the most extreme ideologues and the most belligerent hawks — already in privileged positions of power — have taken command of the world's most powerful country, whose military and technological capabilities seem infinite. Its capacity to destroy and kill is enormous, while its inclination toward equanimity, serenity, thoughtfulness and restraint is minimal. A combination of elements — not discounting complicity by other rich and powerful countries who enjoy similar privileges — prevailing opportunism, confusion and panic, make it almost impossible to avoid a bloody and unpredictable outcome.

The first victims of whatever military actions are undertaken will be the billions of people living in the poor and underdeveloped world. They already suffer unbelievable economic and social problems: unpayable debts and the ruinous prices of their basic commodities; growing natural and ecological catastrophes; hunger and misery; widespread undernourishment of their children, teenagers and adults; terrible AIDS epidemics; malaria; tuberculosis and infectious diseases that threaten whole nations with extermination.

The grave world economic crisis was already a real and irrefutable fact affecting absolutely every one of the big centers of economic power. That crisis will, under these new circumstances, inevitably grow deeper and when it becomes unbearable for the overwhelming majority of people that crisis will bring chaos, rebellion and ungovernability.

The price would also be unpayable for rich countries. For years to come it might be impossible to argue strongly about the environment and ecology, about ideas or the results of research, or about projects for the protection of nature, because that space and opportunity would be taken for military actions, war and crimes as infinite as "Infinite Justice," that is, the name pretending to describe the war operation about to be unleashed.

Can there be any hope left, after listening, hardly 36 hours ago, to the speech made by the president before the US Congress? I will avoid using adjectives, qualifiers or offensive words toward the author of that speech. They would be absolutely unnecessary and untimely, when the tensions and seriousness of the moment advise thoughtfulness and equanimity. I will limit myself to underlining some short phrases that say it all:

> We will use every necessary weapon of war.

> Americans should not expect one battle, but a lengthy campaign unlike any other we have ever seen.

> Every nation in every region now has a decision to make. Either you are with us or you are with the terrorists.

> I've put the armed forces on alert and there is a reason: The hour is coming when America will act and you will make us proud.

> This is the world's fight, this is civilization's fight.

> I ask for your patience... in what will be a long struggle.

> The great achievements of our time and the great hopes of all time, now depend on us.

> The course of this conflict is not known, yet its outcome is certain... And we know that God is not neutral.

I ask every one of Cuba's citizens to meditate deeply and calmly on the ideas contained in several of the above-mentioned phrases.

"Either you are with us or you are with the terrorists." No nation of the world has been excluded from the dilemma, not even the big and powerful states; none has escaped the threat of war or attack.

"We will use every necessary weapon." No procedure has been excluded, regardless of its ethical value, no threat—however fatal—nuclear, chemical, biological or other.

It will not be a single combat but "a lengthy campaign unlike any other we have ever seen."

"This is the world's fight; this is civilization's fight."

"The great achievements of our time and the great hopes of all time, now depend on us."

Finally, a confession never before heard in a political speech made on the eve of war, and in times of apocalyptic risks: "The course of this conflict is not known; yet its outcome is certain. And we know that God is not neutral." This is an astonishing assertion. Thinking about the real or imagined parties involved in the bizarre "holy war" that is about to begin, I find it impossible to determine where the fanaticism is stronger.

On Thursday, before the US Congress, the idea of a world military dictatorship was put forward that would have the exclusive rule of force, irrespective of international laws or institutions. The United Nations, absolutely ignored in the present crisis, would fail to have any authority or prerogative whatsoever. There would be only one boss, only one judge, only one law.

All of us have been ordered to ally either with the US government, or with terrorism. Cuba, with the moral right that comes from being the country that has suffered the most and the longest from terrorist actions, the country whose people are not afraid of anything, because there is no threat or power in the world that can intimidate them, proclaims that it is opposed to terrorism, and opposed to war.

Although the possibilities of doing so are now remote, Cuba reaffirms the need to avert a war of unpredictable consequences, whose very authors have admitted to having not the least idea of how events will unfold. Likewise, Cuba reiterates its willingness to cooperate with all countries in the total eradication of terrorism.

An objective and cool-headed friend should advise the US government against throwing young US soldiers into an uncertain war in remote, isolated and inaccessible places, almost as if they were fighting against ghosts, not knowing where those ghosts are or even if they exist, or whether the people they kill are in fact responsible for the deaths of their innocent fellow citizens killed in the United States.

Cuba will never declare itself an enemy of the people of the United States. Those people are today being subjected to an unprecedented [propaganda] campaign designed to sow hatred and a spirit of vengeance, so much so that even music that is meant to inspire peace has been banned. Instead, Cuba will make that music its own. Our children will sing songs for peace as long as the bloody war that has been announced continues.

Whatever happens, the territory of Cuba will never be used for terrorist actions against the US people and we will do everything within our reach to prevent such actions against the US people. Today we express our solidarity, and also urge peace and calmness. One day, they will admit we were right to do so.

If we are attacked, we will defend our independence, our principles and our social achievements with honor, to the last drop of blood! It will not be easy for them to fabricate pretexts against us. Now, when they are talking about a war that would employ "all the necessary weapons," we would do well to recall that such an experience would not be a new one. Almost four decades ago, hundreds of strategic and tactical nuclear weapons were aimed at Cuba, yet not one of our compatriots lost any sleep.

We are the children of those heroic people, and our patriotic and revolutionary consciousness is more elevated than ever. It is the time for serenity and courage.

The world will become aware of this and will raise its voice in the face of the terrible, dangerous drama that we are about to suffer.

For Cubans, this is the precise moment to proclaim more proudly and more resolutely than ever:

Patria o muerte! [Homeland or death!]
Socialismo o muerte! [Socialism or death!]
Venceremos! [We will win!]

19. ASSESSING HALF A CENTURY OF THE CUBAN REVOLUTION

REVOLUTION PLAZA, HAVANA
MAY 1, 2003

At the May Day rally in Havana in 2003, Fidel Castro summed up the achievements of 44 years of the Cuban revolution.

Distinguished guests;
Dear fellow Cubans:

Our heroic people have struggled for 44 years from this small Caribbean island just a few miles away from the most formidable imperial power ever known by humankind. In so doing, they have written an unprecedented chapter in history. Never has the world witnessed such an unequal fight.

Some may have believed that the rise of the empire to the status of the sole superpower, with a military and technological might with no counter-balance anywhere in the world, would frighten or dishearten the Cuban people. Yet, today they have no choice but to watch in amazement the en-hanced courage of this valiant people. On a day like today, this glorious international workers' day, which commemorates the death of the five [Haymarket] martyrs in Chicago [in 1887], I declare, on behalf of the one million Cubans gathered here, that we will face any threats, we will not yield to any pressures, and that we are prepared to defend our homeland and our revolution with ideas and with weapons to our last drop of blood.

What is Cuba's sin? What honest person has any reason to attack her?

With their own blood and the weapons seized from the enemy, the Cuban people overthrew a cruel dictatorship with 80,000 men under arms, imposed by the US government.

Cuba was the first territory free from imperialist domination in Latin America and the Caribbean, and the only country in the hemisphere, throughout post-colonial history, where the torturers, murderers and war criminals that took the lives of tens of thousands of people were punished.

All of the nation's land was recovered and turned over to the peasants and agricultural workers. The natural resources, industries and basic services were placed in the hands of their only true owner: the Cuban nation.

In less than 72 hours, fighting ceaselessly, day and night, Cuba crushed the Bay of Pigs mercenary invasion organized by a US administration, thereby preventing a direct military intervention in this country and a war of incalculable consequences. The revolution already had the Rebel Army, over 400,000 weapons and hundreds of thousands of militia members.

In 1962, Cuba confronted with honor, and without a single concession, the risk of being attacked with dozens of nuclear weapons.

It defeated the dirty war that spread throughout the entire country, at a cost in human lives even greater than that of the war of liberation.

It stoically endured thousands of acts of sabotage and terrorist attacks organized by the US government.

It thwarted hundreds of assassination plots against the leaders of the revolution.

While under a rigorous blockade and economic warfare that have lasted for almost half a century, Cuba was able to eradicate in just one year the illiteracy that has still not been overcome in the course of more than four decades by the rest of Latin America, or the United States itself.

It has brought free education to 100 percent of the country's children.

It has the highest school retention rate — over 99 percent between kindergarten and ninth grade — of all the nations in the hemisphere.

Its elementary school students rank first worldwide in the knowledge of their mother language and mathematics.

The country also ranks first worldwide with the highest number of teachers per capita and the lowest number of students per classroom.

All children with physical or mental challenges are enrolled in special schools.

Computer education and the use of audiovisual methods now extend to all of the country's children, adolescents and youth, in both the cities and the countryside.

For the first time in the world, all young people between the ages of 17 and 30, who were previously neither in school nor employed, have been given the opportunity to resume their studies while receiving an allowance.

All citizens have the possibility of undertaking studies that will take them from kindergarten to a doctoral degree without spending a penny.

Today, the country has 30 university graduates, intellectuals and professional artists for every one there was before the revolution.

The average Cuban citizen today has at the very least a ninth-grade level of education.

Not even functional illiteracy exists in Cuba.

There are schools for the training of artists and art instructors throughout all our provinces, where over 20,000 young people are currently studying and developing their talent and vocation. Tens of thousands more are doing the same at vocational schools, and many of these then go on to undertake professional studies.

University campuses are progressively spreading to all municipalities. Never in any other part of the world has such a colossal educational and cultural revolution taken place as this that will turn Cuba into the country with the highest degree of knowledge and culture in the world, faithful to Martí's profound conviction that "no freedom is possible without culture."

Infant mortality has been reduced from 60 per 1,000 live births to a rate that fluctuates between six and 6.5, which is the lowest in the hemisphere, from the United States to Patagonia.

Life expectancy has increased by 15 years.

Infectious and contagious diseases like polio, malaria, neonatal tetanus, diphtheria, measles, rubella, mumps, whooping cough and dengue fever have been eradicated; and others like tetanus, meningococcal meningitis, hepatitis B, leprosy, hemophilus meningitis and tuberculosis are fully controlled.

Today, in our country, people die of the same causes as in the most highly developed countries: cardiovascular diseases, cancer and accidents, but with a much lower incidence.

A profound revolution is underway to bring medical services closer to the population, in order to facilitate access to health care centers, to save lives and alleviate suffering.

In-depth research is being carried out to break the chain, mitigate or reduce to a minimum the problems that result from genetic, prenatal or childbirth-related causes.

Cuba is today the country with the highest number of doctors per capita in the world, with almost twice as many as those that follow.

Our scientific centers are working relentlessly to find preventive or therapeutic solutions for the most serious diseases.

Cubans will have the best health care system in the world, and will continue to receive all services absolutely free of charge.

Social security covers 100 percent of the country's citizens.

In Cuba, 85 percent of the people own their homes and they pay no property taxes on them whatsoever. The remaining 15 percent pay a wholly symbolic rent, which is only 10 percent of their salary.

Illegal drug use involves a negligible percentage of the population, and is being resolutely combated.

Lotteries and other forms of gambling have been banned since the first years of the revolution to ensure that no one pins their hopes of progress on luck.

There is no commercial advertising on Cuban television and radio or in our printed publications. Instead, these feature public service announcements concerning health, education, culture, physical education, sports, recreation, environmental protection, and the fight against drugs, accidents and other social problems. Our media educate, they do not poison or alienate. They do not worship or exalt the values of decadent consumer societies.

Discrimination against women was eradicated, and today women make up 64 percent of the country's technical and scientific workforce.

From the earliest months of the revolution, not a single one of the forms of racial discrimination copied from the southern states of the United States was left intact. In recent years, the revolution has been particularly striving to eliminate any lingering traces of the poverty and lack of access to education that afflicted the descendants of those who were enslaved for centuries, creating objective differences that tended to be perpetuated. Soon, not even a shadow of the consequences of that terrible injustice will remain.

There is no cult of personality around any living revolutionary, in the form of statues, official photographs, or the names of streets or institutions. The leaders of this country are human beings, not gods.

In our country there are no paramilitary forces or death squads, and violence has never been used against the people. There are no executions without due process and no torture. The people have always massively supported the activities of the revolution. This rally today is proof of that.

Light years separate our society from what has prevailed until today in the rest of the world. We cultivate fraternity and solidarity among individuals and peoples both in our own country and abroad.

New generations and the entire people are being educated about the need to protect the environment. The media are used to build environmental awareness.

Our country steadfastly defends its cultural identity, assimilating the best of other cultures while resolutely combating everything that distorts, alienates and degrades.

The development of wholesome, non-professional sports has raised our people to the highest ranks worldwide in medals and honors.

Scientific research, at the service of our people and all humanity, has increased several-hundredfold. As a result of these efforts, important medications are saving lives in Cuba and other countries.

Cuba has never undertaken research or development of a single biological weapon, because this would be in total contradiction with the principles and philosophy underlying the education of our scientific personnel, past and present.

In no other people has the spirit of international solidarity become so deeply rooted.

Our country supported the Algerian patriots in their struggle against French colonialism, at the cost of damaging political and economic relations with such an important European country as France.

We sent weapons and troops to defend Algeria from Moroccan expansionism, when the king of that country sought to take control of the iron mines of Gara Djebilet, near the city of Tindouf, in southwest Algeria.

At the request of the Arab nation of Syria, a full tank brigade stood guard between 1973 and 1975 next to the Golan Heights, when this territory was unjustly seized by Israel.

Patrice Lumumba, the leader of the Republic of Congo when it first achieved independence, who was harassed from abroad, received our political support. When he was assassinated by the colonial powers in January of 1961, we lent assistance to his followers.

Four years later, in 1965, Cuban blood was shed in the western region of Lake Tanganyika, where Che Guevara and more than 100 Cuban instructors supported the Congolese rebels who were fighting against white mercenaries in the service of the man supported by the West: [Joseph] Mobutu [Sese Seko], who stole $40 billion and no one knows which European banks they are kept in, or who controls this cash.

The blood of Cuban instructors was shed while training and supporting the combatants of the African Party for the Independence of Guinea and Cape Verde, who were fighting under the command of Amilcar Cabral for the liberation of these former Portuguese colonies.

The same was true during the 10 years that Cuba supported Agostinho Neto's MPLA in the struggle for the independence of Angola. After independence was achieved, and over the course of 15 years, hundreds of thousands of Cuban volunteers participated in defending Angola from the attacks of racist South African troops that in complicity with the United States, and using dirty war tactics, planted millions of mines, wiped out entire villages, and murdered more than half a million Angolan men, women and children.

In Cuito Cuanavale and on the Namibian border, to the southwest of Angola, Angolan and Namibian forces together with 40,000 Cuban troops dealt the final blow to the South African troops. This resulted in the immediate liberation of Namibia and speeded up the end of apartheid by perhaps 20 to 25 years. At the time, the South Africans had seven nuclear warheads that Israel had supplied to them or helped them to produce, with the full knowledge and complicity of the US government.

Throughout the course of almost 15 years, Cuba had a place of honor in its solidarity with the heroic people of Vietnam, caught up in a barbaric and brutal war with the United States. That war killed four million Vietnamese, in addition to all those left wounded and mutilated, not to mention the fact that the country was inundated with chemical compounds that continue to cause incalculable damage. The pretext: Vietnam, a poor and underdeveloped country located 20,000 kilometers away, constituted a threat to the national security of the United States.

Cuban blood was shed together with that of citizens of numerous Latin American countries, and together with the Cuban and Latin American blood of Che Guevara, murdered on instructions from US agents in Bolivia, when he was wounded and held prisoner after his weapon had been rendered useless by a shot received in battle.

The blood of Cuban construction workers, who were nearing completion of an international airport vital for the economy of a tiny island fully dependent on tourism, was shed fighting in defense of Grenada, invaded by the United States under cynical pretexts.

Cuban blood was shed in Nicaragua, when instructors from our armed forces were training the brave Nicaraguan soldiers confronting the dirty war organized and armed by the United States against the Sandinista revolution.

And there are even more examples.

Over 2,000 heroic Cuban internationalist combatants gave their lives fulfilling the sacred duty of supporting the liberation struggles for the independence of other sister nations. However, there is not one single Cuban property in any of those countries. No other country in our era has exhibited such sincere and selfless solidarity.

Cuba has always preached by example. It has never given in. It has never sold out the cause of another people. It has never made concessions. It has never betrayed its principles. There must be some reason why, just 48 hours ago, it was reelected by acclamation in the United Nations Economic and Social Council to another three years in the Commission on Human Rights, of which it has now been a member for 15 straight years.

More than half a million Cubans have carried out internationalist missions as combatants, as teachers, as technicians or as doctors and health care workers. Tens of thousands of the latter have provided their services and saved millions of lives over the course of more than 40 years. There are currently 3,000 specialists in comprehensive general medicine and other health care personnel working in the most isolated regions of 18 Third World countries. Through preventive and therapeutic methods they save hundreds of thousands of lives every year, and maintain or restore the health of millions of people, without charging a penny for their services.

Without the Cuban doctors offered to the United Nations in the event that the necessary funds are obtained — without which entire nations and even whole regions of sub-Saharan Africa face the risk of perishing—the crucial programs urgently needed to fight AIDS would be impossible to carry out.

The developed capitalist world has created abundant financial capital, but it has not in any way created the human capital that the Third World desperately needs.

Cuba has developed techniques to teach reading and writing by radio, with accompanying texts now available in five languages—Haitian Creole, Portuguese, French, English and Spanish—that are already being used in numerous countries. It is nearing completion of a similar program in Spanish, of exceptionally high quality, to teach literacy by television. These are programs that were developed in Cuba and are genuinely Cuban. We are not interested in patents and exclusive copyrights. We are willing to offer them to all of the countries of the Third World, where most of the world's illiterates are concentrated, without charging a penny. In five years, the 800 million illiterate people in the world could be reduced by 80 percent, at a minimal cost.

After the demise of the Soviet Union and the socialist bloc, no one would have bet a dime on the survival of the Cuban revolution. The United States tightened the blockade. The Torricelli and Helms-Burton laws were adopted, both extraterritorial in nature. We suddenly lost our main markets and sources of imports. The population's average calorie and protein consumption was reduced by almost half. But our country withstood the pressures and even advanced considerably in the social field.

Today, it has largely recovered with regard to nutritional requirements and is rapidly progressing in other fields. Even in these conditions, the work undertaken and the consciousness built throughout the years succeeded in working miracles. Why have we endured? Because the revolution has always had, as it still does and always will to an ever-greater degree, the support of the people, an intelligent people, increasingly united, educated and combative.

Cuba was the first country to extend its solidarity to the people of the United States on September 11, 2001. It was also the first to warn of the neo-fascist nature of the policy that the extreme right in the United States, which fraudulently came to power in November 2000, was planning to impose on the rest of the world. This policy did not emerge as a response to the atrocious terrorist attack perpetrated against the people of the United States by members of a fanatical organization that had served other US administrations in the past. It was coldly and carefully conceived and developed, which explains the country's military build-up and enormous spending on weapons at a time when the Cold War was already over, and long before September 11, 2001. The fateful events of that day served as an ideal pretext for the implementation of such a policy.

On September 20 of that year, President Bush openly expressed this before a Congress shaken by the tragic events of nine days earlier. Using bizarre terminology, he spoke of "infinite justice" as the goal of a war that would apparently be infinite as well.

> We will use every necessary weapon of war.

> Americans should not expect one battle, but a lengthy campaign unlike any other we have ever seen.

> Every nation in every region now has a decision to make. Either you are with us or you are with the terrorists.

> I've put the armed forces on alert and there is a reason: The hour is coming when America will act and you will make us proud.

> This is the world's fight, this is civilization's fight.

> The great achievements of our time and the great hopes of all time, now depend on us.

> The course of this conflict is not known, yet its outcome is certain... and we know that God is not neutral.

Are these the words of a statesman or an unbridled fanatic?

Two days later, on September 22, Cuba denounced this speech as the blueprint for the idea of a global military dictatorship imposed through brute force, with no regard for international law or institutions of any kind.

"The United Nations, simply ignored in the present crisis, would fail to have any authority or prerogative whatsoever. There would be only one boss, only one judge, and only one law."

Several months later, on the 200th anniversary of the West Point Military Academy, at the graduation ceremony for 958 cadets on June 3, 2002, President Bush further elaborated on this line of thinking in a fiery harangue to the young soldiers graduating that day, outlining his fundamentalist, inflexible ideas:

> Our security will require transforming the military you will lead — military that must be ready to strike at a moment's notice in any dark corner of the world. And our security will require all Americans to be forward-looking and resolute, to be ready for preemptive action when necessary to defend our liberty and to defend our lives.
>
> We must uncover terror cells in 60 or more countries...
>
> ...we will send you, our soldiers, wherever you're needed.
>
> We will not leave the safety of America and the peace of the planet at the mercy of a few mad terrorists and tyrants. We will lift this dark threat from our country and from the world.
>
> Some worry that it is somehow undiplomatic or impolite to speak the language of right and wrong. I disagree. ... We are in a conflict between good and evil, and America will call evil by its name. By confronting evil and lawless regimes, we do not create a problem, we reveal a problem. And we will lead the world in opposing it.

In the speech I delivered at a rally held in General Antonio Maceo Plaza in Santiago de Cuba on June 8, 2002, in front of half a million people, I said:

> As you can see, he doesn't mention the United Nations once in his West Point speech. Nor is there a phrase about every people's right to safety and peace, or about the need for a world ruled by principles and norms.
>
> Hardly two-thirds of a century have passed since humanity went through the bitter experience of Nazism. Fear was Hitler's essential ally against his adversaries... Later, his fearful military force [led to] the outbreak of a war that would inflame the whole world. The lack of vision and the cowardice of the statesmen in the strongest European powers of the time opened the way to a great tragedy.
>
> I don't think that a fascist regime can be established in the United

States. Serious mistakes have been made and injustices committed in the framework of its political system—many of them still persist—but the US people still have a number of institutions and traditions, as well as educational, cultural and ethical values that would hardly allow that to happen. But the risk exists in the international arena; the power and prerogatives of that country's president are so extensive, and the economic, technological and military power network in that nation is so pervasive that due to circumstances that fully escape the will of the US people, the world is coming under the rule of Nazi concepts and methods.

The miserable insects that live in 60 or more countries of the world chosen by him and his closest assistants—and in the case of Cuba by his Miami friends—are completely irrelevant. They are the "dark corners of the world" that may become the targets of their unannounced and "preemptive" attacks. Not only is Cuba one of those countries, but it has also been included among those that sponsor terror.

I mentioned the idea of a world dictatorship for the first time exactly one year, three months and 19 days before the [US] attack on Iraq.

In the days prior to the beginning of the war, President Bush repeated once again that the United States would use, if necessary, any means within its arsenal: in other words, nuclear weapons, chemical weapons and biological weapons.

The attack on and occupation of Afghanistan had already taken place.

Today the so-called "dissidents" — actually mercenaries on the payroll of Bush's Hitler-like government—are betraying not only their homeland but humanity as well.

In the face of the sinister plans against our country on the part of the neo-fascist extreme right and its allies in the Miami terrorist mob that ensured its victory through electoral fraud, I wonder how many of those individuals with supposedly leftist and humanitarian stances who have attacked our people over the legal measures we were forced to adopt as a legitimate defense against the aggressive plans of the superpower—located just a few miles off our coast and with a military base on our own territory—have been able to read these words. We wonder how many have recognized, denounced and condemned the policy announced in the speeches by Mr.

Bush that I have quoted, which reveal a sinister Nazi-fascist international policy on the part of the leader of the country with the most powerful military force ever imagined, whose weapons could destroy defenseless humanity 10 times over.

The entire world has been mobilized by the terrifying images of cities destroyed and burned by brutal bombing, images of maimed children and the shattered corpses of innocent people.

Leaving aside the blatantly opportunistic, demagogic and petty political groups we know all too well, I am now going to refer fundamentally to those who were friends of Cuba and respected fighters in the struggle. We would not want those who have, in our opinion, attacked Cuba unjustly, due to disinformation or a lack of careful and profound analysis, to have to suffer the infinite sorrow they will feel if one day our cities are destroyed and our children and mothers, women and men, young and old, are torn apart by the bombs of Nazi-fascism, and they realize that their declarations were shamelessly manipulated by the aggressors to justify a military attack on Cuba.

The numbers of children murdered and mutilated cannot be the only measure of the human damage, but also the millions of children and mothers, women and men, young and old, who remain traumatized for the rest of their lives.

We fully respect the opinions of those who oppose capital punishment for religious, philosophical and humanitarian reasons. We Cuban revolutionaries also abhor capital punishment, for much more profound reasons than those addressed by the social sciences with regard to crime, currently under study in our country. The day will come when we can accede to the wishes, so nobly expressed here in the brilliant speech by our beloved brother Reverend Lucius Walker, to abolish such penalties. The special concern over this issue is easily understood when you know that the majority of the people executed in the United States are African American and Hispanic, and not infrequently they are innocent, especially in Texas, the champion of the death penalty, where President Bush was formerly the governor, and not a single life has ever been pardoned.

The Cuban revolution was placed in the dilemma of either protecting the lives of millions of Cubans by using the legally established death penalty to punish [recently] the three main hijackers of a passenger ferry, or sitting back and doing nothing. The US government, which incites common criminals to assault boats or airplanes with passengers on board, encourages these people gravely endangering the lives of innocents and creating the ideal conditions for an attack on Cuba. A wave of hijackings had been unleashed and was already in full development; it had to be stopped.

We cannot ever hesitate when it is a question of protecting the lives of the sons and daughters of a people determined to fight until the end, in arresting the mercenaries who serve the aggressors and applying the most severe sanctions, no matter how unpleasant it is for us, against terrorists who hijack passenger boats or planes or commit similarly serious acts, who will be punished by the courts in accordance with the laws in force.

Not even Jesus Christ, who drove the traders out of the temple with a whip, would fail to opt for the defense of the people.

I feel sincere and profound respect for His Holiness Pope John Paul II. I understand and admire his noble struggle for life and peace. No one opposed the war in Iraq as much and as tenaciously as he did. I am absolutely certain that he would have never counseled the Shiites and Sunni Muslims to let themselves be killed without defending themselves. He would not counsel the Cubans to do such a thing, either. He knows perfectly well that this is not a problem between Cubans. This is a problem between the people of Cuba and the government of the United States.

The policy of the US government is so brazenly provocative that on April 25, Mr. Kevin Whitaker, chief of the Cuban bureau at the State Department, informed the head of our interests section in Washington that the National Security Council's Department of Homeland Security considered the continued hijackings from Cuba a serious threat to the national security of the United States, and requested that the Cuban government adopt all of the necessary measures to prevent such acts.

He said this as if they were not the ones who provoke and encourage these hijackings, and as if we were not the ones who adopt drastic measures to prevent them, in order to protect the lives and safety of passengers, and being fully aware for some time now of the criminal plans of the fascist extreme right against Cuba. When news of this contact on the 25th was leaked, it stirred up the Miami terrorist mob. They still do not understand that their direct or indirect threats against Cuba do not frighten anyone in this country.

The hypocrisy of Western politicians and a large group of mediocre leaders is so huge that it would not fit in the Atlantic Ocean. Any measure that Cuba adopts for the purposes of its legitimate defense is reported among the top stories in almost every media. On the other hand, when we pointed out that during the term in office of a Spanish head of government, dozens of ETA members were executed without trial, without anyone protesting or denouncing it at the UN Commission on Human Rights, or that another Spanish government leader, at a difficult moment in the war in Kosovo, advised the US president to step up the war, increase the bombing and attack civilian targets, thus causing the deaths of hundreds of innocent people and tremendous suffering for millions of people, the headlines merely stated, "Castro attacks Felipe and Aznar." Not a word was said about the real issue.

In Miami and Washington they are now discussing where, how and when Cuba will be attacked and the problem of the revolution solved.

For the moment, there is talk of economic measures that will further intensify the brutal blockade, but they still do not know which to choose, who they will resign themselves to alienating, and how effective these measures may be. There are very few left for them to choose from. They have already used up almost all of them.

A shameless scoundrel with the poorly chosen first name Lincoln, and the last name Díaz Balart, an intimate friend and advisor of President Bush, has made this enigmatic statement to a Miami TV station: "I can't go into details, but we're trying to break this vicious cycle."

What methods are they considering to deal with this vicious cycle? Physically eliminating me with the sophisticated modern means they have developed, as Mr. Bush promised them in Texas before the elections? Or attacking Cuba the way they attacked Iraq?

If it were the former, it does not worry me in the least. The ideas for which I have fought all my life will not die, and they will live on for a long time.

If the solution were to attack Cuba like Iraq, I would suffer greatly because of the cost in lives and the enormous destruction it would cause Cuba. But, this might turn out to be this administration's last fascist attack, because the struggle would last a very long time.

The aggressors would not merely be facing an army, but rather thousands of armies that would constantly reproduce themselves and make the enemy pay such a high cost in casualties that it would far exceed the cost in lives of its sons and daughters that the US people would be willing to pay for the adventures and ideas of President Bush. Today, he enjoys majority support, but it is dropping, and tomorrow it could be reduced to zero.

The US people, the millions of highly cultivated individuals who reason and think, their basic ethical principles, the tens of millions of computers with which to communicate, hundreds of times more than at the end of the Vietnam war, will show that you cannot fool all of the people, and perhaps not even part of the people, all of the time. One day they will put a straight-jacket on those who need it before those people manage to annihilate life on the planet.

On behalf of the one million people gathered here this May Day, I want to convey a message to the world and the US people:

We do not want the blood of Cubans and Americans to be shed in a war. We do not want a countless number of lives of people who could be friends to be lost in an armed conflict. But never has a people had such sacred things to defend, or such profound convictions to fight for, to such a degree that they would rather be obliterated from the face of the earth than abandon the noble and generous work for which so many generations of Cubans have paid the high cost of the lives of many of their finest sons and daughters.

We are sustained by the deepest conviction that ideas are worth more than weapons, no matter how sophisticated and powerful those weapons may be.

Let us say as Che Guevara did when he bid us farewell:

Hasta la victoria siempre! [Ever onward to victory!]

20. IN ANSWER TO THE EMPIRE: LETTERS TO PRESIDENT GEORGE W. BUSH

The Commission for Assistance to a Free Cuba (CAFC) was appointed by President Bush in October 2003 to recommend ways to hasten the demise of the Cuban revolution. After the CAFC released its report, a mass rally was held in Havana on May 14, 2004. The rally marched past the US interests section, where Fidel Castro read his "Proclamation by an Adversary of the US Government." He addressed President Bush again in a letter on June 21. The CAFC, chaired by Secretary of State Condoleezza Rice, released a second report in July 2006.

PROCLAMATION BY AN ADVERSARY OF THE US GOVERNMENT
HAVANA, MAY 14, 2004

Mr. George W. Bush:

The million Cubans who are gathered here today to march past your interests section are just a small part of a valiant and heroic people who would like to be here with us, if it were physically possible.

We have not gathered in a hostile gesture to the US people, whose ethics, rooted in the time when the first pilgrims emigrated to this hemisphere, are well known to us. Nor do we wish to upset the officials, employees and guards of this office, to whom we offer all the safety and guarantees that a civilized and educated people such as ours can give while they serve their terms. This is an outraged protest and a denunciation of the brutal, ruthless and cruel measures against our country that your country has just adopted.

We know beforehand what you believe or want to make others believe about those who are marching here. In your opinion they are oppressed masses who yearn for liberty and who have been forced on to the streets by the Cuban government.

You completely ignore the fact that no force in the world could drag a dignified, proud people, which has withstood 45 years of hostility, blockade and aggression from the most powerful nation on earth, on to the streets like a flock of animals, each one with rope around their neck.

A statesman, or someone who claims to be one, should know that throughout history truly humane ideas of justice have been shown to be much more powerful than force; force leaves in its wake only contemptible ruins, covered in dust; humane ideas leave a luminous trail that no one will ever be able to extinguish. Every era has had its own ideas, both good and bad ones, and they have accumulated over time. But the worst, most sinister and dubious ideas belong to the era in which we live—a barbarous, uncivilized, globalized world.

In the world that you seek to impose on us today there is not the slightest notion of ethics, credibility, standards of justice, humanitarian feelings or the elementary principles of solidarity and generosity.

Everything that is written about human rights in your world, and in the world of your allies who share in plundering the world, is an enormous lie. Billions of human beings live in subhuman conditions, starving, without enough food, medicine, clothes, shoes or shelter and with only a minimal understanding of their tragic situation and the reality of the world in which they live.

Surely no one has told you about the tens of millions of children, adolescents, youths, mothers, middle-aged or elderly people who die every year but who might have been saved in this "idyllic Eden" that is our earth; they cannot have told you how fast the natural conditions for life are being destroyed, and that the hydrocarbons that took the world 300 million years to create have been squandered in a century and a half, with devastating effects.

You have only to ask your advisors for precise data on the tens of thousands of nuclear, chemical and biological weapons, bombs, smart long-range missiles, battleships and aircraft carriers, and the conventional and non-conventional weapons in your arsenals which are enough to wipe out all life on the planet.

Neither you nor anyone else would ever be able to sleep again. And nor would your allies, who are trying to emulate your military build-up. If your allies' lack of responsibility and political talent, the inequality between their respective states, and their infinitesimal inclination to reflect in the time they have left between protocol and meetings are taken into account, those who have the destiny of the world in their hands can harbor few hopes when, half puzzled, half indifferent, they gaze upon the real madhouse that world politics has become.

The purpose of these words is not to offend or insult you; but since you have set out to intimidate, to terrorize this country and eventually to destroy its socioeconomic system and independence, and if necessary its very physical existence, I consider it my elementary duty to remind you of a few home truths.

You have neither the morality nor the right — none whatsoever — to speak of freedom, democracy and human rights when you have sufficient power to destroy humanity and are attempting to install a world dictatorship, side-stepping and destroying the United Nations, violating the human rights of any and every country, waging wars of conquest to take over world markets and resources, and installing decadent and anachronistic political and social systems that are leading the human race into the abyss.

There are other reasons why you should not mention the word "democracy"; among these is the fact that everyone knows you became president of the United States through fraud. You cannot speak of freedom because you cannot conceive of a world other than one ruled by fear of the lethal weapons which your inexpert hands might rain down on humanity.

You cannot speak of the environment because you are completely ignorant of the fact that the human race is in danger of disappearing.

You label a dictatorship the economic and political system that has guided the Cuban people to higher levels of literacy, knowledge and culture than those in the most developed countries in the world. The same system has reduced infant mortality to a rate lower than that of the United States and provided the population with health care and educational facilities and other extremely important social and human services free of charge.

Listening to you talk of human rights in Cuba has a hollow, absurd ring. This, Mr. Bush, is one of the few countries in this hemisphere where not once in 45 years has there been a single case of torture, a single death squad, a single extrajudicial execution or a single ruler who has become a millionaire through having held power.

You lack the moral authority to speak of Cuba, a dignified country that has withstood 45 years of a brutal blockade, economic war and terrorist attacks which have cost thousands of lives and ten of billions of dollars in economic losses.

You are attacking Cuba for petty, political reasons, trying to obtain electoral support from a shrinking group of renegades and mercenaries who have no ethical principles whatsoever. You lack the moral right to speak of terrorism because you are surrounded by a bunch of murderers who have caused the death of thousands of Cubans through terrorist methods.

You do not hide your contempt for human life, because you have not hesitated to order the extrajudicial death of a secret, unknown number of people in various parts of the world.

You have no right whatsoever, except for that of brute force, to intervene in Cuba's affairs and, whenever the fancy takes you, to proclaim the transition from one system to another and to take measures to make this happen.

This people can be exterminated — you should know this — or wiped off the face of the earth, but it cannot be subjugated or be once again put into the humiliating position of a US neocolony.

Cuba fights on the side of life in the world; you fight on the side of death. Whereas you kill countless people with your indiscriminate, preemptive, surprise attacks, Cuba saves the lives of hundreds of thousands of children, mothers, old and sick people all over the world.

The only thing you know about Cuba are the lies that spill forth from the ravenous mouths of the corrupt and insatiable mob of former Batista supporters and their descendants, who are experts in electoral fraud and capable of electing as president of the United States someone who did not obtain enough votes to claim victory.

Human beings are not aware of — and cannot be aware of — freedom in a regime of inequality like the one you represent. No one is born equal in the United States. In the black and Latino ghettos, and on the reservations for the people who once inhabited that land but were exterminated, there is no equality other than that of being poor and excluded.

Our people, educated in solidarity and internationalism, do not hate the US people, nor do they want to see young white, black, Native American, mestizo or Latino soldiers from that country die, young people driven by unemployment to enlist in the military, to be sent to whatever corner of the world in traitorous, preemptive attacks or in wars of conquest.

The unbelievable torture applied to prisoners in Iraq has rendered the world speechless.

I do not seek to offend you with these words, as I have already said. My only hope is that in your leisure time one of your advisors might bring these truths to your notice, even though they may not be completely welcome.

Since you have decided that the die is cast, I have the pleasure of saying farewell like the Roman gladiators who were about to fight in the arena: Hail Caesar, those who are about to die salute you!

My only regret is that I might not see your face, because in that case you would be thousands of miles away, while I would be in the frontline, ready to die fighting in defense of my homeland.

In the name of the Cuban people,

Fidel Castro Ruz
May 14, 2004

SECOND EPISTLE
HAVANA, JUNE 21, 2004

Mr. Bush:

I must be calm but very sincere. I have absolutely no intention of insulting you or launching personal attacks. But it is cynical to include Cuba in a list of countries involved in the illegal trafficking of persons. And what is even more outrageous and abhorrent in this arrogant report that the State Department feels obliged to issue every year is the claim that Cuba promotes sex tourism, even with children.

You are in a position to be informed that Cuba has signed two immigration agreements with the United States in the interests of family reunification. The US administration failed to honor the first of these, signed in 1984. Ten years later, instead of the 20,000 visas promised, only about 1,000, that is, 5 percent, were issued every year. Following the immigration crisis that broke out in 1994, our country signed a new agreement with the US government, which was expanded the following year and is still in force. In spite of this, and although its provisions have been basically met with regard to the number of visas, they have not been met regarding the fundamental, inescapable obligation to avoid any incitement to illegal emigration.

With no justification whatsoever, the murderous Cuban Adjustment Act is still in place, implacable, and indeed, new incentives [for illegal immigrants] have been added to it. This absurd and immoral act has cost an incalculable number of lives, including the lives of many Cuban children. And it was as a result of this same law that the loathsome traffic in immigrants emerged using speedboats that come from Florida to points anywhere on our coastline. Cuba punishes these acts severely, whereas US administrations, for very well-known political reasons connected with the state of Florida, have just folded their arms.

No country in the world has given as much physical and moral protection, as much health and education to its children, as Cuba has. You should know that a higher proportion of children die in their first year of life in the United States than in Cuba. One hundred percent of children and adolescents in our country, including those afflicted by some kind of physical or mental disability, attend the appropriate schools and are able to study.

How can you claim not to know that while in the United States there are, on average, 30 students to a classroom; in Cuba the ratio is less than 20 and our educational results are better than those in any developed country?

Our health care services have raised the life expectancy of each child from about 60 years in 1959, according to estimates, to 76.13 years today.

In spite of the US blockade and the collapse of the socialist bloc, unemployment in Cuba is only 2.3 percent, which is several times lower than in your own country, the richest and most industrialized in the world.

You should be ashamed of trying to economically asphyxiate the Cuban people, who, blockaded and subjected to more than four decades of economic warfare, armed aggressions and terrorist actions, have achieved such feats. You can show us nothing like this in your own country.

You are trying to strangle our economy and are threatening war against a country that has shown itself capable of having 20,000 doctors currently offering their services in 64 countries of the Third World. Your administration, in spite of possessing the resources of the richest power on earth, has not sent a single doctor to the most distant corners of these countries, as Cuba does.

On your conscience, and on those of the leaders of the world's richest states, lies the genocide which is implicit in the death, every year, of more than 10 million children and tens of millions more people who could be saved. These deaths are the result of the pillaging and robbery practiced against Third World countries through the unjust and unsustainable world economic order that the rich countries have imposed to the detriment of 80 percent of this planet's population.

Someone should inform you of these problems and these facts, instead of constantly spreading intrigue and lies.

As for Cuba, you allow yourself to be driven by the fanatical belief that your reelection in November [2004] depends on the support of a mob of well-known old terrorist émigrés and their descendants, a large section of whom were Batista's embezzlers and war criminals who sought refuge in the United States with their booty on their backs and their crimes unpunished. Others have grown rich through many years of service to acts of terrorism and aggressions that have caused our people much bloodshed. These groups are becoming increasingly discredited and their influence is diminishing. Everyone remembers what happened in Florida, where they committed all kinds of electoral fraud—in which they are real experts—still you carried the state by only 518 votes. I do not wish to humiliate you by digging up this sordid and unpleasant matter. I will rather limit myself to telling you, with all sincerity, that the errors into which your commitment to this mob lead you may decisively backfire in the next elections.

The US people are already fed up with the embarrassing influence that these groups exercise over the foreign and domestic policy of such an important country. Your dependence on these groups will end up losing you a lot of votes, and not only in Florida, but all over the country.

When you forbid Americans to travel to Cuba under the threat of brutal repression, you are violating a constitutional principle and a right of which your country's citizens have always been proud. Moreover, it shows political fear.

While Cuba, with no hesitation or fear (with very few exceptions), has opened its doors to masses of [Cuban] immigrants so they can visit their country of origin, and, recently, has authorized them to do so as many times as they wish through the simple procedure of renewing their passports every two years, you are implementing ruthless and inhumane measures against Cuban families that deeply offend their ancestral culture and traditions. It is indescribably cruel to forbid resident Cubans, naturalized or not, to visit their closest relatives for a period of no less than three years, even if these relatives are at death's door. Quite a few Cuban Americans are already thinking of campaigning for a protest vote.

For purely electoral reasons, and ignoring resolutions passed by almost all members of the United Nations, you have just adopted new, harsher economic measures against the Cuban people that world public opinion and the immense majority of the US public find appalling.

The worst thing about your ridiculous, clumsy anti-Cuba policy is that you and your closest advisors have brazenly proclaimed your goal of forcibly imposing what you call a "political transition" on Cuba if I die in office, a transition which you do not, of course, hesitate to admit that you will try to hasten. You are very well aware of what that means in the language of the mob.

However, perhaps the most shameful thing you did was to announce that the first hours will be decisive, since the idea is to go to any lengths, under any circumstances, to prevent a new political and administrative leadership from taking charge of our country. You would do this completely ignoring the Cuban constitution, the powers of the National Assembly and of our party's leadership, and the powers that the constitution and the highest institutions of the people have bestowed — as is the case all over the world — on those whose responsibility it is to assume this task immediately.

Since you can only do this by sending troops to occupy key positions in the country, you are, in fact, announcing your intention to launch a military intervention in our homeland. This is why, on May 14, I "hailed" you in advance for the role of Caesar you are playing, as did the gladiators who were forced to fight to the death in the ancient Roman circus.

Today, I think it is only right to add a few more things.

You should know that your march on Cuba will be anything but easy. Our people will stand up to your economic measures, whatever they may be. Forty-five years of heroic struggle against the blockade and economic war, against threats, aggressions, plots to assassinate its leaders, sabotage and terrorism have not weakened but rather strengthened the revolution.

Forty-three years ago the treacherous invasion at the Bay of Pigs was routed in less than 66 hours of relentless combat, against the predictions of brilliant experts.

Some of us who are leading this revolution went through the singular experience where a handful of combatants, who at first had only seven rifles, managed, using weapons taken from the enemy in battle, to defeat Batista's armed forces, which were equipped, trained and advised by the United States and which numbered 85,000 troops.

In October 1962, a year and a half after the Bay of Pigs, not a single Cuban fighter batted an eyelid at the thought of the very real threat of a nuclear strike. Not a single inspection of our country was allowed, in spite of the agreement between the two superpowers.

Dozens of years of dirty war, sabotage and terrorism, in which many of your current friends from Miami played such a notable role, could not bring Cuba to her knees.

The collapse of the European socialist bloc and of the Soviet Union itself, which deprived us of markets, fuel, food and raw materials, compounded by a blockade made harsher by the Torricelli and Helms-Burton laws and other measures, did not break the Cuban people, and what seemed impossible came to pass: We stood firm! This is something that is now in the blood and tradition of patriotic Cubans, who in the last war against Spanish colonialism, clashed with, wore down and virtually defeated 300,000 Spanish soldiers; this is the spirit of fighting against impossible odds and winning.

It is not my intention, Mr. President of the United States, to torment you or upset you with these memories. It is simply my desire to give you an idea of what Cuba is all about, of what a genuine and deep revolutionary process signifies and of what the people you look down on condescendingly are really like.

Today, Cuba has the most cultured and politically aware population of all the countries in the world. Our people are not fanatics, our people defend ideas. This is not a country of illiterate or semi-illiterate people; it is a country where higher education is being made accessible to the whole population and where courage and patriotism are becoming common traits. Experience and knowledge go hand in hand with dreams of a society where justice and humanism can prevail, something that yourself, with your fundamentalism and messianic ways, will find very hard to understand.

Today, we are not just a handful of men and women determined to win or die. We are millions of women and men with enough weapons and over 200,000 well-trained officers and leaders who know perfectly well how to use them under conditions of modern, sophisticated warfare. We have a huge mass of combatants who are similarly well aware of the strengths and weaknesses of those who are threatening us, despite their enormous military resources and the technological superiority of their weapons.

Under the present circumstances in Cuba, and in case of an invasion of our country if I cease to exist — either from natural or other causes — this will not in any way inflict the least damage on our capacity to fight and stand firm. Every political and military chief at every level, and every individual soldier, is a potential commander-in-chief who knows what they must do, and in a given situation each person can become their own commander-in-chief.

You will not have even one day, one hour, one minute or one second to prevent the political and military leadership of the country from taking charge immediately, for the orders on what should be done have already been given. Every man and woman will be at his or her combat station without wasting a second.

On May 14, in front of one million Cubans who marched past your interests section, I told you very clearly what I had to do and would do. That is my job. Today, I reiterate it and I suggest that you and your advisors do not concoct any vicious plan for vengeance against our people. Do not try crazy adventures such as surgical strikes or wars of attrition using sophisticated techniques, because you could lose control of the situation. Undesirable things could happen that are not good for the Cuban people or for the US people. You might shatter the immigration agreement and provoke a mass exodus that we would not be in a position to prevent and you might unleash an all-out war between young US soldiers and the Cuban people. That would be very sad.

Yet, I assure you that you would never win that war. You will not find here a divided people, conflicting ethnic groups or profound religious differences, nor will there be traitorous generals commanding our troops. You will find a people solidly united by culture, feelings of solidarity and social and human achievements that are unprecedented in history. You will not win glory with military action against Cuba.

Our people will never give up their independence, nor will they ever give up their political, social and economic ideals.

Cuba showed full solidarity with the US people after the painful and unjustifiable attack on the Twin Towers. That same day we expressed our point of view, which today is being confirmed with almost mathematical precision. War is not the way to put an end to terrorism and violence in the world. That tragic event has been used as a pretext to impose on the planet a policy of terror and force.

Your measures against the Cuban people are atrocious and inhumane. Cuba can prove that you want to destroy a country whose medical services have saved and continue to save hundreds of thousands of lives in poor countries around the world, a country that could even save as many lives of poor US citizens as the 3,000 who died in the Twin Towers.

You surely know that 44 million people in the United States lack medical insurance and that at some point in a two-year period, 82 million Americans had no insurance and could not afford the astronomical costs of essential health-care services in your country. A very conservative estimate indicates that many tens of thousands of lives are lost every year in the United States because of this, perhaps 30 or 40 times the number that died in the Twin Towers. Someone should calculate this exactly.

In a brief five-year period, Cuba is prepared to save the lives of 3,000 poor Americans. It is perfectly possible today to forecast and prevent a heart attack that could be fatal, and to alleviate illnesses that lead inevitably to death. These 3,000 Americans could come to our country accompanied by a relative and receive medical treatment absolutely free of charge.

I want to ask you a question, Mr. Bush, about ethics and principles: Would you be willing to give those people permission to come to Cuba on a program designed to save a life for every life lost in that horrendous attack on the Twin Towers?

And, if they accepted the offer of those services and decided to come, would they be punished?

Show the world that there is an alternative to arrogance, war, genocide, hatred, egoism, hypocrisy and lies!

On behalf of the Cuban people,

Fidel Castro Ruz
June 21, 2004

EPILOGUE: FIDEL CASTRO ON THE CUBAN REVOLUTION AFTER FIDEL

On November 17, 2005, Fidel Castro gave a lengthy address to students and professors in the Aula Magna of the University of Havana. In this speech, Fidel Castro remarked on the bitter experience of the loss of the "first socialist state," the Soviet Union, and the spread of corruption, inefficiency and inequality in Cuba. He stated that the primary threat to the revolution today came from within and not from outside Cuba. He then put the following provocative questions to his audience:

Is it that revolutions are doomed to fall apart, or do human beings cause revolutions to fall apart? Can individuals or society prevent revolutions from collapsing? I could immediately add another question: Do you believe that this revolutionary socialist process can fall apart, or not? Have you ever given this any thought or deeply reflected about it?

Were you aware of all these inequalities [in Cuba] that I have been talking about? Were you aware of certain generalized habits? Did you know there are people who earn 40 or 50 times the monthly salary of one of the doctors over there in the mountains of Guatemala, who are part of the "Henry Reeve" Contingent? Or in far-off Africa, or in the Himalayas at an altitude of thousands of meters, saving lives and earning 5 or 10 percent of what one of those dirty little crooks earns selling gasoline to the nouveau riche, diverting resources from our ports in trucks by the ton-load, stealing in the dollar shops, stealing in a five-star hotel by exchanging a bottle of rum for another of lesser quality and pocketing the dollars for which that person sells the drinks.

Just how many ways of stealing do we have in this country?...

I asked you a question, compañero students. I ask this in light of historical experience and I ask you all, without exception, to reflect on it: Can the [Cuban] revolutionary process be reversed, or not? What are the ideas or what level of consciousness would make the reversal of the revolutionary process impossible? When those who were the forerunners, the veterans, start disappearing and making room for new generations of leaders, what will happen and what will be accomplished? After all, we have witnessed many errors, and we didn't recognize them.

A leader has tremendous power when he enjoys the confidence of the masses, who have complete trust in his abilities. The consequences of errors committed by those in authority are terrible, and this has happened more than once during revolutionary processes.

Such is the stuff for meditation. One studies history, one meditates on what happened here or there, on what is happening today and on what will happen tomorrow, on where each country's process might lead, what path our own process will take, how it will get there, and what role Cuba will play...

Our country has endured limitations in resources, many limitations; but this country has also wasted resources thoughtlessly... Some thought that socialism could be constructed with capitalist methods. That is one of the great historical errors.

I don't wish to discuss this, I don't want to theorize. But I can give any number of examples of many things that couldn't be resolved by those who called themselves theoreticians, who immersed themselves from head to toe in the books of Marx, Engels, Lenin and many others.

That was why I commented that one of our greatest mistakes at the beginning of, and often during, the revolution was our belief that someone else knew how to build socialism.

In my opinion, today, we have relatively clear ideas about how one goes about building socialism, but we need to be extremely clear and you will need to find answers to many questions because you will be the ones responsible for the preservation of socialism in the future.

How can we not be aware of this, so that our heroic island, this heroic people, this nation, which has written pages in the history books like no other nation in the history of humankind, might preserve the revolution? Please, do not think I am speaking as a vain man or a charlatan, or someone inclined to bluff.

Forty-six years have passed and the history of this country is well known, and the people of this nation know this history well. They also know our neighbor very well, the empire's size and power—its strength and its wealth, its technology and its control over the World Bank, the IMF and the entire world of finance. That country has imposed on us the most incredible, iron-clad blockade, which was discussed at the United Nations where 182 nations supported Cuba, despite the risk entailed in voting against the empire.

The island has survived, not just during the days when the European socialist countries stood together with us, but after the socialist camp had disappeared and the Soviet Union had fallen apart. We forged this revolution alone, against all risks, for many long years. We realized that if the day ever came when we would be directly attacked by the United States, no one would ever fight for us and we would never ask anyone to do so...

The empire might have tanks to spare, but we have just what we need, not one to spare! All their technology will collapse like ice-cubes in the noon-day sun in summer. Once we possessed only seven guns and a handful of bullets. Today, we possess much more than those seven guns. We have a people who have learned how to handle weapons; we have an entire nation, which, in spite of our errors, has such a high degree of culture, education and consciousness that it will never allow this country to become a colony again.

This country can self-destruct; this revolution can destroy itself, but they can never destroy us. We can destroy ourselves, and that would be our fault...

Let there never be a Soviet situation here, or a broken, dispersed socialist bloc! The empire will not come here to set up secret jails in which to torture the progressive men and women from other parts of this continent who are rising up today to engage in their second and final fight for independence!

Before we go back to such a repugnant and miserable existence there had better not be any memory — not even the slightest trace — of us or our descendants.

I said we are more and more revolutionary and I said this for a reason. Now, we understand the empire much better, and we are increasingly aware of what they are capable of...

We have to be resolute: we must defeat these deviations and strengthen the revolution by destroying any of the illusions that the empire may have. That is to say: either we radically defeat these problems or we die. We must repeat the motto: *Patria o muerte!*...

There must be an end to stupidity in the world, the abuses and the empire based on might and terror. It will disappear when all fear disappears. Every day there are more fearless countries. Every day there will be more countries that will rebel and the empire will not be able to keep its infamous system alive any longer.

Salvador Allende once spoke of things that would happen sooner or later. I believe that sooner rather than later the empire will disintegrate and the US people will enjoy more freedom than ever; they will be able to aspire to more justice than ever before; they will be able to use science and technology for their own benefit and for the betterment of humanity; they will be able to join all of us who fight for the survival of the species; they will be able to join all of us who fight for the human species.

It is only just to struggle for that cause, and that is why we must use all our energy, all our effort and all our time to be able to say with the voice of millions, or hundreds of thousands of millions of people: It is worthwhile to have been born! It is worthwhile to have lived!

* * *

Facing major intestinal surgery, on July 31, 2006, Fidel Castro temporarily handed over all his responsibilities as Cuba's head of state and leader of the Cuban Communist Party to his brother Raúl Castro, minister for defense and first vice-president of the Council of State. He sent the following message to the Cuban people from hospital, published in *Granma* on August 1:

I very much appreciate all the messages sent by our compatriots and by many people throughout the world. I feel sorry for having caused so much concern and bother to our friends around the world.

I cannot make up good news, because that would be unethical; and if there were bad news, this would only be of benefit to the enemy. Given the specific situation Cuba faces and the plans designed by the empire, the information about my health condition becomes a state secret that cannot be continuously disseminated; and my compatriots should understand this. I cannot let myself be trapped by the vicious circle of the health parameters that are constantly changing during the day.

I can say that my condition is stable, but only with time will I be able to speak about the true state of my health.

The best I can say is that my condition will remain stable for many days to come before I can give a verdict.

I feel in very good spirits.

The important thing is that everything in our country is proceeding and will continue to proceed very smoothly.

The Revolutionary Armed Forces and the people are ready to defend the country.

Our compatriots will have complete information in due course, as was the case when I had a fall in Villa Clara.

We must struggle and work.

* * *

Although not resuming any official governmental duties, from March 2007, Fidel Castro began to write regular columns for the Cuban newspaper, *Granma*. On June 23, 2007, in response to a message from the Union of Young Communists, he wrote:

…What is a life bereft of ideas worth? Martí once said that "trenches of ideas are more valuable than trenches of stones." Are ideas born of human beings? Do they perish with an individual? Ideas have come into being throughout the history of the human species. They will exist as long as our species does. Never before have we faced such a serious threat, due to the combination of society's political underdevelopment and the fruits of technology. While the possibilities of technology appear limitless, our capacity for self-destruction is beyond all reason. Genocidal wars, climate change, hunger, thirst and inequality are everywhere we look.

Human beings need to cling to hope and seek a means of survival in science itself. This is only natural. There should be no room, in that brighter future, for the horrible injustices bred by today's developed capitalist system run by a worldwide dictatorship.

Shakespeare wrote in one of his plays, "To be or not to be." That is the alternative young people now face. To ignore this would be to choose to live in the most idyllic of worlds, but for only a couple of decades, which represent less than a few seconds in the history of time…

If young people fail, everything will fail. It is my deepest conviction that young Cubans will struggle to prevent this. I have faith in you.

* * *

A year after temporarily relinquishing his positions, on July 31, 2007, Fidel Castro published a "reflection" titled "The Eternal Flame":

This is a political reflection. To be more precise, it is another proclamation. Exactly one year ago today, on July 31, 2006, I issued the first proclamation. But the year gone by is worth 10, for I have had the opportunity to live a unique experience which has afforded me information and knowledge on vital questions facing humanity, knowledge I have conveyed to the people of Cuba with the utmost honesty.

Today, I am bombarded with questions as to when I will take up again what some call "power," as though that power were possible without independence. The world knows a real and destructive power, wielded by a decadent empire that threatens everyone.

Raúl has already explained that as I recover I am consulted about every important decision. What will I do now? I will fight tirelessly as I have done my entire life.

One year after the first proclamation, I can share with the people of Cuba the satisfaction of seeing that what was then promised is reflected by today's undeniable reality: Raúl, the party, the government, the National Assembly, the Union of Young Communists and grassroots and social organizations, headed by the workers, move forward, guided by the unshakable principle of unity.

With the same conviction, we continue to struggle relentlessly to have the five heroes, who provided Cuba with information on the anti-Cuba terrorist plans of the United States, released from their cruel and merciless imprisonment.

The struggle against our own deficiencies and against the insolent enemy that seeks to take possession of Cuba must be unrelenting.

On this point, I am obliged to insist on something that the leaders of the revolution can never forget: It is our duty to work untiringly to strengthen our defensive capability and preparedness, under the principle that, regardless of the circumstances, an unpayable price must be paid for any invasion.

No one should entertain the slightest illusion that the empire, which carries within it the genes of its own destruction, will negotiate with Cuba.

Though we have said, again and again, that our struggle is not against the people of the United States—and this is absolutely true—those people are not in a position to curtail the apocalyptic impulses of their government or the foul, insane call for what they label a "democratic Cuba," as though leaders here in Cuba nominate and elect themselves without the support of the overwhelming majority, which is the inflexible filter embodied by an educated and cultured people

In a previous reflection, I invoked the historical figures of Martí, Maceo, Agramonte and Céspedes. To keep alight the memory of the innumerable people who fell in combat, of those who fought and sacrificed themselves for the homeland, Raúl lit a flame that shall burn for eternity, 50 years after the death in combat of Frank País, the young, 22-year-old hero whose example moved all of us.

Life is meaningless without ideas. There is no greater joy than to struggle in their name.

* * *

Fidel Castro addressed the closing session of the 7th congress of the Cuban
Communist Party on April 19, 2016.

Fidel opened by pointing out to the assembled delegates out it takes
"a superhuman effort to lead any people in times of crisis," but to be a
revolutionary is a great privilege and an honor. Answering the question
of why he became a socialist and a communist, he explained he had had
to study Marxism-Leninism on his own, but was greatly influenced by the
history of the Russian revolution. He expressed confidence that humanity
would again produce further examples of magnificent social revolutions
like that in Russia that had marked a huge step in the struggle against
colonialism and its inseparable companion, imperialism.

"The greatest danger hanging over the earth today," he said, was "the
destructive power of modern weaponry which could undermine the peace
of the planet and make human life on earth's surface impossible." The
human species itself "might disappear like the dinosaurs," and maybe,
he speculated, "new forms of intelligent life" will emerge. He wondered
whether all the governments that signed the Paris accords on climate change
would keep to their commitments. "We must constantly hammer away at
these issues," he said.

He concluded his remarks by saying, "I shall soon turn 90, such an
idea would never have occurred to me and it was never the result of any
plan—it was sheer chance. I will soon be like every other human being. We
all reach our turn, but the ideas of the Cuban communists will remain as
proof that on this planet, working with fervor and dignity, one can produce
the material and cultural wealth that humans need, and we must fight
relentlessly to achieve this. To our brothers and sisters in Latin America and
around the world we should convey the conviction that the Cuban people
will overcome."

INDEX

Afghanistan, 24, 435, 489

Africa, 11, 12, 19, 21, 22, 24, 141, 144, 160, 169, 171, 174, 175, 177, 239, 242, 245, 361, 384, 386, 387, 390, 395, 427, 429, 435, 441, 486

African National Congress (ANC), 15, 19

Agramonte, Ignacio, 100, 325, 331, 333, 354

agrarian reform, 64, 144, 145, 146, 151, 168, 203, 249, 360

Agrarian Reform Law, 144

AIDS, 474, 486

Algeria, 11, 168, 173, 174, 180, 303, 429, 483

Allende, Salvador, 14, 355, 381

Almeida, Juan, x, 3, 4, 313

Alpha 66, 308

American revolution, 97

Angola, 18, 386, 428, 430, 435, 484

anticommunism, 434, 444

apartheid, 18, 19, 385, 386, 437, 441, 484

Árbenz, Jacobo, 3, 154, 454

Argentina, 17, 25, 168, 252, 392, 455

arms race, 170, 178, 182, 397, 402

Arteaga, Cardinal, 90

ASEAN, 455

Associated Press (AP), 147, 163, 164, 170, 272, 280

Ayacucho, battle of, 456

Baraguá Protest, 127, 332, 351

Batista, Fulgencio, ix, x, 1, 2, 3, 4, 7, 41, 47, 53, 56, 57, 58, 70, 72, 73, 74, 76, 80, 86, 87, 89, 90, 94, 95, 99, 104, 105, 106, 107, 108, 110, 112, 115, 117, 118, 124, 129, 131, 139, 141, 142, 143, 146, 149, 172, 197, 199, 282, 346, 378, 443, 460, 462, 498, 501, 503

Bay of Pigs, 9, 12, 18, 191, 194, 249, 263, 366, 367, 377, 413, 415, 424, 425, 437, 480, 503

Bishop, Maurice, 16, 17

blockade against Cuba, 10, 21, 26, 27, 265, 301, 302, 303, 305, 345, 393, 414, 431, 432, 442, 445, 448, 480, 486, 492, 496, 498, 501, 503, 504

Bolívar, Simón, 248, 447, 452, 455, 456, 457, 469, 472

Bolivia, 12, 13, 18, 22, 27, 59, 168, 252, 322, 392, 439, 485

Brazil, 20, 24, 168, 421

Brigade 2506, 9, 185

Bush, George W., 25, 26, 487, 488, 489, 490, 492, 493, 495, 498, 500, 506

Cabral, Amilcar, 484

Camp Columbia, 56, 57, 72, 104, 107, 111, 115, 116, 117, 118, 119, 120, 124, 129, 142

CARICOM, 453

Carmichael, Stokely, 289, 290

Carter, Jimmy, 15, 25

Castro, Raúl, x, 3, 4, 27, 52, 311

Catholic church, 205, 215, 375

Central America, 187, 250, 468, 469

Central Intelligence Agency (CIA), 3, 6, 7, 8, 9, 14, 246, 306, 308, 367

Céspedes, Carlos Manuel de, 100, 324, 325, 329, 331, 333, 336, 353, 354, 438

Chávez, Hugo, 23, 24, 26, 443

Chibás, Eduardo, 2, 54, 90, 460

Chile, 14, 168, 355, 356, 359, 361, 364, 365, 367, 374, 375, 378, 379

China, 7, 8, 96, 177, 178, 179, 180, 441, 453, 471

Cienfuegos, Camilo, x, 4, 5, 6, 120, 132, 191, 314

Clinton, Bill, 22

Cold War, 474, 487

Colombia, ix, 168, 257, 392

Columbus, Christopher, 69, 202, 471

Commission for Assistance to a Free Cuba (CAFC), 495

Committees for the Defense of the Revolution (CDRs), 8, 12, 419

Congo, 12, 168, 170, 172, 173, 174, 180, 284, 429, 483

constitution of 1940, 5, 62, 91, 92, 98, 199, 200, 201

constitution of Guáimaro (1869), 98, 329, 351

Costa Rica, 154, 155, 168, 392

Council of Mutual Economic Assistance (CMEA), 14, 19

Cuban Adjustment Act, 12, 500

Cuban American National Foundation (CANF), 22

Cuban Communist Party, x, 11, 15, 18, 20, 22, 271, 278, 288, 413

Cuban Family Code, 14

Cuban Film Institute (ICAIC), 221, 226

Cuban People's (Orthodox) Party, ix, 2, 460

Cuito Cuanavale, 18, 484

Declaration of Independence, the US, 99

Declaration of San José, the, 7, 182

Demajagua, 13, 323, 351

Díaz-Balart, Lincoln, 492

Díaz Lanz, Pedro Luis, 6

disarmament, 170, 175, 176, 177, 178, 385

Dorticós, Osvaldo, 6

Echeverría, José Antonio, 3

Ecuador, 168, 392

Egypt, 11, 168, 170, 389, 390

Eisenhower, Dwight D., 6, 7, 8, 161, 171, 175

Elián González, 23

El Salvador, 168, 435, 441

Engels, Friedrich, 240, 279, 438, 458, 459, 460

English revolution, 97

ETA, 492

Ethiopia, 429

European Union, 455

fascism, 179, 242, 362, 363, 379, 432, 490

Federation of Cuban Women (FMC), 419

Federation of University Students (FEU), 4

French revolution, 97, 233, 273, 357, 372, 456

García, Calixto, 105, 331, 336, 337

General Agreement on Tariffs and Trade (GATT), 398

Gómez, Máximo, 100, 325, 326, 331, 334, 337, 429, 438

Gorbachev, Mikhail, 17, 18, 20, 433

Granma (boat), x, 3, 120, 282, 311, 312, 378, 437, 459

Granma (magazine), 278

Grau San Martín, Ramón, 1, 56

Great Depression, the, 139, 398

Grenada, 16, 17, 392, 485

Group of 77, 11, 17, 23, 399, 403, 410

Guantánamo, 20, 21, 24, 120, 163, 164, 165, 166, 250, 266, 326, 393

Guatemala, 3, 144, 154, 168, 312

Guevara, Ernesto Che, x, 3, 4, 5, 6, 8, 9, 10, 11, 12, 13, 22, 120, 281, 282, 284, 311, 348, 429, 439, 484, 485, 493

Guiteras, Antonio, 345, 436

gusano, 347, 350

Haiti, 20, 154

Hatuey, 346

Helms-Burton law, the, 22, 486, 504

Hernández, Melba, 2, 45, 77

History Will Absolve Me, ix, 2, 41, 101, 123, 461

Hitler, Adolf, 91, 179, 202, 361, 437, 488, 489

immigration, 12, 61, 135, 272, 273, 274, 500, 505

Integrated Revolutionary Organizations (ORI), 9, 10, 278

International Monetary Fund (IMF), 23, 301

Iran, 168, 169, 392

Iraq, 169, 489, 491, 492, 499

Israel, 303, 304, 388, 389, 390, 483, 484

Italy, 66

Japan, 180, 185, 187, 414, 453

Jesus Christ, 205, 491

Johnson, Lyndon, 272, 273, 274, 275, 276, 284, 285, 306, 308

July 26 Movement, ix, x, 2, 3, 4, 9, 106

Kennedy, John F., 8, 9, 10, 11, 166, 167, 187, 202, 265

Khrushchev, Nikita, 147, 163, 170, 203

Kosovo, 492

Latin American Solidarity Organizations (OLAS), 12, 289, 290, 294, 305, 309

La Coubre, 7, 149, 250

Lenin, Vladimir, 240, 432, 438, 458, 460, 461

Lincoln, Abraham, 180, 181, 332

literacy, 8, 10, 203, 249, 486, 497

literacy campaign, 8, 10, 156, 191, 203, 249, 251, 480

López, Narciso, 328

Lumumba, Patrice, 173, 483

Maceo, Antonio, 59, 60, 82, 100, 316, 325, 326, 331, 332, 334, 335, 336, 337, 353, 425, 427, 437, 438

Maceo, José, 326

Machado, Gerardo, 1, 56, 75, 131

Malvinas [Falkland] Islands, 17, 391

mambises, 59, 127, 280, 323, 336, 337, 340, 347

Mandela, Nelson, 19, 21

Martí, José, 4, 45, 48, 63, 68, 69, 70, 75, 78, 100, 101, 122, 194, 237, 238, 316, 325, 326, 328, 333, 334, 335, 336, 337, 338, 348, 351, 353, 374, 423, 438, 446, 447, 455, 456, 457, 459, 461, 481

Marx, Karl, 170, 240, 241, 279, 293, 438, 448, 451, 458, 459, 460

Matos, Huber, 6

Matthews, Herbert, 3

McCarthyism, 255, 444, 460

McNamara, Robert, 306, 308

Mella, Julio Antonio, 345, 436

Mexico, x, 3, 17, 153, 168, 181, 272, 345, 392, 455

Military Intelligence Service (SIM), 42, 82, 90

Miranda, Francisco, 456

Miró Cardona, José, 5

Mobutu Sese Seko, Joseph, 172, 173, 484

Moncada, ix, 2, 19, 42, 44, 55, 62, 72, 73, 74, 79, 207, 338, 436, 459, 460, 465, 467

Movement of Nonaligned Countries, viii, 9, 16, 20, 22, 383, 384, 387, 390, 393, 394, 397, 401, 402, 403

Mozambique, 386

Namibia, 386, 387, 429, 484

Nasser, Gamal Abdel, 8, 175, 390

National Assembly of Cuba, 15, 21, 22, 25, 433, 469, 503, 513

National Council of Culture, 209, 219, 220, 221, 224, 225, 227

National Institute of Agrarian Reform (INRA), 6, 228

Neto, Agostinho, 484

New Jewel Movement, 16

Nicaragua, 16, 19, 139, 153, 435, 485

Nixon, Richard, 5, 8, 167

Nkrumah, Kwame, 175

North Atlantic Treaty Organization (NATO), 251, 433

October Missile Crisis, 265, 266, 272, 308, 366, 437, 503

Organization of African Unity (OAU), 387, 388

Organization of America States (OAS), 7, 10, 153, 154, 155, 156, 166, 247, 250, 251, 309

Orthodox Party, ix, 2, 460

País, Frank, 3, 4, 123

Palestine, 388, 389

Panama, 19, 24, 26, 154, 168, 180, 246, 254, 392, 435

People's Movement for the Liberation of Angola (MPLA), 484

Peru, 168, 392

Philippines, 137, 169, 435

Platt Amendment, 137, 162, 238, 337, 339

Polisario Front, the, 388

Pope John Paul II, 22, 491

Popular Socialist Party (PSP), 9, 460

Prío Socarrás, Carlos, 70, 72, 77

Puerto Rico, 137, 168, 238, 266, 273, 335, 391, 392

Punta del Este, 9, 10, 248, 249, 250, 251, 257

racism, 5, 24, 275, 332, 385, 386, 389, 437, 463, 482

Rebel Army, x, 4, 104, 118, 129, 142, 197, 458, 480

Revolutionary Armed Forces (FAR), 5, 277, 428, 437

Revolutionary Student Directorate (DRE), 4, 9

Roosevelt, Franklin D., 433

Roosevelt, Theodore, 337

Rousseau, Jean-Jacques, 98, 240

Rubido, Colonel Rego, 103, 110, 111, 115, 117, 118, 120

Russian revolution, 233, 273

Sandinista National Liberation Front (FSLN), 16, 19, 392, 485

Sandino, Augusto, 154, 248

Santamaría, Haydée, 2, 77

Santa Clara, 5, 22, 314, 439, 441

Santiago de Chile, 14, 355, 366

Santiago de Cuba, ix, 2, 3, 4, 5, 9, 41, 52, 55, 57, 60, 70, 74, 75, 78, 80, 89, 103, 104, 105, 107, 108, 109, 110, 111, 112, 113, 115, 116, 117, 118, 119, 121, 126, 129, 335, 336, 337, 421, 443, 445, 465, 488

September 11 terrorist attacks, 24, 473, 486, 487, 505, 506

slavery, 284, 327, 328, 329, 334, 342, 343, 351, 352, 357

Smith, Adam, 451

Southern Africa, 441

South Africa, 21, 22, 24, 174, 386, 387, 390

Soviet Union, 7, 8, 10, 11, 13, 17, 18, 19, 20, 135, 147, 150, 152, 154, 155, 163, 166, 170, 175, 176, 179, 181, 198, 242, 265, 267, 268, 300, 301, 371, 372, 390, 414, 432, 435, 446, 450, 458, 464, 465, 486, 503

Spain, 26, 136, 137, 178, 179, 180, 261, 272, 327, 336, 337, 430, 471

Sucre, General José Antonio, 455

Syria, 429, 483

Ten Years' War, 332, 333, 334, 348

Third World debt, 398, 400, 402, 403, 404, 406, 434, 474

Torricelli Act, the, 21, 486, 504

Touré, Sékou, 175

Tricontinental conference, the, 12, 305, 316

Trujillo, Rafael Leonidas, ix, 1, 6, 123, 139, 447

UNEAC (the Union of Writers and Artists of Cuba), 224

Union of Young Communists (UJC), 419

UNITA, 435

Unitary Action Party (PAU), 90

United Fruit Company, 64, 146, 154, 168, 199

United Kingdom, 17, 97, 139, 169

United Nations (UN), 8, 11, 14, 16, 19, 21, 23, 27, 133, 134, 135, 144, 153, 155, 156, 159, 161, 167, 168, 169, 171, 172, 174, 178, 179, 180, 383, 385, 386, 387, 388, 389, 390, 393, 397, 400, 405, 407, 409, 410, 411, 476, 485, 487, 488, 492, 497, 502

United Party of the Socialist Revolution (PURS), 10, 278

United Press International (UPI), 146, 164, 170, 280

UN Commission on Human Rights (UNHRC), 492

UN Conference on Trade and Development (UNCTAD), 11, 397, 398

Urban Reform Law, 8, 206

Urrutia, Manuel, 5, 6, 108, 116, 118, 119, 122, 128

Venezuela, 5, 15, 23, 24, 168, 253, 298, 392, 443, 452, 456, 457, 463, 464, 468, 469, 470, 471

Venezuelan Communist Party, 300

Vietnam, 8, 11, 12, 251, 273, 281, 284, 322, 372, 441, 484, 493

Walker, Reverend Lucius, 490

Warsaw Pact, the, 433

Western Sahara, 388

World Bank, 396, 404

World Trade Organization (WTO), 23

Yara, cry of, 60, 323, 351

Zanjón Pact, the, 331, 332, 338

Zimbabwe (Rhodesia), 386, 387

FURTHER READING

The most important, comprehensive and authoritative source of speeches and writings by Fidel Castro is the website of the Cuban Council of State. An expanding archive can be found at: www.cuba.cu/gobierno/discursos

In the near future the archive will contain every speech and document by Fidel Castro. Other websites purporting to do the same are frequently unreliable and some are even based on US-government transcriptions and translations of Fidel Castro's speeches (an open project of the US intelligence agencies!).

Another reliable source are the archives of *Granma* and *Granma International*, official publications of the Cuban Communist Party. Since 1965, *Granma International* has published a significant number of English translations of the speeches of Fidel Castro.

Ocean Press has several titles by Fidel Castro and information can be found at the web site: www.oceanbooks.com.au

Ocean Sur, the Spanish-language sister publishing house of Ocean Press, has embarked on a major multi-volume project to publish thematic anthologies of Fidel Castro. Information about these titles can be found at the web site: www.oceansur.com

THE BOLIVIAN DIARY
Authorized Edition
Ernesto Che Guevara; Introduction by Fidel Castro

"Thanks to Che's invariable habit of noting the main events of each day, we have rigorously exact, priceless, and detailed information on the heroic final months of his life in Bolivia." — *Fidel Castro*

This is Che Guevara's famous last diary, found in his backpack when he was captured by the Bolivian Army in October 1967. It became an instant international bestseller. Newly revised, with a preface by Che's eldest son Camilo and extraordinary, previously unpublished photos, this is the definitive, authorized edition of the diary, which after his death catapulted Che to iconic status throughout the world.
ISBN 978-1-920888-24-4 (paper)
ISBN 978-1-921700-80-4 (e-book)

REMINISCENCES OF THE CUBAN REVOLUTIONARY WAR
Authorized Edition
Ernesto Che Guevara

A classic, new edition of Che's reminiscences of his transformation from troop doctor to guerrilla fighter in the Cuban revolutionary war, published in association with the Che Guevara Studies Center, Havana. This includes an extraordinary selection of photos and a new foreword by Che's daughter Aleida.

The dramatic art and acute perceptiveness evident in Che Guevara's early diaries fully blossom in these highly readable and often entertaining stories.
ISBN 978-1-920888- 33-6 (paper)
ISBN 978-1-921700-82-8 (e-book)

AWAKENING OF LATIN AMERICA
A classic anthology of Che Guevara's writing on Latin America.
Ernesto Che Guevara

The name Che Guevara is synonymous with Latin America. This classic anthology on Latin America shows the Argentine-born revolutionary's cultural depth, rigorous intellect and intense emotional engagement with a continent and its people.

Selected from his family's personal archives, this book offers the best of Che's writing: examples of his journalism, essays, speeches, letters and even his poetry, revealing the evolution of an extraordinary mind from that of an impressionable young medical student to the "heroic guerrilla," brutally assassinated in Bolivia.
ISBN 978-0-9804292-8-2 (paper)
ISBN 978-1-921700-91-0 (e-book)

FIDEL CASTRO
An Intimate Portrait / Un Retrato Intimo
Alex Castro

Many photographers have tried to capture the elusive and enigmatic figure of Fidel Castro—the man behind the beard. This book presents a unique and intimate perspective of the Cuban leader through the camera lens of his son, Alex Castro, revealing the gaze of a photographer as well as that of a son.

Fidel Castro. An Intimate Portrait offers 90 photographs that bear witness to the final years of life of the former president of Cuba, capturing visits from close friends, among whom were heads of state and international personalities from the fields of culture and politics. Included in this book are never-before-seen photographs of Fidel Castro with members of Robert Kennedy's family and President Carter.
ISBN 978-1-925019-93-3 (Cloth)

GUANTANAMO
Why the Illegal US Base should be returned to Cuba
Fidel Castro

How is it that the large slice of land around Guantánamo Bay, Cuba, seized after the Spanish-American War over 100 years ago, is still held by the United States as a naval base? President Obama proposed to close the prison for those captured in the "war against terrorism," but Fidel Castro argues here that the illegal occupation of the territory should end immediately.

This book also features a comprehensive chronology of the base's history and extensive appendices, including some key historical and recently declassified documents through which Washington has justified its continued occupation of the territory.
ISBN 978-0-9804292-5-1 (paper)

COLD WAR
Warnings for a Unipolar World
Fidel Castro

Who won the Cold War? CNN's astonishingly frank interview with Fidel Castro, in which he makes some remarkable revelations about the conflict that took the world to the brink of annihilation. Far from being a proxy for Moscow, Fidel Castro explains that Cuba's support for liberation movements in Latin America was a "constant source of disagreement" with the Soviet Union. "If a Soviet-Cuban master plan had really existed, we would have won the Cold War!" he says. Fidel's reflections on talk of US preemptive nuclear strikes during the 1962 Missile Crisis are frighteningly familiar today.
ISBN 978-1-876175-77-1 (Also available in Spanish ISBN 978-1-876175-91-7)

FIDEL & RELIGION
Conversations with Frei Betto on Marxism and Liberation Theology

In an intimate 23-hour dialogue with Brazilian liberation theologist Frei Betto, Fidel Castro revealed much about his personal background and candidly discussed his views on religion. The result was an extraordinary reconciliation of revolution with religion, as Fidel remarks: "There are 10,000 times more coincidences between Christianity and communism than between Christianity and capitalism." Frei Betto responds: "Socialist societies that create better living conditions for the people are unconsciously carrying out what we men of faith consider God's projects in history."

As Betto explains in his introduction to this new edition, this book—having already sold over a million copies worldwide—paved the way for Pope John Paul II's historic visit to Cuba in 1998 and the Cuban Communist Party's decision to accept as members those practicing their religious faith.

ISBN 978-1-920888-45-9 (Also available in Spanish ISBN 978-1-920888-77-0)

CHE: A MEMOIR BY FIDEL CASTRO
Edited by David Deutschmann

Fidel Castro writes with great candor and emotion about a historic revolutionary partnership that changed the face of Cuba and Latin America, vividly portraying Che—the man, the revolutionary, and the intellectual—and revealing much about his own inimitable determination and character.

This book documents Che's extraordinary bond with Cuba from the revolution's early days to his final guerrilla expeditions to Africa and Bolivia, and includes Fidel's speech on the return of Che's remains to Cuba 30 years after his assassination in Bolivia in 1967 and his frank assessment of the Bolivian mission.

ISBN 978-1-920888-25-1 (Also available in Spanish ISBN 978-1-921235-02-3)

MY EARLY YEARS
Fidel Castro

Here, Fidel Castro, one of the century's most controversial and private figures, reflects on his childhood, youth and student activism. In this unprecedented selection of his most personal musings, Fidel discusses his family and the religious and moral influences that led to his involvement in politics from an early age.

This book includes excerpts from Fidel's letters from prison after the failed Moncada attack and some rare photos of Fidel as a child and youth. It also features an introductory essay by Gabriel García Márquez.

ISBN 978-1-920888-09-1 (Also available in Spanish ISBN 978-1-920888-19-0)

CHE GUEVARA READER
Writings on Politics and Revolution

More than just a guerrilla strategist, Che Guevara was a profound thinker who made a lasting contribution to revolutionary theory. This bestselling anthology, prepared in association with the Che Guevara Studies Center in Havana, is the most complete and authoritative collection ever published of the work of Che Guevara that includes some of his most famous speeches and lesser known writings and letters.

ISBN 978-1-876175-69-6 (Also available in Spanish ISBN 978-1-876175-93-1)

CUBAN REVOLUTION READER
A Documentary History of Fidel Castro's Revolution

The Cuban revolution was one of the defining moments of the 20th century, reaching far beyond the shores of the tiny Caribbean island. From the euphoria of the early years of the revolution, to the devastating economic crisis that followed the collapse of the socialist bloc in the 1990s and beyond, this book provides a sweeping vision of revolutionary Cuba—its challenges, its defeats, its impact on the world. Covering decisive moments such as the Bay of Pigs invasion and the 1962 Missile Crisis, this edition also features more recent events such as the demise of the Soviet Union, the visit of Pope John Paul II to Cuba and the crisis over the child refugee Elián González.

An outstanding resource for scholars and all those interested in gaining an understanding of Cuba's remarkable experience over the last half century.

ISBN 978-1-920888-89-3 (Also available in Spanish ISBN 978-1-920888-08-4)

JOSÉ MARTÍ READER
Writings on the Americas

This classic anthology presents the writings, poetry and letters of José Martí, one of the most brilliant and impassioned Latin American intellectuals of the 19th century.

Teacher, journalist, revolutionary and poet, José Martí interweaves the threads of Latin America's culture and history, condemning the brutality and corruption of the Spanish colonizers as well as the increasingly evident predatory ambitions of the United States.

This book features bilingual text of some of Martí's best-loved poems.

ISBN 978-1-920888-74-9

oceanpress

e-mail info@oceanbooks.com.au
www.oceanbooks.com.au